# EGYPT'S FOREIGN POLICY IN TIMES OF CRISIS

# EGYPT'S FOREIGN POLICY IN TIMES OF CRISIS

## My Testimony

**AHMED ABOUL GHEIT**

The American University in Cairo Press
Cairo New York

First published in 2020 by
The American University in Cairo Press
113 Sharia Kasr el Aini, Cairo, Egypt
One Rockefeller Plaza, New York, NY 10020
www.aucpress.com

Translated by Abeer Mustafa and Wafya Ibrahim
Translation revised by Mohamed Helal

English translation supported by the Arab League Educational, Cultural, and Scientific Organization (ALESCO)

Dar el Kutub No. 10919/19
ISBN 978 977 416 960 1

Dar el Kutub Cataloging-in-Publication Data

Gheit, Ahmed Aboul
    Egypt's Foreign Policy in Times of Crisis: My Testimony / Ahmed Aboul Gheit.—Cairo: The American University in Cairo Press, 2020.
      p. cm.
      ISBN 978 977 416 960 1
      Egypt—Foreign relations
      327.62046

1 2 3 4 5   24 23 22 21 20

Designed by Adam el-Sehemy
Printed in the United States of America

# CONTENTS

Foreword to the English Edition *Francis J. Ricciardone*                    ix

Introduction                                                                1

1.  The Assignment                                                         11
2.  Upbringing and Preparation                                             44
3.  Understanding the Situation and the General
       Framework for Action                                                89
4.  Challenges and Responses: The United States                           117
5.  Challenge and Confrontation: An Attempt to Expand
       the Security Council                                               169
6.  The Nile River: Challenges and Attempts to
       Reach an Understanding                                             195
7.  Challenges of Sustaining Status: Egypt and Africa                     243
8.  Challenges of Division: Sudan                                         260
9.  Egypt and the Challenges of the Arab World                            292
10. Egypt and the Challenges of the Region                                339
11. Challenges of Expanding the Framework of the
       Egyptian Movement: Egypt and the World                             362
12. Challenges of a Peaceful Settlement                                   386
13. Challenges of the Final Forty-five Days                               441

Conclusion: Challenges of the Past and the Future                         455

Index                                                                     463

To Laila,

My dearest and most loyal friend, the one who sincerely criticized, praised from the heart, and always supported me. Smiling and optimistic Laila who did her very best to raise the two precious jewels in our lives, my sons Kamal and Ali. Laila, the one who made me a proud father.

To you, my life companion, my dear wife, I dedicate this book.

# FOREWORD TO THE ENGLISH EDITION

*Francis J. Ricciardone*
*President, The American University in Cairo*

I first met Ahmed Aboul Gheit at the Fairmont Hotel near Cairo International Airport in late January 1999, on the first stop of Secretary of State Madeleine Albright's tour of the Middle East to introduce me as the new "Special Coordinator for the Transition of Iraq." My appointment represented the Clinton Administration's response to the strong bipartisan Congressional intent, as expressed in the "Iraq Liberation Act" of October 1998, to use overt diplomatic means to "remove the regime headed by Saddam Hussein from power in Iraq and to promote the emergence of a democratic government to replace that regime." The Clinton Administration was well aware of the Arab world's wariness of such a proposition, and it approached that proclaimed objective with due sobriety.

Aboul Gheit was about to deploy to New York as Egypt's Permanent Representative to the United Nations, the next jewel in the crown of an illustrious career in his country's diplomatic corps. He listened intently to Secretary Albright's explanation of my role before focusing his questions on the ramifications for Egypt. His skepticism was as penetrating as his courtesy was unshakable.

This stage is worth setting because it illustrates the relative roles and self-concepts of the Egyptians and Americans in world affairs at that point in their modern histories. Engaging with the world's preeminent power at the height of its fin de siècle influence, Aboul Gheit personified both his country's confidence in its weight in world affairs and its war-weary historical perspective on their dynamics.

*Egypt's Foreign Policy in Times of Crisis: My Testimony* reveals Aboul Gheit's thinking behind his mission as foreign minister only a few years following that fateful unilateral American initiative to intervene in shaping the future of this turbulent and complicated region. His career as a leading Egyptian statesman was approaching its climax just as the age of Egyptian giants of war and peace—Nasser and Sadat—was rapidly receding. Yet even then, the United States, at the height of its influence, took no steps in the broader region without at least checking in with Egypt. The country was the dominant political, military, and cultural leader of the Arab world, enjoying a historical phase of economic advancement borne of sustained domestic stability and regional peace.

The book brings the English reader behind the curtain of Egyptian statecraft—an apparatus historically capably staffed but also traditionally dominated by the vision and will of the head of state. Aboul Gheit's rejection of the idea that foreign ministers or a "deep state" drove Egyptian foreign policy is based not on modesty but on the reality that he portrays. In a government so centralized and so dependent on the President, Aboul Gheit explains, the foreign minister and other related departments were merely "executors in this realm." Successful foreign ministers were those whom the President fully trusted—and who were humble enough to shun credit for their accomplishments. This historical and political context makes Aboul Gheit's own professional accomplishments, even if often rearguard or defensive efforts, stand in sharper relief.

Whether in New York or Cairo, some Western counterparts found Aboul Gheit's approach aggressive. Those who understood and respected his authentically Egyptian historical and nationalist perspective, however, found him a disciplined, willing, and creative problem manager, when the parties were not otherwise able to resolve problems with finality. As the United States ambassador to Egypt during several years of Aboul Gheit's lengthy tenure as foreign minister, I was privileged to observe firsthand how his deep patriotism, scholarly appreciation of history, and confidence in his country's identity and historical role, invariably shaped his dealings with foreign counterparts. Aboul Gheit was unrelenting in upholding President Mubarak's vision of Egypt's national interests as well as Egyptians' keen sense of national dignity. Their direct experience of war and peace with Israel, and of the United States' roles in both, contrasted with the indirect historical knowledge and often ideologically driven decision-making of the Americans. By contrast, Aboul Gheit's and Mubarak's direct dealings with Israeli counterparts were qualitatively different, even if cooler: they shared with their erstwhile enemies the searing experiential affinities both of all-out war and often vexatious peace. In all his dealings with foreigners as I observed them, Aboul Gheit appeared instinctively to reflect the outlooks and sentiments of the great mass of his countrymen, at all levels of education.

Since leaving office as Egypt's foreign minister in the aftermath of the national upheaval of 2011, Aboul Gheit's patriotism, erudition, intelligence, and personal discipline continue as always to characterize his long career of public service, now as secretary general of the League of Arab States. His story offers essential insights for contemporary and future generations of foreign diplomats, scholars, businesspeople, and all who seek to deal mutually successfully with Egyptian counterparts. Theirs is a courteous, welcoming, and seductive country. This book, however, bears witness nonetheless to Egypt's tenacity, even ruthlessness, in the pursuit of its national interests as Egyptian leaders proclaim them.

As one of the very few firsthand accounts in English of service near the pinnacle of Egyptian statecraft, Aboul Gheit's memoir is compelling and exceptionally important. The American University in Cairo Press is honored to bring to an English readership this provocative, personal testimony of a leading Arab statesman, as part of our educational mission to advance mutual understanding across barriers of culture, language, history, and geography.

# INTRODUCTION

With the historic day of the October 6, 1973 approaching, I realized the need to record everything that I witnessed at the time, so that I could write about that period later on. I was inspired to do so by my readings, over many years, of the writings of historical figures, including generals, political leaders, ministers of defense and foreign affairs, and even ordinary soldiers who fought for their countries. Those figures journaled on a daily basis. They recorded their ideas and evaluated the strategies that their countries implemented in the wars they waged, and kept track of battles that were fought during these wars, traced the conflicts among the peoples and ideologies of their time. Back then, I predicted that the impending war would definitely leave its imprint on the history of Egypt, the region as a whole, and the world. Hence, I decided to record everything I witnessed, as well as my thoughts, starting from October 5. I kept all my papers and documents for later use, I chronicled my reflections and conclusions about the unfolding events, and worked hard to ensure that my recollections of that period were intact in my memory. Since then, my career progressed on an arduous path during which I achieved many successes and faced innumerable challenges. As the years passed, I realized—at a particular moment in 2009—that I was allowing time to slip by

1

without writing my observations, which could help my fellow countrymen to continue to serve Egyptian society in the fields that I believe I mastered, or to be more accurate, have learned to master. Therefore, I wrote a series of articles on war and peace based on what I began recording on that fateful day, October 5, 1973. Then I incorporated this whole experience in my book entitled *Witness to War and Peace*.

Upon my appointment as minister of foreign affairs in 2004, it was only logical to adopt the same approach that I had used during my work in 1973 and in the many years that followed, namely, fully and thoroughly documenting what I did and witnessed throughout my time in office. I was told that Dr. Boutros Boutros-Ghali, Egypt's minister of state for foreign affairs from November 1977 to the end of December 1991 and the former United Nations (UN) secretary general, recorded every night the events of the day, preparing himself to write about his experience for future generations. I imagined that I, too, could record everything in a similar manner in preparation for writing after leaving office, which I knew would inevitably come one day. For days, or maybe for weeks, I did my best to do so. Gradually, however, the pressures and responsibilities of leading Egypt's diplomatic corps caught up with me. I found that I was starting my day at 5:30 a.m. and continuing to work until 10:00 p.m. almost every day. I realized that I would not be able to record my thoughts or the events of the day in a quarter or half an hour, nor would I be able to keep it up for years, so I stopped.

Instead, I decided to make use of the modern technologies that have revolutionized human life in recent decades. I kept copies of all my communications and correspondences on a series of compact discs (CDs). These CDs cover my entire tenure as Egypt's foreign minister, and have provided the wealth of information that forms the foundation for this book.

Despite the deluge of information made possible through modern technology and the availability of news and information from all sources on the internet, I have always felt that there was something missing as I was writing this book: the recovery of my own thoughts, notes, and personal evaluation of the events of the seven years I served as minister of foreign affairs. I genuinely regretted the fact that I did not record my feel-ings and the summaries of my thoughts throughout those years. I should have pressed myself more to write them down at the time. Consequently, I had to rely on the documentary record of my years of service and my own memory of these events. For years, I had been working to sharpen my memory and deepen my understanding of the complex policy challenges that I faced during my years of service in preparation for the day I needed it. That day has come as I began writing this book.

In August 2009, I received a request from the editor in chief of *al-Musawwar* magazine to write an article about the tenets of Egyptian national security from my perspective. This was a good opportunity to write down initial ideas that could be developed in the future as a part of a book about Egyptian foreign policy and national security, and this is what I have actually done in this book. In that article, I noted that I would endeavor to present my thoughts briefly, but without making the mistake of too much summarizing, and that I would only present general ideas about various matters to give the reader the chance to reflect on them and come to his/her own conclusions concerning the issues I covered. I also made it clear in that article that we should not confuse the concept of national secu-rity with the role of security agencies, or matters that need to be urgently addressed with those that may be less urgent but that are nonetheless of a strategic nature, and thus more important in the long term. I warned that the objectives of Egyptian national security policy must be articulated in a manner that accords with the capabilities and resources of Egyptian society, because otherwise these objectives would become unattainable.

When I wrote those words, I was thinking of those people who were carrying out a campaign, which I believed was totally unfounded, about what they called the loss of Egypt's leading role in organizations on the international, regional, Arab, African, Mediterranean, and international levels. At the time, Egypt was active and capable of both interacting with other nations and taking the initiative on various issues, but within the limits of its economic, financial, and other capacities and potentials. It was important, however, not to raise or discuss these capacities and potentials in too much detail, so that our adversaries could not exploit anything that we might unintentionally reveal. One might be led to compare Egypt in this respect with other similar countries, in the region or further away, which have the same capabilities but not the same political and strategic circumstances. Most probably you would come to the conclusion that Egypt's successes or failures in carrying out its foreign policies have always depended on the limitations to its potential, and on the fact that the available resources were limited and could not be wasted. We have always taken into consideration previous experiences that endangered Egyptian national security and exposed it to serious risks; these have included the occupation of Egyptian land for extended periods of time.

My article in *al-Musawwar* tackled three core tenets of Egyptian national security. The first was the internal front, which includes everything within the country's geographical borders, especially the importance of providing the necessary resources to enable the Armed Forces to secure these borders. This aspect of national security also includes those internal measures needed to ensure the stability of the country. Guaranteeing security for Egypt's citizens within Egyptian borders is a condition sine qua non to ensure development, a decent life, and national cohesion of against attempts of foreign intrusion. It also includes working hard to resolve internal contradictions, concentrate on points of strength, and address points of weakness: the poor versus the rich, religious extremism, health, education, transportation, housing, job opportunities, care for the elderly, and many other issues. To do this, we need a good administration with a great sense of responsibility, capable of securing suitable financial resources and spreading an atmosphere of trust that stresses the value of citizenship as a major factor in assigning duties and responsibilities.

The second aspect of national security is its regional dimension. I said in the article that due to improvements in transportation and communication, the world has increasingly become closer and more entangled than ever. What a Chinese or a Brazilian citizen sees on television can be seen at the same moment by an American or an African or a European or anyone in the world. What happens far away from our borders can endanger the safety and security of our country. There are many examples of this, some of which I mentioned in the article:

- How to ensure that Egypt gets enough water to cover its needs and facilitate its development. This, of course, requires developing our relationship with upstream countries along the Nile and rationalizing our water consumption. I did not explain in the article that the threats that faced us at that time were being addressed through diplomatic endeavors and have in fact helped us to achieve these goals. Ensuring that Egypt gets its fair share of water also requires that projects involving the Nile must not be carried out without Egypt's consent. Lying, delaying, evasiveness, and failing to address the root causes of these challenges will no doubt lead to frightening losses that will cause future generations to suffer. There were many things that could have been said concerning this matter, but there were also things that could never be revealed, for reasons of national security.

- How to handle the Israeli issue—not to mention the Palestinian problem—since Israel has always represented the most direct military security threat to Egypt since its founding in 1948 and until the 1973 war and the conclusion of the 1979 peace treaty, and Israel's withdrawal from the Sinai, which it occupied twice, in 1956 and 1967, and briefly encroached on its territory in 1949. There was a lot to be said about this matter that the article did not include. In the article I wrote: "The Israeli issue is still without a comprehensive and satisfying solution due to the absence of a just solution to the Palestinian problem. Our northeastern borders will remain under full and close surveillance on our part in order not to create a loophole in our national security." Anyone who read these words back in 2009, or who reads them today, will understand their intention. There is no more to be said about Israel and its relationship to Egypt, now or in the future, as long as the Palestinian issue remains unresolved.

- How to deal with the threats to the southern approaches to the Red Sea, especially in Yemen, Somalia, and Bab al-Mandeb. Tensions in these areas, whether on land or on sea, such as piracy, could have detrimental effects on the security of the Suez Canal with its strategic and economic importance to the country. This book includes several chapters that deal with these threats in general and with the ways we addressed them—or kept silent about them, in the case of matters that cannot be further disclosed.

- How to deal with the Arabian Gulf region, which can affect Egypt directly or indirectly despite its geographical distance. The article did not deal with certain issues that I discuss in this book about addressing the Arab situation in the Gulf. Some of these issues are Iran and its nuclear program, how it relates to the Israeli program, and the future of nuclear and conventional armaments in the region extending from Iran in the east to the shores of the eastern and southern Mediterranean. In this book, the chapter that discusses these matters also addresses the dangers of nuclear proliferation and the limits and possibilities of success or failure in either making the Middle East, including Israel and Iran, free from weapons of mass destruction, or adding to them an Egyptian or Arab nuclear arsenal, with all the implications for safety, stability, and development in Egypt and the whole region.

- How to work within the framework of the Mediterranean basin, which is our northern border and one of the most important links to the countries that surround it, both the Arab countries in North Africa and the countries of southern Europe, the latter being our most important commercial partner. There are also the countries to the east of the Mediterranean, the Levant and Black Sea countries, with whom we have sensitive relations.

The third component of Egyptian national security policy relates to global issues and Egypt's relations with the great powers. To quote from the 2009 article: "We recognize that issues of the environment, climate change, and global financial turmoil are all issues that affect the quality of life and our vital interests and eventually our national security." Some of the specific issues that I noted in this context are:

- The exceptional role of the United States as the greatest world power now and for many decades to come, and the ways to deal with it and adjust our relationship with it, especially considering that it is the major supplier of weaponry to Egypt and plays a vital role in the Israeli issue and the Palestinian problem.

- The weight of the world economic and financial powers, especially the ones that are geographically close to us, like the European Union on the economic and political levels, and the Gulf Cooperation Council on the political and financial ones.
- Emerging economic powers like China, India, Brazil, Mexico, and other countries. We must reshape our relations with them, make use of their experiences, and relate to them within a modern scientific framework.
- Our potential ability to improve the status of the Islamic world within the international community, especially if we succeed in controlling rogue elements who adopt violence as a method.

The article came to the conclusion that the protection of the constitution—that is, providing security for citizens, combating chaos, and ensuring the role of law and justice—is the main goal of domestic national security. Securing the Egyptian borders is also a sacred duty, the importance of which cannot be underestimated, as is the need to secure enough water to encourage development and progress. The article also concluded that the strength of our regional ties, in terms of cultural, economic, religious, and civilizational elements, is the real guarantee of the international status of Egypt and the source of its security.

One of the greatest assets of Egyptian society, as mentioned in the article, is the Egyptian human presence outside its borders, whether in the form of permanent emigration or a temporary work force. Egyptian communities abroad are one of the major arteries of the country and a source of its pride, and whenever these communities faced problems, they are wisely tackled and their negative consequences are contained. At the end of the day, Egypt's Foreign Ministry and its diplomatic corps are among the executive tools of the country, adopting the motto "Egypt Comes First," without any distinction between Muslims and Christians or rich and poor. They execute the policies of the country according to an accurate evaluation of reality that do not involve exaggeration or intimidation on the one hand, or negligence and underestimation on the other. They strike a balance between the country's resources and its international aspirations, and seek to calmly achieve the goals of Egyptian society to the greatest possible degree.

This summary of the article in *al-Musawwar* encompasses the rules and governing lines of my viewpoint on foreign policy issues as they relate to all aspects of interior affairs. During the years that preceded January 25, 2011, much was said about coming up with new routes of development for Egypt and widening the frameworks of its communication, presence, and influence. For me, the pretense that we could reinvent the wheel, as the proverb goes, was not an option. I believed that the scope and direction of movement were predetermined in accordance with Egypt's history, geography, and culture, and that we have already done what is required within the available capacities without wasting or withholding any effort.

The conviction that Israel represented a permanent threat until a just settlement of the Palestinian case is reached was then, and still is, widespread, and the article in *al-Musawwar* testifies to this conviction. The sacredness of Egyptian land and the idea that nothing is ever more important than its security were closely adhered to regardless of the intentions of the enemy or the feelings of friends or brothers. The concluding chapter of this book will reveal a running theme and a clear connection among all the points mentioned in this introduction—that is, the relationship between the setting of goals and the ability to achieve them according to the resources available to the decision-maker.

This book is made up of thirteen chapters, in which topics are addressed through combination of a thematic approach on the one hand and a chronological one on the other.

I discuss many things that have not been formerly disclosed, but I have tried to avoid, as much as I possibly could, revealing any strategic secrets that could harm Egypt and its foreign affairs in the future. I focus on the way decisions were made during these years, on the tools that were used in the national security field, and on the relationship between them. I also deal with the secretive approach of some of these tools and how they kept their movements and attitudes hidden, which caused a lot of harm or undermined the successes that could have been achieved otherwise. The conclusion that the book makes clear is that administering the foreign affairs of a country with the stature of Egypt with its varied and multifaceted interests all over the world is a very complicated matter that should be neither misrepresented nor underestimated, since the consequences could be hazardous. Adventurism in this field or irresponsible calls for wars without a vital strategic necessity are also dangerous, and their effects on the country could extend for decades, maybe centuries. Many telling examples of this can be seen in Egypt.

The book also deals with the methods of the Egyptian president in managing this foreign policy system. I would like to add here that Mustafa al-Nahhas, the renowned Egyptian prime minister, and Gamal Abd al-Nasser had the same motivations, starting points, and objectives. Similarly, Anwar al-Sadat and Hosni Mubarak were not different from one another, or from the other two politicians mentioned, except in their style or in the degree of maneuverability they enjoyed as a result of the different strategic and political circumstances that each of the four had to handle.

I have always believed that Amr Moussa or Mohamed Hassan al-Zayyat, to mention two of Egypt's foreign affairs ministers following the 1952 revolution, were a natural extension of Mohamed Salah al-Din or Ahmed Maher and other Egyptian ministers before 1952. Even though they might have used different methods, their objectives were always the same: defending Egyptian interests and ensuring its preeminent status. Again, I must underline the role played by the available resources. These always had a major impact on the view of the decision-maker and the way he took the necessary actions while not exposing Egypt to any potentially serious harm or losses.

During the republican era, Egyptian foreign policy has witnessed the supremacy of the president's authority as the decision-maker who determines and establishes the baselines, starting points, and orientation of Egyptian foreign policy, while the foreign minister, supported by other components of the Egyptian national security system, implements them according to the instructions they receive—or, at least, this is how it should work.

Nasser, Sadat, and Mubarak used to determine the overall direction and objectives of foreign policy, each following his own decision-making method, and then the implementation mechanism was launched. During my term from 2004 to 2011, there were restrictions and obstacles that hindered the movement but, at the same time, there were situations and elements that facilitated it. All of this is part of the complicated nature of decision-making and implementation of foreign policy for a big country like Egypt.

Readers who are familiar with the decision-making processes in foreign policy for superpowers or other large countries during the twentieth century will understand what I mean by the complications and difficulties of this process. Those responsible for foreign affairs often think about resigning, as I did myself. In the course of our work, all of us make a lot of calculations that involve both personal and public factors, whether internal or external. If the challenge is simply too difficult, that resignation may become possible, or even certain. But if it involves many struggles and conflicting points of view or methods, then committing to work for the purpose of achieving the goals is the best solution to prove the validity of the calculations and the strength of the position. I should note that, at a time when public decorum has deteriorated in Egypt, throughout this book I refer to President Mubarak as 'the president.' I do so out of respect for Egypt and its people and out of respect for the office of Egypt's head of state.

I have included some personal photographs of myself and my family and left out many of my photographs with presidents, prime ministers, and foreign affairs ministers because, to be honest, such photographs mean nothing except for the fact that I have met the individuals in question. Actually, I have met hundreds of high-profile officials over the period of my work as a diplomat and a minister.

I have always been ready to serve my country's flag, and no other. Hence, throughout my diplomatic career and during the years I spent in the service of my country I never considered working for any international organization, such as the UN, though I have had the chance to do so if I wanted.

In conclusion, I hope my readers find what they are looking for in the pages of this book.

# 1

# THE ASSIGNMENT

I entered my office in the headquarters of the Egyptian permanent mission to the United Nations at 344 East 44th Street in New York at 3:45 p.m. on Friday, July 9, 2004. In less than five minutes, the phone started ringing and my Nigerian secretary, Stella, said, "This call is for you from Cairo." She told me the name of the caller—someone who was part of the inner circle of the president's staff. He said that he was making the call from the Heliopolis Sheraton hotel, not from his home or office, because he did not want anyone to know about it at present. I had been selected as the minister of foreign affairs in a new cabinet in Egypt that would be announced within days. He added that I should not talk about it to anyone and that I would get a phone call from the prime minister-designate about this position. I thanked him for the news and for his enthusiasm about it.

The previous night, at dawn on Thursday, July 8, a well-connected former ambassador in the Ministry of Foreign Affairs who was on good terms with various members of the Egyptian elite had called my New York apartment to relay the same news. He said that he was certain that the decision had already been made about my appointment as minister of foreign affairs and successor to my lifelong friend Ahmed Maher. Maher had already succeeded our friend Amr Moussa on May 15, 2001, when the latter was elected as secretary general of the League of Arab States, replacing

Dr. Esmat Abdel Meguid, who had held that position for ten years during which Amr Moussa had been the foreign affairs minister.

I kept thinking about the calls and began to think that the news might be true. I had been told that since Amr Moussa left the ministry in 2001, President Mubarak had been thinking about some names and that mine was at the top of his list. Even more, just after the announcement that Egypt intended to nominate Moussa as secretary general of the Arab League, the Saudi newspaper *Asharq al-Awsat* reported from London in the middle of April 2001 that "Aboul Gheit is the candidate most likely to get the position." However, I thought that the president might choose someone else closer to him since he did not know me really well. Until then, I had met the president personally only twice throughout my service as a diplomat. The first time was during his visit to Italy in November 1994 when I was the Egyptian ambassador there. The Italian authorities had decided then that it was dangerous for him to stay in a hotel in Rome because they had intercepted suspicious phone calls during that period when Egypt was confronting serious terrorist threats. Thus, the president spent his night at the Villa Savoya—the headquarters of the Egyptian Embassy—where Italian monarchs had lived during and before the Second World War, and where the Italian Carabinieri had arrested Mussolini during his visit to the king of Italy, to discuss the progress of the war and the possibility of the withdrawal of Italy to save itself a crushing defeat. The president's visit was a success, and later, one of the inner circle of the president's officials told me in a phone call that the president liked the warm hospitality and expressed his satisfaction, commenting on my wife and myself as "a really exceptional and excellent couple." The second time I met the president was before I left to New York as the permanent representative of Egypt to the United Nations in 1999; it was in the Heliopolis Presidential Palace and lasted for twenty minutes in the presence of Amr Moussa, the minister of foreign affairs at the time.

Since 1989, I had heard from high-profile friends in the government that the president kept asking about personnel in the Ministry of Foreign Affairs who could be promoted. They often mentioned my name and he would answer that he was sure about my good reputation and wide experience, in addition to the fact that my father was one of his acquaintances and they had served together in the air force. However, he would sometimes add, "Isn't he a bit young for the position?" I found President Mubarak's age-sensitivity when it came to decisions about promotions and assigning positions strange; seniority clearly meant a great deal to him.

When President Mubarak asked Dr. Esmat Abdel Meguid about someone to replace Ambassador Amr Moussa, the permanent Egyptian representative, upon the latter's return from New York in April 1991, Abdel Meguid suggested my name. Again, the president's response was that he found Aboul Gheit "young for the position," although I was forty-nine years old at the time! I found this attitude extremely provocative, and I was even more vexed and exasperated after Amr Moussa was assigned to succeed Esmat Abdel Meguid as minister of foreign affairs and Moussa's recommendation to the president to extend the service of a group of Egyptian ambassadors for years beyond their normal retirement age. I firmly believed that extending their service, even though I never doubted their efficiency or denied their competence, denied opportunities for many high-caliber people that my friend and colleague Dr. Mustafa al-Fiqi called "the generation of the mezzanine floor" (that is, the lost generation). I had already decided never to follow that path myself, and I assured the president, when I became foreign affairs minister, that I had no intention or desire to approach him in the future with a recommendation to extend the service of any ambassador, whether inside Egypt or abroad, beyond the retirement age. In fact, there had been attempts in the years following my appointment that I firmly resisted. The president's wife had tried to extend the service of some of the women ambassadors beyond the retirement age and I refused; the president was supportive, despite the pressures I believe he had felt from his family.

The first six months of 2004 were rife with many of the usual rumors about the Ministry of Foreign Affairs, among which was that Ahmed Maher would not continue for long at the helm of Egyptian diplomacy, especially after his visit to Jerusalem, which was not a success. Some Palestinians allied to an extremist organization gathered and protested against his visit to the al-Aqsa Mosque in a repugnant manner that displayed their ingratitude for Egypt's efforts and sacrifices on behalf of the Palestinian cause and its support of the Palestinian people to claim their rights in Palestine generally, and particularly in Jerusalem, for decades. These rumors spread widely after Ahmed Maher suffered from a severe illness in 2004 that caused him to be rushed to a hospital in Cairo; he was thus unable to accompany the president on a visit to America.

Maher had actually suffered two major health crises. The first was in 1983 when he was the Egyptian ambassador to Belgium and the European Community in Brussels; the second happened in 1993 when he was ambassador to Washington. In both cases, he underwent major heart surgeries that required him to remain under close medical supervision. However, he had always found ways to dodge doctors' instructions and escape the supervision of his wife in her continuous attempts to make him follow those instructions by supervising his meals and activity.

During the years 2002–2003, when I was the permanent representative in New York, Ahmed Maher, the-then minister of foreign affairs, visited many times and seized the opportunity to undergo some medical checkups in the main hospital of Cornell University. Most of his tests were concerning, and I often asked the Egyptian physician not to talk about them to anyone to keep his image intact. I did not know then whether Maher himself had told anyone in Cairo about the results of his tests or not, but I was sure that some official and personal reports were sent to Cairo, whether to the president's office or to some other Egyptian government agencies. I was also aware that when President Mubarak chose Ahmed Maher to succeed Amr Moussa, he was worried that his responsibilities would indirectly affect his already vulnerable health. Nevertheless, the president preferred to choose someone known for his efficiency, and whom he had known well for many years during his work in Washington from 1992 to 1999 and in Moscow from 1988 to 1992.

Returning to the subject of my nomination to the position: I have always believed that the Egyptian permanent representative to the United Nations, whether personally known to the president or with no direct relation to him—as in my case—was invariably one of the candidates for the position of foreign affairs minister in case unexpected changes happened at the head of this ministry. There had been many instances of this kind, starting with Dr. Mahmoud Fawzi in 1953 and followed by Mahmoud Riyad in 1964, Mohamed Hassan al-Zayyat in 1969, and Dr. Esmat Abdel Meguid in 1984, who was succeeded by Amr Moussa in 1991. Therefore, I believed that there was really a strong possibility of my appointment to that position.

President Mubarak came back to Cairo a few days before July 10 after undergoing major spine surgery and staying in Germany for some weeks. It was then rumored that a major cabinet reshuffle was expected in Cairo shortly. On July 8, an editorial by Ibrahim Nafie was published in *al-Ahram* in which he severely criticized the policies of the Egyptian government and the performance of the Ministry of Foreign Affairs. This led me to conclude that there was a serious possibility that the minister of foreign affairs would be replaced.

I monitored the matter closely, not only because I was a potential candidate for the position, but also because I did not wish to serve under a minister who was either younger than myself or whom I outranked in the diplomatic corps. Therefore, I had to be prepared to go back to Cairo and enjoy a relaxed life after thirty-nine years of hard work during which I devotedly served my country's diplomacy. I was then sixty-two years old and had already received three presidential decrees to extend my service beyond the retirement age, each decree granting one additional year.

What I felt that day, July 9, was a sense of anticipation. I decided to call my wife, Laila, via the direct connection between my office and the residence of the Egyptian ambassador on Park Avenue. I told her about the phone call I had received from one of the members of the president's office, and of course she already knew about the earlier call from the retired Egyptian ambassador. She cried and said that she did not want me to take this position because of its overwhelming responsibilities that would take me away from her for however long I served in that post. She also said that the years of our lives had gone by far too quickly and that we were not getting the chance to rest, relax, and enjoy each other's company. I replied that if what I had been told about my imminent appointment was true, I could not refuse the president's trust, since neither my personality, work ethics, nor training as an Egyptian diplomat allowed me to do so. I assured her that I was absolutely convinced that men must accept responsibilities and never run away from them, especially if they are sufficiently qualified. I firmly believe that this philosophy governs the conduct of all diplomats and other high-profile officials when they receive a request from their president to perform a certain task, whether big or small. I was following Al Jazeera television while talking to my wife and suddenly I saw my photograph and name on the screen, together with the news that I was to be the next Egyptian minister of foreign affairs.

Phone calls poured into the headquarters of the delegation from colleagues in the Ministry of Foreign Affairs, our embassies abroad, and my family in Cairo. I decided to leave the building and go out with one of the young members of the delegation, the well-qualified Mohamed al-Farnawany. We leisurely strolled through New York's streets for hours, looking at shop windows and entering bookstores. I arrived home in the evening to find that my wife had disconnected most of the phones in the apartment, especially since it was just after dawn in Cairo and no one was expected to call. She said she had received dozens of calls, and that was just a sample of how our future life would look.

It might be relevant here to narrate a funny story that happened to one of the diplomats in our delegation, Counselor Mahmoud Sami. I accompanied him one Friday from the office to my apartment to discuss some matters and have a light lunch, then go back. It was a hot and humid day and we walked about three kilometers; when we arrived, he was soaking with sweat and in bad shape. We finished talking and had lunch, then I showered quickly and we were all set to go back. When I suggested that we go on foot, he firmly refused and said that he never refused any of my requests but he could not stand walking in the heat and humidity. I started teasing and threatening him, and he said that he knew that I would most probably be the minister of foreign affairs within days or even hours, but he would not walk in the heat no matter what happened. So he went back in my car and I walked to the office. As soon as he heard the news on Al Jazeera, he came to tease me, suggesting that, now that I had become foreign minister, he was prepared to walk back and forth from my home to the mission many times and make it a daily routine, and we laughed.

I tried to sleep that night but slept only fitfully. On July 10, 2004, I received a phone call at 6:00 a.m. from the Cabinet switchboard in Cairo and was told that Dr. Ahmed Nazif wanted to talk to me; then General Abu Talib, Dr. Nazif's chief of cabinet at the Ministry of Communication, also said that Dr. Nazif wanted to speak to me. I waited on the line for a couple of minutes and did not hear anyone so I hung up. The Cabinet headquarters called again and Dr. Nazif was on the line; he courteously said that he still remembered his last successful visit to New York the previous year when he came on an official mission related to the Ministry of Communication. He said that he was calling to deliver the "president's appeal" for me to accept the position of the minister of foreign affairs in the next cabinet. I was surprised by his cordial style in handling the subject. I thanked him and asked him to thank the president for his trust. He said that I was expected to arrive in Cairo before Sunday noon for the swearing-in, which was expected to be on Monday, July 12. I jokingly commented that the position had already started to weigh heavily on me and that I would spare no effort to leave New York on Saturday, July 10.

I requested a farewell meeting with all the members of the delegation and wrote a short note to the secretary general of the United Nations, apologizing for my unexpected departure. I also prepared a memorandum to be sent to the ambassadors of all countries, notifying them of the circumstances of my departure, as was the customary method of diplomatic communication in such cases. While my wife was packing my summer clothes, I got ready to travel via the EgyptAir flight leaving for Cairo at 10:00 p.m.

We agreed that my wife would stay in New York for a few weeks to tend to our personal belongings before coming back to Cairo. This created a small problem: my son's fiancée was expected to arrive in New York with her sister on the same day I was to leave. Thus we met at the airport; she arrived and I left. To give my wife her due, I must admit that I have always burdened her with a lot of responsibilities, or to be exact, all familial responsibilities. For the thirty-six years of our marriage up to 2004, she raised and nurtured our children, Kamal and Ali, and supervised their education. My sole duty has been to work, and I am sure that had it not been for her constant support, I would not have achieved the success I did in my professional career.

The EgyptAir flight took off on time, and though I was very exhausted, I could not get a wink of sleep. I recalled many of the stages in my professional career, and how things developed from June 1, 1965, the day I joined the Egyptian Foreign Affairs Ministry, to the day I left New York to go home to be the foreign affairs minister. I also thought about the coming mission and the great responsibilities it entailed. Egypt is a big country with major status, significant responsibilities, and an important role in the Middle East, Africa, the Mediterranean, and the Red Sea. Furthermore, Egypt has a visible presence in all global policy circles, especially at the United Nations and its various specialized agencies, and is actively engaged in discussions on a wide range of issues. Egypt has shouldered many responsibilities and still does, especially when it comes to dealing with the Arab–Israeli conflict, both during the armed confrontation period and in the quest for a peaceful settlement, as we have witnessed since Sadat's visit to Jerusalem in November 1977.

Based on my reading of Egypt's history and its role in international developments over the last two hundred years, I was deeply convinced that Egypt has great international importance, not only because of its geographical location, but also because of the vitality and vigor of its people under any visionary and effective leadership. This was the source of Egypt's ability to influence its vital sphere and the wider interests of many superpowers whenever it got the chance. As an Islamic country, Egypt's magnitude attracts the attention of millions of Muslims. As an Arab country, Egypt has been at the forefront of defending an Islamic and Arab region, which was for centuries subjected to violent attacks from the Christian west, including the Crusades, the appearance of the Portuguese in the Red Sea and the Arabian Gulf in the sixteenth century, the fleets of Venice and Genoa in the Mediterranean at the end of the Mamluk era, and until the beginning of the Ottoman dominance. Egyptian leaders and rulers have always been required to lead its foreign policy and protect its security and interests in the midst of incessant competition between the great powers, which always projected their power and exercised their influence in the region.

When Mamluk Egypt came under the control of the Ottoman Empire for several centuries, efforts were made, from time to time, to escape this dependency within the limits of the circumstances prevailing at that time. For centuries, the rulers of Egypt made more than one attempt to achieve a degree of independence, and then to influence developments in its immediate surroundings, especially in the Mediterranean. Ali Bey al-Kabir, for example, attempted to escape the complete dominance of the Ottoman Empire and allied himself with Russia in order to exert pressure on the Ottomans. Another example is Muhammad Ali Pasha's conflict with the Ottoman Empire and his rapprochement with France. Then came Gamal Abd al-Nasser and the revolution of 1952, thwarting the plans of the western powers—the United States and the Anglo-Saxon allies—and getting closer to the Soviet Union.

All these ambitious attempts on the part of the rulers of Egypt to expand its external influence and regional clout failed. Despite the initial success of leaders such as Ali Bey al-Kabir, Muhammad Ali Pasha, and finally Gamal Abd al-Nasser in expanding Egyptian geopolitical influence into areas such as the Arabian Peninsula, the Red Sea and its southern approaches from the Horn of Africa and the Eritrean lands, and as far as the headwaters of the Nile, these leaders ultimately failed to ensure sustained Egyptian influence over these areas.

Tracing Egyptian diplomacy over a period of two hundred years from 1775 to 1975, I came to the conclusion that in its attempt to achieve its goals, Egypt leveraged the global balance of power and the interests of the great powers to serve its own interests. Ali Bey al-Kabir took advantage of Tsarist Russia's ambitions in the Mediterranean and its desire to gain access to warm waters and control the Black Sea straits to help Egypt escape Ottoman domination. However, this attempt, which entailed a great deal of Egyptian effort, failed for several reasons, the most important of which was the interference of the greatest navy in the world at that time—that of the British Empire. One more possible reason for the failure of Egypt's efforts was its early extension beyond its own borders, which revealed its intentions prematurely before it could build up its internal front.

Muhammad Ali Pasha, on the other hand, took the Egyptian project further by strongly aligning himself with France. Neither this alliance nor that of Ali Bey al-Kabir with Russia can be discussed in detail here. Both France and Russia were major land powers competing with the greatest naval power of the age, Britain. However, these experiences provide valuable strategic lessons that should be instructive to Egyptian decision-makers today in finding and securing a vital role for Egypt in nearby regions or those under its strategic, cultural, religious, and political influence.

The British naval forces challenged Muhammad Ali Pasha's project and defeated it. As a consequence, Egypt was subjected to British colonization for more than eighty years. As Gamal Abd al-Nasser sought to articulate a role for Egypt in combating imperialism and the receding colonizing forces, together with the burden of the Arab confrontation against Israel which was led by Egypt, he had to gradually get closer to the Soviet Union, the heir of Tsarist Russia. The Nasserist project was thwarted in turn by the greatest naval force of the time, namely that of the United States, during the Cold War. I have tried to study and evaluate these experiences, and I have often asked myself: Why didn't the Egyptians and their rulers try to support their ambitious projects through a more profound study and a thorough understanding of international developments and conditions? Why did they not understand the influence of the strategic concepts and principles of Admiral Mahan on the impact and importance of sea power, which disproved the views of Professor Halford Mackinder, who argued that land power and the control of the Eurasian heartland were the keys to global power? Why did they not notice that sea powers, especially in the modern age, have the greatest influence? These questions led to another question: Why did not we seek to ally ourselves with these global sea powers at the beginning of all of our geopolitical projects, and come to an understanding about their objectives and ambitions in relation to ours?

All these philosophical questions weighed heavily on my thoughts and the way I evaluated Egypt's circumstances over the previous decades, especially since June 5, 1967, when the Egyptian–Russian coalition was dealt a heavy blow. Though I knew that answering these questions was hard and complicated, I could not get them out of my mind for decades. I sometimes asked myself an even tougher question: Why did we repeatedly join allies that led to our defeat? We offered naval support to the Persians against the cities of Greece in ancient times; we fought with Hannibal and the Carthage fleets against Rome; we allied with Venice against Portugal in the war of the Indian Ocean and in the Battle of Dewey near Bombay.

As I reflected on Egypt's history and its past political experiences, I became convinced that geography played a central role in determining our actions. In addition, cultural imperatives also affected our policy choices and shaped our political destiny. These are complex historical and philosophical questions that require deep reflection and discussion. When I consider these questions today, I am seeking to encourage people to think deeply about the requirements and tenets of Egyptian foreign policy, based on its deeply rooted and extended history and exceptional geographical location. I believe that Gamal Hemdan's encyclopedic work is a must-read for any Egyptian official in the position of making decisions or administering Egypt's foreign policy, as it explains so clearly how history and geography influence Egypt's status and foreign policy.

I have often reflected on the philosophy of President Sadat and his posture toward the United States, the greatest naval power of the twentieth century. I felt that Sadat's policies echoed my own convictions about our foreign policy. Consequently, I have always been preoccupied with the way we should deal with the United States as the leader of the Christian, western world with absolute power to influence world policies and control countries and societies since the collapse of the Soviet Union, which used to be a safety net for many of our countries. The withdrawal of the Soviet role led to an overwhelming emergence of the United States and its unrivaled dominance over international affairs. Unfortunately, the United States exhibited a degree of prejudice against Islam and engaged in an extended confrontation with certain political and cultural currents in the Muslim world, causing serious harm to Muslim societies.

During the ten-hour flight to Cairo, my mind kept wandering through many of my deeply rooted convictions about Egyptian foreign policy. I thought about Egypt and the way it viewed the region and its role within it. Egypt has been a major Islamic power ever since it successfully confronted the Crusaders, the Christian western invasions of the region, and the attack of the Tatars on the Middle East. The Battle of Hittin of 1187, during which Saladin defeated the invading Crusaders, and the Battle of Ain Jalut of 1260, where Egypt vanquished the Mongul hordes, are unforgettable and illustrious marks in the consciousness and history of Islamic Egypt. But what about today, in a world of divided Islamic countries and western hegemony? On the one hand, there is Shi'i Iran, and on the other, there is Sunni Turkey with its Ottoman history; what should we do about both of them? These are the twin Islamic powers that have historically combated one another for dominance and influence over the region. Their mutual antipathy has lasted for some six hundred years and the history of their conflict remains vivid in memory. The invasions of Tamerlane and his destruction of Islamic civilization in the Caucasus, Central Asia, and Iran is a tale to be told for generations, as is the conflict between Shah Abbas of the Safavid Empire and Sultan Selim I of the Ottoman Empire. Finally, there is the Ottoman invasion of Syria and Egypt and the destruction of the Mamluk Sultanate, whose leaders, although Muslim, belonged to Iranian, Turkish, Azeri, and Central Asian ethnic groups. The history of the Muslim region is one of continuous internal conflicts. The challenge is how to change this sad reality into one of cooperation and mutual support in defense of the Islamic region in this era of western aggression and domination.

I have been preoccupied by these thoughts ever since the shock of the defeat of Egypt and the Arabs in 1967. I was searching for a true Islamic coalition but I was unfortunately led to the sad conclusion that such a coalition is an unachievable dream. How can it be achieved when relations between Iran and Turkey have always been marked by considerable animosity? When Egypt is preoccupied by a sense of responsibility to defend the region, including addressing security threats from Israel and ensuring the security of the Gulf area? When Turkey is solely driven by its economic and commercial interests, especially after the emergence of its economy and its need for markets? Moreover, Turkey insisted on building a relationship with the west and joined NATO, which made NATO an immediate neighbor of the Arab world in Iraq and Syria. All of these elements would leave their imprint on Egypt and its foreign policy.

I was of the opinion that we should spare no effort to build up a framework of cooperation among Egypt, Turkey, and Iran in order to establish security for the whole region and help to balance the influence of Israel and its relation to the west, thus fortifying the Islamic world's resistance capabilities. But can we succeed in achieving this goal? Would revolutionary Shi'i Iran agree to reach an understanding with both Egypt and Turkey? How far would Turkey be willing to go in order to build such a relationship without harming its essential interests with the western world, NATO, and Europe? All these questions need to be answered.

During the time of Sadat, Egypt took an opposite direction in dealing with Saudi Arabia from the one Gamal Abd al-Nasser had followed. Egyptian–Saudi cooperation after the defeat of 1967 contributed to restoring a degree of stability in the region, especially after the end of the conflict with Israel. However, the growth of Saudi economic and financial capabilities over the past forty years and the expected continuous development of the Saudi status in the coming decades on the one hand, and the continuing deterioration of Egypt's economic capabilities over the same period on the other, undoubtedly affected Egypt's willingness to accept a partner with such a big influence on the destiny of the region. As soon as I took up my position as minister of foreign affairs, I sensed the difficulty of this situation. I came to realize that the Egyptian–Saudi relationship is truly profound; it transcends the religious ties that shape the views of Egyptians about the Hijaz region.

Within this context, I monitored the financial and economic assistance that Saudis use in order to influence many Egyptian positions and decisions. This came in the form of financial deposits during Egypt's times of need, or as grants, at Egypt's request, in the form of wheat purchases worth hundreds of millions of dollars to cover Egypt's annual wheat requirements. I soon found out that Saudi Arabia's views are very influential in Egypt, especially because the support it offers comes not only from within the kingdom itself, but from the Emirates, Kuwait, and other countries of the Gulf Cooperation Council (GCC) as well.

After the defeat of 1967, Gamal Abd al-Nasser asked for the financial and economic support of Saudi Arabia and ended the Egyptian presence in

Yemen by an almost complete withdrawal. Egypt had its eye on the Saudi–Iranian rivalry at the time, and it was believed that building new bridges with the Saudis or mending the old ones was more beneficial to Egypt than cooperating with revolutionary Iran. For my part, I felt the need for answers to these complex questions based on political and economic realities.

Iraq had been attacked the previous year—2003—and Syria was now under threats and pressures. Iraq was, of course, lost the day it invaded Kuwait, on August 2, 1990. The Egyptian–Syrian axis did not endure for long in its attempt to support the GCC, nor did the Damascus Declaration, despite the fact that this declaration and the states that adopted it could have succeeded in restoring the region's ability to forge its own future in a period of conflict between Iran and the Arab region. It could also have helped to confront any attempt to penetrate the region by western powers. There remained one additional question: What could be done about Israel, which continued to expand into Palestinian lands and extinguish the aspirations of the Palestinians? How could we address the tragic situation of the Chairman of the Palestinian National Authority, Yasser Arafat, who was isolated and besieged in his headquarters in Ramallah, without any serious support from any Arab, Islamic, or international power? It was always possible to make dramatic announcements but, as we witnessed in previous eras, this was no longer possible nor constructive in confronting the aggression of Israel.

My thoughts wandered away from the Middle East, conflicting Islamic viewpoints, and the relations between Islam and the west, to the arena I was leaving at the time, that is, the United Nations, of which I had a deep knowledge and understanding. I believed that Egypt has had a real presence and continuous influence in this international arena for several decades, perhaps since the breakout of the 1948 war and certainly since the organization had become occupied with the Middle East because of the birth of the State of Israel. But there were new elements to be considered in 2004: the probability that other major world powers like Germany and Japan—powers that regained influence after their defeat in the Second World War in 1945—would seek to gain permanent membership in the Security Council. This, of course, would lead to substantial changes in the mapping of power relations in the United Nations and consequently leave its mark on the world in the twenty-first century. I concentrated on figuring out ways to protect our interests, to deal with India and Brazil and other countries that sought to introduce themselves into this international arena, and to consider the question of African representation on an enlarged Security Council.

It was no secret that Egypt had a great influence in Africa during the period extending from the consolidation of Nasser's rule in Egypt in 1955 until his confrontation with western powers and his ultimate defeat in 1967 at the hands of Israel. As a result of that defeat, Egypt began to retrench and reduce the extent of its commitment to supporting Africa against western interests, including by supporting revolutions against colonialism and the western imperial powers in Africa.

For decades, various African powers ascended or descended. Algeria, Ghana, and Nigeria, in particular, were considered favorably until the rise of South Africa in the mid-1990s, after the fall of the apartheid regime. At that point, Nigeria and South Africa were regarded as the best candidates to represent Africa in the UN Security Council: South Africa because of the strong emergence of democracy, and Nigeria because of its attempts to reach an acceptable democratic form of rule in such a large and diverse country. The Arab–African dimension, on the other hand, faded away out of the sight of the west, or perhaps was ignored, either because of western hostility to Islam or the fear of the possible appearance of extremist Islamic powers that might have a negative influence on the United Nations arena.

I believed that this matter should be one of the top priorities on the Egyptian foreign affairs agenda in the future. I was sure, however, that Egypt's economic power and its ability to serve the aims of Egyptian foreign policy was the main element in determining its success or failure to influence not only the region but Africa as well. With this economic strength established, a strong and influential image of Egypt would be guaranteed on the international level.

International relations at the time were ripe with many trends and ideas for the new millennium. The Millennium Development Goals had been adopted, various thematic conferences were being held at the

United Nations, and the annual High-Level Segment of the United Nations General Assembly meetings provided an excellent opportunity for heads of state to meet and confer. But for reasons that I did not know, the president of Egypt never made an appearance there. I decided that we must convince him to attend and participate, and I did my best to do so, but he adamantly refused. His refusal, it was said, was due to security concerns. To me, this situation was unclear; I believed that not paying enough attention to such issues and refusing to actively engage in international events and policy gatherings caused us much harm at the time, despite all the efforts that were exerted in order to secure active and effective Egyptian participation.

As for Sudan, I had the feeling that this country, which has always been described as Egypt's twin, was on the verge of explosion and that it would be divided not only into north and south, but into various provinces. Therefore, I believed that we must pay more attention to it, not only because it is an Arab and African country, but because of its African connections, which could be an advantage for Egypt. Sudan also had its disagreements with other African countries, which was a problem in its own right. Then there was the issue of Nile water security, and how to guarantee a sustainable supply of water for Egypt and defend Egypt's share of Nile waters in accordance with historical agreements. All these elements, of course, had their considerable importance, but the key to managing them was, as we have previously pointed out, great economic power, together with an Egyptian commitment to make a big comeback on the African scene like the one achieved during the Nasser era. I knew that would be a real challenge, considering the huge difference between what Abd al-Nasser had done for Africa and the current situation. Since the liberation wars were over, Africans no longer needed weapons, military training, external headquarters for anticolonial resistance, or international support for independence. What they needed from Egypt now was food, financing, investment, and development, all of which exceeded Egyptian capabilities.

Concerning the field of Egyptian–African relations, I believed that Boutros Boutros-Ghali exerted significant efforts during the period from

1977 to 1991. He established the Egyptian–Africa Cooperation Fund in the Ministry of Foreign Affairs. He made several tours and engaged in many activities in African countries, which undoubtedly helped him to become secretary general of the United Nations. But I was aware also that the fund's budget in 2004 did not exceed ten million dollars per year, a very small sum of money that could by no means be effective in advancing Egyptian relations with other African countries.

President Mubarak refused to participate in any of the African summits from 1995, following the assassination attempt against him at a summit in Addis Ababa, until 2004, when I was appointed foreign affairs minister. Egyptian security agencies increasingly insisted upon the danger of the president's visiting Africa. As a result, the Egyptian role in Africa began to recede despite the great efforts exerted by other Egyptian agencies, efforts that the president refused to participate in or lead. Once again, I sensed the need to exert more effort in order to contain the situation in Africa and encourage the president to reclaim an active role on the African scene. The following years actually witnessed an improvement in the president's viewpoint, as he started to show more interest in Africa. He participated in the African Union Summit more than once, in Nigeria, Ghana, and Libya, and sent the Egyptian prime minister to participate in summits. I must point out in this context that the concept of presidential participation in such summits and conferences is the key to opening doors on the African level. Unfortunately, many of these doors had been locked between 1995 and 2005.

I had a firm belief in the importance of keeping positive relationships with western powers, especially with the United States, the most influential world power, and the European Union, which had started to open up to the Middle East in its Mediterranean region through the cooperative framework of the Barcelona Declaration. The power relations between these two camps, that is, the American and the European, did not escape my notice at the time. Even though I believed that both of them actually represent one strategic and political bloc, I realized that they undoubtedly had political and economic rivalries, which would allow Egypt to move back and forth between them to pursue its interests.

I also estimated that the gross national product of Egypt reached around $150 billion in 2004, while that of the European Union and of the United States amounted to around $12 trillion each. Such comparisons are necessary in order to put economic issues in their due context.

I supported the opinion that we should maintain strong ties to the United States, and that these ties must be based on respect for the Egyptian viewpoint, no matter how different it was from that of the Americans. Yet it was also important for us to open up to and support other horizons of foreign relations with Asian powers like China, India, Indonesia, and Malaysia. Though I believed that China's complete rise as an Asian power needed at least three more decades, I was sure, even in 2004, that it was already an open field for Egyptian national security. We could benefit from the Chinese experience as a substitute for the west or as a parallel to it when it came to our need for weaponry and technology. I was also fully aware that we were partially open to China only in some limited fields at the time.

Like China, the Soviet Union was accessible to us and ready to play a major role in the balance of the region, thanks to its extended experience since 1955. Besides, Russia wanted to continue relating to the region by selling its weaponry. This could be a winning card for Egypt, which did not want to rely on the west as the sole supplier of weapons. That was a sensitive issue in our relationship to the United States, the country which, I believed, would continue to be the most influential world power and in particular would control the Middle East for decades, especially the Palestinian issue and the performance of Israel. Besides, it was clear that the United States—enraged after the destruction of the Twin Towers in New York on September 11, 2001—was pressuring the Arab and Islamic world in order to change the conditions that led to the emergence of world terrorism. Hence, we were in need of maneuverability and precise calculations so as not to lose the United States or be harmed by it in any way.

During my stay in New York in the mid-1980s I monitored the American preoccupation with ensuring the continuity of its global dominance and hegemony. When I returned to work in New York once again at the end of the 1990s, I found that this preoccupation had turned into some sort of obsession for the American elite, who were concerned about America's strategic relations with both rising and traditional powers that were likely to have influence in the twenty-first century. I consequently realized the importance of quiet diplomacy and sobriety in order to reinforce our relations with these powers.

I studied thoroughly the Egyptian approach of constantly seeking to declare the Middle East a zone free of weapons of mass destruction, and supporting the accession of Israel to the Nuclear Non-Proliferation Treaty. I believed it was important to us to continue following this approach despite the conflict it could entail with the United States. Back then, I believed that the Egyptian attitude did not represent a big problem to the west as long as they were still able to protect Israeli interests and to keep it out of the Nuclear Non-Proliferation Treaty, and I still hold the same belief today.

As the plane flew above the Atlantic, I thought about the institutional apparatus that oversaw and implemented Egyptian foreign policy. I noted that personal influences played a great role in managing this system. The Egyptian president, whether in the time of Nasser, Sadat, or Mubarak, was the principal actor and most influential decision-maker. There were also institutions and individuals that appeared and disappeared according to the will of the president. I have followed this matter throughout my career, first with the Egyptian national security advisor in July 1972, and then with the foreign affairs ministers Mohamed Ibrahim Kamel, Mustafa Khalil, Kamal Hassan Ali, Esmat Abdel Meguid, Amr Moussa, and finally with Ahmed Maher, and then when I became minister of foreign affairs in 2004. Naturally, I could not monitor or follow all the currents and competing forces of Egyptian diplomacy during the terms of Mahmoud Riyad, Morad Ghalib, Mohamed Hassan al-Zayyat, and Ismail Fahmy, due to my subordinate position at that time. In 2004 I considered that Osama El-Baz, who was very close to the president over the period from 1976 to 2004, still played an influential role in the decision-making process and the implementation of Egyptian foreign policy. I had to decide my attitude toward him accordingly and start playing with him!

El-Baz worked closely with deputy prime minister Ismail Fahmy from 1972 until Fahmy's resignation in November 1977. Supported by Fahmy, El-Baz succeeded in becoming close to the vice-president, Hosni Mubarak, who was assigned by President Sadat to perform certain foreign policy tasks that Fahmy needed to be aware of. Ismail Fahmy thus encouraged Osama El-Baz to offer advice by accompanying the vice-president on his missions abroad, and at the same time to keep an eye on the activities of Hosni Mubarak, who had to depend on the foreign policy institution and mechanisms to successfully perform his tasks.

Osama El-Baz continued to have a decisive influence during the terms of Mohamed Ibrahim Kamel, Mustafa Khalil, Kamal Hassan Ali, and Esmat Abdel Meguid as foreign affairs ministers. However, he was exceptionally keen on helping Amr Moussa, the new minister in May 1991, to achieve great success. In fact, Moussa enjoyed El-Baz's support for many years, since they began working together in 1974. El-Baz's willingness to help Moussa was particularly obvious when I participated with them in a meeting with the Syrian minister Farouk al-Sharaa in Damascus in June 1991. The Egyptian and the Syrian parties met to discuss Saudi and Gulf attempts to revise the Damascus Declaration and dilute the military and security role assigned to Egypt and Syria in the Arabian Gulf pursuant to this declaration when it was signed on March 6, 1991. I noticed that El-Baz kept silent all the time, unlike his meetings with other foreign affairs ministers; he was used to interfering in discussions all the time in a manner that annoyed them sometimes. I remember that on this particular day, and perhaps because of my experience in the preparation of the Damascus Declaration and my participation in all the meetings that led to its signing, I intervened with some views and comments that were agreed upon by Farouk al-Sharaa, who had headed the Syrian diplomatic corps during the drafting period. Dr. El-Baz came to me after the meeting and said, "Oh, Ahmed, please keep in mind that we have to help Amr Moussa and give him the chance to show his potential." I then realized how self-denying El-Baz was when it came to helping Amr Moussa.

I kept thinking about this situation. It was said that El-Baz's influence within Egypt's political system was receding and that the president was no longer inclined to depend on him as he did in the 1980s and 1990s. My relationship with El-Baz was based on deep respect for his capabilities and his practices, and I sensed that he too appreciated my experience and my role in helping many foreign affairs ministers to accomplish their tasks efficiently.

When I was appointed foreign affairs minister on June 14, 2004 and started shouldering my responsibilities, I quickly detected that El-Baz had already receded and ceased to have a decisive influence on the president. Besides, he was no longer among the close circle of the political advisors of the president, nor did he write the president's letters to other presidents or remain in direct contact with him as he had been in the past. For many years during which I worked with a large group of Egyptian foreign affairs ministers, I have monitored El-Baz's performance and his relationship with the president. Back then, he had been the person with the most decisive influence on the president's decisions in foreign affairs; his influence immensely exceeded the normal authority of the position of the principal undersecretary of the Ministry of Foreign Affairs to which he clung so tightly. I can safely say that the role Osama El-Baz played sometimes exceeded the roles of foreign affairs ministers and that the tasks assigned to him by Egyptian presidents were equivalent to those of both the national security advisor and the president's secretary for political and diplomatic affairs.

I did not attempt to learn the reasons for this quick fading out of El-Baz's influence. It could have been due to the appearance of other persons or parties within the realm of Egyptian foreign affairs, or health problems, or even mistakes on his part that I do not know of but which led the president to gradually push him away. The history of Egyptian foreign policy will, I believe, find answers to these questions.

On arriving in Cairo on Sunday, July 11, 2004, I was met by Ambassador Sameh Shoukry, whom I had decided to make my chief of cabinet and principal assistant. I asked if he had heard anything about whether the position of the minister of state for foreign affairs, held at the time by the respected Fayza Abul Naga, would remain, and he answered that he had no idea. I preferred that this position be removed, since it had been proven, through long years of experience, to lead to many complications in the conduct of Egyptian diplomacy, especially during the term of Ahmed Maher. As a young diplomat, I had observed the role of Morad Ghalib, Sameh Anwar, Mohamed Riyad, Hafiz Ismail, and Mohamed Fa'iq, all of whom were ministers of state for foreign affairs who worked with foreign affairs ministers like Mahmoud Riyad and Ismail Fahmy, and I had seen that it was the cause of many problems. Later on, I worked in a more effective position and got closer to Mohamed Ibrahim Kamel, Kamal Hassan Ali, Esmat Abdel Meguid, and finally Amr Moussa while Boutros Boutros-Ghali was the minister of state. I witnessed several conflicts and contradictory viewpoints. There were occasions when the minister of foreign affairs presented his opinion in front of the Council of Ministers (Cabinet), then the minister of state offered a different opinion on behalf of the Ministry of Foreign Affairs in front of the same council, and sometimes during the same session.

I was convinced beyond any doubt that the position of minister of state for foreign affairs is actually a source of non-stop conflict and strife that should not be allowed. I had been informed by Minister Ahmed Maher back in 2002 that he had resisted the idea of appointing a minister of state for foreign affairs and talked to President Mubarak about this in August 2001. When Maher learned that the president insisted on having it because he was worried about Maher's health and wanted to make things easier for him, he suggested my name as a candidate and proposed that the title should be 'minister of state in the Ministry of Foreign Affairs,' instead of 'minister of state of the Ministry for Foreign Affairs.' This way, the position would not have the status it had previously had in the ministry. But the president refused both suggestions and appointed Abul Naga as minister of state. The president, I believe, had calculated that the person in this position, especially with Ahmed Maher, would face many problems in his relation to the foreign affairs minister, and he imagined that choosing a lady for the position would ease the tensions between the two ministers. Abul Naga actually succeeded in handling Ahmed Maher's anger, but her wisdom did not completely prevent the conflicts and maneuvers of which the president knew; he thus preferred not to keep this position when appointing a new minister whose personality and style were not known to him despite all the written reports and the opinions he had received about me.

At the time, I told Ahmed Maher, as we were strolling in Central Park in New York, that I would not have been happy to be appointed minister of state and work with him, despite all the good feelings and respect I had for him, because he would have treated me as "the minister whom I chose" or as "the third secretary who had worked with me" when we both served in the national security advisor's office. I told him that I would not have accepted that position after I had worked as Egypt's permanent representative to the United Nations for more than five and a half years. Strange as it was, my close friend Mohamed Assem Ibrahim called from Cairo while I was still in New York and said that he had heard that I was chosen as minister of state for foreign affairs to assist Ahmed Maher. I was annoyed and told him decisively that I would not accept this position, that Maher had discussed it previously with me in 2001 and I had refused, and that I still had the same attitude.

Back to my evaluation of President Mubarak's vision of how the Egyptian Ministry of Foreign Affairs should implement its policies to achieve its aims: Mubarak was convinced of the importance of the position of minister of state. It is noteworthy that this position had existed ever since Mubarak was appointed vice-president in 1975; hence, it was not strange that he would try to find a qualified diplomat to fill it and replace Boutros Boutros-Ghali, who left Cairo on January 1, 1992 to take up his responsibilities as secretary general of the United Nations. I often discussed this issue with Amr Moussa and told him that he had to be prepared with a list of suggested names in case the president obliged him to have a minister of state. In May 1992, the president tried to appoint one candidate or another, but Amr Moussa resisted the attempt and maneuvered until the subject was forgotten for a while. When the relationship between Moussa and the president started to develop difficulties in the late 1990s, discussion of this subject was resumed.

Since the beginning of 2006, I had been told by the prime minister that the president often expressed his sympathy with the minister of foreign affairs for having to travel for long distances all the time, and repeated that it was important to find some way to help him. I would reply to this rather coldly, saying that I could not tolerate such a situation because it would complicate matters and cause endless conflicts within the ministry and in managing Egyptian foreign policy elsewhere. However, I would add that

I was ready to accept the appointment of a deputy foreign minister who worked under a clearly defined system of leadership. I even presented a list of suggested names of current and former ambassadors to the prime minister, and proposed that they be assigned certain missions according to the vision and priorities of the foreign affairs minister.

At the beginning of 2006, I traveled to Latin America for a whole week. During those seven days, I represented Egypt in a two-day Latino–Arab summit, which the president and prime minister decided not to attend, spent three days on bilateral visits to Brazil, Argentina, and Chile, and spent a total of two days traveling. When I returned to Egypt, I met the president in Sharm al-Sheikh. He calmly pointed out that I had been away for a while and that he needed to have a foreign affairs minister who would be available whenever he wanted him. He also mentioned that he was concerned for my health, with all the pressure I was under. I told him I was aware that he had suggested the need for a state minister for foreign affairs, and that it was my duty to tell him honestly that this position had its complications and that it had often led to conflicts and strife. I added that my experience throughout my work with several foreign ministers proved that it was always difficult to achieve the needed balance and agreement between the two ministers. He replied that he did not feel comfortable with having a deputy minister and that he had no candidates for any additional position in the ministry. I did not suggest any names myself and the subject was closed for good.

From the time I was Egypt's ambassador in Rome in 1992, and throughout the 1990s, I heard that the role of Omar Suleiman, director of General Intelligence, was becoming more influential, especially after the assassination attempt on Mubarak in Addis Ababa in 1995. I could see the growth of his role myself in April 2001 when he accompanied the president on a visit to Washington. He arrived earlier than the president and contacted all the American agencies, including Secretary of State Powell, despite the presence of Amr Moussa—who was getting ready to leave his position as minister of foreign affairs to go to the Arab League the following month—in the same delegation.

I was also aware that the Egyptian General Intelligence had had a great influence in implementing certain missions in Egyptian foreign policy ever since it was established in 1957. Though this had always been true with respect to Egyptian relations with Arab counties, this influence became even more manifest in our relations with Libya after Colonel Qadhafi's 1969 coup, and in our relations with Algeria since its independence in 1963. In spite of the fact that we had well-informed and active ambassadors in these countries, the intelligence officer served as an additional observer for the administration in Egypt to help it discern and evaluate the conditions in these countries. This has been the case throughout all those years no matter who the foreign affairs minister was or how strong his influence was on the president.

Sudan was an obvious example of this after its June 1989 revolution. The Egyptian intelligence representative in Sudan had a particularly powerful presence. The Sudanese tried to change him, to no avail, after Egyptian–Sudanese relations became more complicated in the early 1990s. They succeeded in doing so only once, when they demanded the replacement of Magdy Abd al-Moneim Omar, first undersecretary of the Egyptian General Intelligence, who was nominated in 1989 to be Egypt's ambassador in Khartoum, and Cairo had to accept their demand, as the relationship between Cairo and Khartoum had deteriorated to the point where Cairo could not insist on its choice of ambassador.

Though the influence of the Egyptian General Intelligence was strong for decades, it was limited only to the specific files of a few neighboring countries, especially Sudan, Libya, and Israel, and the degree of influence depended on whether the administrations in these countries accepted or resisted it. It was certain that Sudan and Libya encouraged this kind of relationship and influence at certain periods, while Jordan, Syria, Iraq, and all the Gulf countries sought to prevent it, since they believed that Egyptian interference had its risks. However, there has been no such interference since the end of Abd al-Nasser's rule, especially after the defeat of June 1967, which led to many strategic reconciliations and the withdrawal of the Egyptian Intelligence in these countries.

The importance of the role of Intelligence and its men, according to my own vision, was always about collecting data and news and analyzing them to help the decision-maker. Therefore, introducing recommendations and suggestions about the country's policies or how to tackle one issue or another was acceptable. Still, this role should never have extended to the executive realm as it did during the decades of Mubarak's rule. No matter how efficient the General Intelligence was, claiming an executive role would take it away from its essential role of collecting and analyzing news and data.

As for Omar Suleiman's role: he worked more closely with the president once he became the head of military intelligence in the Egyptian Armed Forces in 1988. His relation to the president became even closer after May 1991, when he was appointed head of the Egyptian General Intelligence. His authority and influence were wisely, calmly, and cautiously growing and expanding. The "traditional" influence of the General Intelligence increased in areas such as relations with Sudan, Libya, Israel, the Horn of Africa, and the Palestinians.

When I came back home in 2004 and assumed my duties as minister of foreign affairs, I realized that this influence was not due to institutional conditions only, but mainly due to the personality of General Omar Suleiman himself and the extra effort he put into his work, day and night, together with the president's trust in his personal judgment. I also noticed another phenomenon that did not happen during my work with Esmat Abdel Meguid or Amr Moussa: Suleiman started to meet ministers of foreign affairs and major officials visiting Cairo after Ahmed Maher started to work in 2001. His viewpoints became influential and his impact became powerful in the field of foreign policy, especially in relation to the Palestinian issue. When the U.S. Central Intelligence Agency was assigned to manage the relationship between the security agencies of the Palestinian National Authority and Israel right after the outbreak of the Second Intifada, the Egyptian General Intelligence too played a large, if subordinate, role. This, in turn, enhanced Omar Suleiman's relationship with George Tenet, director of the U.S. Central Intelligence Agency, and his successors. It also boosted Suleiman's personal status with the Americans and his relation to American secretaries of state who had a role in Palestinian affairs. I was preoccupied with all these thoughts about him during my flight and throughout the first weeks of my work as foreign affairs minister.

My first mission during the first week after my return to Cairo was to travel to Libya to get acquainted with Colonel Qadhafi, at his request. He had phoned President Mubarak about it and Omar Suleiman was sent with me. During the flight to Libya we discussed this mission, and it was then that I noticed many traits about his personality; he was honest, well-seasoned, and admirably organized in his thinking and his speech. As soon as we landed at Sirte Airport, Libyans affectionately celebrated his arrival, and when we entered Colonel Qadhafi's tent, it was obvious that the Libyan leader was greatly interested in Suleiman's opinions.

Two days after our visit to Sirte, we had another mission: traveling together to Khartoum to meet President Omar al-Bashir, then to Darfur to witness the deteriorating situation there. The Sudanese too showed their affection and interest in him and it was clear that he possessed prolific knowledge about this country as well.

I felt greatly embarrassed when we traveled on missions together. According to Egyptian protocol, which was based on the seniority of office, the minister of foreign affairs came ahead of the director of general intelligence. Suleiman, however, was eight years my senior and enjoyed considerable political influence. He had been a high-profile official while I was still gradually moving up the ranks. Although all parties dealt with us in accordance with the seniority protocol, Suleiman was satisfied with his position as number two in that protocol, even when we traveled with President Mubarak. I often brought up the subject with Suleiman during our travels, and I told him I was surprised that President Mubarak did not promote him or give him the title or position of deputy prime minister, so that he would be senior to many of the ministers who otherwise preceded him in the seniority protocol and in forming Egyptian delegations accompanying the president. To tell the truth, the man would keep silent and continue working out of a sense of patriotism, transcending any personal goals despite the authority and influence he had and the fact that many people resorted to him for advice or if they had complaints.

My relationship with Omar Suleiman dated back to 1992 when I was appointed ambassador in Rome and visited him at the headquarters of Egyptian General Intelligence to listen to his views concerning our relations with Italy and to establish the responsibilities of the 'liaison officer' from the agency in relation to the Italian authorities. It was a warm meeting.

I met him again before starting work in New York in 1999, to discuss the international scene and Egypt's relationship with the international community. I could detect his clear vision, analytical skills, and well-developed viewpoints on many international problems over the years that he held that position, from 1991 to 2011.

From the start of my mission, I decided to cooperate with Suleiman and with the General Intelligence, and I never regretted it. He soon became an open book to me and we exchanged thoughts and ideas all the time, until we came to the point that he would find it strange if we did not call one another on a daily basis. He would then seize the first chance to get in touch and complain about the loss of contact between us. President Mubarak had always expressed his satisfaction about the way we and our agencies cooperated to effectively boost Egyptian foreign policy during these years. Our close relationship continued until the end of President Mubarak's rule in 2011. Suleiman did not keep any secrets from me when it came to matters concerning the Ministry of Foreign Affairs and its staff, and often disclosed to me reports he had received about the performance of ambassadors or other members which might negatively affect our reputation or viewpoints. In most cases, he did this verbally without sending written notes or letters, unless there was something very serious. I used to listen to him and study the situation, then react according to my obligations toward the country, its foreign policy, or the staff member in question. Sometimes I needed to protect staff members and defend them against malicious rumors. On the other hand, I used to give him, verbally or in writing, depending on the gravity of the subject, the ministry's opinion and evaluation of the performance of officers of the General Intelligence Agency who worked for ambassadors.

We trusted one another highly and exchanged opinions about almost everything. During one of our trips to Sudan, we discussed Gamal Mubarak's chances of ruling Egypt and what the president could do to settle that issue. Both of us, of course, were against this form of presidential succession and were sure that the Egyptian army and its leadership would never accept such a situation. During the flight, Suleiman said that in 2003 and 2004, there was some talk of replacing Ahmed Maher with a younger minister who could understand Gamal Mubarak. The person said to be under consideration at the time was our ambassador in Washington, but the president's opinion prevailed, and I was chosen because of my seniority and my experience.

It was only natural that my thoughts would next lead to my relationship with the president and with his high-profile officials, including the head of the Presidential Cabinet and the president's secretary for information, who was usually a member of the Egyptian diplomatic corps, and thus theoretically affiliated with me.

I had closely followed the relationship between the president and the ministers of foreign affairs I had worked with through the phone calls they made in my presence. While working with Kamal Hassan Ali in 1982, I detected that the president was very decisive in his words and instructions and that both Esmat Abdel Meguid and Amr Moussa received his calls attentively. I had also attended meetings with Kamal Hassan Ali and Esmat Abdel Meguid with foreign leaders abroad, in which the president had headed the Egyptian delegations. The way he talked to them revealed his energy, decisiveness, and presence; he closely followed the conversation and what had been agreed with them.

Consequently, I expected many challenges in my mission and in my relationship with him. However, I was surprised that when I started working with him in 2004, he appeared to be a different person; he looked old, and his enthusiasm, decisiveness, and concentration had waned with the passage of the years. This gave me some freedom of movement, despite the fact that the presidential authority and his central method of management held firm to the end.

As the years passed, we faced many crises, both inside Egypt and on the level of the foreign affairs, and I gradually came to the conclusion that the president could not control or grasp the details of the issues at hand. Hence, it was important to have an influential vice-president who could organize and manage issues before presenting them to the president. This, however, did not happen until the last ten days of the president's rule; it should have happened in the previous five years, or even ten.

The traditional information channel with the president has always been through an information secretary, a veteran diplomat from the Foreign

Affairs Ministry. For that reason, I realized from the start that it was vital to keep in touch with this diplomat, to supply him with all the information and analysis that he needed, and to follow up as he presented them to the president. Therefore, I showered those diplomats with countless documents and ideas over the course of seven years, a practice that often made them complain about the load they received from the Ministry of Foreign Affairs that had to be presented to the president. On many occasions, I mentioned during my conversations with the president that we had already sent him those ideas. He would then ask the information secretary about it, which put him under severe pressure all the time.

In the course of figuring out my new situation, I eventually came to the role of the head of the presidential office, which was getting bigger as the president aged. I believed that maintaining a positive and professional relationship based on mutual respect with him was essential to preserve our interests and our relations with other countries. This was especially important when foreign officials visited Egypt and asked to meet the president, and when making arrangements for the president's visits to other countries.

The president was aging, as I have already pointed out. Accordingly, the president's office increasingly tried to lighten his burdens and decrease the number of daily and weekly visits, which often caused some trouble with the head of the office. I was able, however, through my relationship to him, to soften him up and facilitate the visits, and thus keep good ties with countries and individuals. Nevertheless, there had been some pitfalls that complicated international relations that should not have been damaged. The concept of protecting the president, reducing his obligations, and accommodating his decreasing concentration span, took priority over all other matters.

On the evening of my arrival in Cairo on Sunday, June 11, I received a call from the Council of Ministers inviting me to meet Dr. Ahmed Nazif. The next day, we met for a very brief time. It was well known in Egypt that the prime minister did not interfere with the work of the foreign affairs minister, or at least that was very obvious during Mubarak's rule. This, of course, led to many problems between both parties, as could be particularly seen in the relationship between Kamal Hassan Ali and Dr. Fouad Mohieddin at the beginning of Mubarak's rule, during the years 1981–84, and between Amr Moussa and Kamal El-Ganzouri. Naturally, prime ministers wanted to assert their status, while foreign affairs ministers assured everyone that the leadership chain of foreign affairs ended at the president and that prime ministers had nothing to do with it, unless it directly affected a matter that was within the jurisdiction of the prime minister.

My first meeting with Dr. Ahmed Nazif was characterized by courtesy and nothing more. Throughout the years I was foreign affairs minister, I did not have substantial problems with him, except once or twice, which I will come to later. On the day I met him, I received a warm welcome call from Omar Suleiman and another from Dr. Osama El-Baz expressing his great enthusiasm.

My oath of office was on Wednesday, July 14. I went to the president's office in Heliopolis Palace. Members of the new government lined up with the prime minister in the front, followed by the ministers in order of seniority. When my turn came and I was face to face with the president, I took the oath and shook hands with him; what I saw that day was a tired and bored face. Then a meeting was held for the whole government in which he talked very briefly and gave general instructions before ending the meeting quickly. I expected to be asked to meet with him, especially because I knew that he gave special priority to foreign affairs and tended to manage it directly through the foreign affairs minister or the head of the intelligence and other national security agencies—that is, the Ministries of Defense and Interior Affairs. But the president did not ask to meet me, and I was surprised; how would I start my work without getting any directions from him or talking about his vision of what was to be achieved in this new stage, and what the specific goals of the new government were? I left the Presidential Palace—also referred to as 'Ittihadiya,' meaning 'unity.' It used to be the headquarters of the Union of Arab Republics during President Sadat's years or the headquarters of the central government of the United Arab Republic during the three years from 1958 to 1961 when Egypt and Syria were united.

I reached the Ministry of Foreign Affairs and took up my job anyway. As soon as I entered the building, I asked for the coming week's schedule, June 14–21; I already knew that a ministerial meeting of the countries bordering Iraq and Egypt was to be held on June 20.

Since this meeting was my first, I wanted the preparation for it to be properly done. Sameh Shoukry, the assistant minister, gave me a memorandum about the arrangements, which I read very carefully to learn all the aspects and background details, and I wrote some specific instructions for preparing for the meeting.

As soon as I finished reading the memorandum, I received a phone call from the presidency's number, which I have known since my early years of work with Minister Mohamed Ibrahim Kamel in 1977 and the rest of the foreign affairs ministers. I heard the voice of the president's secretary on the other end saying that the president wanted to speak to me. That was my first call with him. I waited for a while until I heard his voice, which was calm and courteous but very feeble; I wondered if his recent spine surgery had affected him that much. He said that he knew a meeting would be held in Cairo in a few days and hoped that I would take care of it. He did not talk much and I thanked God that I had finished reading the report about the meeting right before receiving his call and was therefore able to brief him about it and explain what we intended to do. I could sense that he was relieved; he added that we would meet soon to discuss other foreign affairs matters. I told him I was ready for any direction from him; but weeks and months passed by and we did not meet.

I participated in other meetings that were headed by the president, but I was not given the direction I expected from him. I had to work on my own, according to the general line of Egyptian foreign policy that I had known and practiced for decades.

In June 2004, I recalled the news I had heard about the president's loss of interest in many foreign policy issues and international personalities, and I could actually see it was true. He no longer showed enough interest in important rising powers like India, with its accelerating capabilities or China, which possessed massive economic power, or Brazil, the emerging Latin American power, or in the relationships between all of them, on the one hand, and the old western powers, on the other. My analysis of this was that the president's long years of dealing with foreign affairs had diminished his interest and made him feel there was nothing new. On the other hand, the president was captive to his relationships with major personalities, including all the French presidents, German chancellors, and high-profile Italian officials, all of whom took a great interest in Egypt and were eager to visit it, meet the president, and exchange views. Thanks to the president's long years of experience, there was a feeling of tiresomeness, a sense that we had been through all of this before and there was nothing new to be done. Though this attitude was not very encouraging, I decided to do my best according to my own vision and analysis of international developments as I had studied them throughout the early years of the new millennium to see how they affected Egypt, the Arab region, the Arab–Israeli conflict, and the role of the regional powers, such as Iran or Turkey, in that conflict.

# 2
# UPBRINGING AND PREPARATION

I graduated from Masr al-Gadida Secondary School in July 1959. My grades were reasonable enough to allow me to be admitted to various colleges, except the schools of medicine or engineering, neither of which I was interested in anyway.

At the time, my father was in Bonn, where he was serving as the chief procurement officer for the armed forces in Germany. I sent him a letter telling him that I wanted to join one of the military academies, either the Air Force Academy or the Military Academy, which had been my dream since childhood. I received his firm and final refusal saying that he would not only refuse to let me apply for any of them, but would also do his best to see that I failed the interview required for these colleges. I argued with him for weeks, but to no avail, until the application deadline had passed and I thought that there was no chance for me to join the military. Angry, frustrated, and desperate, I entered the Faculty of Science, Ain Shams University, feeling that my hopes were gone and the efforts I had exerted for ten years, reading and trying to grasp military affairs, had been wasted.

My father, Ali Ahmed Aboul Gheit, had been a pilot in the Royal Air Force since 1939, and had been transferred among different Egyptian air bases, which were limited in number back then. He and other Egyptian fighter pilots participated in the Palestine War in May 1948, especially in bomber operations that raided Israeli airports, cities, and other establishments. I was six years old then, and strangely enough, despite my young age, I was somehow aware that there was war, that Egypt was fighting the "Jews" in Palestine, and that my father was taking part in it. Maybe that was why all my toys and my interests at that age had to do with airplanes, tanks, and war. I often reenacted my father's role when playing, especially when I met with other pilots' families and their kids. After the war ended, my father traveled to Britain on a scholarship to study air navigation, which was a new science at that time, and left us in our apartment on Sohag Street in Heliopolis near Almaza Airport, which was the main air base of the Egyptian Air Force. I remained with my mother, Fatma Mohamed al-Messiri, and my sister, who was not yet a year old. My father had met my mother through his brother, who was married to her stepsister. The two sisters, and thirteen other children, were the daughters and sons of General Mohamed al-Messiri of the Egyptian Ministry of Interior, who had worked for years as Khedive Abbas Hilmi's adjutant at the beginning of the First World War.

My father came back to Egypt from Britain at the beginning of 1950, where he had received advanced training on air navigation. He was transferred to Alexandria to establish and manage a new air navigation school at al-Dekhaila Airport. We all moved to live with him in the airport officers' residence, and I entered Moharram Bey Model School. Living at the airport, I noticed hundreds of pieces of broken equipment: cars, airplanes, and tanks that had been collected in the airport or outside its walls since the end of the Battle of al-Alamein in October 1942 and the withdrawal of the Axis Forces from Egypt. I spent hours, and sometimes days, in this huge warehouse of rundown broken military equipment.

My parents had a dreadful premonition that I would have an accident or touch something that I should not. Thus, a conscript was always assigned to accompany me. My interest in war and military life started to grow. I came across a collection of military books that belonged to one of my uncles; I had five who served in the Armed Forces, some of whom took part in Egypt's several wars with Israel. One of them, Vice Air Marshal Nabih al-Messiri, was the chief of staff of the Egyptian Air Force during the October 1973 War. All the books dealt with war and strategy in general and the Middle East wars in ancient history, or during the First and Second World Wars in particular. They were profound, fascinating books, which the Egyptian Army had translated to enrich its library as soon as the Second World War ended. I also believe that these books were given to the military personnel free of charge. Some of these books, which consisted of several volumes of three hundred pages each, dealt with North African campaigns of the Second World War during the period from 1940 to 1943. These books outlined the strategic objectives of the belligerents, the leaders of the various armies, and the weapons they used. They also detailed the overall political goals of the Axis powers in the Mediterranean and the threat they posed to western dominance over Syria and Iraq reaching Iran, and threatening the oil reserves and their supplies to the Allies. I started to get acquainted with the term 'strategy,' its meaning and purpose. I also read several books on the First World War, on the western theater and Russia, and in the Palestine region between the Turks and the British. These books influenced my understanding of matters when Egypt was engaged in its series of wars with the rising Israeli entity in Palestine. I noticed that in its translation of these marvelous books, the Egyptian army focused on desert warfare, its tactics, the kind of weapons used in them, and the leaders who fought these wars, their experiences and concepts, as well as the effectiveness of specific weapons and their impact on the desert: tanks, planes, anti-tank artillery, and tactical and strategic camouflage and deception.

I found it strange that none of these works were written by Egyptian military authors. I noticed, however, that some of the books on the strategy of the Middle East in particular had been written by some of the rising Egyptian military figures, one of whom was Mohamed Hafiz Ismail, or by civilians like Mohamed Hassanein Heikal.

My father was transferred to Cairo at the start of the Egyptian Revolution in July 1952, and started a ten-year journey during which he took over the command of several military bases. Then he took a training course to obtain a General Staff degree from the Royal Air Force Staff College in Andover in southern England. When he returned, he was appointed as deputy commander of the Eastern Air Command. It was at that time that the British departed the Suez Canal region. As he moved from one place to another, he was accompanied by the whole family. On many occasions, I sat silently in our dining room, whether in the officers' residence in Heliopolis or in our apartment in Andover in southern England, to follow my father's conversation with his Egyptian or foreign pilot colleagues as they discussed air operations and practices and military projects that they were assigned. My passion for the army, aviation, the Armed Forces, and war in general increased.

One of my cousins had married a young Moroccan man who had studied in Egypt, then traveled to Cambridge University for further study. Before leaving, he left at my family's house a huge number of books dealing with conditions in North Africa, and the Arab people's attempts to achieve independence from colonizing western powers. I read all these books when I was only thirteen or fourteen years old. I was thus exposed to the state of affairs in the Arab world and I became aware of the nationalist sentiments motivating Arabs to demand their independence and end centuries of foreign domination. Among these books, I read two translated books published by al-Helal publishing house. The first was about Mustafa Kemal Atatürk, written by a British-Indian author. The second was about Genghis Khan and the Mongol wars in Asia, and how they moved to the Arab regions and then the Mediterranean; it also dealt with the fall of Baghdad and Damascus and how Egypt regained control of them in the battle of Ain Jalut.

Whenever I met my cousin in Cairo or in Morocco years later, I would talk about the influence of the books and papers that her husband—the late Mohamed al-Sadany, who later became a renowned ambassador in the Moroccan Ministry of Foreign Affairs—had left behind, and how they left their imprint on my personality and broadened my horizons. I owe this man much gratitude.

The personality of Atatürk inspired my feelings and thoughts and encouraged me to get to learn about this leader and his struggle to establish modern Turkey. I lived under the influence of this personality for years, especially during the years after Nasser's revolution in 1952 and his attempts to establish a modern and developed society. In later years, I read many books about this legendary figure, and I visited his tomb and the museum attached to it in Ankara whenever I went there to meet Turkish leaders.

Through the other book about Genghis Khan, I was introduced to Asia, China, and Japan, Tatar and Mongol tribes, and migrations of the populations and peoples and tribes of Central Asia to the Middle East and Eastern Europe. These readings introduced me to European history: the Greeks and their conflict with Persia's Achaemenid Empire, and the Peloponnesian War between Sparta and its allies on the one hand, and Athens and its supporters from the Greek cities on the other. This led me to study land power and its influence, with its freedom of movement in the face of sea power. This paved the way to other readings in the history of Macedonia, Alexander the Great, and Rome, both the republic and the empire. This gave me a comprehensive view of history.

When I entered the Faculty of Science at Ain Shams University in 1959, I started to study subjects that I was not passionate about. Many of my friends and acquaintances had entered military academies, since it was a period of escalating nationalism. I studied zoology, botany, entomology, and physics, as well as geology and rocks; none of these subjects were what I had hoped for, nor would ever be. My passion lay completely elsewhere. When my father came back after an eighteen-month mission in Bonn, West Germany, I started complaining and nagging him about it, which intensified the conflict in the family. My father did not like the idea of my joining the air force; he had lost many of his pilot friends over the years. He wanted to prepare me, his only son, for a less dangerous career. Many of his friends from the military intervened to help convince him to let me join the Armed Forces, and he gradually started to soften. But he still insisted that I should not enter the Air Force Academy or the Military Academy. He finally relented, and allowed me to join the Military Technical College, which first opened in September 1959. He went to meet Field Marshal Abdel Hakim Amer in December 1959 and asked him to make an exception to admit me to the college halfway through the academic year if I could pass the medical examination, and he agreed. Thus, I was admitted to the Military Technical College on December 19, 1959 after passing the medical examination. I was four months behind my first-year colleagues, which, of course, affected my studies, and I could not keep up with some of the important subjects, especially mathematics and geometry. I remained in the third brigade of the Khalid bin Walid battalion for several weeks in one of the barracks, going through the daily routines of sleeping, waking up, and going to the dining hall for meals, without studying enough, which naturally decreased my chances of success. I was also aware that I had not attended basic training like the rest of my colleagues. That was a very tough period, during which I felt I could never catch up with them when it came to the technical sciences. I could not make it into the second year of the college and I had to choose between starting all over again in September 1960 or transferring to the Military Academy, which my father adamantly refused. One of my uncles, Ambassador Ahmed Mohamed al-Messiri, could sense the predicament my father and I were in, and he suggested that I go back to university and seek a degree that would lead to the diplomatic corps. That suggestion hit a nerve with me, and I left the college in a haze of burning tears. Though the year, or rather, the eight months I spent in the Military Technical College were harsh, they were actually beneficial in the way they influenced my personality. I developed a sense of discipline, hard work, and being well prepared for any situation. My slogan remained the same for ever after: "Duty, honor, homeland," which is the slogan that Gamal Abd al-Nasser had given to the Military Technical College when he inaugurated its buildings and its headquarters in Heliopolis during his visit in 1958.

I returned to Cairo University in September 1960, but this time I was enrolled in the Faculty of Commerce. I had set a goal of entering the Ministry of Foreign Affairs. When I graduated in 1964, I applied for the entry exam for diplomatic attachés which the Ministry of Foreign Affairs had announced would be held on September 12, 1964. I had to race in order to get ready for the exam by reading up on the topics. I had no prior knowledge of international law, which was one of the major subjects of the exam. I have to admit here that my earlier readings about strategy and international relations positively influenced my personality and facilitated my entry into the Egyptian diplomatic corps. The four years of university study gave me the chance not only to read for the degree, but also to do more influential reading in other subjects. I read extensively on Marxist thought, Soviet history, the era of Stalin, and the Cold War. I also read about the Nazi era, fascism, and the emergence of the United States on the international scene.

At this point of my life, I was deeply impressed by socialist philosophy and the concepts of social justice, and the need to establish a society based on them. These were my political leanings throughout the Nasser era until the shock and disillusionment of June 1967. Therefore, I always wanted to work in Egypt's embassy in the Soviet Union under the leadership of the great Egyptian ambassador Morad Ghalib, who was a close friend of my father.

On October 1, 1964, I received a phone call at home: one of the employees of the Diplomatic and Consular Corps Affairs Department in the Ministry of Foreign Affairs, the department in charge of human resources at Egypt's foreign ministry, informed me that I had successfully passed the written exam and that I had to come to the ministry on October 12 for an oral exam and a personal interview. My father drove me to the Ministry of Foreign Affairs in Tahrir Square on the evening of that day to join a group of other young men and women taking the exam. I completed it confidently because I had such a wealth of knowledge, and went home to wait for the results. Days and months passed, during which I did more intensive reading for several hours each day on a variety of topics. I considered that I was in a race with everyone else, and that this was a period to collect information and prepare myself for the future. On May 24, the same official called and told me to go to the ministry the next morning to get the application for the medical examination, to be done at the medical commission of the Egyptian Ministry of Health. I was told that I had passed the exams, and I joined the diplomatic corps officially on June 1, 1965. I later learned that the seven-month lapse of time was due to the need to conduct police and security investigations about me and all the other applicants before the final approval. It was ridiculous that these investigations were done by humble individuals from the Egyptian police force, mostly detectives, who relied on the information given by craftsmen who worked for my family, like the man who ironed our clothes, the butcher, the vegetable seller, or the drivers who worked for my father. I thought back then that maybe our home phones in both Cairo and Alexandria were under surveillance for the same purpose. These investigations might also have been done at the university, especially by the university police.

Perhaps this is the moment to speak honestly about the issue of joining the Ministry of Foreign Affairs, which people often believe is based on nepotism and connections, so that the sons and daughters of personnel in the diplomatic corps or in other senior administrative positions have an advantage over other individuals. The truth is—and I say this with all honesty—that all these assumptions are completely false and that the truth is completely different. There have always been equal opportunities for everyone; the written exams have always been top secret, and passing them was based solely on the abilities of the applicant and his or her experience. The oral exam served the purpose of choosing the best candidates and, on many occasions, the sons and daughters of important ambassadors failed because they were not well prepared or because their capabilities were not suitable for the needs of the ministry.

On that day, June 1, 1965, I was assigned to work in the Eastern European Affairs Department. I remained there for over a year, and was then transferred to the press department. I started to acquire information and attempt to understand the Ministry of Foreign Affairs and its various currents, the severe internal competition, and the working conditions.

I learned that serving in the minister's or deputy minister's office is the key to opening doors to influential positions in embassies or major Egyptian diplomatic missions, and ensuring chances to make oneself visible and prove oneself.

I had the sense that all the posts I held for the first two or three years in the ministry would not lead me to a great career. Despite this, I refused to resort to nepotism to improve my status, though I could have done it through my father's connections with influential people, especially the ministers and deputy ministers from a military background who were transferred to the Ministry of Foreign Affairs in the first half of the 1960s. I remained in the press department of the ministry from October 1966 until the day I was transferred abroad in 1968. But every cloud comes with a silver lining; when the 1967 war broke out and I was still in the press department, I had the chance to read many documents, reports, and journalistic studies about this war and its various aspects. Together with my colleagues in the department, I used to prepare these materials in the form of reports to be distributed among the rest of the members of the ministry. I also had the chance to discuss what I read and learned with many promising diplomats, who listened attentively to my opinions. Among these high-profile figures were Ambassador Abdul Raouf El Reedy, Minister Ahmed Maher, and others. The defeat of 1967 was a shock that surpassed anything I had ever experienced up to that point in my life. As the size and magnitude of the defeat became apparent, I thought about committing suicide, but I overcame this notion with reason and decisiveness.

As my third year of service in the ministry approached, I was due for a transfer. I wrote to Ambassador Morad Ghalib in Moscow and asked him to request that I work with him. He and my father were good friends, as I mentioned before, and I had met him many times at home and talked to him about important matters. Though I was young and had limited experience, he used to listen attentively, talk, and exchange opinions with me. He replied that I was welcome to work with him, and invited me to meet him at Cairo Airport before he left for Moscow after a short visit he paid to Egypt. I took my fiancée Laila, who was then twenty years old, so that he and his wife could get acquainted with her.

The reason I wished to serve in the Soviet Union in that period—the spring of 1967—was my desire to work in a country that had gigantic influence on world policy. Moreover, I was motivated by my deep reading about Marxism and the Soviet political system to experience the country firsthand. On April 1, 1968, the diplomatic assignments, which is an annual administrative decree that transfers the members of the diplomatic corps to Egyptian embassies and missions abroad, were announced.

I was severely disappointed when I was informed that I had been assigned to Nicosia, Cyprus. Cyprus was nowhere on my list of interests; it would neither help me acquire wide experience nor improve my chances to make a powerful impression within Egypt's diplomatic corps. I felt my world spin with a heavy sense of desperation.

I wrote a sad letter to Morad Ghalib, expressing my deep regret for missing the chance to work under his supervision and learn from him. The seasoned ambassador, originally a pediatrician who had taught at the Faculty of Medicine at Alexandria University, was known to have worked with President Nasser as his office manager for diplomatic affairs from the mid-1950s until he was appointed Egypt's ambassador to Congo during its crisis with Belgium in 1960–61. Later on, he was appointed as Egyptian ambassador to the Soviet Union in 1961, a time when Egypt was opening up to this country. Therefore, his relationship with the Soviet leaders was very strong and the ties he had with them had a personal quality, especially because he had become extremely fluent in Russian since the early years of his service in the mid-1950s, when he worked in Moscow with Lieutenant General Aziz al-Masri.

The next part of the story will prove again that every cloud comes with a silver lining. I have always believed that the wife of a diplomat is an essential partner who helps him advance in his career. I was eager to become better acquainted with the lady whose destiny would be tied to mine and who would share my journey toward the success I aspired to. I had met her in our apartment: Laila Kamal al-Din Salah, my sister's friend and the daughter of Ambassador Kamal al-Din Salah who was martyred in Mogadishu, Somalia in April 1957. The Ministry of Foreign Affairs commissioned a statue of him, which was placed at the top of the main staircase in its headquarters in Tahrir Square in 1965. This statue was a token of respect and appreciation for the first Egyptian diplomat to have been martyred while on official mission. I liked Laila and wanted to know her better and to meet her on every possible occasion. Our relationship deepened gradually, and her mother, Mrs. Amina Ahmed Morad, began to suspect that her daughter was developing feelings for someone whom she talked to on the phone for long periods. She adamantly forbade our relationship, saying that I had no future and that my income was too small to take on the responsibility of supporting her daughter. But Laila insisted on her choice, and after a lot of debate, some family friends who were ambassadors and colleagues of her father knew what was happening. Two of them, Ambassador Ali Khashaba and Ambassador Gamal Mansour, decided to interfere. They assured her mother that this young man had a promising career and that everyone was aware of his good traits. She agreed, and we were married and traveled together to Cyprus on September 2, 1968.

I have always believed that the wife of a diplomat is the backbone of his success, and therefore I have always advised young diplomats to choose wisely in this respect. I also advise them to develop certain habits that will ensure success and advancement in their careers. I tell them to be persistent and never stop working hard at any stage of their life; to read extensively and acquire knowledge in all fields; and to broaden their horizons, since these are the foundations for the sound judgment and evaluation of political and diplomatic situations that enables them to serve Egypt best. I also add a fourth aspect—luck—which is the gate that enables the other three aspects to achieve their goal.

In my own personal case, I have always sought to have these three elements: a good wife, hard work, and acquiring knowledge and culture. However, I sometimes felt that I did not enjoy enough luck. As it turned out, I should not have complained about the absence of luck, or to put it more accurately, divine intervention. I should have understood back then that rising in the Egyptian diplomatic corps always requires ten to fifteen years of hard work and highly visible activity, in order to gain recognition in this demanding profession. It takes this long for the corps to accurately evaluate their capabilities, behavior, moral attitudes, psychological balance, flexibility, decisiveness, and self-respect. I traveled to Nicosia feeling wronged. Other diplomats had been transferred to New York, Washington, London, Moscow, Paris, Delhi, and Beijing, while I got a small city in a small country. However, I decided not to feel broken or to assume that my rise in the Egyptian diplomatic corps was being disrupted.

During my work in our embassy in Cyprus, a dangerous event that could have negatively affected my career took place in Cairo. A large number of Egyptian army officers were arrested on charges of contacting the Iraqi Baath Party and plotting to overthrow Gamal Abd al-Nasser because of the June 1967 defeat. Some of them were my close friends, and I was told by one of them, who was acquitted months later, that investigators had asked them about their civilian friend Ahmed Aboul Gheit, who was always with them in 1968–69 before traveling to Cyprus. My friend assured them that I had nothing to do with military matters and could not have been involved in this matter. I must admit, though, that I had felt I was being watched during my visits to Cairo for vacations in 1969 and 1970.

Serving in Cyprus allowed me to develop my relationship with my wife and to start a healthy family in a calm atmosphere. Working in a small embassy with a limited staff gave me the chance to work on many different projects and tackle different specializations. I got to know budget and financial matters when I substituted for the only administrative attaché when he left for his annual vacation. I also worked in consular affairs, and got to know the citizens' problems and needs and the hardships that came their way because of cumbersome Egyptian procedures and the slow service they received from the Egyptian government. On the other hand, I discovered that some of our citizens harm the rest of the Egyptians in a particular country or city with their misbehavior. This, of course, pushes the authorities in foreign countries to take precautionary measures, or leads the Egyptian authorities to refuse to help them.

On many occasions, I was assigned by Ambassador Salah Sha'rawi— my head of mission in Cyprus—to handle cultural and media-related issues. I became acquainted with many Cypriot and foreign media personnel and could get accurate information about events in Cyprus, which helped in preparing political and media reports. It also opened my eyes to the important role of the press and media in any country.

Work in Cyprus during this period was characterized by many challenges for the embassy and its diplomats. The Cold War affected everyone; the embassies and diplomats of socialist countries and the Soviet Union competed with the representatives of western countries. Military personnel in the form of military attachés investigated the behaviors, interests, and priorities of other countries' personnel. The British bases on that island attracted the attention of all parties, including Egypt, Syria, and Lebanon, which were the only Arab countries represented in Nicosia.

The Cypriot issue, the conflict with Turkey, the attitude of Greece, and the responsibilities of Britain—one of the countries that guaranteed the independence of Cyprus—put pressure on the government of Archbishop Makarios. I provided political coverage of all these subjects.

There was also the role of Israel in Cyprus, which was strong because of Israel's geographical proximity to the island and its dependence on it as a nearby exit route. For us, this proximity was very interesting, especially with the circumstances of war and the confrontation going on between Egypt and Israel from 1968 to 1970. This was an opportunity to learn about the role of the secret service division of the Egyptian General Intelligence. Readers of my book *Witness to War and Peace* will know much of what was going on in Cyprus and how it was carried out.

Everything that happened in Cyprus during my service was a step toward my rise after my return to Cairo in 1972. This period revealed weak points in my professional training and preparation and showed me that I would have to work hard to overcome them. Through my membership in the Young Diplomats Club, where diplomats affiliated with different embassies in Cyprus met twice a month for a business lunch or a social dinner, I realized that diplomats of superpowers received much better training than what we had in the Egyptian Foreign Affairs Ministry. Though I had always imagined that I exerted enough effort to read and be informed of foreign affairs to be able to compete with foreign diplomats, I realized I was mistaken. This realization showed me that my wife and I needed to work hand in hand to overcome the weaknesses in our training. I believe we have managed to achieve this goal over the course of many years.

Upon my arrival in Egypt, I was surprised to be assigned by the Diplomatic and Consular Corps Affairs Department to work in one of the less visible departments: The General Affairs department, which is responsible for issuing permits for foreign aircraft to land and for ships to enter Egyptian ports. I felt desperate again because I felt I was not being given the chance to make the kind of big achievements that would advance my career. At the time, I came to the conclusion that maybe I would have to follow in the footsteps of all the diplomats before me and use connections with acquaintances and friends—and my father had many of them—to achieve that goal. I felt sad about this since I had been determined not to resort to nepotism and to make my way up the ladder without depending on my family or their friends. My father talked to Morad Ghalib, minister of foreign affairs at the time, and requested that I work with him, and the minister promised to act on it as soon as he came back from a meeting of non-aligned countries in Guyana in Latin America.

Everything suddenly changed and matters took an unexpected turn when my friend and colleague Ismail al-Qattan, who was then working in the Diplomatic and Consular Affairs Department and was well-informed about upcoming personnel transfers, said that he had heard in the department that the president's office would ask me to work there. He had overheard Minister Wagih Marzouk talking to someone over the phone—an important figure from the president's office, as my friend could tell. I thought deeply about this and assumed that I might be chosen to work with Ashraf Marwan, who was then President Sadat's secretary. It was no secret that he also held other jobs and many responsibilities. Marwan was one year younger than I, and had been my companion at the Masr al-Gadida Secondary School and the Heliopolis Sporting Club. I thought that it would not be appropriate to work with him in the information secretariat, if I was asked to.

Then I thought about another possibility. It was being said that Ahmed al-Messiri, the fiancé of President Sadat's daughter and also one of his guards, was going to work in the president's office as the head of the Arab Affairs Department, and that he was going to ask some members from the Foreign Ministry to serve with him. I also decided that I would not accept any of these nominations.

The way matters developed, however, proved that my assumptions and expectations were mistaken. Ambassador Marzouk called the next day to ask me to go immediately to meet Dr. Abdel Hadi Makhlouf in Abdin Palace. He had left my name at the gates of the palace so that I would be easily admitted. I had absolutely no prior acquaintance with him; I did not even know what his job was or what he did there. I asked the manager of diplomatic affairs for more details about him. He replied that I was a candidate for a position with the Egyptian national security advisor, Mohamed Hafiz Ismail, and that they wanted to see me and speak to me. I drove my blue Volkswagen at top speed toward Abdin Palace and went through the gate for the first time in my life. I was mesmerized by the beauty and grandeur of the building with its corridors, carpets, furniture, and cleanliness. I entered Dr. Makhlouf's office, which is next to the office of the national security advisor. Dr. Makhlouf said that two of his assistants had suggested my name. The first was Ahmed Maher, whom I had known before and during the 1967 war and I used to accompany him in his car after a long day of work. The second was First Secretary Ehab Wahba, who had visited Cyprus during his mission as a diplomatic pouch courier, and we had spent a day and a half talking and exchanging views on international and regional issues. The director of the office of the national security advisor and I conversed for over an hour, during which time he was assessing my personality and my psychological makeup. He said that he wanted me to work with him, and I told him I appreciated the opportunity. He said that I should start the next day, and that he would inform the Ministry of Foreign Affairs about my new assignment. That was the first time that I felt that luck and divine intervention were on my side.

Before leaving the office, I was stopped by Dr. Makhlouf, who looked me in the eye and asked, "Have you ever joined any of the youth organizations affiliated with the Arab Socialist Union?" I answered in the affirmative, saying that I had joined one in 1966 after entering the Ministry of Foreign Affairs and had spent a training period in a camp in al-Haram district. Then he asked whether I was a member of the pioneer organization. I said that some of the members of the organization had attempted to convince me to join it before the 1967 war, but I refused because I disliked their style of secrecy within the ministry. I also told Dr. Makhlouf that for a long time I was fond of Marxist and socialist thought, which was natural for young people. I added that I left the youth organization in anger after the defeat of 1967, which had revealed many weak points in Egyptian society. Dr. Makhlouf praised my honesty. In the months and years that followed, I realized his great animosity toward the rule of President Nasser and his political philosophy.

On my way out of the palace, I met Ahmed Maher, whom I had not seen since he was transferred to Kinshasa, Congo. We talked for a long time and I had the feeling that our old friendship was still on track. We went back to Heliopolis and he promised to pass by my home the next morning to take me with him to Abdin Palace to start my work with Hafiz Ismail.

I was assigned to an office prepared for me and one of my colleagues, Farouk Baraka, who had recently returned from a diplomatic assignment in Colombia. We were both summoned around noon, and Dr. Abdel Hadi Makhlouf accompanied us to meet Hafiz Ismail together with a third colleague, Taymour Serry. Dr. Ismail's office reflected the exquisite taste of the Egyptian royal family. Extremely elegant and well-dressed, with features and a posture that expressed a stern character, he remained standing while talking to us. He said that working in the office of the Egyptian national security advisor was a big responsibility that required alertness, vigilance, accuracy, and secrecy, which were, in his opinion, very sensitive matters. He added that the period Egypt was going through in its confrontation with Israel required great efforts and long working hours, and that getting precise and mature analysis of the conditions and attitudes in the geographical regions and political issues assigned to us was very important.

For almost two years I worked closely with the national security advisor. I was responsible for Arab affairs. During this period, I closely followed Egypt's preparation for war with Israel in 1973, then the war itself, and the negotiations and consultations that followed it. It was a hard, yet wonderful period, about which I have written extensively in *Witness to War and Peace*. Throughout my service with Dr. Ismail, I could see the depth and breadth of his political and military knowledge and his strategic thinking. I often discussed with him wars and armed conflicts generally, and the First and Second World Wars in particular, which were not directly related to my work with him. He gladly responded, however, and showed great interest in such discussions, which, as I could see even then, took him away from the pressures of his responsibilities and allowed him to discuss subjects that he loved and wrote about. These discussions were really valuable. I was very much interested in his knowledge, and had spent many nights during my service in Cyprus reading the history of the world in the past and the present and the philosophy of human history.

When I first worked with him, Hafiz Ismail's mission involved informing President Sadat of all circumstances and summing up all the reports and documents that we received from various Egyptian government agencies and sources, such as the military, the Ministry of Foreign Affairs, the

General Intelligence, and the Ministry of Interior Affairs, each according to its specialization. The views and information we received from these sources were fused together so that Hafiz Ismail could approve them. He wrote reports of the evaluations himself on many occasions. He concentrated on the issues of the Middle East and ways to deal with the Arab–Israeli conflict. However, his top priority was the regional situation and Egypt's relationship with Arab countries, specifically all suggestions concerning the promotion and development of these relations so that Egypt could get all the support it needed. The next priority was, of course, our relations with Turkey and Iran and how to achieve cooperation with them despite their relationship with Israel, the west, and the United States. Hafiz Ismail also paid close attention to our relationship with Russia, Egypt's main supporter; with the United States, Israel's loyal friend; and the relationship between the two powers and how these relations affected Arab–Israeli relations.

The American–Soviet summits attracted much interest and followup, especially the increasing détente between them and its influence on what was then called military pacification and self-restraint in dealing with regional problems.

Toward the end of 1972, work in the office of the national security advisor developed to include members from General Intelligence who had a great deal of experience with analysis, political evaluation, and national security issues. It also included some military personnel from the Presidential Guard to monitor military affairs, and members of other Egyptian ministries and agencies interested in the economy. It was clear that Hafiz Ismail was widening his circle of interests; he did not limit himself to the small group of Egyptian diplomats in his service, which at first did not exceed five members but later expanded a little more as the 1973 war approached. In March 1973, Hafiz made many calls to a number of Egyptian figures. He was very discreet about it, though we, as members of his office, knew that the president had assigned him to lead the new government that he would be in charge of during the battle. Then, suddenly, he stopped all his consultations. Dr. Abdel Hadi Makhlouf told some of us at the time that President Sadat had informed Hafiz Ismail of his decision to take on the responsibility of leading the Cabinet himself and to appoint Dr. Abd al-Qader Hatem as deputy prime minister and acting head of government. I was disappointed that Hafiz Ismail was not assigned this prestigious post.

Hafiz Ismail's responsibilities, both as the national security advisor and as the general secretary of the National Security Council, were governed by a republican decree that determined his duties. When it was first established, the Council worked within the framework of the specialized councils, but it was separated at a later stage.

I must say here that Hafiz Ismail had been extremely active and engaged throughout his work, which is why I was astonished when President Sadat decided early in 1974 to disband the National Security Council and not to appoint another security council advisor to replace Hafiz Ismail. Ismail's views on promoting a peaceful settlement and negotiating with Israel diverged from the president's own views.

During my service in Moscow from 1979 to 1982 I thought that the new president, Mubarak, would reestablish a national security council along the lines developed by Hafiz Ismail. But Mubarak followed the lead of his predecessor and relied for political advice on an information secretary who provided him with a summary of the documents received from other national security agencies: the military, the Ministry of Foreign Affairs, and the Interior Ministry. Unfortunately, this secretary did not have enough experts of a high enough standard to provide adequate counsel on issues of foreign affairs or national security.

Hafiz Ismail avoided any clash with the Ministry of Foreign Affairs or General Intelligence. He was eager to present their views to the president, accompanied by specific suggestions based on what they provided or from the wealth of information available to him from his own staff. These agencies, therefore, were eager to cooperate with the national security staff, especially since Hafiz Ismail had been minister of state for foreign affairs and head of General Intelligence from 1969 to 1971.

I should mention here that as soon as I became the minister of foreign affairs in 2004, I made it my goal to remedy this absence of authority on all levels. I believed that there was an inherent weakness in the evaluation of information and the presenting of options in Egyptian foreign policy due to the absence of a strong and effective national security staff.

Therefore, I always believed it was important to include all the relevant government agencies, each according to its specialty and responsibility, in handling foreign-policy issues through joint meetings in the headquarters of the various ministries. Anyone who attended such meetings during these years must have noticed the presence of military personnel from the Ministry of Defense and the Ministry of Interior, and members of the General Intelligence, in the corridors and offices of the ministry throughout the week. The example of Omar Suleiman during the years when he led General Intelligence is important. President Mubarak had granted him a broad mandate to work in foreign affairs issues. However, to provide the appropriate institutional setting for this and to avoid the impression that General Suleiman and the General Intelligence Service were undermining the Foreign Ministry or impinging on its areas of expertise, it would have been necessary to appoint Suleiman as national security advisor in addition to his position as director of General Intelligence. This would have been appropriate given the fact that he was already in frequent contact with the national security advisers of foreign countries.

Our work with Hafiz Ismail came to an end on February 12, 1974 and I went back to the Ministry of Foreign Affairs and waited to be transferred abroad again. Dr. Abdel Hadi Makhlouf, who was still influential in diplomatic and consular circles, called and asked about the next place I would like to serve in. I asked to be located in Moscow, which was still my dream workplace. He made some calls and came back saying that my dream had come true and that I would be transferred to Moscow within a month. I was satisfied and hopeful and I felt that I was finally shaping my own future and having some luck.

The date of the new diplomatic transfer list, April 1, 1974, was approaching. Ambassador Omar Sharaf, brother of Samy Sharaf who was President Nasser's information secretary and a close friend of my father, called me at home on March 24. He told me that the minister of foreign affairs, Ismail Fahmy, had changed my assignment from Moscow to New York, to work in Egypt's permanent mission to the United Nations. As happy as I was to hear this news, which would change the course of my life, I also regretted losing the incomparable opportunity to work in the Soviet

Union and get first-hand information about the politics of a superpower that had such a great influence on world policy.

Before leaving for New York, my wife and I were blessed with a second child, Ali, in addition to our first son, Kamal. (Our family is now made up of my wife and myself, two sons, and four grandchildren, two boys and two girls.)

I met with some Egyptian diplomats who had formerly served in New York, and with whom I worked after having served on the National Security Council staff, which ended on March 1, 1974 and I returned to the ministry. These were Counselor Mahmoud Kassem and First Secretary Mohab Mokbel, both of whom had just returned from four years' service in New York. They gave me advice about the work style, the importance of efficient performance, and the value of being in such a location and the experience I could get out of it. I started to read up on international law, the United Nations, its principal organs, its charter, its history, its relationship to the League of Nations, and its major crises so far. I read many books in preparation for the coming challenge, and I approached the position with much fear and apprehension.

I arrived in New York on July 15. Almost immediately, the attempted coup d'état against the Greek Archbishop Makarios, the president of the Republic of Cyprus, and the Turkish invasion of the northern part of the island took place. I took part in the Security Council's deliberations on this situation, and I considered it my first battle experience in the United Nations. It was followed by many other battles over the years.

I met Dr. Esmat Abdel Meguid, who was Egypt's permanent representative to the UN at the time, after his return from a vacation in Cairo at the end of August 1974. I immediately noticed what I had often heard from others, that he was one of the most professional and conservative diplomats who followed the traditional line, since he had worked for many years with Dr. Mahmoud Fawzi, one of the most famous ministers of foreign affairs during the time of Gamal Abd al-Nasser. He asked me to come to his office in the last week of September while the twenty-ninth session of the General Assembly was being held. When I entered his office, he asked if I was married to Laila Kamal al-Din Salah. When I answered in the affirmative, he was astonished and asked why I had not told him. He added that her father was one of his best friends and mentors in the Ministry of Foreign Affairs. From that point on, he took a special interest in my career and made a point of training me for the challenges of working at the United Nations.

My years of service in the Egyptian mission to the UN in New York were the basic foundation of my career. I started to work there when I was thirty-three years old and came back with new experience and a good understanding of the UN and the role of this organization in the world. I was aware that my work in the delegation would be under scrutiny, and that I needed to make a good impression in order to prove my position within this small group of remarkable Egyptian diplomats. Therefore, I worked very hard, and found that I was appreciated by Dr. Esmat Abdel Meguid. He later asked me to join him when he was summoned to Cairo to partic- ipate in the peace negotiations with Israel in December 1977, and I joined the working group assigned to follow up this issue.

My service in New York, like that in Nicosia, taught me much about the Egyptian diplomatic corps and the performance of individual diplo- mats. My contacts with western, Indian, and Pakistani diplomats showed me that, despite all our efforts, they were superior to us in the fields of languages, general knowledge, and the information their countries made available to them. I concluded that we could improve the quality of our university graduates who join the Ministry of Foreign Affairs by intensi- fying their training and putting more emphasis on languages. I paid great attention to these things when I became the minister of foreign affairs.

On October 1, 1977, I returned to Cairo after Ismail Fahmy, who was then minister of foreign affairs and deputy prime minister, issued a decree ending the work of any diplomat who had worked for three or more years abroad, as a cost-cutting measure. Strangely, the same decree included the transfer of an equal number of diplomats abroad, which of course increased expenses instead of cutting them. This decree reflected a state of confusion and lack of understanding in the management of diplomatic affairs. It was simply a response to President Sadat's discontent about diplomatic spend- ing—or, as it was said, that he was dissatisfied with the way the minister of foreign affairs managed the negotiations with Israel.

I was assigned to work in the Department of International Organizations, which was headed at the time by Counselor Amr Moussa, one of the rising diplomats who worked closely with Ismail Fahmy, the minister of foreign affairs, and Osama El-Baz, the minister's chief of cabinet. Once again, I felt that luck was on my side and that I was on the right track to a great future. All I needed, I believed, was to move cautiously and perfect my work on the one hand, and to continue to enjoy divine support on the other. Although I was satisfied with my status after coming back from New York, I was still trying to figure out ways to work with Ismail Fahmy, which I thought would put me in a better position in the long term to depend on myself and be less dependent on the help of others.

Because of the three-year limit on working abroad, Ahmed Maher came back from Paris, where he had been transferred in 1974 after his work with Hafiz Ismail ended. We used to meet, talk, and analyze situations. The group of diplomats working in Ismail Fahmy's office were efficient and experienced. Most of them, or maybe all of them, either served in Egypt's missions to the UN or were appointed as permanent representatives to the UN in later years. These diplomats included Nabil al-Arabi, Amr Moussa, Mounir Zahran, Mohamed ElBaradei, Hussein Hassouna, and Mervat al-Tellawi.

Everything was turned upside down by President Sadat's announcement of his intention to travel to Jerusalem and speak before the Knesset. Ismail Fahmy resigned, followed by Mohamed Riyad, the minister of state for foreign affairs. Except for the seasoned and capable Osama El-Baz, there was no one to maintain stability in the Ministry of Foreign Affairs. In addition to his responsibilities as the chief of cabinet of the resigned minister of foreign affairs, he was also the director of the office of the vice-president. We waited until Esmat Abdel Meguid returned to Cairo to head the Egyptian team appointed to negotiate with Israel in the Mena House talks that were held in December 1977, and I joined him. I imagined that Abdel Meguid would be chosen as foreign affairs minister. Instead, Sadat chose Mohamed Ibrahim Kamel, who had been very close to him, since they were imprisoned together following a famous criminal case in the 1940s. He thus chose someone whom he personally trusted over a more qualified person, because of his anger and dissatisfaction with Ismail Fahmy and Mohamed Riyad.

When Mohamed Ibrahim Kamel was appointed, Ahmed Maher appeared on the scene once again; he had served with Ibrahim Kamel in the Congo from the beginning of 1967 to 1971. When Ahmed Maher came back to Cairo, I accompanied him to the minister's office. The negotiation period with Israel from December 1977 until the Camp David summit in September 1978 was charged with many challenges and involved a great deal of hard work. I have dealt in considerable detail with this whole period in *Witness to War and Peace*. Ahmed Maher had been appointed the minister's chief of cabinet on December 24, 1977, and started to work efficiently as usual. Osama El-Baz—whom the vice-president had appointed first undersecretary of the Ministry of Foreign Affairs and manager of his own office as a compensation for the loss of the position and responsibilities of chief of cabinet of the minister's office—later came to clear out his office and told Maher that many of the diplomats who served with Ismail Fahmy were anxious about the new situation. Maher replied that they need not be, and that they would soon be transferred, each in his turn, to good destinations that would guarantee their well-being and their professional security.

In less than nine months from his appointment, Mohamed Ibrahim Kamel resigned at Camp David in protest against the agreement which, he believed, was harmful to Egypt. We returned to Cairo feeling like orphans. After Mohamed Ibrahim Kamel's resignation, the position of foreign minister remained vacant until Dr. Mustafa Khalil was appointed in February 1979. That period felt like an extended hibernation. We were serving in a minister's officer without a minister. We undertook all of our normal tasks, but given the circumstances, we did not feel particularly effective. The vacuum at the helm of the ministry meant that Osama El-Baz regained his responsibilities and steered the operations in the ministry, especially since Boutros Boutros-Ghali, who was minister of state, was not very familiar with the less public aspects of the work, the history of the issues, or even the people in the ministry. This period of almost ten months, from September 1978 to June 1979, is also dealt with in *Witness to War and Peace*. During this time I continued to work with Ahmed Maher, the minister's chief of cabinet, serving the minister whom we never saw. In the last week of February 1979, Dr. Mustafa Khalil, the prime minister, became minister of foreign affairs in order to arrange Egyptian–Israeli meetings under the supervision of the Americans in Camp David, in an attempt to overcome the disagreements about the phrasing of the peace agreement. It was rumored at the time that Dr. Boutros-Ghali was dissatisfied, even angry, at not being entrusted with the task of preparing for the Camp David negotiations, which would have made him the counterpart of Moshe Dayan, Israel's foreign minister at the time. President Sadat was upset by Boutros-Ghali's reaction, and suddenly decided to appoint Dr. Mustafa Khalil as foreign minister and asked him to go to Camp David to meet with President Carter. I have to admit here that Dr. Khalil did a very good job and firmly confronted the Israelis, even though he had little prior diplomatic or foreign affairs experience. He continued to hold the position of foreign minister until he handed it to Kamal Hassan Ali on February 15, 1980. Documents from this period reveal that Egyptian diplomacy, under Khalil's guidance, adopted a strong stance in the interpretation of the Egyptian–Israeli peace agreement. An official book was issued at the time, explaining the Egyptian standpoint.

It was time for me to be transferred abroad again, a systematic and monotonous process. An Egyptian diplomat spent three to four years abroad, then returned to Cairo to spend a year or two years in the ministry's headquarters. It is a tiring process that places endless psychological strain on a diplomat and his family, although those who do not work in the Ministry of Foreign Affairs view it as a wonderful opportunity to travel the world and visit different countries. The truth is that it is an extremely difficult process that involves finding new schools for the children, buying furniture or shipping it from Egypt, renting houses, and buying a car and other necessities. In effect, it involves starting a new life only to end it four years later.

I tried to move to Moscow again. This time I got what I wanted, and later wished it had never happened. I traveled to the Soviet Union on July 17, 1979 on an Aeroflot TU 154. It was a short journey—no more than three hours from Cairo to Moscow—but the chaos before boarding the plane, showing no consideration for the comfort of the passengers, was a warning of things to come. I landed in Moscow Airport with my family and that of the Egyptian chargé d'affaires, Hassan Kandil. We had to stay in the airport for a long time while the Soviet officials inspected our passports and other documents, and probably they were also inspecting our luggage. At last we headed into the city, to the famous Ukraina Hotel. I noticed that the road was narrow and the lights were dim, conditions which hardly seemed to reflect the capabilities and resources of this superpower. In the hotel, the furniture looked a hundred years old, despite the fact that it was built between 1946 and 1949 by Germans who were kept captive by the Soviets years after the Second World War ended. The services offered by the hotel were very primitive. On every floor there sat an old Russian lady, who looked at everyone's passport and other documents and decided who was allowed to be on that floor and who was not. We stayed in this hotel for three months because there were no apartments to move to. During its honeymoon with Russia, Egypt got a fairly good number of apartments that were described as being the size of football courts. When the Ministry of Foreign Affairs started its policy of reducing the number of diplomats in order to appear to be saving money, the Soviets decided to withdraw the huge apartments, and many of the Egyptian diplomats suffered for years because of the lack of suitable housing. I learned from this short-sighted decision to travel to Moscow that it is really necessary to study all sides of a situation before making any decision that might affect the whole family.

Moscow, as I saw it, was a sprawling city with spacious streets, huge gardens, and buildings dating back to the 1920s and 1930s, and some even to the previous century. I noticed a strict order in all aspects of life: the behavior of citizens, the buses and metros, times for opening and closing shops, and the traffic in the streets. I also noticed that the Russians feverishly attempted to imitate the west in everything, though they lacked the resources to match the consumption levels of westerners.

I obtained a small apartment, around sixty-six square meters—previously occupied by the embassy's chef, who now had an even smaller apartment—and started to work. I immediately felt that the Russian giant was suffering greatly, despite the huge potential of its heavy industry, electrical power, and technology stolen from the west or developed at home, which made its great military performance possible. It produced 180 to 200 million tons of grains and around 250 million tons of iron and steel per year, and sold from eight to ten million barrels of petroleum daily to the west, but its services were deteriorating and the zeal of its citizens was waning. Both the government farms and the cooperative farms reflected the failure to apply Marxist theory. As a result, more grain needed to be imported in order to guarantee even a minimum standard of living for the citizens. It was clear to me that this society could not remain in this state, or it would be unable to compete with America and the west. The Soviets did their best to maximize the use of their economic resources, constantly compared themselves to the United States, and believed they would catch up with it within a few years. They kept repeating that even though their economy was half the size of the American economy, it was growing at a faster rate than that of the United States. In the 1970s, the Soviets were also pursuing an expansionist foreign policy in several regions of the world. Their influence was not limited to one or two Arab countries in the Middle East, but was moving into Africa, Asia, and Central America, and their navy was competing with western powers in all regions of the world.

The Soviet Communist Party and its political offices were controlled by a group of flabby elders like Leonid Brezhnev, Alexei Kosygin, Mikhail Soslov, and Yuri Andropov. They were very proud that one of the members of this political office, named Arvid Pelshe, had been working there ever since the reign of Lenin in the 1920s.

Western writers started to monitor and express the drawbacks of the Soviet system and the need for liberating the society. But Brezhnev and his colleagues had a firm grip on everything. Then the Soviets fell into the trap of invading Afghanistan, becoming victims of an expansion that exceeded their limited capabilities. Prime Minister Kosygin died, as did many other members of the political establishment, most of whom ranged in age between seventy-five to eighty during the years 1980–82. While western shops were full of personal computers and other electronic goods, the Soviets remained captive to the technologies of the 1940s or even the

1920s. Their military and missile powers, which were huge, were nonetheless connected to the weakness of the economy, decaying politics, the lack of creative thinking, and the insistence on ruling with an iron fist. In November 1982, Andropov, the head of Soviet intelligence, came to power, and then died in less than thirteen months. He was followed by a weak figure, a former assistant of Brezhnev named Konstantin Chernenko; he, too, died within a few months.

Mikhail Gorbachev then took office, and matters started moving in another direction. I returned to Cairo after finishing my term in Moscow. Studies conducted within the next few years revealed that the estimates made by Soviet experts and professors in the west were correct. According to these studies, Soviet capabilities did not live up to their ambitions, especially their spending on arms and on expansion abroad; they believed that the Soviet star was fading away. Some documents and studies showed that the Soviet GDP did not exceed $400 billion in 1990, while the American figure was five trillion dollars—ten times that of the Soviets. The Soviets spent 30 to 50 percent of their GDP on military and space projects. The Americans had managed to drag them into an arms race that led to economic implosion. This was accelerated by the collapse of petroleum and gas prices in the mid-1980s, sharply reducing the country's income.

I watched these developments in astonishment, earnestly attempting to understand what was going on. I had always believed that a vigorous Soviet Union was a safety valve for many countries and many peoples against the greed of the west.

I returned to Egypt in July 1982; I took a train from Moscow to Kiev, then to Odessa on the Black Sea, where I boarded a ship to Alexandria. As I contemplated this broad land and its rich possibilities, it also struck me how poor the country's services were, on the trains and everywhere else. Although they were regarded as the world's second superpower, capable of wrecking the west and destroying the United States with their nuclear capability, the Soviets reflected nothing in their services and livelihoods but a Third World society seeking a way out of its dilemma. It had the advantages of a well-educated population and a wealth of raw materials. What was missing was a political regime that could unleash its energies.

As I traveled home, I reflected on my three-year stay in Moscow. Those were years of severe suffering: a small apartment, threadbare services, expensive schools. In addition, half of my salary was paid in Egyptian pounds and kept in Cairo. Getting access to this money required a complicated process of exchanging it for U.S. dollars on the Egyptian black market and transferring it to Moscow, so that we could afford to buy, from outside the Soviet Union, the many commodities that were not available within it.

Egyptian–Soviet relations were affected by President Sadat's signing of the Camp David Accords, which excluded the Soviets and marginalized their influence in Middle East policies. The accords limited the Soviets' influence to mobilize those Arab governments opposed to the Egyptian–Israeli peace agreement and create a united front against the peace process.

Egypt had no ambassador in the Soviet Union at the time. There were only myself and the chargé d'affaires, the loyal and honorable Hassan Kandil, struggling to protect these relations from further deterioration, to no avail. On the other hand, and despite the suffering, those three years of service gave me the opportunity to become acquainted with the Soviet Union, and to observe it on its deathbed. The difficulty of life in Moscow brought out the best in the Egyptian wives, who bore many burdens and hardships while we, the diplomats, were working to defend the interests of our county under very difficult political and personal circumstances.

The route of my ship took me past Istanbul, Limassol in Cyprus, and Latakia in Syria. The voyage gave me a rare chance to be away from the pressures of work and to think deeply about future plans and many other matters. As the Russian ship entered the Bosporus, I recalled my readings of the renowned British historian Arnold Toynbee, who discussed the influence of the location of a city or a port on its potential historical impact. The choice of the Roman emperor Constantine of the location of the city of Constantinople immortalized his name in world history and Christian history in a way that he himself never imagined. The palaces and fortresses of the city expressed the strength and the influence of the Eastern Roman Empire and its Orthodox Church, and of the Ottoman Empire for many centuries until its collapse at the end of the First World War.

As the ship was passing out of the Sea of Marmara through the Dardanelles, I stood up and looked closely at the hills on both sides of the strait, which had been defended by Muslim Turkish soldiers under the leadership of Mustafa Kemal Atatürk against a naval campaign planned by the British First Lord of the Admiralty, Winston Churchill, in 1915 and carried out by troops from Britain, Australia, and New Zealand. The campaign sought to occupy the strait, seize Istanbul, and force Ottoman Turkey to surrender. I was always fond of reading about this confrontation, which lasted for months with great suffering on both sides and proved beyond any doubt that a determined leadership, defending a critical goal, would always succeed when supported by equally determined and loyal troops. The land of Islamic Turkey was the target of a western enemy, and it was gloriously defended by the Ottoman Turkish people.

The voyage continued for seven days, during which I followed with great concern the development of the Israeli attacks on south Lebanon and the land and air clashes between Syria and Israel. I was consumed by Israel's operations against Arab countries, and in particular against Syria, which had been our partner and twin sister in the war of 1973. It seemed to me that we were witnessing a new era for which we needed to be prepared. Israel was capable of conducting extensive military operations against Arab countries without opposition because of the absence of Egypt, which could apparently do nothing more than protest and condemn the Israeli actions.

Back in Cairo, I started working with the deputy prime minister and minister of foreign affairs Kamal Hassan Ali in the first week of July 1982. Counselor Mohamed Assem Ibrahim, who was the minister's personal secretary for two years and was known to be supportive of the younger staff, had nominated me to work with him.

Assem Ibrahim was about to be transferred abroad at the time. He introduced me to the minister of foreign affairs as soon as I arrived in Cairo from Alexandria. My impression of the minister before seeing him face to face was that he was a bit stout, but I realized after meeting him that he was short, and not as stout as the photographs made him look, and that what really distinguished him was that his head was big compared to the rest of his body.

I continued to work with him for three years, from July 1982 to July 1985, during which our relationship was firmly established. I was a press secretary for some months; then I became a personal and political secretary from July 1983 until he was appointed Prime Minister in July 1984. I finally moved with him, and with one of my unforgettable friends, Mohamed Hassan Gawally, to the headquarters of the Cabinet for another year.

Kamal Hassan Ali was a very kind man; it hardly seemed possible that he had spent almost forty years in the Egyptian Armed Forces. Still, he was decisive and firm enough to be able to settle any situation by making a decision and insisting on carrying it out, with flexibility and revision as needed. Despite his three years of experience as the director of the Egyptian General Intelligence, with all the information this position made available, plus his work as the minister of defense for almost a year and a half, he was wise enough not to pretend that he was knowledgeable about everything, especially when it came to politics and foreign policy. On many occasions, he would ask about subjects without being concerned about what others might think. Moreover, his military training allowed him to evaluate situations quickly and suggest logical solutions.

On one of the hot summer days of 1982, I came back to my apartment in Heliopolis around 4:00 p.m. and received a call from the employee on duty in the press department in the minister's office. He said that news agencies were reporting a huge massacre in the Palestinian Sabra and Shatila camps in Beirut. Thousands of Palestinians had been killed under the eyes of the Israeli army, which occupied parts of Beirut and threatened the whole city. I quickly began to evaluate the situation and formulate some ideas that I could suggest to the minister of foreign affairs to deal with the tragic situation.

I called the minister of foreign affairs at home, as I usually did every evening at 7:00 p.m. since I started working with him, to keep him updated on the latest developments. One of the employees of the house said that he was asleep; I asked him to wake him up but he refused. I asked to talk to his wife. She tried to avoid waking him up but I insisted, and I was right to do so. I heard the minister's faint voice at the other end and I started reporting the events; he kept silent but I could sense he was disturbed. During the rest of the call I tried to provide him with an analytical review of the consequences of what had happened and my perceptions of its impact on the overall situation in the region. Then I suggested a number of initiatives, among which were a statement from the Ministry of Foreign Affairs or the president to condemn the incident, and an instant message to the secretary general of the UN about the seriousness of the situation and the necessity of the international community intervening in order to stop the massacre, investigate it, and bring the responsible party to justice. Though he agreed with all my suggestions, he asked me to talk to Dr. Boutros Boutros-Ghali, minister of state for foreign affairs, and discuss my proposals with him.

I called Dr. Boutros-Ghali and woke him up from his nap as well. He listened attentively, said that he agreed with all my suggestions, and added that he was happy I had returned from Moscow and was pleased with my work in such a sensitive position. We had maintained a good relationship since I started working with Minister Mohamed Ibrahim Kamel and accompanied him and Dr. Boutros-Ghali at the Camp David negotiations in September 1978; we often talked about international relations and world history. Though Dr. Boutros-Ghali was minister of state for almost thirteen years, he essentially remained a university professor with profound knowledge of international matters and was always wholeheartedly ready to discuss them with any diplomat, no matter how young he was.

I called the minister again, but before I could tell him about my conversation with Dr. Boutros-Ghali, he said that the president had just called him and that he had accepted my suggestions. He requested that I go to his house that evening, where he planned to meet the Israeli ambassador, whom he had summoned to protest against the situation. That too was one of the suggestions I had proposed to him in my first call.

I entered Dr. Kamel's apartment on Ammar bin Yasser Street in Heliopolis in front of the Military Academy for the first time. He was very welcoming and looked quite satisfied with the achievements of the day. When the president called him, he knew about all the developments of the situation and had his opinions and suggestions ready. From that day, I understood the complexity of the relationship between them: although the minister of foreign affairs was politically subordinate to the president, he had outranked the president in the military. Seniority was a matter of great importance to all military personnel. Moreover, over the years 1978–80, the minister of foreign affairs had been closer to President Sadat than Vice-President Mubarak was. In addition, their daily schedules were quite different. The president woke up very early and started his work immediately, then headed to the gymnasium of the Air Force headquarters next to his residence at about 2:00 p.m. and exercised until 5:00 p.m., then went home, worked until 10:00 p.m., and went to bed. On the other hand, Kamal Hassan Ali woke up around 8:00 a.m. and went to the Medical Rehabilitation Center in the Agouza district of Cairo to practice some sports and exercises to help ease his chronic rheumatoid arthritis. He would come to his office to work after 10:00 a.m. and go home around 5:00 p.m. to rest for a few hours before he started an evening of social visits—weddings, funerals, or ordinary visits—that usually ended late at night. This difference in working hours and habits affected the interactions between the two men and governed the timing of calls between them. Sometimes I heard whispers among the officials working with the president that he was annoyed at not being able to instantly contact the minister whenever he wanted. Maybe that explained why Kamal Hassan Ali was satisfied with the work that was done on the day the Sabra and Shatila massacre was revealed, since he was not surprised by the president but instead was ahead of the events and had all the relevant information.

The second point I noticed about the relationship between President Mubarak and Kamal Hassan Ali, and all the other ministers of foreign affairs I worked with was that he loved to call them the moment he learned of an important local or international event. The ministers would call to inform me how proud the president was when he surprised them by knowing the latest events and developments before they did. He believed that, as ministers of foreign affairs, they should know about all events first; it was part of their work. Throughout my work with these ministers—Kamal Hassan Ali, Esmat Abdel Meguid, and finally Amr Moussa—I was eager to provide them with the latest developments and my analysis of them, so they could be ready to answer any question related to foreign affairs.

Egyptian diplomacy became deeply involved in dealing with this massacre, attempting to address the situation in Lebanon in isolation from a unified Arab response, since the other Arab countries had cut off diplomatic ties with Egypt in the wake of the Camp David Accords. Our focus was on three essential dimensions: The United States, France, and the UN, represented by its secretary general. We prepared ourselves to accompany the minister of foreign affairs on a visit to Paris, Washington, and New York.

Parallel to the Egyptian action, we were actively engaged in the process of evacuating Yasser Arafat and the forces of the Palestine Liberation Organization (PLO) from Beirut. This involved considerable effort and communication with all these parties in addition to Israel, on which Egypt exerted strong pressure.

While preparing for this mission, I suggested to the minister of foreign affairs that we fully familiarize ourselves with the Palestinian position so that we could relay it to the Americans. Accordingly, we asked the Palestinian leadership to send an envoy to meet our foreign minister in Paris at the residence of the Egyptian ambassador, Samir Safwat. They sent Mustafa Natsha to discuss this matter with us.

As we were walking to the car that would take us from the VIP hall in the Paris airport to the French plane to leave for Washington, we noticed that Farouk al-Qaddumi, head of the External Affairs Department of the PLO, was entering the hall. He pretended that he did not see us, an act of hostility that astonished me. Being the strict and decisive person he was, Kamal Hassan Ali stopped him and scolded him harshly, saying that what he did was not acceptable and that it was his duty to inform us of the latest developments of the situation. Qaddumi's reply was brief so that the minister would not miss his plane. It was clear that he did not know anything about the ongoing communication between us and the PLO or about the important Paris meeting.

We were received warmly in Washington. Kamal Hassan Ali met with President Reagan, Vice-President George Bush, and U.S. Secretary of State George Schultz and his top aides.

Lebanon and Palestine were the main topics of the talks. We presented our own perspective and the viewpoint of the PLO, and the importance of a speedy withdrawal of the Israeli army from Lebanon in order to end the unprecedented tension caused by the invasion, which threatened an Arab capital for the first time in the history of the Arab–Israeli conflict. The Americans complained about the actions of the Israelis and confessed that controlling their irrational acts was difficult. We agreed on a series of steps to control the situation and on the steps the United States and other western powers could take to facilitate the Israeli withdrawal. We also discussed strategies to gradually de-escalate the situation between the Israelis and the Palestinians on Lebanese territory.

We then moved on to discuss the regional situation more broadly. It became obvious that the Americans were quite interested in discussing the Iran–Iraq war and the situation in the Gulf area. They were obviously against Iran and its revolution and very willing to do whatever it took to counter it. It must be said here that all of Kamal Hassan Ali's missions to Washington during 1983–84 focused primarily on regional matters and rarely dealt with Egyptian–American relations, which were smooth during that period. Egypt and Israel had already started implementing the peace treaty between them, and Israel had withdrawn from the occupied Egyptian land in Sinai. Thus there was nothing to be discussed in that context. Hoping to acquire maritime, air, and land facilities in Egypt, the United States was obviously trying to convince the Egyptian leadership to agree by magnifying the regional military threats and the importance of defending Egypt and the region. On our side, all the Egyptian authorities strictly refused and resisted these American attempts to acquire a military foothold in Egypt. An American presence in Ras Banas, an Egyptian military area on the Red Sea in southern Egypt, was repeatedly refused by Egypt throughout the period of 1982–84. So was the U.S. suggestion of using the area as a storage site for military equipment, lest it later be used as a pretext for perpetual occupation, as Kamal Hassan Ali put it. To the Americans, Kamal Hassan Ali was the Egyptian general who negotiated the peace treaty with the Israelis and was right at the heart of Egyptian authority as the director of armored corps, assistant secretary of defense, head of General Intelligence, and then minister of defense. Therefore the Americans had great respect for him and they listened attentively to his views.

In New York we met with UN Secretary General Javier Pérez de Cuéllar, who was not very effective despite the fact that he was obviously supportive of the Palestinians and the Lebanese situation. As expected, the man did not have a magic wand to end the situation in Lebanon. Only the great powers could reach an understanding among themselves and impose a decision on Israel to withdraw from Lebanon. We summoned the French ambassador to the UN to the residence of the Egyptian ambassador in New York, where Kamal Hassan Ali asked him to deliver a message to Claude Chaisson, the French foreign minister, informing him about Kamal Hassan Ali's latest communications and his evaluation of the situation. Then we returned to Cairo via London.

Most Arab countries had already cut their diplomatic relations with Egypt because of the peace treaty with Israel. Therefore, the axes of Egyptian diplomatic action revolved around Africa, on the one hand—with Boutros Boutros-Ghali shouldering the responsibility of communicating in this area—and Europe and the United States on the other. It was Kamal Hassan Ali who focused on this latter axis, and had numerous missions to Rome, London, Paris, Bonn, and other European capitals. During this period, Egypt also intensified its communication with India, China, and Japan to expand the range of Egyptian diplomatic activity and to show the Arab countries opposed to Egypt's regional policies that Egypt was capable of overcoming the boycott imposed on it by its fellow Arabs. This state of siege gradually started to weaken in 1983 through a threefold Egyptian movement. First came the Summit of the Non-Aligned Movement in Delhi in March 1983, which was attended by the president, the minister of state for foreign affairs, and a large Egyptian delegation of seasoned members who had the ability to defend Egypt and ensure that what happened in Havana in September 1979 would not be repeated. Back then, Egypt's position was targeted and there were attempts to suspend our membership in the Non-Allied Movement. Amr Moussa was the hero of the Egyptian delegation, confronting Arab and Cuban attempts to weaken the role of Egypt on the international scene in response to the signing of the peace treaty with Israel a few months earlier.

The Foreign Ministry laid out the Egyptian situation in detail, both before and after the Delhi summit. Many of the members of the Non-Aligned

Movement came to understand the Egyptian policies and principles. I was once accompanying Kamal Hassan Ali in a car in the middle of February, 1983, and we talked about the formation of the Egyptian delegation to the upcoming summit in Delhi, which was less than a week away. I suggested that we should assemble very influential people for the delegation and that Amr Moussa, the Egyptian deputy permanent representative to the UN in New York, should accompany Kamal Hassan Ali to India so that we could use his great mobility and his unmatched capabilities for negotiating to fend off any attempt to undermine Egypt's position, as had happened in Havana three years earlier. The minister accepted my suggestion, and also agreed not to include the permanent representative in the delegation, so that the deputy permanent representative, Amr Moussa, would not feel any restraint during the meeting. That meeting in Delhi marked the beginning of the Egyptian comeback in the Non-Aligned Movement.

The second important Egyptian initiative intended to overcome the effects of the Arab boycott at the time was the decision to seek a two-year non-permanent membership to the Security Council in 1984–85. The decision was announced by Kamal Hassan Ali after meeting with Amr Moussa and the Algerian permanent representative, who assured him that his country would not compete with Egypt for that seat. Egypt enjoyed considerable support despite the opposition of the Soviet Union, the socialist bloc, and some of the Arab countries. I did not know back then, as we were preparing for this battle for a Security Council seat in 1984–85, that I would become the deputy permanent representative at the Council for five months, from August to December 1985. I remember arriving early in the morning the day we received the Egyptian delegation's cable about Amr Moussa's talks with the Algerian delegate. I called Kamal Hassan Ali hurriedly and talked to him about the importance of this suggestion and the necessity of moving quickly to take advantage of it. I also told him that I doubted the Algerian delegate was accurate in his understanding of the situation of his country. Despite everything, Kamal Hassan Ali made a fast and firm decision without checking with the president.

These two diplomatic successes on the part of Egypt were followed by a third successful move involving Morocco. King Hassan II committed himself to helping Egypt reinstate its membership in the Organization of the Islamic Conference (OIC), which was to meet in Casablanca in early 1984. Egyptian delegations went to most of the member countries of the OIC, and detailed arrangements were made with Morocco. The summit was held and Egypt regained its membership after a glorious battle led by Ahmed Sékou Touré, president of Guinea, and King Hassan II. Egypt gradually and calmly began to resume its role in the organization. The tireless efforts of Kamal Hassan Ali and of King Hassan in preparing for this comeback must be gratefully acknowledged.

On May 28, the director of the diplomatic and consular corps affairs, Ambassador Omar Serry, said that the deputy prime minister and foreign minister wanted to transfer me and my colleague Mohamed Hassan Gawally abroad. I was worried and asked him if we had made some big mistake. Serry denied this, and stressed that the minister greatly appreciated our selfless efforts in doing our job. He added that the minister might leave the Ministry of Foreign Affairs soon and did not want to leave us behind in an insecure position, especially since he hoped to take us with him wherever he would go.

Without thinking, I said that I would like to be transferred to New York and Gawally to Washington, and Omar Serry commented that Kamal Hassan Ali had expected these exact choices from us.

Up to that point, I had spent almost two years working with the foreign minister, during which I was determined to gain his trust and do my best so that he would appreciate my effort. Every day I read all the important incoming and outgoing cables and other correspondence and suggested ways to handle them depending on my experience of their subject matter. Sometimes I communicated with other members or departments in the ministry in order to understand the background of these subjects and asked for their suggestions; I would later inform the minister of their suggestions and give them the credit for them. I could sense that he greatly appreciated the effort and commitment that my colleague Gawally and I exerted willingly on a daily basis and sometimes around the clock.

Kamal Hassan Ali could tell how happy I was to go back to the headquarters of the UN when he visited the secretary general in November

1982. He knew I was greatly interested in all that was related to the UN and its role worldwide. We had many discussions about the roles, attitudes, and experiences of the ministers who preceded him and about their understanding of the UN.

I used to tell Kamal Hassan Ali that from my own point of view, I believed that New York was the gateway to the position of minister of foreign affairs, and he would smile and say that a person has to do his best but there were no guarantees that things would always go your way. I went to his office to express my thanks, and he said that he had known my decision beforehand but he wanted to let me choose. A few days later, on June 5, I traveled with him to Sudan to deliver a message from the Egyptian president to the Sudanese president, Jaafar Nimeiry. At that time, the first sparks of the second civil war in Sudan had erupted, which would ultimately lead to its division into North and South in 2011.

We had frequently visited Sudan in the previous months to help President Nimeiry resolve the situation in his country. Once, as we sat with him, a member of the Egyptian General Intelligence entered carrying a small piece of paper, which he handed to the Egyptian foreign minister, who was stunned when he read it. He told President Nimeiry that the death of Egyptian Prime Minister Dr. Fouad Mohieddin had been announced in Cairo and that we had to leave immediately.

We boarded the small plane to Cairo. During the flight, Kamal Hassan Ali said that the president had had a business breakfast with his top assistants the day before I was transferred to New York, in which he had informed them of his intention to reassign the top executive positions in the Egyptian government. Dr. Fouad Mohieddin, who was the prime minister, was supposed to move to the People's Assembly and Kamal Hassan Ali would become the prime minister. I asked him about the nominee for the position of foreign minister, and he replied that it might be Esmat Abdel Meguid or Ashraf Ghorbal. Esmat Abdel Meguid had spent eleven years in New York as Egyptian permanent representative to the UN. Ashraf Ghorbal had been Egypt's ambassador to Washington for eleven years. Both diplomats had spent these years working hard defending Egyptian and Arab interests. Both of them were renowned and highly appreciated figures in the Foreign Ministry with whom I had good relations, and they had kept in touch with me since their return from the United States. Whenever they wanted to deliver a message to Kamal Hassan Ali and failed to reach him directly, they called me.

In addition to these two figures, there was another group of younger rising stars who had a chance to get the top position: Amr Moussa, Nabil al-Arabi, Abdel Raouf El Reedy, Ahmed Sidqi, Mohamed Shaker, and Mounir Zahran.

When we landed in Cairo, our press office informed me, while we were still in the airport, that the president had met Esmat Abdel Meguid but had not announced anything about a new position for him. I guessed that it would most probably be that of foreign minister, since Kamal Hassan Ali would be the prime minister. I called Dr. Esmat Abdel Meguid in the evening and congratulated him, and he said that had just been on the phone with the next prime minister. He asked me to go to his office the next day in the Cairo Arbitration Center, which he headed, and requested a thorough report about the situation in the Ministry of Foreign Affairs. I had the permission of Kamal Hassan Ali to give him an oral report, which I did.

Abdel Meguid said that he would be happy to have me work with him. I apologized and told him that I had been transferred to New York and that I thought that Kamal Hassan Ali would probably request that I stay with him for at least a year. Abdel Meguid asked me who could be relied upon to manage the Foreign Ministry. I suggested two people who came to my mind immediately: Mohamed al-Zu'eibi and Said Rifaat. I assured him that I was confident that they were capable of managing the work in the minister's office. He said that he would choose Mohamed al-Zu'eibi. As he prepared for his official appointment as prime minister on July 17, 1984, Kamal Hassan Ali moved from the Foreign Ministry to the Cabinet building.

As the appointment of the new cabinet approached, the president called Kamal Hassan Ali—his prime minister-designate—and they discussed the choice of the next minister of foreign affairs. Mohamed Hassan Gawally and I were in the room with Kamal Hassan Ali, and the three of us were astounded when the president fired a bombshell when he asked, "How about Ashraf Ghorbal?" While the discussion continued, I could tell that Kamal Hassan Ali was a little annoyed, since he and the president had already informed Abdel Meguid that they intended to choose him for the post. Later in the call the president said that he would go with the first choice, Abdel Meguid, after all, and appoint Ashraf Ghorbal as minister of tourism. Ghorbal, however, adamantly refused this post.

Mohamed Gawally and I guessed that the purpose of this maneuver on the part of the president was to pick Ashraf Ghorbal as a substitute, thus making him a future candidate for the Ministry of Foreign Affairs. The same thing had happened with Ismail Fahmy, who was appointed as minister of tourism in March 1973 and moved after six months to the Ministry of Foreign Affairs.

The new government started to work hard, and I worked in the Cabinet building as advisor to the prime minister for one year. During that period, I got to know the work in the government headquarters and the way that state business was run. Years later, I realized that this was a very beneficial experience for me. Today I can see that my experience in the president's office with the Egyptian national security advisor from 1972 to 1974, and in the office of the prime minster from 1984 to 1985, greatly deepened my understanding of the state's internal and external affairs and the relationships among all the Egyptian institutions working in the fields of domestic and foreign policy and national security. These experiences proved very useful when I became foreign minister of Egypt in July 2004.

I left for New York in the middle of July 1985 to take up my responsibilities as a counselor in the Egyptian mission to the UN. I spent four years in that post, which unfortunately did not add much to my knowledge of the working mechanisms of the UN. They did, however, considerably enhance my position in later years whenever the position of UN ambassador was vacant and new names were suggested to fill it, which is what happened when I was appointed as Egypt's permanent representative in 1999. At the beginning of 1989, as my posting to New York was ending, Dr. Esmat Abdel Meguid asked me to work with him. Indeed, upon my return from New York in August, I joined his office and worked with him until he left on May 15, 1991 to become secretary general of the League of Arab States, while Amr Moussa became minister of foreign affairs on the same date.

Those three years from 1989 to 1991 witnessed two important series of events and developments. The first was Iraq's invasion of Kuwait in the early hours of August 2, 1990. The second was the events related to the interests of the American administration, under the leadership of George H.W. Bush, in advancing peace efforts in the Middle East and starting a negotiation process between the Palestinians and the Israelis. My memoir, *Witness to War and Peace*, contains the details of these developments, which affected the situation in the Middle East for years to come.

Saddam Hussein's invasion of Kuwait made me extremely angry. It revealed Hussein's ignorance of the development of power relations during that period. The Soviet Union was in retreat, while at the same time there was a stunning rise of unchallenged North Atlantic influence on the international stage. I was also surprised at Jordan's reaction, which gave the impression that they were sympathetic to Iraq's motivations. My immediate analysis at the time, which I discussed with both Dr. Esmat Abdel Meguid and Osama El-Baz, was that if the invasion continued, Egypt would be in an embarrassing situation. Iraq would appear as the most influential and boisterous power in the Arab world, while Egypt would subside into the position of a worn-out country that no one would pay any attention to. Therefore, I believed that it was necessary to reverse the situation to the status quo ante bellum and to ensure a complete Iraqi withdrawal from Kuwait. Later on, I believed, we should attempt a reconciliation between the conflicting parties.

Egypt exerted real efforts to control the situation and to convince Iraq to show flexibility; Iraq proved to be intransigent and determined to annex Kuwait.

There was a sharp debate between Dr. Esmat Abdel Meguid and Saadoun Hammadi, the Iraqi minister of state for foreign affairs, in a meeting between them that I attended. Hammadi threatened that if Egypt failed to fully support Iraq, it would cost Egypt dearly and that whoever lent a hand to change the situation would have this "hand" cut off. Abdel Meguid replied with a great deal of self-restraint: "I am afraid, brother Saadoun, that Iraq's hand is the one that will be cut off." In the emergency meeting of Arab foreign ministers held in Cairo on August 1–2, 1990, Egypt advocated the condemnation of the Iraqi action and demanded the withdrawal of Iraqi troops from Kuwait. The vote showed a sharp split in the positions of the Arab states. It was followed by an Arab summit that adopted a resolution on August 9, which further deepened that split between the Arab states.

As soon as the invasion took place, Egypt realized that allowing it to continue would weaken its influence and its role in the Arab world, and therefore the situation needed to be reversed to the state of affairs before the invasion. Egypt began laying the groundwork for building an Arab and international coalition for the purpose of restoring things back to normal. I recounted the complete story of this crisis in *Witness to War and Peace*. It is noteworthy that this period not only harmed the Arab political system and undermined the potential for Arab cooperation but also complicated the relationship between the Palestinian leadership as represented by Yasser Arafat, on the one hand, and Egypt and the Gulf Cooperation Council (GCC), on the other. These effects lasted for a long time. As the views of Syria and Egypt on the Iraqi invasion became closer to those of the GCC, Syrian Foreign Affairs Minister Farouk al-Sharaa came up with the suggestion of issuing a statement expressing the views of the three parties on the Arab situation in general and ways of defending Arab interests with a plan for cooperation. The foreign ministers of Egypt, Saudi Arabia, and Syria began holding meetings in Cairo, Riyadh, and Damascus. The armed conflict started on January 17, 1991 and ended with the expulsion of Iraq from Kuwait on February 25, 1991. The Damascus Declaration was signed on March 6, 1991. The Egyptians and Syrians thought that the declaration would establish an institutional framework that would enable greater cooperation among its parties: Egypt and Syria, on one hand, and the GCC, on the other. A few months later, however, Saudi Arabia demanded the withdrawal of the Egyptian and Syrian forces from its lands. Of course, Egypt promptly removed its forces, which had participated in the liberation of Kuwait as part of the international coalition. Then Saudi Arabia requested a modification of the Damascus Declaration in a way that suited the new Arab situation, but Egypt was not enthusiastic about this. The Damascus Declaration, which was a serious attempt at securing real Arab cooperation in the Gulf area, receded and was almost forgotten.

Throughout this crisis, I was in the middle of the action in the Egyptian foreign ministry and bore many responsibilities, especially when Dr. Esmat Abdel Meguid was hospitalized after a serious car accident on the highway between Cairo and Alexandria. Being at the heart of the dilemma, I believed that the Iraqi leadership had made one of the most serious mistakes in modern Arab history, which cost Iraq long years of losses. I also believed that Egypt had no other path but the one it took by allowing the formation of an international coalition and facilitating the transfer of its forces and equipment to the Gulf, and contributing a large Egyptian force.

After attacking the Iraqi occupying forces and liberating Kuwait, the United States put forth an initiative for peace in the Middle East. This initiative was not the first American attempt toward a political settlement of the Arab–Israeli conflict and it was by no means the last. Egypt was immersed in these efforts through its foreign minister at the time, Abdel Meguid, and his successor, Amr Moussa, both of whom I worked with closely.

The confrontation with Iraq and the need to form this broad international coalition led to a nearly unprecedented Egyptian–American convergence, equaled only by the signing of the Camp David Accords on September 17, 1978. In the middle of this cooperation, I received an advisor from the American Embassy in Cairo, who said that he was trying to find out whether the Egyptian foreign minister wanted to run for the post of secretary general of the UN. The post was expected to become vacant by the end of 1991 with the expiration of the second term of the Peruvian Pérez de Cuéllar. I talked with Dr. Esmat Abdel Meguid, who agreed to open a secret channel with the Americans to find out more about his chances of winning the post. I secretly informed the American official that Abdel Meguid did not mind exploring his chances. He replied that James Baker, the U.S. secretary of state, was enthusiastic about the idea and that the United States was ready to start official discussions with us and begin securing support for the nomination, since the election was to take place before the end of 1991—only a few months away. I conveyed this message to Dr. Esmat Abdel Meguid, suggesting that he should discuss the topic with the president. All of a sudden, the minister of foreign affairs asked me to immediately prepare letters from President Mubarak to the leaders of Arab countries informing them of the nomination of Dr. Esmat Abdel Meguid for the post of secretary general of the Arab League. He also wanted to end all discussions with the Americans and to inform them that Dr. Abdel Meguid would not be available. Then fate played its role: Dr. Boutros Boutros-Ghali became the UN secretary general through extremely hard work and unprecedented good luck.

The Madrid Conference for peace in the Middle East was held at the end of October 1991 to push for a continuing peace process. The Egyptian delegation worked very hard and made a serious attempt to achieve a real settlement for the Palestinians, but Israel continued its maneuvers and prevarication. Years and decades passed by and nothing came true but what Yitzhak Shamir, the Israeli prime minister and foreign minister at the time, told Amr Moussa arrogantly: that Israel would negotiate for ten years or more and the Palestinians would never get anything from them unless they wanted to give it.

In October 1992, I left for Rome as the Egyptian ambassador. I came back to Cairo in 1996 to work once again with Amr Moussa on the gloomy peace process. In 1999, I was transferred to the United States as the permanent representative of Egypt to the UN, thus realizing one of my biggest aims. I owe thanks to Amr Moussa for both transfers, to Rome and to New York. While I was working at the UN, my anger and irritation built up as time went by; I was almost fifty-seven at the beginning of 1999, which meant I might soon be required to retire without achieving the kind of breakthrough that I had hoped for in my professional career. In 2004, however, I returned to Egypt as minister of foreign affairs, the ultimate goal for any serious Egyptian diplomat. The so-called "peace process" was still being handled by various parties, but whenever a real chance came up, it was immediately aborted by Israel, which had no desire for peace with the Palestinians except on its own terms.

It was a long and arduous journey from June 1, 1965 to the day of my appointment as minister of foreign affairs on July 14, 2004. Life was not always a bed of roses; we have been through trauma, grief, suffering, and despair, but we have also experienced happy moments, success, true friendship among colleagues, hard work, loyalty, discipline, truthfulness, and a feeling of responsibility for our words and actions. As the proverb goes, March winds and April showers bring forth May flowers. Through this long path, full of hardships and blessings, I was accompanied by my dear wife Laila, who always had my back and was always by my side, supporting me in every possible way. When I became minister of foreign affairs, she had a major role in restoring the splendor of the buildings and clubs of the ministry and of many of the embassies. I will be forever indebted to her.

# 3

# UNDERSTANDING THE SITUATION AND THE GENERAL FRAMEWORK FOR ACTION

As I entered the Ministry of Foreign Affairs on the afternoon of July 14, 2004, I received a phone call from Amr Moussa, the secretary general of the Arab League, who extended his cordial congratulations on my appointment as foreign minister. He added that he would be arriving in minutes at my office. I met him in front of the entrance to the main building of the ministry in Maspero. When I proposed that we sit together in the lounge, he adamantly refused and insisted on seeing me seated in the minister's chair at Khedive Ismail's old wooden desk, where all the Egyptian foreign ministers of the twentieth century had sat. I felt embarrassed but he insisted. I realized how much Amr Moussa appreciated that he had been succeeded by a colleague whom he had helped promote over the past ten years. Amr Moussa left without attempting to suggest certain policy positions regarding the issues that I was about to tackle as minister.

I then received another phone call from Ahmed Maher, my distinguished predecessor, inviting me to lunch at his home the following day. I had called him as soon as Dr. Ahmed Nazif had informed me of my new appointment, on July 10 at daybreak in New York. He wished me well and expressed his certainty of my success in this major task in my career.

At that point, I had served in the Egyptian diplomatic corps for more than thirty-nine years. I had worked with all the Egyptian foreign ministers since 1977 as a staff member at the headquarters in Cairo whenever I was there, and was thus acquainted with the working methods of the minister of foreign affairs, particularly his communications and relations with the president, the presidential staff, the prime minister, and all the other ministers, especially those of defense, interior, and intelligence. However, I had been out of the country for five and a half years, from the beginning of 1999 until July 2004, during which many internal transformations had occurred in Egypt that had affected the working methods, and thus I needed to study the situation precisely and attentively.

I was disappointed that the president had been absent from the major summits that were held at the UN General Assembly in September every year, especially the Millennium Summit in which most of the leaders of countries, large and small, participated. I felt that it was one of my duties to urge the president to participate in the upcoming summit in September 2004. I was also dissatisfied that the president had stopped attending any of the African summits since the Addis Ababa assassination attempt in 1995. This negatively affected the general image of Egypt's interest in Africa in the minds of many African leaders. Nonetheless, the Egyptian national security agencies—the Ministry of Foreign Affairs, the General Intelligence, and the Ministry of Defense—had maintained constant contact with African countries generally, and especially the Nile riparian states and those African countries that were contiguous to Egypt.

On the other hand, many political groupings and axes were being formed among pivotal countries with the purpose of expanding their influence and improving their status in the international system. I also noticed that neither the Egyptian government nor the president personally observed or interacted with them in a manner that would secure a place for Egypt among them. These included, most importantly, the Group of Eight (G8: the United States, the Russian Federation, Britain, France, Germany, Canada, Italy, and Japan), to which various countries representing the regional economic groupings were invited annually. The Egyptian president turned down all invitations except one, out of respect for the French president, who invited him to the summit in the city of Evian. The IBSA Forum (India, Brazil, South Africa) was founded in 2002 while Egypt was not present. Observing the situation from New York at the time, I believed that we had a problem that needed to be dealt with. Egypt did have a certain international stature and influence. Although we had not sat on the Security Council since 1998, we had maintained a strong UN presence on the issues of disarmament, nuclear nonproliferation, and other political questions. Egypt's influence, and its ability to act within the Non-Aligned Movement (NAM) and the Islamic, Arab, and African groupings, carried its weight in the deliberations of the Security Council and the General Assembly. Egypt was present at all the social, economic, and environmental discussions handled by the UN, and everyone was eager to hear its opinion regarding the legal issues, human rights and the landmine conventions, terrorism, and other matters.

I believed that the president should be encouraged to actively participate in all kinds of international activities. It's true that I was talking about a president who was over seventy-five years old in 2004; on the other hand, the security issues that were so often cited to explain his absences were overblown. I decided to keep maneuvering in order to get him to participate more. I gathered several opinions and views that argued that the president was becoming politically isolated and sent them to the president, hoping that this would spur him into action. I admit that I succeeded at certain points and failed in others, as will be recounted hereafter.

I started to work out how to do my job with a president who had been in office for twenty-three years by then, further complicated by the fact that we had not been personally acquainted. I admit that it was a difficult relationship in the beginning. I had only been in office a little more than two weeks when the president left Cairo for Ras al-Hikma on the North Coast for recovery from surgery during the month of August. When he returned to Cairo at the beginning of September 2004, I noticed that he called once or twice a day, usually in the evening. Thus I made certain to be available at these times and to be fully updated on all the international or regional events that had taken place in the previous few hours, so I could discuss them with him. He asked questions and demanded immediate answers. I always answered that I had sent the information the day before, or that I had mentioned my evaluation of this or that problem in a memo that had been presented to him. As time passed, it became obvious that he preferred direct phone calls and wanted to have me available at all times, avoiding the use of the mobile phone, which he distrusted for security and safety reasons.

Air Vice-Marshal Samir Ramadan, who was my father's friend and had maintained good relations with my family for decades after my father's death, used to talk about his experience with President Mubarak when he was the commander of the Egyptian Air Force. Mubarak was then strict, serious, stern, a maneuverer, and always eager to learn everything. Answers must be ready and correct or one should not bother to inform him, for he would investigate the matter and come back to point his finger at the person who had given inaccurate answers, and possibly to punish him. I came to understand these characteristics over the years and listened to endless stories about him, which turned out to be true. When the president came to visit Rome in 1994 and I, as the Egyptian ambassador, received him, I noticed that he kept asking about the Italian luxury car, the armored Maserati, in which he rode, inquiring about its horsepower, shielding, the steel used in its manufacture, its speed, and its price. I answered quite cautiously and promised to get answers for his questions promptly. Within three hours of his arrival, he was riding the car again on his way to meet Oscar Luigi Scalfaro, the Italian president, at the Italian presidential palace, Quirinale, and was asking again about the car. I had already received the answers from the Italians and he was satisfied. He then began discussing the Italian cars, Lancia and Alfa Romeo, used by the Italian officials, and their armor. This showed that he was aware of the discussions in Egypt about buying European armored cars for some of the senior Egyptian officials as an anti-terrorist measure in the early 1990s. The president said that they had settled on French cars because their shielding was thicker than that of the Italian ones. From our discussion during the trip, I inferred that he was well acquainted with the details and very much concerned with the financial costs. From my observations during his trip, I would say he was a very good listener; he listened carefully to my oral report on the situation in Italy at the time and about the problems of Prime Minister Silvio Berlusconi.

Through our communication, I found out that the president trusted people and their actions. While we were in the car, I brought out some tasty

Italian mint tablets and offered him one, which he accepted. That evening his secretary asked me to provide him with a whole package. I sent him a box containing several packages for long-term use.

I began to get accustomed to a certain method of working with the president. I would send him feedback on a certain political issue, then call him on the following day to discuss it after I had sent the memo to his secretary of information, so that his staff members would have time to study the proposal before I defended this point or that. Experience showed the president's perseverance and interest in learning everything, even without reading the documents but depending on summaries, on the one hand, and the secretary of information's oral report, on the other.

I was extremely clear and honest in reporting situations to the president. I remember that I once nominated a competent ambassador, who had retired more than a year earlier, to a mission, and the president was angry. He called to oppose the appointment, and to object to what he perceived as an attempt on my part to twist or ignore his standing orders of not assigning missions to retired officials. I answered politely and firmly, "Mr. President, please trust that I only seek the general interest, and any nomination or suggestion that I come forward with is offered after meticulous thought. There is no place for favoritism or a wish to do a friend or an acquaintance a favor. This will never be my way of working with you." I felt that the president appreciated the straightforwardness, boldness, and politeness in my words, and never questioned any of my nominations to foreign positions or my views on public or personnel issues again.

During my almost seven years in office, he neither refused nor changed any of my nominations for Egyptian ambassadors, or recommendations to transfer an ambassador due to inefficiency or disreputability. He even inquired occasionally about the competency of one ambassador or another for a public position.

I also became aware at once that the method the president and his staff members adopted for managing foreign relations at the president's level had not changed for the past two decades. If the president wished to travel abroad, the presidential staff or its chief were assigned to make the necessary arrangements. For security reasons, they contacted the Egyptian ambassador in the country concerned, or that country's ambassador in Cairo, to discuss the details of the visit: its date, duration, topics, and the like. Our ambassadors used to call the ministry to inform us that they had been contacted to arrange for the visit and had been instructed not to tell anyone, not even their immediate leadership.

I noticed that the same procedures also extended to the president's wife and his son Gamal. We often learned of trips and meetings that were arranged by the foreign ambassadors in Egypt or our ambassadors in foreign capitals. Years of work proved that there were continuous attempts to conceal the president's son's foreign activities and his meetings with officials of other countries in Egypt or abroad. From 2006 onward, this became quite obvious when foreign senior officials met with him unannounced in his office. We did not know what went on behind the closed doors. During his visits abroad, our ambassadors were often contacted, especially our ambassador in Washington, D.C., to arrange meetings, including those with the American national security advisor and other officials. He even had a meeting with U.S. President George W. Bush, which was arranged at a time when we were having difficulties with the American administration. The American president entered the national security advisor's office during his meeting with the Egyptian president's son for a brief discussion.

Many ambassadors of other countries in Cairo, who were contacted to prepare for one visit or another, spoke to the Egyptian foreign affairs officials informing them that the presidential office had made certain requests relating to these visits. This put us in an awkward and frustrating position. On my part, I talked to the chief of the presidential staff, who confirmed that these were the president's instructions in order to maintain the confidentiality of all communications and movements. I told him that I would always know every action involving our ambassadors abroad or an ambassador in Cairo the minute it happened, and there was no need to treat me in the same way my predecessors had suffered. I also noticed that some of these foreign contacts were aimless, their sole purpose being to maintain for Egypt or the president an image of persistent action toward powers or personalities we favored. For decades, our reaction at the ministry was to work on giving a meaning to each visit and expanding its substantive aspects by focusing on the details of the relationship between the two countries and seeking to gain or offer benefits. We thus managed to give these visits and contacts a certain impetus that Egyptian foreign policy could then take advantage of.

Examining President Mubarak's pattern of the foreign operations and private visits he made since I had worked with Dr. Esmat Abdel Meguid and Minister Amr Moussa, I found that he decided to travel abroad on some mission every six to eight weeks, to either a European or an Arab country, visiting more than one country at a time, two or three being the optimum number. The dates would be set for the main destination, then the president's office would decide on the second and third destinations. These visits were actually well received by the countries. I often pointed out to Minister Amr Moussa that we were getting close to the fifth or sixth week and had to expect the president to travel abroad soon. As the president's confidence in the efforts made by the Ministry of Foreign Affairs increased after 2004, this method began to diminish gradually, and the presidential office became more dependent on the ministry for its operations.

On the Arab front, Egypt relied primarily on its relations with the Gulf states, especially Saudi Arabia, which is the principal power in the Gulf, while maintaining close ties to the Emirates, Kuwait, Bahrain, and Oman, which had enjoyed particularly close relations with Egypt since President Sadat's years in office.

Egypt also maintained dynamic relations with Syria while totally understanding its role in Middle East policy, even though the president always felt suspicious of the Syrian perspectives and aims from the time I came into office until he stepped down in 2011.

It was quite obvious that whenever relations with Syria became complicated, Egypt turned toward Jordan, with which, together with Saudi Arabia and the Emirates, it had developed closer communications since the Israeli invasion of southern Lebanon in 2006.

Sudan and Libya were of major interest to Egypt. A few days after I came into office, I received a phone call from the president asking me to travel the following day to meet Muammar Qadhafi, who wanted to get to know me in the presence of General Omar Suleiman. The president was brief; he did not give any instructions or have a specific vision of the meeting or its purposes. This was a trait I noticed as soon as I got to know him. When he spoke, he was concise and expected his subordinates and officials to be fully aware of his instructions and guidelines, a problem I quickly overcame by depending on General Omar Suleiman's experience, or by reviewing my observations with the former ministers of foreign affairs with whom I had worked: Kamal Hassan Ali, Esmat Abdel Meguid, and Amr Moussa. I also noticed that when he wished to inquire about some matter, he would ask directly, "About that?!" or "That guy who finally came and told me about the matter." I usually needed some time to figure out what he meant. Omar Suleiman said that he had the same problem. Perhaps this was the reason Kamal Hassan Ali, Esmat Abdel Meguid, and Amr Moussa were always so alert when the president talked to them over the phone.

On the following day, we left on the presidential Mystère plane for Sirte. After we landed at the military airport, the Libyans took us to a spot in the desert twenty kilometers from the Mediterranean coast, where there was a very small lake with a fountain in the middle to symbolize the activity of "The Great River," a project on which Libya had squandered billions to supply water through pipes from the aquifer in the Sahara to northern Libya. We waited for two hours for the Libyan leader to meet us. During this time we talked with Abdel Rahman Shalgham, the Libyan foreign minister, who seemed uncomfortable with the long wait, or with Moussa Koussa, head of the Libyan intelligence agency. The Libyan leader finally appeared. He welcomed us and asked us to accompany him to an open tent to have breakfast together. It was then around two o'clock in the afternoon. The breakfast lasted about one hour, during which neither Omar Suleiman nor I talked. Muammar Qadhafi did the talking. He attacked Saudi Arabia ferociously, explaining that it was destined to disintegrate into small republics. He criticized the Saudi royal family, which he considered responsible for undermining the Nasserist project. Omar Suleiman tried to express our views, especially when Qadhafi accused us of being submissive to Saudi Arabia when formulating our foreign policy, but Qadhafi was very aggressive. It was interesting that the two of us sat at a table by ourselves while he sat at another one, set for him alone, two meters away. We exchanged remarks across the open tent. It was scorching hot and the flies were all

over the place attacking our plates, which were filled with a simple breakfast of bread, cheese, and honey that I had to cover with a paper tissue to
keep the flies away. The Libyan officials left us before Qadhafi's arrival for
breakfast and did not participate in the conversation. The visit ended and
we left Sirte. When I expressed to Omar Suleiman my deep sorrow as well
as my surprise at the conduct of the Libyan leader, who had been ruling
Libya since 1969, he explained that I would be witnessing a lot of strange
things, and that in order to protect Egyptian interests, we were required to
show resilience and put up with the tragicomedies.

When the plane landed at Almaza Military Airport, which was the
main base for the Egyptian presidential planes, I received a call from the
president's secretary, who said that the president wanted me to call him
immediately on a secure line. I called as soon as I arrived at my apartment,
which is almost adjacent to the airport in the suburb of Heliopolis. He
asked, "So how was it?" I answered clearly and precisely, "Qadhafi wants to
use us in order to attack Saudi Arabia, and the purpose of his request to get
to know me personally is to send us a message not to get much closer to the
Saudis. He attacked both the king and the Saudi foreign minister fiercely.
We listened but did not comment or argue with him." I felt that the president was satisfied with our performance. I said that although Qadhafi was
well-read, as shown in his conversation with us, he was still living a harsh
desert lifestyle, and added that, to my surprise, he was not well dressed
when we met; his clothes were obviously dirty and his nails were long and
untrimmed. I commented at length on the visit and its main character. The
president listened quietly to my detailed account, then he remarked, "It's
just the tip of the iceberg!" He explained that Qadhafi was shrewd and sly
as a fox, and that we needed to coexist in order to protect our various interests in Libya. Still, it was important that we should not let him complicate
our relations with Saudi Arabia or the rest of the Gulf countries.

Omar Suleiman and I visited Libya several times to meet with Qadhafi, either with the president or by ourselves. His strange, unrealistic views
ceased to surprise me, but the president sometimes remarked that some of
Qadhafi's views were logical enough to be considered, and that we should
not take whatever he said in our presence seriously for he sounded more

reasonable in their private meetings. Qadhafi often criticized our policies with respect to our relations with Europe, especially concerning the Barcelona Process and the Union for the Mediterranean, and our relations with the Gulf. I even felt that some of his interruptions were rude enough to embarrass Mubarak. We reacted reasonably, sometimes firmly, but gently. Qadhafi was not comfortable with the freedom that the Egyptian media had to criticize the authorities. He repeated, "This is dangerous and will have its consequences for you, and definitely for us too in Libya."

Egypt's interests in Libya, as well as our desire to acquire Libyan investments, forced us to contain these situations. Mubarak repeatedly warned Qadhafi not to trust the Americans' attempt to open up to him, and that he had to be very cautious and not to allow their new embassy in Tripoli or their mission in Benghazi to allow too much American access to Libyan territory. Qadhafi used to say that he was certain of his ability to control the U.S. presence on his territory and that he would be vigilant.

The president gave special attention to Sudan, since it is considered an inseparable partner in the Nile Valley with the strongest ties to Egypt. In our conversations, he repeatedly said, "It's Sudan . . . the river passes through its territory." I remember that on the morning of July 15, 2004 I received a phone call in my office at around nine o'clock from the president's secretary, who seemed upset, asking, "Where are you, sir? We called you at home but nobody answered." I, who had been in office for just one day, answered, "I've been in my office since seven o'clock in the morning. That's been my way of working my whole life." He said that the president requested that I go immediately to his residence in Heliopolis, where he would receive the Sudanese president Omar al-Bashir fifteen minutes later, and since he was accompanied by the Sudanese foreign minister, the president thought it necessary for me to attend the meeting. I went quickly to the president's residence. The meeting had already started when I arrived. President al-Bashir had come for a mere courtesy visit to see how the president was doing after major surgery on his spinal cord. Nothing came of this visit except al-Bashir's invitation for me to visit Sudan.

This surprise visit was a good example of the Arab way in which the presidential or palace staff in some country would contact the presidential staff in Egypt to arrange for visits or meetings, without consulting the ministries of foreign affairs of either country. As soon as they learned of the arrangements, the ministries would then have to work hard to prepare for these visits and to add some sort of value that would help develop the relations between the two countries.

A few days after al-Bashir's visit I asked for the president's permission to travel to Sudan, because conditions in Darfur were deteriorating significantly and Sudan was at risk of disintegration; the Sudanese army and regime were exhausted from the lengthy civil war between the southern and the northern parts of the country. The president approved the trip, and asked me to go with General Omar Suleiman.

I mention at this point that the president in Egypt, like any country with a presidential political system, sets the general strategic objectives of the country's foreign policy. The administration of foreign policy and pursuing the strategic objectives set by the president, however, are matters that are executed by the Foreign Ministry. The president rarely intervened in technical diplomatic issues or the day-to-day management of the Egyptian foreign ministry.

We took off from Almaza Airport to Khartoum to meet President al-Bashir, his vice-president, and his minister of foreign affairs. Then we left for Darfur to monitor the situation on the ground and meet with the tribes and some of their leaders, and finally returned in the evening. It was a remarkable visit, the first of frequent visits to Sudan, to Khartoum in the north or Juba in the south, to discuss Sudanese affairs and attempt to find a solution for our dear neighbor's crises.

As soon as we landed back in Cairo, I was informed of the president's wish to receive my oral report. I made the phone call, which became one of our daily rituals, and informed the president of my first impressions. I explained that I had warned the Sudanese president of the dangers that could result from ignoring the charges presented by the prosecutor of the International Criminal Court (ICC), which would place him under the penalty of law. I added that I had told President al-Bashir that it was important for him to respond to the demands of the international agencies and the Security Council, and to arrange to interrogate some Sudanese officials who were accused of committing crimes in contravention of international humanitarian law. Otherwise, he would be held accountable. I had the impression that President al-Bashir was surprised at the harshness embedded in my message despite the courtesy I tried to show. I told him that the west wanted Sudan to disintegrate, and that Britain felt it had made a mistake when it kept Sudan as a unified country in 1956. There were also influential Christian interests in western or European circles aiming at establishing a state in southern Sudan, and powerful investment interests hoping to make use of Sudan's resources if they could be removed from a strong central rule. He should take action to thwart these interests. I assured him that Egypt was closely observing the situation in Sudan at the time, and that we were aware that there were neighboring African and regional parties who were not keen on preserving the unity of Sudan.

President Mubarak listened calmly to my report. I believe that he had already got used to my direct way of speaking with the regional parties we were concerned with to maintain Egyptian national security.

My reports, oral or written, which were sent to the president over the next months and during the years 2004 and 2005, gave my predictions concerning the possibility of secession in Sudan, and the indictment of President al-Bashir by the ICC. The president approved many of our proposals on the best way to advise Sudan on dealing with the ICC, and providing the Sudanese with legal experts. Chief among these was Dr. Nabil al-Arabi, the international judge, who was well acquainted with the intricacies of the ICC, and who met with Sudanese officials several times to offer legal advice and to explain the steps that Egypt might take to address the threats.

To help Sudan overcome its problems, it was agreed to intensify Egyptian economic activity in both northern and southern Sudan, as well as its military presence within the UN peacekeeping operations on the Sudanese stage. In spite of all this Egyptian support, which placed heavy burdens on the Egyptian treasury at a time when Egypt itself suffered from difficult economic conditions, the aim would not be achieved as long as the Sudanese leadership did not take the preservation of the unity of the country seriously. Our natural concern with Sudan and its affairs caused some tensions between us and our brothers in Khartoum. The southern leaders regarded Egypt with suspicion despite all the scholarships they had been given that had allowed some of their officials to study in Alexandria. They assumed that, in our quest to maintain the unity of Sudan, we would support the government in the north against their interests. We actually wished to promote the option of unity, but we also needed to take into account that both the northern and the southern parts are our partners in the Nile Valley. When some northern leaders expressed dissatisfaction with this attitude, we explained that we would not take sides unless one side was aggressive or unjust to the other. As a result, there were difficulties in our relations, even though the northern leaders continued to ask for our help to ease the tension whenever it flared up. I should here express my gratitude to our ambassador in Khartoum at the time, Mohamed Assem Ibrahim, for the oral and written reports he gave me, and whose close relations with General Omar Suleiman made it possible for all of us in our two agencies to share the same views regarding the situation in Sudan.

If our first priority was opening up to the Arab world, Africa was the second. I paid several visits to African countries, alone or accompanied by the president, during 2004. The president was quite aware that Egypt needed to become more involved at the continental level, and from his responses during our talks about African issues, I believe he came to realize that his absence from earlier African visits and summits had had a negative effect on us.

All the visits I paid to African countries were welcomed, especially those that sought to improve communication with the Nile Basin countries. Because of my persistent demands, the president disregarded the security considerations that were raised occasionally whenever there was a possibility of attending an African summit or visiting an African country. He participated in the African Summits in Abuja, Nigeria in January 2005 and Ghana in July 2007, and then visited Senegal for a few hours, as well as South Africa, Uganda, and Khartoum and Juba in Sudan.

To compensate further for his absence from the African scene, which gave the false impression that we took no interest in the continent, the president agreed to host a large number of African leaders in Cairo over several years, and to hold a number of summits for African leaders in Sharm al-Sheikh, which improved Egypt's image in Africa. Still, it must be admitted that our poor trade and economic relations with the African countries resulted in limiting the impact of Egypt's influence. I have to admit, too, that I frequently felt that the president received the African leaders with great formality and lack of enthusiasm, not even attempting to put on an act which would have built closer ties within the African context, taking into consideration the fact that many of these relationships depended on personal recognition and direct communication among the heads of state.

The interest and concern of the Egyptian president focused on certain Arab capitals, such as Riyadh, Damascus, Kuwait, and Abu Dhabi. He also made frequent appearances on the European stage, in Rome, Paris, and Berlin. The president did not visit London during the period from 2004 to 2011, due to merely personal reasons, as far as I could tell. I sought to expand the breadth of Egypt's contracts and interaction with Europe and the Arab world, so as not to be restricted to a small selection of countries. We deepened our contacts with Eastern Europe and the Balkans, and visited Moscow, thereby creating a greater Egyptian presence on the European stage. The president also traveled to Morocco, Algeria, all the countries of the Gulf Cooperation Council (GCC), and Syria.

I continually advised Mubarak to open up more to the Asian world and its rising powers, especially since everybody was talking about a shift of international power to China, the Indian subcontinent, and the Far East. Some of the people surrounding the president seemed annoyed by the idea, claiming that he could not physically bear all that stress. Even so, he agreed to visit China, India, and Kazakhstan.

It was generally thought that the president had no wish or strength to travel abroad frequently and be present at the international level. He felt that the minister of foreign affairs and several other ministers should instead intensify their physical presence as well as their communication with the foreign capitals. Heads of states and their senior officials were to be encouraged to visit Cairo. At the same time, the resort town of Sharm al-Sheikh was being transformed into a focal point for conferences and international summits, such as the Non-Aligned summit, African summits, the China–Africa summit, and France–Africa summit and other major conferences, even though the president was always worried about the expense.

We set out to broaden the Egyptian framework of movement with the principal powers. With Brazil, an annual strategic dialogue at the level of foreign ministers was agreed upon. With Turkey, our relationship was strengthened by agreeing on a document for strategic relations and annual meetings between the two leaderships. It was well known that under the dual rule of Erdogan and Gul, Turkey was seeking to extend its influence over the areas where the Ottoman Empire had historically had relations and influence, but we were not particularly sensitive to these Turkish efforts. Our aim was mainly to encourage the Turkish economic and investment abilities to serve Egypt's economic growth targets. Turkey was also seeking to play a role in the settlement in the Middle East, which we felt could be harnessed to assist our role in this regard.

We strengthened our relations with Russia and agreed on a framework for deepening our strategic relations by holding annual meetings between the leaders of the two countries and an annual meeting of the foreign and defense ministers. Russia was used to conducting such dialogues with only a very limited number of countries, such as the United States, India, France, and Italy. I asked to have Egypt added, and it was only with great effort that the Russians accepted. Some of us resisted the idea and prevented the implementation of these agreements with Russia out of fear of provoking the United States, but I did not understand the reason for this reluctance until I left office in March 2011.

During my first few months in office, our main aim was to emphasize the Egyptian prospects and secure a presence for Egypt on the international scene in a way that would provide it with a distinct, influential position, making it possible to join the small group of countries that enjoyed international economic influence. Thus, in case of an expansion of the UN Security Council, Egypt would seek a part in it. We actively tried to gain entry for Egypt into the IBSA grouping, which includes India, South Africa, and Brazil, whose capitals I visited several times. I also convinced the president to travel to India, which he last visited in 1983. He also visited South Africa. We were planning for him to visit Brazil, Argentina, and Mexico, but family and health issues kept him from traveling, which disappointed all parties, especially me. In many instances, foreign relations were advanced through personal relations and contacts. For example, the president refused to visit India for years for reasons unknown to me, in spite of my persistence. He also stopped visiting Britain after 2004 because of an unpleasant experience he had on his visit to its capital in 1994, or for what he thought was cold treatment offered to his spouse when she was visiting London alone.

Great efforts were made to join the group of emerging economies known as BRIC, which includes Brazil, Russia, India and China. The attempts continued for years, ending only when the group decided to open up to South Africa instead, on the grounds that it was economically stronger than Egypt. It must be admitted that many diplomatic policies and attitudes are, in fact, influenced by the economic capacities of the country. No matter how active a country's diplomatic corps is, the world today regards economic impact as the key to unlock closed doors. I observed these developments with great concern, particularly because I thought that an agreement to expand the membership of the Security Council could happen at any moment if the international consensus in which we participated took place, as will be mentioned later. I was aware that Egypt competed with nations whose economic capacities far exceeded its own. Brazil had four times the gross domestic product (GDP) of Egypt, and Mexico three and a half times, while in Africa, South Africa had double the GDP with half the population. In the Arab world, Saudi Arabia had triple the Egyptian GDP or slightly less with one-third of the population; the same applied to Qatar. The economic vision of the international community always dominated its political relations and shaped its evaluation of countries and communities. Yet Egypt's diplomats maneuvered skillfully, took the initiative, and achieved success, thus managing to conceal the structural weaknesses inherent in Egypt's economic capacities, especially Turkey and Iran, the former having triple Egypt's GDP and the latter double, with smaller populations.

I believed in the soft power of Egypt and the ability of Egyptian culture and higher education to attract thousands of Arab and African students to enter Egyptian universities and institutes. Nonetheless, I saw the strong performance of many other countries in fields such as providing health facilities to African and Arab citizens, in which I had thought we were competitive. We were no longer at the top in this field or many others. The annual international reports of competitive rankings revealed a steady deterioration of Egypt's position. I truthfully presented these reports to all the Egyptian state agencies—the president, the prime minister, and other concerned ministers—but it was clear that no one was interested. Lack of enthusiasm was common in spite of great improvement in specific fields, which had a positive effect on the national economy.

Due to his age and the obsession with the security procedures needed for his protection at all times, as well as the wish of those surrounding him to protect him by keeping him isolated, the president was absent from many summits, not only at the UN or the African Union (AU) but also at the Asian–African Summit, known as "50 years after Bandung," in April 2005; the Non-Aligned Movement Summit in Havana in 2006; and the Arab–Latin American Summit in Brazil in 2005.

A few days after my return to Cairo to take up my duties as foreign minister, a conference of the foreign ministers of the neighboring countries of Iraq was held. This was the conference President Mubarak had asked me about in our first phone call after I was sworn in. It achieved its objectives with the cooperation of all participants, the foreign ministers of Iraq, Turkey, Iran, Jordan, Kuwait, Saudi Arabia, and Syria, as well as Egypt in its pre-eminent Arab and regional role. I began to build bridges of communication with the foreign ministers of Turkey and Iran since I was convinced of the importance of maintaining positive communication with these two parties because of their regional importance, even though the president took a cautious view of Turkey and its Ottoman tendencies, as well as Iran, whose interests tended to be contrary to ours. I met with the U.S. secretary of state Colin Powell on the margins of the meeting, and we both stressed the importance of continuing our cooperation and attempting to settle the regional issues, notably the Palestinian issue, which was not on the agenda of the Bush administration then. In our meetings, I felt that there was no problem with the bilateral relations, and that things were the same as they had been for decades. Time proved that I was wrong and that the United States had critical problems with the regime in Egypt. I will be dealing with the relations between the two countries in the following chapters.

In my conversations with Colin Powell, I discussed the importance of the United States making a serious effort to deal with the stalled peace process. The United States could not be active in the region after Iraq's invasion and its threats to Syria, and could not expect its policies in the region to succeed in the absence of real solutions to the Palestinian–Israeli confrontation and Arafat's siege in Ramallah.

As for Iraq, Powell said that he knew that many of the comments I had made as the Egyptian ambassador to the UN were against the American military operations, yet he asked me to understand the situation and help them to get Iraq out of its difficult condition.

In New York, months before the invasion, when the American intentions toward Iraq were being discussed, I was certain that the United States would defeat the Iraqis and occupy Baghdad and the whole country in a matter of six weeks, after which it would enjoy a period of respite, even of welcome, of six months. After that period, however, I predicted that there would be six years of resistance to the U.S. occupation of Iraq after which U.S.–Iraqi relations would suffer for six decades, and that the entire experience would be remembered in the Arab world for generations. I kept warning of the dangers of direct American military intervention in Iraq, an act that would appear to be directly serving Israel's interests. Powell referred to this attitude of mine at a seminar held at the Carnegie Institute in New York, saying that the invasion of Iraq was like swallowing a razor blade that the United States would suffer greatly from. I commented that it was not my statement, but that of Prince Zeid bin Ra'ad, the Jordanian delegate, although I agreed with him.

I also worked on restoring my vital relationship with the Saudi foreign minister, Prince Sa'ud al-Faisal, and the Syrian foreign minister, Farouk al-Sharaa, who both knew me since I had worked with Esmat Abdel Meguid and Amr Moussa during the Second Gulf War and in the preparation for establishing the group of countries of the Damascus Declaration. I strengthened my communications with the Jordanian foreign minister,

Marwan Muasher, and the Kuwaiti foreign minister, Sheikh Dr. Mohamed al-Sabah, both of whom had worked as their countries' ambassadors in Washington, D.C., when we frequently met in connection with political seminars and other occasions in New York. Finally, I maintained a positive relationship with the Iraqi foreign minister, Hoshyar Zebari.

In our regular phone conversations, the president seemed satisfied with the meeting and its outcomes. It came to my knowledge from my contacts and from the chief of the General Intelligence Service (GIS), Omar Suleiman, that the president followed my work closely, even though he was recovering from surgery. When he was back at work, I cautiously revived our relations and gave him the opportunity to get to know the way his foreign minister worked. Just as he learned my opinions on the phone, he also learned about my personal situation, my behavior at work, and my views on foreign policy and life in general. He seemed satisfied, but still we were reserved in our relations for years. They became less reserved only after the shocking incident in which he lost his grandson and the major surgery he had in 2010.

I naturally attended with the president the meetings held with the leaders of other countries, their senior officials, and their foreign ministers, whether in Cairo or abroad. His comments often showed that he had knowledge of every detail of my life. He said admiringly, "Ahmed walks into his office at seven in the morning even though he lives in Toukh in the Nile Delta, forty kilometers away." He added that he knew that his foreign minister read all the information received at the Ministry of Foreign Affairs daily, knew all the Egyptian ambassadors abroad, and so on.

The president was cautiously reserved in his relations with his subordinates. I received a phone call from his chief of secretariat only one hour after my return from the swearing-in, urgently asking to see me. I received him in my office and was anxious to hear what he had to say. With a little embarrassment, he explained that my wife and I were probably unaware of the practices of the president and his spouse. He advised that we should keep our distance and be "formal," especially with his spouse. I quietly told him that my wife had no interest in authority or formal communication. She preferred to keep a low profile and look after her own affairs and her farmland. So the president and his spouse were the ones to take the initiative.

During the first few months of my job, I worked on rapidly building relationships with the principal parties on the international scene. I had several meetings in Cairo and New York while attending the session of the UN General Assembly in September 2004 with a large number of state officials and foreign ministers of the major powers, such as Russia, China, Britain, France, and Germany. Unfortunately, I failed to convince the president to participate in another important summit in New York. His reasons were that he had to attend the ruling National Democratic Party's conference, and also that he needed to rest. The big international ministerial meeting held in Sharm al-Sheikh in November 2004 to help Iraq was a good opportunity to meet with representatives from countries such as Japan, Indonesia, Malaysia, Pakistan, India, and a number of European countries.

I observed at once that major changes had occurred in the conduct of Egyptian foreign policy since I had left in 1999. General Omar Suleiman personally had considerable influence on all the state agencies that had any connection with the foreign policy process, and there were many of these. The General Intelligence, its officers, and its departments were convinced that they had the right to inquire or comment on many issues that they might not be fully acquainted with. This could have adversely affected relations between the Foreign Ministry and the General Intelligence Service. I often turned to General Omar Suleiman, pointing out some difficulties we faced, and he would decisively deal with the problems. Because of his intervention, these two major agencies—the Foreign Ministry and the intelligence service—were able to work constructively together to bring others, such as Defense or Interior, around to support their views regarding particular issues that required security approval. Here, I have to admit that these difficulties were numerous. The Egyptian foreign policy organizations frequently disputed with each other, causing Egypt to lose opportunities that could have been used productively in favor of Egyptian interests and foreign policy. As a case in point, Egypt was absent from deliberations about counter-piracy efforts in Somalia due to the resistance of one department or another. Iran's attempts to dominate the Gulf and the policies of the Gulf Arab countries would have been a good opportunity for Egypt to offer support and promote its own interests, but excessive caution and internal conflicts hindered this. Egypt failed to formulate a coherent policy toward the threats in the Red Sea or to increase cooperation with the coastal countries, despite all the efforts made in these matters.

During my first weeks in office, I noticed that the president's secretary of information had come to be in full control of communications with the foreign ambassadors and other foreign officials in Cairo. The president did not mind sending information and messages directly to his office. I knew that this situation was undesirable, since the secretary of information was not sufficiently well informed to provide the president with the complete picture. Some of the communications were done without acknowledging the Foreign Ministry or its officials at all.

The president often received calls from senior officials and heads of state without discussing them with me or asking the secretary of information to brief me. I found out about them later, either in conversations with him days later—if we happened to talk about them—or through our ambassadors' communications with the decision-making circles in one country or another. I believed then, and I still do, that the management of Egyptian foreign relations during the years of Presidents Nasser, Sadat, and Mubarak gave the president the sole authority for making and directing foreign policy. The foreign minister and the other related departments were merely his tools in this realm. Thus I rejected, and still do, the claims of some Egyptian foreign ministers that "their" foreign policies were aiming at this matter or that, or this foreign policy that "they" established achieved so and so. These claims do not reflect the truth of the Egyptian presidential regime. My assertion is that all the foreign ministers implemented and managed foreign policy as instructed by the presidents, using different methods and ideas that varied from one minister to another according to his convictions, the challenges he faced, his competencies, and his experience. Since I had worked with the Egyptian national security advisor in 1972, I believed that the best management of foreign policy requires, in addition to an efficient foreign minister who enjoys the president's trust, a national security council with a national security advisor who works with all parties who contribute to the formulation of foreign policy. The absence of this concept during President Mubarak's rule and his dependence on the secretary of information represented a weakness in the Egyptian foreign policy-making process. The role of Omar Suleiman should be mentioned here, since part of his job made him appear to be acting as the national security advisor. However, if the president's secretary of information were given a larger staff from the various government agencies, he could have fulfilled this role and ensured that the president was well-informed and fully briefed on the recommendations of the various government departments, thus enabling him to compare the available options and policies and make better choices. He would, in effect, be serving as the national security advisor. The president chose not to adopt this concept. Instead, he could have depended on a secretary of information with a large number of assistants and deputies—a choice he refused—or else distributed the functions of the post among several persons, such as press secretary, speechwriter, and others, who would coordinate with the secretary of information. Having said this, I should mention that I maintained a good relationship with Ambassador Suleiman Awad, the president's principal policy advisor and spokesperson and his secretary of information, a prudent, efficient diplomat who was put under unbearable pressure.

On the other hand, I agree with the criticism that Egypt focused on a limited number of foreign political issues and gave them priority—first and foremost the Palestinian cause and the Arab–Israeli dispute, then the Arab and African issues. I insisted on updating the president on a daily basis about many other international issues, such as climate change; environment; energy; oil, gas, and transportation lines; the financial and economic policies of other countries and of major international and regional groupings; and technological developments in different fields. I was certain the Ministry of Foreign Affairs was capable of providing sound opinions in all these fields. Occasionally the secretary of information informed me that the president asked for the data received from the Ministry of Foreign Affairs to be sent to other state entities for followup. Once, when I was on my way back from New York after the UN General Assembly in September 2004, I read a collection of important articles published in the Fall 2004 issue of *Foreign Affairs* that discussed the dangers of the avian flu. I sent a short memo on the subject to the president and the head of the cabinet, and as a result, the state launched a number of measures to contain the risk.

I perceived that Egypt faced serious challenges at the regional as well as the international level, especially when confronting western powers. In the fall of 2004, Yasser Arafat was under siege in Ramallah; the situation in Somalia and Sudan was deteriorating; the U.S. presence in Iraq was causing tension in both Syria and Iran; and the situation in Afghanistan was deteriorating as well. Egypt was always concerned with these countries. I felt from the start that our reaction had long been extremely cautious, and some of the proposals and initiatives offered by the Ministry of Foreign Affairs to maintain a regional presence for Egypt were stifled due to the differences among the various departments. I firmly believed we needed a national security advisor who could analyze a situation, formulate it, and present it to the president in the form of graded options.

My work at the UN from 1999 to 2004 gave me the ability to evaluate international and regional problems. When I returned to Egypt, I recognized the importance of being acquainted with all of our region's situations, problems, and conditions. After a total of almost fourteen years in the United States, my previous expertise was mainly in the UN and/or the United States and its foreign policy, as well as European policies and Russia's foreign relations. I therefore asked for numerous memos and briefings on the sensitive subjects I would now need to deal with, such as Sudan and the Nile River issues, partnerships with the European Union, the Barcelona Process, and relations with the NATO.

My interests as the new foreign minister were not limited to promoting my ideas for revitalizing Egyptian interests in various places, or getting acquainted with the issues unfamiliar to me, but extended to introducing new working methods and improving performance and efficiency, believing, like Amr Moussa and Ahmed Maher, that a minister should maintain a firm grip on the bureaucratic management of his ministry. This is probably why I arrived at the office before all the staff every morning and made it a point to visit the different departments within the Foreign Ministry and to walk through the different floors of the large building that houses it. I always made sure that the building was clean and that staff members were hard at work and that the different support services were efficient and available. I also read all the incoming cables and faxes, not just their summaries, for I depended on this raw material to reach my conclusions without being influenced by other people's opinions. This approach differed from that of some other foreign ministers, who preferred to exercise general supervision, give specific instructions, and let their staff do the rest. My method of management did not restrict the freedom or authority of others. On the contrary, I allowed my subordinates to act, but I had to be fully informed of all details.

Just a few hours after I took up my duties, I asked the Code and Communications Department within the Foreign Ministry to implement a new process by which all our missions could correspond with headquarters and inform any other mission abroad of the situation in the country it was covering. I have to admit here that when I paid visits to foreign diplomats at their mission headquarters in the different places where I served, I was always amazed by their full knowledge of events that had taken place only a few hours ago, and they showed me dozens of filed cables concerning developments in the different countries we were discussing. The technologically advanced countries obviously used more up-to-date tools than we did, for while any European ambassador could directly inform more than one hundred of his country's missions of an important incident via cable, the Egyptian missions had to send the information to Cairo headquarters, which might or might not resend it to other missions that were relevant to the issue. This was really disruptive. The communication experts explained that the process I wished to implement would far exceed our budget. Still, I was persistent in finding a solution. As so often happens in such cases, a young Egyptian engineer in the Code Department came up with some suggestions that were quietly applied after a careful study. In a few weeks, we managed to set up a process that would do what was needed at the lowest cost. Thus our embassies and missions were able to have at least occasional correspondence among themselves, which was very useful and led to major improvement in our work. The clever computer engineer got a bonus of not more than ten thousand pounds and some missions abroad, and we still saved millions.

It was necessary to boost the morale of the ministry staff—both administrators and diplomats—so I held a series of meetings with them. I stressed my refusal of favoritism or recommendations by senior officials concerning the transfer of personnel abroad, and my full commitment to the rules of the ministry, which would be applied with no exceptions. Some of the special advantages the personnel enjoyed were left intact. One of these was the sensitive matter of sending certain employees on a brief mission abroad as a social and economic contribution from the ministry when they were facing particular difficulties in life. This practice had been in use since 1980. Although I felt that it was unfair, there were hundreds of workers who benefited from it. Thus I decided not to alter it, in order to avoid unnecessary tension in the way work was conducted at the ministry, in spite of a lot of criticism and personal attacks in the media. The practice was still in effect when I left office in March 2011, and none of my successors changed it, despite the gossip about corruption and favoritism passed along to the media by those who did not benefit from the policy. We also began to quietly raise the salaries of the ministry workers, which made the employees feel more secure. In return, they regarded the Ministry of Foreign Affairs as their safe haven, and defended it against all confrontations and challenges.

I was eager to give priority to technology and the development of communication. Internet services at the ministry had deteriorated for unknown reasons between 2001 and 2004. In a few months, we succeeded in improving the system and made it accessible to a larger number of workers.

Having taken care of the humanitarian side, and improved the technological, technical, and communications performance, we began to pay more attention to the training of our diplomats and administrators. We decided not to allow anyone to travel abroad unless he had successfully completed a training period that included all the responsibilities he would deal with.

We were instructed to focus on attracting investment, promoting Egyptian trade in the outside world, encouraging tourism, and doing our best to assist the Egyptian economy. We also had to look after our citizens' interests abroad, a task which, I believe, was difficult due to the conditions in some the countries they were living in. However, it was necessary in order to preserve their pride and make them feel appreciated by their homeland. During my years of service, I frequently had officers and workers abroad transferred if it was proven that they had mistreated our citizens.

There was the problem of fishing vessels entering the territorial waters of neighboring countries. We always tried to handle this matter in a way that would not negatively affect our relations with our neighbors. Incidents happened to our citizens in Arab countries with which we were trying to improve relations, and the media then attacked these countries and the ministry. In these situations, our attempts to achieve the often-contradictory objectives of preserving relations with these countries, calming the media maelstrom, and protecting our citizens was like walking a tightrope.

I was concerned with controlling costs and not wasting state resources, using them constructively and according to rational, agreed-upon priorities. In this way, we were able to supply the missions and the headquarters with new, advanced equipment. Missions abroad, and participation in conferences and delegations, were rationalized to save money while maintaining effectiveness and achieving the objective of training the diplomats, especially low-ranking ones. Many people had their own ideas about this rationalization, especially when the missions in certain countries were being considered for reduction or termination. Bureaucracy strived to survive. Everyone was maneuvering to maintain these missions in order to save the jobs.

The studies that we undertook revealed that if we shut down missions in more peripheral countries, they would, in turn, close their missions in Cairo, which would affect the city's image as a capital of major international attraction and influence. In order to bring down expenditures in these cases, we instead reduced the number of workers in several missions; thus we could rationalize the expenditure without weakening the Egyptian diplomatic presence globally. We also downgraded a large number of 'general consulates' to 'consulates' only, which reduced the level of support required from the Egyptian government. Diplomatic representation was reduced in cities such as Aden, Rio de Janeiro, London, Paris, Kaduna, Lagos, and Zanzibar.

Egyptian society should certainly be well informed of the true status of our embassies, the number of their staff, and their budgets, so that no one, especially those with authority or influence in society, can reach a false conclusion that could have a harmful impact on conditions for Egyptians in foreign countries.

We have about 135 missions abroad. The budget of the Ministry of Foreign Affairs is around $200 million, while the Egyptian consulates provide revenues of up to $70 million per year; thus the net cost of the ministry in the state budget is around $130 million. There are around 480 diplomats and 300 administrators in the missions abroad. The remaining 500 diplomats, or slightly fewer, work at the headquarters in Cairo.

Some ministry officials have suggested modifying the organization of the ministry, which was established by Amr Moussa during his first days as foreign minister. It is based on the concept of 'desk,' meaning the person responsible for all aspects of a particular country or topic. I resisted the modification proposal and stressed that it was important to continue using the existing system, which gave the ministry officials more control over the issues presented, and the young staff opportunities to hold midlevel positions that would provide them with experience, thus making it easier for the ministry to select the best-qualified ones for promotion.

I noticed that after the 1967 defeat the ministry stopped dispatching periodic inspection missions to check the efficiency of operations and the performance of individuals in missions. I decided to revive these missions. An incoming ambassador received a letter from the foreign minister stating the priorities of the mission and the specific tasks he was expected to perform. Any inspection that took place during his tenure would focus on these clearly stated goals. The ministry also asked every ambassador returning home at the end of his term to write a full report on his mission, describing his performance, the obstacles he met, how he overcame them, and his recommendations for his successor. For years, we had been doing our best to amend the laws pertaining to the diplomatic and consular corps to attract the best-qualified Egyptian youth, and provide them with a competitive opportunity based on their potential and professionalism. We also established an exam for mid-career promotion, as is the case in other well-run foreign ministries, an achievement whose worth will be seen in the future.

Egyptian diplomats and officials often encountered difficulties in obtaining diplomatic visas to enter European countries, the United States, and Canada. In such cases, it was normal to reciprocally refuse entry to diplomats from these countries at our airports. Some Egyptian citizens also asked to have ordinary citizens of these other countries refused entry, too. They did not understand the risk of applying this method when we were trying to promote tourism. I did not suggest any ideas to the Cabinet regarding this matter. My only request was that we insist that tourist visas should be issued only by our embassies and missions abroad, not upon arrival at the airport; the visa fee at the airport was almost half the fee charged by the Egyptian missions. By insisting on advance visas, the Egyptian treasury would double its visa income. The minister of tourism rejected the idea, and the tourist companies claimed that this extra amount would discourage tourism. In my opinion this was funny and pathetic at the same time. Nobody took my side in the Cabinet, and the status quo was maintained until I left office.

The European and western countries eventually began to apply biometric security measures to all citizens of Arab countries who wished to travel to these countries, including the officials traveling on government business; the only exceptions were the president of the country and his foreign minister. We informed the countries in question that we would, in turn, apply the same rules, and so we bought the equipment and established a strict system.

The ministry provides its employers with many benefits, which enable them and their families to maintain a decent standard of living in missions abroad or at the headquarters at home. Yet there are always discrepancies among different countries in the standards of living, the degree of comfort or difficulty the employer faces at work, and the sustenance of his family. Consequently, it is always necessary to be impartial in staff transfers, benefits, salaries, and all other staff affairs. I was always concerned with providing the employees dispatched to areas where living conditions are difficult with services and benefits that would encourage them to accept the situation and not regard it as a punishment. This helped to maintain the morale of the ministry staff and motivated them to act in the best interests of their homeland.

# 4
# CHALLENGES AND RESPONSES: THE UNITED STATES

S erving in the Egyptian mission to the UN in New York and living in the United States intermittently for over thirteen years, from July 1974 to July 2004, made me fully acquainted with American politics, especially since I had decided not to confine myself to UN affairs but to try to understand the history of the American political system and its foreign policy since its independence two centuries ago. I focused mainly on foreign policy and international affairs since the end of the Second World War and through the period of the Cold War, and the related global conflicts. No Egyptian or Arab diplomat could afford to ignore U.S. relations with the Middle East region and the Arab–Israeli conflict. Thus, when I was about to become foreign minister in 2004, I felt well versed in the complexities of Egyptian–U.S. relations and well prepared to manage this multifaceted relationship—its serious as well as its less pressing components.

Although I had worked with the Egyptian national security advisor before and during the October 6, 1973 war, I had no direct contact with Egyptian–American relations. However, I began to be exposed to U.S. policy toward Egypt when I joined the office of Minister Mohamed Ibrahim Kamel, which was led by his office director, Ahmed Maher. My involvement in managing this file deepened when I worked with the deputy prime ministers and foreign ministers Kamal Hassan Ali and Esmat Abdel Meguid from 1982 to 1991. As the liaison officer in the office of the minister of foreign affairs, I had close connections with the U.S. embassy in Cairo, with the ambassador—or, rather, the political counselor—in particular, and with the Egyptian Embassy in Washington, D.C. I was attuned to the developments of the relationship and became aware of its subtleties and many complex details, which evolved over years. The chief Egyptian official responsible for the management of the relationship, after the foreign minister, was Osama El-Baz, who had worked as advisor to the president and director of presidential political affairs for decades.

Since the signing of the Camp David Accords, Egypt and the United States have had a stable relationship of cooperation and balance of interests, though it might have been shaken a little during the crisis of the *Achille Lauro* cruise ship in 1985, when the relations between the Egyptian president and the American president, Ronald Reagan, were complicated. The relationship intensified during the tenures of Presidents George H.W. Bush and Bill Clinton, covering twelve years of understanding and joint work from January 1989 to January 2001. Egypt tended to support the election of George W. Bush in the 2000 election, and everyone was happy about his success. Then came the shock of the attack on the World Trade Center in New York on September 11, 2001, followed by the so-called War on Terror in which the United States confronted what it considered to be terrorist groups coming from the Middle East. As a result, the United States plunged into war. It invaded Afghanistan and Iraq, and escalated pressure on Pakistan, Iran, Syria, Sudan, and even its closest Arab friend in the Middle East, Egypt. President Mubarak could hardly believe that a group of young Arabs could attack the World Trade Center on their own, insisting that it would be difficult to attack buildings with planes operated by individuals with little experience in aviation. The president implicitly expressed his belief in a conspiracy that would create a disaster in order to give the United States an excuse to interfere in the affairs of the Arab and Islamic states.

As I took up my duties on the afternoon of July 14, 2004, I received a message from the U.S. embassy in Cairo that Colin Powell, the U.S. secretary of state, wished to call to congratulate me. I asked them to find out whether he intended to discuss other matters, and they replied that he would mention his wish to visit Cairo. He called at 8:30 that same evening warmly saying, "Congratulations, Mr. Minister. I know it's a difficult task but I'm certain that your extensive service will help you succeed in your mission." He hoped to secure a permanent Egyptian–American understanding and joint cooperation. He also acknowledged that even though it was not necessary for the United States and Egypt to always agree about our bilateral relations or the situation in the Middle East, our thirty-year friendship would certainly help to ensure that both countries would reach an understanding on issues of mutual concern, which would be in both countries' interests. He asked if he could call me by my first name, Ahmed, in the future as a sign of friendship between the two countries. I told him that would be fine, but I insisted that I would always call him "General" as a sign of respect.

I had previously met with General Powell twice, in 2001 and 2002, when Ahmed Maher met him at the UN in the course of their work at the General Assembly. I then met him for a moment on the day he arrived, accompanied by a large number of officials from the new U.S. administration, to address the Security Council and unjustly accuse Iraq of possessing weapons of mass destruction. Before giving his famous statement, he gave me a message for the Egyptian president and foreign minister, in which he expressed the U.S. expectation of Egypt's support for its vision. I promised to pass it on.

Once I became foreign minister, Colin Powell and I agreed that he would come to Cairo within just a few days, in connection with the meetings being held by the countries neighboring Iraq. Powell had already been the secretary of state for three and a half years when we met in Cairo, and President Bush's intention to name a new secretary had not been announced yet. This change took place as Bush started his second term in January 2005.

Powell's visit turned out to be both revealing and deceptive. He focused intensively on the regional situation. He discussed what the United States was doing in Afghanistan and Iraq and its objectives there. He severely criticized Syria, accusing Damascus of complicating the U.S. situation in Iraq by allowing Arab and Islamist elements fighting in Iraq to cross the

Syrian–Iraqi border, and hosting elements of the Iraqi Ba'th Party in Syria. He put particular emphasis on Syria, and said that he expected Egypt to assist the United States in every way possible during this sensitive period, when the U.S. army was appearing, for the first time in its history, as a direct participant and element in the Middle East equation.

As soon as they invaded Afghanistan, the Americans asked all friendly parties to join the alliance of the forces fighting with them in this Islamic country. They clearly did not understand the situation of Egypt and the sensitivity surrounding sending Egyptian troops to fight in an Islamic land, especially in aid of western or NATO forces. Although Egypt resisted the U.S. demands for military support, in order to help the Afghan people it decided to send a big field hospital to be set up at the NATO air base in Bagram. With the invasion of Iraq, the United States asked Egypt again to send troops, or at least to work toward maintaining stability in this Arab country. Egypt refused to make any military contributions. Thus, when Powell came, he focused on explaining the U.S. point of view and attempted to draw Egypt into the U.S. activity in West Asia and Iraq. We quietly resisted, made no commitments, and explained our views. Over the next few months the Americans came to Egypt asking to have the Afghan military personnel and policemen trained in Egypt and to supply them with light weapons. The Afghans were to send symbolic forces, like many other parties, to participate in the Bright Star maneuvers in 2004. We did not mind doing this, since Egypt would not be asked to send trainers or troops to Afghanistan. In the end, none of these ideas were implemented, and eventually it became clear that the Americans were only trying to entangle Egypt in the net of these relations. When it became obvious that Egypt would not play the requested role, the Americans lifted their pressure for a while, as will be shown later.

As for Syria, Powell mentioned in our conversation, as he did in his public statements, that the United States had an aversion to Syria and was seeking to subdue it. We explained that we doubted that Syria meant to stir up trouble for them on the Iraqi border. Still, we would inform the Syrians of the U.S. views. The Americans asked us to advise Syria to stop playing a negative role in the situation. President Mubarak passed on the

U.S. viewpoint to President Assad without making any recommendations as to Syrian actions. Subsequent developments revealed that not only had Washington directly focused on changing Syria's Middle East policies, but that it had also sought to contain Syria to the point of regime change.

Powell was satisfied with the U.S.–Egyptian relationship and hoped that we would take positive steps toward internal reform as soon as possible. I pointed out that we were aware of the importance of this. Powell ended his visit and left. We met again in New York during the High-Level Segment of the UN General Assembly in September 2004. The following year Powell left office. We had a distinct relationship in spite of its shortness. He was a professional military officer who was well aware of Egypt's capabilities and its role in the Middle East and the Islamic world, and his post as chairman of the Joint Chiefs of Staff and his previous work with President Reagan and President George Bush Senior made him familiar with the extent of Egyptian–U.S. cooperation and the need to maintain that cooperation and to preserve the relationship. I also believe that he recognized some of my personal traits and my interest in military affairs and history, making it easier for us to have a constructive dialogue that was useful for our bilateral relations.

Condoleezza Rice succeeded Powell on January 20, 2005. I called her on the following day and decided that I would visit her in Washington, D.C. Thus, on February 12, 2005, I became the first Arab foreign minister to visit her. Hopes were raised for a healthy, active relationship, based on the communications and visits of all the Egyptian foreign ministers to Washington since 1977, including Mohamed Ibrahim Kamel, Kamal Hassan Ali, Esmat Abdel Meguid and Amr Moussa, in which I had participated. The various departments of the ministry were directed to prepare for the visit. I regarded this trip as very important, both because it would be my first as foreign minister and because I would be meeting with a U.S. secretary of state whom I did not expect to be as well informed about Middle East affairs as her predecessor.

While I was attending the ministerial meetings of the African Union (AU) held in Abuja in Nigeria, and expecting the arrival of President Mubarak, whom I had convinced with great effort of the importance of taking part again in African activities and summits, I was shocked by the harsh U.S. criticism of the arrest of Ayman Nour, a member of the Egyptian Parliament on the previous day, January 28, 2005. I was not acquainted with the situation or its background. I assumed that it would affect my upcoming visit to Washington, D.C., on which Omar Suleiman and I were counting to convince the administration to pay attention again to the Middle East, the Palestinian cause, and the settlement with Israel after a four-year period of inattention and inaction.

The president arrived in Abuja on January 29, accompanied by General Omar Suleiman and a large delegation. I did not mention the matter of Ayman Nour to him because I preferred to focus on the African affairs that were being discussed at the AU summit, which the president had not attended for a long time. I did, however, inquire about the circumstances of Ayman Nour's arrest from the intelligence chief and the chief of presidential staff. When I returned to Cairo, I turned my attention to the matter and talked with the president and General Omar Suleiman, with whom I was supposed to travel to Washington, D.C., to discuss our project for the revitalization of the Palestinian–Israeli settlement, and to calm the Americans' feelings toward Syria. I updated the president orally on the U.S. situation and how upset the Americans were as a result of Nour's arrest. In view of my imminent trip to the United States, I asked the president to consider releasing him pending investigation. He listened quietly. I repeated the request on the following day and throughout the first week of February, and stressed the importance of Nour's release for the success of my visit to Washington.

Finally, the president clearly indicated in our phone call that he did not exclude the release of Nour within a few days, and certainly before the visit to Washington. General Omar Suleiman called and apologized for dropping out of the trip for work reasons. Then the U.S. ambassador in Cairo came to see me three days before I left, to warn me that there was some tension in the United States over the issue and that people there were keeping a close eye on it. I informed the president of the situation, but did not ask to postpone the visit, since he had said that Nour would be released a few days before I left.

I traveled to Munich to participate in a conference on European security and its connection with the Middle East, which was attended by many American and international figures. There I found myself ambushed. Nour's arrest was the reason. All the U.S. officials brought the matter up. Senator John McCain, who was attending with a large number of senators and congressmen, harshly attacked the Egyptian president, accusing him of planning to have his son succeed him and publicly calling him a dictator while we were on the podium together. It was upsetting. I replied quietly, explaining the Egyptian situation in a few words, then focused on the Egyptian vision for achieving peace in the Middle East and the various threats to the region. After the conference I met Senator McCain again, who acted as if he had not criticized the president in public, and we had a normal conversation in which we talked about his experience as a prisoner of war in Vietnam and his relations with his father and grandfather, who had been senior officers in the U.S. Navy. Since I did not have all the facts regarding Ayman Nour's situation, I avoided discussing the case. Unfortunately, I was inclined to believe that he was arrested in order to remove a qualified rival to the president's son in case the latter ran for president. However, I did play a major part in Nour's release later, as will be mentioned.

Upon my arrival in Washington D.C., I met again with Senator McCain, whose tone was completely different from the one he had used in our private bilateral meeting in Munich. He resumed his attacks on the president and his policies. Ayman Nour had not been released yet, contrary to the impression I had received from the president. Perhaps McCain's public attacks at the seminar in Munich made President Mubarak rethink his decision after all.

During the following years Mubarak sharply criticized Senator McCain and his attitudes toward the Middle East in his private talks and his meetings with Egyptian and foreign dignitaries. He might even have deliberately tried to complicate some situations during McCain's presidential campaign to make it easier for his Democratic rival, Barack Obama.

I held several meetings at the Senate and the House of Representatives and respective committees on foreign relations. The actions taken against Ayman Nour were strongly criticized, as was the attitude of the

Egyptian government toward the International Republican Institute, the National Democratic Institute, and Freedom House. The latter had been denied a license to work in Egypt and its internal movements had been restricted. They also hinted that they were considering the reduction of the annual economic aid to Egypt. Members of Congress had different views; some suggested the reduction of the aid or its elimination, while others, including the Zionist Congressman Tom Lantos of the Foreign Relations Committee, were willing to propose transferring the amount of $400 million from military aid to economic aid in order to help Egypt address its economic and development problems. It was apparent that the U.S. administration was behind these attacks and threats, which, I must admit, I found appalling. It was a premeditated U.S. decision and a strategic attitude toward Mubarak and his regime, that started at the beginning of President Bush's second term. I felt it was an inquisition. During my meeting with the Appropriations Committee, the committee's chair said that they would be meeting with the U.S. secretary of state as soon as that meeting ended, and would be discussing with her the reduction of the economic as well as the military aid. I had had a meeting with her before they did and already knew how critical the situation was.

The purpose of my mission to Washington was to promote positive relations between Egypt and the United States. My specific assignment was to strive to preserve the U.S. military aid for the Egyptian Armed Forces, without which, I believe, Egypt's vital defensive abilities would be greatly affected. I also had to convince the Congress to approve a commitment made by the U.S. Department of Defense to the Egyptian Ministry of Defense to increase military aid by over $100 million for the deployment of Egyptian forces and units on the Israeli border in order to prevent smuggling and military operations against Israel launched from Egyptian territory.

I was deeply concerned as a result of these discussions and the aggressiveness displayed by the congressmen. I considered it the worst situation to face any Egyptian foreign minister since the end of the October 1973 War regarding relations with the Americans and the change of Egypt's foreign-policy orientation from the Soviet Union to the United States.

Having been in office barely six months, I did not want it to be said that I had gone to Washington and ruined the relationship, reduced U.S. aid to Egypt and complicated the situation for Egypt, and returned!

The congressmen began talking about their wish to have Egypt contribute troops in Iraq and Afghanistan. After all, the United States was facing significant challenges in these two Islamic states, and it expected its friends to lend a hand, which in turn would be rewarded by the United States! The deal they were offering sounded like "You should send troops and decide to stand by our side in the war; then we will consider reaching an agreement on issues that we are concerned about: democracy, human rights, Egyptian civil society, and the right of our nongovernmental organizations to work in your country." In the beginning these demands had been subtle and implicit and the deal had been quietly proposed before Ayman Nour's arrest, but after Nour's arrest the tone became sharper and clearer.

From my first day in office in July 2004, I was aware that with regard to our relations with the Bush administration, which were damaged by the September 11 attacks, we were dealing with a sensitive equation that had to be calculated accurately. In spite of Egypt's attempts over the years to separate the issue of Egyptian–Israeli relations from Egyptian–U.S. relations, which had to stand on their own apart from Israel, the United States had laid emphasis on the three-sided relations of the Camp David Accords for its own benefits and interests with respect to Egypt, Israel, and the region as a whole. Israel, and the pro-Israel lobby in the United States, and the Congress promoted this attitude so that they could prevail over Egypt and its foreign policies, especially when confronting Israel at the UN and addressing the issues of nuclear non-proliferation and weapons of mass destruction. Egypt has a specific strategic attitude toward all of these issues, with the sole objective of defending Egyptian national security.

The second part of the equation consisted of the U.S. perspective on Egypt's domestic record on democracy and human rights, and ways to use it as a tool to pressure Egypt. The fact that these matters were used as political instruments of pressure against Egypt is apparent when comparing U.S. attitudes on these issues with other Arab countries that are completely under U.S. control. There is no need to name such countries here.

The third and last part of the sensitive equation was the regional effect of U.S. activities. Egypt insisted on maintaining its own viewpoint in order to preserve its identity.

From the start, it was important to deal with all three parts of the equation, and even to add a fourth one by enlarging the range of Egypt's global relations to include other competitors to the United States, mainly Russia and China. Such competitors were few, but they were influential both regionally and globally, and thus, deepening relations with these countries could be useful in managing relations with the United States.

We went along with the U.S. proposal to launch the Qualifying Industrial Zone (QIZ) to build Egyptian export capacity with economic input from Israel, thus promoting bilateral cooperation between the two countries in the eyes of the United States. We also agreed to manage the Egyptian border in Sinai according to American wishes by increasing the available Egyptian facilities via an Egyptian–Israeli protocol. Otherwise, Egypt refused all the other Israeli and U.S. demands. The Ministry of Foreign Affairs continued to strongly support Egypt's attitude, known for years, toward all other regional and international political issues, such as: nuclear nonproliferation, demanding that Israel sign the Treaty on the Non-Proliferation of Nuclear Weapons, declaring the Middle East a nuclear-weapon-free zone, and the various concerns of the UN and its specialized agencies. Egypt became one of the UN members who clashed most often with the United States on resolutions. Both the U.S. and the Israeli sides raised several complaints with other Egyptian agencies working in foreign policy, including the president's office. These agencies did not even bother informing us of the Israeli attitude, for they knew that the entire Egyptian government shared the same views.

I discussed with the president the importance of moving a little toward the western powers and assuring them that we understood their intentions in the Mediterranean Sea and the Middle East in a way that would emphasize our influence. I had in mind a rapprochement with the North Atlantic Treaty Organization (NATO), since Egypt is considered the major Arab country overlooking the strategic routes in which NATO is interested. NATO considered us a "non-member ally" and wished to increase its communications with us, although we were acting so slowly that we may have given the impression of being apprehensive of the alliance. I explained to the president that we could not trust NATO's intentions, which was trying to become the military arm of the UN, or the new concepts being applied in international politics, such as the Responsibility to Protect, the right to intervene, and the right to prevent Iran from developing nuclear capabilities. I also stated that it was up to us to decide whether to get closer or not, but it was important for the United States and the other western powers to know that the openness of the Arab powers in the Mediterranean Sea and North Africa was in our hands. The president agreed to greater openness, an approach that had already been initiated by Amr Moussa in 1992 and had gradually been promoted until May 15, 2001 when he left office. I therefore announced my participation in a meeting of NATO foreign ministers to be held in Brussels on December 11, 2004, at the invitation of the NATO secretary general. Other Arab countries accepted this invitation only after Egypt did, because Israel was represented by a former minister of Russian Jewish origin, Natan Sharansky, who had been implicated in George W. Bush's interference in Egyptian human rights and democracy.

In Brussels, I met Colin Powell during the ministerial meeting. We had a straightforward conversation. I demanded that the alliance change its policy toward the region and said that we would cooperate with them if they would try to establish mutual confidence. I visited NATO headquarters again in March 2007. The secretary general received me and our meeting aroused the interest of the Mediterranean countries, the European members of NATO, and the United States. My third visit was in December 2007, when the NATO–Mediterranean Dialogue Ministerial Meeting was held. In the meantime, a high-level Egyptian parliamentary delegation had visited NATO headquarters in June 2006. We also encouraged the alliance officials to visit Egypt. The deputy secretary general and the chairman of the military committee visited Cairo during the first half of 2005, and the secretary general participated in a symposium on Mediterranean dialogue in October of the same year. The image of the alliance among the Arab nations began to improve gradually, and we signed some agreements that would ensure the training of the Egyptian officials working in different agencies in several areas of common interest.

At the regional level, the United States had its own concept of the greater Middle East, extending from Afghanistan and Pakistan in the east to Morocco and Mauritania in the west—in other words, the Islamic Middle East and its non-Arab periphery, but excluding all those who did not cooperate with the United States, notably Iran and Syria, while including its NATO ally Turkey.

Egypt was invited to participate in this initiative and the president approved, despite concerns that he and agencies that were part of the policy-making process harbored about this initiative. Our decision to participate was based on my own belief that Egypt should be present in any such forum to help guide the discussion. I participated in the first meeting in Rabat on December 12, 2004. The Egyptian contribution on governmental and nongovernmental organizations (NGO) was effective. Some people in Egypt were prepared to accept the increasingly common idea that the United States was willing to spend unlimited amounts of money on the development of Islamic societies. I was aware that, despite the vast U.S. capabilities, they were strictly limited to military commitments to the war in Afghanistan and Iraq, and that we were talking about no more than a few hundred million spread among all these Islamic states. The focus of the conference was on strengthening civil society and the NGOs, on which the United States wanted to rely in order to achieve actual development. This idea was regarded as acceptable as long as it was done within the laws of each individual country, or at least that's what we thought was the case. I met Colin Powell for the fourth time and he was very friendly and cooperative, far more than I had expected. Thus, when I visited the United States in February 2005, I was shocked by the strong language used by the U.S. officials in our talks.

I agreed with Powell to hold a large meeting in Cairo on the larger Middle East initiative and invite the members of the G8, as well as various international and regional parties, to support the U.S. vision. The U.S. was fully cooperative and Powell encouraged all the invited countries to participate in the conference, which was held in Cairo on March 3, 2005.

Egypt flatly refused to send any troops or personnel to take part in the armed confrontation in Iraq or Afghanistan. But because of the pressure of U.S. demands since 2002 and 2003, we expressed our readiness to train Iraqi or Afghan troops in Egypt instead of sending trainers into combat areas. I repeatedly explained our attitude to Congress and other U.S. officials I met. We were also willing to train Afghan judges in Egypt or to send Egyptian legal experts to Kabul. We had a diplomatic mission in Iraq that had not been recalled during the U.S. invasion in March 2003. The Americans asked us to strengthen the mission and convert it into a full embassy, but the extent of our interests in Iraq did not require this change, not to mention the danger to our diplomats and other personnel. One of our intelligence officers had been kidnapped in Baghdad a few days after I took office, and was fortunately set free. The head of our mission, the martyr Ihab al-Sherif, was not so fortunate; I will deal with his tragedy later.

This was how Egyptian–U.S. relations stood when I visited Washington, in February 2005. On the evening of February 15, I went to meet the new secretary of state, Condoleezza Rice, after two days of tough as well as tense and unpleasant discussions with members of Congress on February 14 and 15. The meeting lasted from 5:00 to 6:00 p.m., and dinner, a normal courtesy between foreign ministers, was not included. Its timing was also fixed so that I would face Congress and top administrators before meeting with the executive level represented by the secretary of state.

My meeting with Rice could not be described as cordial as the traditional meetings between Egyptian foreign ministers and their U.S. counterparts. According to the agenda agreed upon, Rice started discussing the Palestinian–Israeli situation and expressed her wish to maintain the momentum from the Sharm al-Sheikh summit between the Israeli prime minister, Abu Mazen, the president of the Palestinian National Authority, and the Egyptian president in February 2005 after the death of President Yasser Arafat. This momentum provided an opportunity to stop Israeli–Palestinian clashes and to give the Palestinians time to recover from the deteriorating conditions. Rice praised our performance in this matter and emphasized the importance of the Egyptian efforts for the Palestinians in facilitating the Israeli withdrawal operation from Gaza and the northern

West Bank, which the Israeli prime minister Ariel Sharon had already started to execute at the time, and in rehabilitating the Palestinian security establishment. She also stressed her country's interest in our joint work. I replied that we would work on empowering the Palestinians and supporting the new Palestinian president. I also referred to the importance of establishing a mechanism for consultation among the actors to quickly contain any crisis during the Israeli post-withdrawal period from Gaza, and the need to formulate a policy with a clear goal and a time frame for the Palestinian peace process. I highlighted the fact that the resolution of the Palestinian cause was the key to security and stability in the area, and to the elimination of terrorism and extremism in the Middle East; I emphasized that the U.S. role was decisive in this matter, and strongly backed her intention to activate it and to visit the region soon. She remarked that she agreed with me regarding the Palestinian path, but that she could not immediately initiate negotiations for a permanent settlement, since Sharon and Abu Mazen were still in a critical situation and had to focus on their current tasks. Starting negotiations at such an unpropitious time would only lead to failure. In the chapter dealing with the Palestinian settlement, I will discuss in detail the joint U.S.–Egyptian efforts to advance the peace process and the philosophy that lay behind our aim. It is important to mention these discussions here, however, because they were a constant feature and were often repeated in meetings between the foreign ministers of the two countries throughout the period from the end of hostilities in June 1967 until I left office on March 5, 2011 with regard to the disputes over the Palestinian settlement.

Following the agenda of the meeting, Rice and I discussed the Syrian issue. Egypt decided to help Syria overcome its problems with the United States, which was placing considerable pressure on Damascus in a variety of ways. I mentioned that I had received a phone call from Farouk al-Sharaa, the Syrian foreign minister, a few minutes before our meeting; he sent her his greetings and asked to have the Americans defer the withdrawal of their ambassador from Damascus in protest of the assassination of Rafik Hariri, the Lebanese prime minister, the day before. I added that we were ready to arrange a meeting for her with the Syrian minister in Cairo during her attendance at the meeting of the greater Middle East countries to be held on March 3, in order to develop their bilateral relations. In her response to this offer, Rice mentioned two points. The first was that, frankly speaking, the Syrians talked a lot about improving their relations with the United States, but they were actually going in the opposite direction, and they had to understand the situation fully. She referred specifically to the crossing of militants from Syrian territory into Iraq in order to attack U.S. troops, and denied that the withdrawal of the ambassador was connected to the assassination because they did not make a snap judgment concerning the identity of the assassin. Instead, she asserted, the withdrawal was a natural consequence of the direction that Syrian–U.S. relations were taking. She concluded that if Syria was interested in moving forward with the peace process, the United States wanted to know how Syria planned to put an end to its errant policies. From her words I sensed that we were about to start a difficult period that would further complicate the relations between the United States and Syria. Yet this would not discourage us from protecting Syria and maintaining its role as an Arab country, especially with the fall of Iraq and the U.S. presence there in the heart of the region.

Rice's second point had to do with the meeting in Cairo on March 3—a meeting which, I believed, would serve the objectives of our own foreign policy more than it would help the United States, since it could have been held anywhere else. She thought that there were problems, the most important of which was the agenda of the meeting, which she felt did not satisfy the minimum requirements of the approach agreed upon by the G8 at the Sea Island summit in 2004. She did not know yet whether she herself would be attending the meeting or not. Having realized the intentions of the United States to exert pressure on us regarding the meeting, for which I had suggested the title "Stability, Peace, Development," I told her that her absence would cause a big problem and that she, as a new secretary, would lose an important chance to meet with the Arab ministers to discuss all the reform and development issues she was concerned about. I notified Cairo of my belief that Rice saw her attitude as a way to apply pressure on us in response to our handling of the Ayman Nour case as well as an attempt to influence the agenda of the meeting in Cairo. This point was also brought up by the U.S. national security advisor in his talks with me, as I will discuss later.

This larger meeting, attended by several representatives from both sides, ended, and Rice said she would like to have a separate talk with her assistant for the Middle East present. I asked our ambassador to join us, saying out loud, "She'll be talking about Ayman Nour's case." Rice confirmed this, adding that the administration was in a difficult position because the U.S. president had political freedom at the top of his priorities and would continue to inquire about the progress achieved in this area in Egypt, a friendly country that led the region in various respects. She explained that Ayman Nour's arrest represented a real and unacceptable problem and that it would be difficult for the United States to maintain its credibility if it ignored this issue, and she insisted on the necessity of his release. She also emphasized the concern of the international community with good governance, since such issues would always be at the top of their priority list, and added that the United States would not be able to overlook these issues. She also noted that she understood the considerations that restricted us, by which she might have been referring to political Islam in Egypt and the surrounding region. She hoped that Egypt would continue its positive steps toward political reform, in which she was certain that it had already made progress. Her most decisive point was that Egyptian–U.S. relations would undoubtedly continue, but that Egypt's attitude toward such issues as good governance would have its effect on the warmth of the relations.

I replied that I had listened to her speak frankly and would now speak likewise. I emphasized that Egypt was committed to development, enlightenment, and reformation in all aspects—economic, social, and political—and that it hoped for an active, lasting dialogue, always taking into account our wish to maintain the stability of our society. Thus, development would continue as fast as possible while maintaining stability. I explained Ayman Nour's legal situation and how the Egyptian legal process worked, and expressed my wish to have him either released or tried promptly before the Egyptian judiciary system, which was well known for its integrity and independence, concluding that it would be advisable to deal with this matter quietly and not via the media channels. She said that there would be a press conference following our meeting in a few minutes; that she expected to be asked about this matter and would reply that Nour should be released immediately. I told her that she should be aware of the personality of President Mubarak and Egypt's self-image; anyone who tried to tell us what to do would get completely opposite results. Rice listened to this decisive statement, thought for a while, then said that she needed two minutes to discuss the matter with her subordinates at the back of the room. When she returned, she said that if she was asked about that matter, she would reply that she hoped he would be released as soon as possible. I commented that this phrasing would express the U.S. attitude without sounding as if she were dictating to Egypt. We decided to go to the press conference hall next to her office.

The press conference went as usual, inquiring about the regional situation, peace efforts, and what Egypt and the United States would do to restart negotiations between the Palestinians and Israelis. Just as the conference was coming to an end, an American journalist asked the expected question, which I was sure the State Department officials had told him to do, and Rice answered as agreed. None of the journalists, Americans, Egyptians, or other Arabs, asked me to comment. I felt it would look awkward if I volunteered to comment and possibly cause a crisis between the two sides in front of the media, threatening a thirty-year relationship. I left the Department of State with a feeling of coldness toward the secretary of state and her staff. At the gate there were some Egyptian and Arab correspondents, to whom I briefly stated that the case of the Member of Parliament Ayman Nour would be decided upon according to the Egyptian judicial system. I returned to the hotel and went through the cables sent from the news agencies, which revealed the ambush I was exposed to by the media. It stated that while Rice had strongly criticized Egypt's situation, the Egyptian minister did not confront her. No one mentioned the statement I made when I left the building regarding the legal status of the case.

On February 14, the day following my arrival, I met with Vice-President Dick Cheney and the national security advisor, Stephen Hadley, each individually. Although the talks were to have focused mainly on the peace process in the Middle East and the need to make a joint Egyptian–U.S.

attempt to advance the peace efforts, the internal Egyptian affairs and Ayman Nour's case completely dominated the discussions. Cheney had asked early for an individual meeting, during which he said that reform in the Middle East was of great importance for President Bush personally, and that Nour's case put the administration in an awkward position, especially before Congress and his opponents, who accused him of failing to implement his plans for promoting reform in the Middle East. This, he added, would make it difficult for the administration to defend its relations with Egypt against its critics. He affirmed that it was our close friendship that led him to discuss this matter, stressing the necessity for Egypt to implement serious political reforms. He also referred to the story going around in Egypt and the region about President Mubarak's wish to have his son Gamal succeed him as president, and its implications for the democratic process for electing the president in Egypt. First, I commented on the issue of Ayman Nour, saying that the matter was in the hands of the prosecutor general and that I hoped the investigation would end soon. I still wished to have him released pending investigation. Second, as for the son succeeding his father, I mentioned that the president continually repeated that he did not wish to have his son as president, in spite of certain indications to the contrary, including Gamal's obvious presence on the political scene. Even so, I could only believe what the president said. I cautiously added that I knew of Vice-President Cheney's friendship with President Mubarak since the Gulf War in 1991 when Cheney was the secretary of defense; I knew that the president trusted him, so he could discuss this matter with him. I did not include this part of our talks in the cable I sent to Cairo, preferring to discuss it with the president personally when I returned.

I had the same conversation with Steve Hadley, the U.S. national security advisor, as if he and Vice-President Cheney were reciting the same words, with the exception of Hadley's mention of his hope that Ayman Nour's issue would not affect the relations between our countries. He clearly hinted at a connection between Nour's case and the G8 Foreign Ministers Conference to be held in Cairo on March 3. He expressed concern that the agenda of the meeting did not include all the points the United States believed were necessary for the political reform issue, and thus they might not encourage Rice's participation.

On the third day of my visit I had multiple meetings with members of Congress and their committees. They presented the same attitude toward the issue of Ayman Nour and the need for democratic reform in Egypt, and the same criticism I had heard before. In my report to the president I wrote that in spite of everyone's concern with maintaining well-developed, positive relations between Egypt and the United States, and the warmth and friendliness that had marked conversations between the president and U.S. senators in the past, the subjects of political reform and Ayman Nour's case would cast a shadow over the relationship and remain on the agenda of U.S.–Egyptian relations for the foreseeable future.

Flying to Cairo on the evening of February 16, I was annoyed, maybe even angry, about what I had faced in Washington as a result of the Nour case. After analyzing all I had been through during my visit, I came to the conclusion that the American administration had decided to open fire on Egypt, either in defense of the U.S. principles of democracy in the most influential Arab country, or in order to use Ayman Nour's issue to criticize Egypt for the difficulties the United States was facing in the region. The goal, I thought, was to force Egypt to change its policy and become involved militarily, a course that the Egyptian leadership absolutely rejected. Consequently, I expected a difficult period in the relationship between the two countries. I decided to openly discuss all aspects of the situation with the president.

I had an appointment at midday on the day following my return. I frankly explained to the president the whole situation and my analysis of what the United States was demanding with respect to democracy, Ayman Nour, and increased Egyptian involvement in the U.S. military maneuvers in the Islamic area. I pointed out the clear, profound change in their attitude toward us, and my anticipation of a difficult period, during which we would have to decide on our reaction. Strong U.S. pressure was coming and we had to resist it. I stressed the importance of reaching a conclusion in the Ayman Nour case so that our foreign relations and our reputation in the international community would not be affected. The president's tone changed while discussing Nour's case. He explained that it was out of his hands, since it was a criminal case for the judicial system to decide. He asked whether I had any recommendations for dealing directly with this matter. I replied that the people in Washington were aware of the importance of the March 3 conference, and would try to make it fail by reducing the level of their representation. I suggested postponing, and then canceling, the meeting. We could also make a show of indifference toward the issues the United States was most concerned about, such as the greater Middle East forum; continue to emphasize the Egyptian view of nuclear disarmament and the Middle East as a nuclear-weapon-free zone; and stir up trouble for the United States and Israel during the next Review Conference of the Parties to the Treaty on the Non-Proliferation of Nuclear Weapons (NPT), to be held in New York in May 2005.

I finally got closer to the sensitive topic of the president's successor, which Vice-President Cheney had discussed with me. President Mubarak looked very concerned and, I felt, a little bit sad. He said that he would look into my recommendations, and I asked to leave. Then the president said that he wished I commented on Rice's words at the press conference. I explained that I did not want a public clash to occur, which would result in a further deterioration of relations and thus give our enemies an opportunity to sow discord.

The papers in Cairo were severely criticizing Rice for her interference in Egyptian affairs, while many articles in the so-called independent papers admonished the Egyptian minister—me—for not "standing up to" the Americans. I tolerated the situation since I was against public confrontation, even though I knew that the Egyptian regime, like other regimes in comparable countries, often relied on a firm public stance forbidding anyone to meddle in its affairs. However, the weeks and months following the Washington disturbance proved that I was correct, and that keeping our temper provided both sides a chance to try to resolve their differences.

To my surprise, the president accompanied me as I walked toward the door of the large reception salon on the ground floor of the Ittihadiya Palace, and, as if he were thinking out loud, said, "I do not exclude the idea that the Americans wish to remove me from office," words uttered spontaneously, which I was shocked to hear and had never heard mentioned to anyone before.

On this specific issue I should recall the following incident: U.S. Vice-President Dick Cheney came to Cairo later, in 2006, and met individually with the president over breakfast. The president later told me that Cheney focused on the American position in Iraq and Afghanistan, and the need for unspecified Egyptian assistance to overcome the difficult situations in both countries. Cheney also briefly referred to their hope of further promoting democracy in Egypt. If I take the president at his word about the content of his conversation with Cheney, then I think the United States should have clearly informed him that they would not support the transfer of authority from father to son in Egypt or any other country. Paradoxically, throughout this period and in the following years, the Americans continued to welcome the president's son on his visits to the United States and his meetings with top officials during my tenure as foreign minister.

Returning to my first visit to the United States, after I had briefed the president, I left the Ittihadiya Palace to meet the Austrian foreign minister for lunch at the Sheraton Heliopolis. As soon as the lunch and the press conference ended, I received a phone call from the president's secretariat, informing me that he wished to speak to me. I told them that I was about to go home and I could call them from there on a secure line, the closed circuit of the presidential communication network. But the president's secretary said he wished to talk to me immediately. The president said firmly, "I agree to postpone the G8 foreign ministers meeting in Cairo and not to schedule another time."

I promptly sent dozens of cables to several capitals, informing the invitees that the meeting had been postponed upon the request of several of them, due to the pressure of work. In the evening, I received another phone call from the president checking on the situation and the procedures taken, revealing his great concern to respond to the Americans. I told him that the meeting had already been postponed. He asked what reason I had given, and I told him that I had informed them that some of the foreign ministers had requested it. He asked whether that was true. I said, "I am lying." He was surprised by my straightforwardness and asked, "Are you really lying?"

I answered, "Yes," expressing my amazement at his surprise. He said, "They [the Americans] listen to everything. They will try to find out what everyone thinks of this, and we will have to cover up our attitude with some kind of message." Throughout that evening I contacted some ministers I was on good terms with, and the matter was arranged in a way that would make the Egyptian attitude look reasonable. The president inquired about the situation again at 10:00 p.m. I updated him, and he sounded relieved. From that moment on, I started to hear him saying, "Count on the Americans and you will be vulnerable." In particular, he often said this when discussing the situation in Pakistan after General Pervez Musharraf's resignation from the presidency in 2008.

The day after the abrupt cancellation, I headed to the Ittihadiya Palace to attend other meetings along with the president. There I met the head of the special secretariat, who asked in distress, "What did you tell him yesterday? He seemed nervous, upset, and furious too." I answered that the visit to Washington was quite terrible. He commented that he already knew it and feared that my usual frankness of speech made it hard to keep the facts from the President, which was what had made him angry. In a low voice, I calmly said that it was my responsibility to inform the head of state of all the circumstances surrounding us and not to keep any information from him at all.

In the following days, I came to know that some of the people surrounding the president—family members or assistants—tried to make things look less painful or hold me responsible, while others, led by General Omar Suleiman and his friends, told him that the foreign minister had made his point very well and had given him the information he needed to properly evaluate the crisis facing the Egyptian–U.S. relationship in a way that would lead to a solution. I always believed in the importance, or rather the vitality, of the relationship, which was not limited to Egypt's regional position, or to economic and military aid, but extended to a long list of common interests. On the one hand, we had to make the Americans respect our will and freedom to decide on matters essential for us, while, on the other hand, we had to constantly encourage a positive U.S. attitude toward Egypt that would pave the way for trade, investment, and a significant presence among the large, influential countries that could help or hinder Egypt in every respect, especially in the economic field.

Our economy was making great strides, and the western nations and the Gulf countries were opening up to the emerging Egyptian economy. It was up to us to provide the maximum possibilities for more initiatives. Hence, I was certain that in spite of his anger at the Americans, the president would contain his anger and work on creating smoother relations, once we had duly responded to the conduct of their administration. I continued to follow developments. The initial U.S. reaction to the postponement of the G8 ministerial meeting was a mixture of surprise and annoyance. When they inquired about the new date, we did not reply. Then I traveled to London to attend the Meeting on Supporting the Palestinian Authority, held on March 1, 2005. This was a meeting agreed upon by the European Union, the UN, the United States of America, the Russian Federation, and other important countries for the purpose of helping the Palestinians. While preparing for the visit, I avoided requesting a meeting with Rice outside of the conference, though I met with many other foreign ministers. During the reception hosted by the British foreign secretary I avoided getting too close to her so that we would not have to engage in conversation. Later, our eyes met across the meeting hall and we coldly exchanged greetings. I avoided attending her address before the conference. Some of her assistants asked the Egyptian delegates the reason for the coldness, and they answered that the meetings in Washington had not been productive and had had a bad effect on the relations.

The period from February to the end of June 2005 witnessed attempts by some in Egypt to reconcile Egypt and the United States, believing that the Ayman Nour crisis could be overcome and that the whole situation resulted from the performance of the foreign minister, not from the U.S. demands on Egypt. The Egyptian prime minister went on a visit to Washington that the media made much of, claiming unprecedented achievements in the relations between the countries or a belief that the U.S. demand for political reform in Egypt could be overlooked. In fact, I believe that as a result of our reaction to various issues following my recommendations to the president, the Americans became aware that they needed to deal with the Egyptians in a slightly different way, even though the U.S. objectives remained the same, as later developments would prove. The U.S. media responded favorably to the personality of the Egyptian prime minister. Yet, I felt that, in spite of the Egyptian media clamor, the president might have been dissatisfied with the outcome of the visit and its perceived success, which might undermine the relationship between the president and the prime minister and also question the prospect of the president's son of running for the presidency. The president might have also believed that some people in the United States might have reached the conclusion that Ahmed Nazif could become a viable candidate to succeed the president. Thus the prime minister did not visit Washington again for six years.

Some Egyptian ministers who had strong ties to the president's son imagined that they could take advantage of their connections with the administration via the financial or international monetary organizations, or the U.S. business sector, to try to alleviate the situation, and some of them asked for the president's approval to meet with the U.S. vice-president while they were preparing for their visits to Washington. They also approached the president's secretary of information about obtaining approval to meet the U.S. secretary of state and, surprisingly, the U.S. national security advisor as well. All these communications were done without seeking the foreign minister's opinion or his evaluation of the situation.

I was really surprised at their naiveté, knowing quite well that they were not well acquainted with the circumstances surrounding the bilateral relations, the regional situation, and the issues that Egypt and the United States were concerned about.

When I expressed my surprise at these maneuvers to the president, he firmly decided that there would be no interventions from the government. Only Omar Suleiman and I were responsible for U.S.–Egyptian relations. Matters such as trade, investment, and international cooperation were dealt with by the relevant ministries only after coordinating with both of us. The same thing happened with the European Union during the difficult negotiations conducted by the Ministry of Foreign Affairs in coordination with several Egyptian agencies to reach a comprehensive agreement for partnership with the Europeans. Some tried to complain about the toughness of the ministry, explaining that the economic interests required immediate action. I discussed this matter with the president, who firmly determined not to sign any agreement with the EU before ensuring the maintenance of our interests and the reciprocity of the relationship. Hence my relationship with the president was stable from mid-2005, and no more irritants arose in the execution of foreign policy.

Condoleezza Rice planned her first visit to Egypt in June 2005. We were all anxious not to have a confrontation, but at the same time we needed her to show consideration for our position. I sent direct and indirect messages to this effect, and they assured us that they were not looking for a fight. However, Rice wished to give a speech before an Egyptian audience, and the American University in Cairo (AUC) invited her to make a statement before its students. We insisted that she would meet with the president, the foreign minister, and the intelligence chief before giving her speech, and that the meetings would be held in Sharm al-Sheikh. Thus, to her inconvenience, she would have to travel to the coastal city first before going to Cairo for her speech.

When Rice arrived, I received her at the airport as a show of comity, since I did not intend to invite her for a working lunch or dinner, due to lack of time as well as to her lack of hospitality during my visit to the United States in February. Although previous Egyptian foreign ministers had been eager to receive their counterparts, the Americans in particular, and to bid them farewell at the airport, I no longer did this, in order not to waste time in Cairo traffic. Besides, we were rarely treated likewise abroad.

Rice's visit focused on the regional situation and the Palestinian issue without reaching any final conclusion. Thus the visit was not really fruitful, but it served the purpose of demonstrating U.S. interest in the Middle East, forming one of the sides of the regional equation. She briefly alluded to Ayman Nour's situation. I believe she did so in case she was asked about it by the media. There was not much to say about her meeting with the president. At the press conference that we attended before she left for Cairo to give her speech at the AUC, I intended not to miss the chance to comment on any of the topics we had covered: regional matters, Egyptian–U.S. relations, or the internal situation in Egypt. We pelted each other politely with words. One of our senior journalists described this meeting and our subsequent meetings with the media as a rough table-tennis match. This was the exact description of all our meetings until Rice left office in January 2009.

Rice's visit in June confirmed a lot of assumptions, regardless of the fact that it did not reach any agreement. The Americans obviously intended to frame the topic of political reform in Egypt cautiously so that they would not lose our friendship, especially when the Egyptian regime was moving to amend its constitution and have a presidential election as well as other developments. The importance of Egypt, and America's need for its cooperation, certainly had an impact on the idea of political reform apart from Egyptian–U.S. cooperation at the regional level and the Palestinian issue. I also believe that the conditions in Lebanon, Iraq, and Afghanistan forced the United States to turn to Egypt for cooperation and help. The aggravating Iranian attitude, which pressured Lebanon, Iraq and the Gulf, and the nuclear issue with its risks and consequences, were influencing the Americans as well.

As a result, the Americans seemed to reassess their situation and the messages they sent became indecisive. They demanded that U.S. civil society and nongovernmental organizations be allowed to work in Egypt. Our position remained ambiguous regarding these requests. We did not officially approve the requests for these organizations to operate in Egypt, but we never took decisive action against them either. The president refused to give an approval and insisted on being the one in charge of decisions concerning these organizations, which quietly did their job of training Egyptians and Egyptian nongovernmental organizations. They included the Republican Institute, the Democratic Institute, and Freedom House. There were many factors to take into consideration. Their operations were restricted, but they were not completely prohibited. In 2005 and subsequent years, the Americans decided to allot a certain amount of their economic aid to the operations of these organizations in cooperation with their Egyptian counterparts. They started with about $25 million annually, according to what was announced at the time, then increased to about $50 million annually. Egypt was aware of this but still made no definite decision. I told the president that the amount was equal to 250 million Egyptian pounds per year or more, quite a large amount by Egyptian standards, and that the organizations might have ulterior motives other than their publicly stated purpose of providing training in elections, democracy, and similar matters. He was concerned but remained utterly indeterminate until he stepped down. I often thought about this incomprehensible attitude, and came to the conclusion that the issue of his succession had had its impact and that he wished to keep the possibility of reaching an understanding on that point with the Americans or the Congress. He also did not want a new crisis to arise that would exert pressure on his tense relations with President Bush. I may add that he took into account the issue of the provision of armaments for the Egyptian Armed Forces, especially since, if Egypt cracked down on these organizations that were working without permission within its territory, the Americans would immediately re-evaluate their military aid to Egypt, a turn of events that would be harmful for both sides.

The Ministry of Foreign Affairs seized every possible opportunity to protest to the United States that the work of these organizations should cease, but to no effect. A resident American director of one of these institutes made a foolish mistake by saying that they would proceed with their operations and impose change in Egypt even if the Egyptian authorities objected. When we protested, they withdrew him at once and removed him from Egypt. Anyone who followed the Egyptian media during these years would conclude that there was an acute problem within the government and Egypt was incapable of making a conclusive decision. During the Forum for the Future, which was part of the U.S. Broader Middle East Initiative that was held in Bahrain in November 2005, the United States blatantly revealed its objectives when the vice-president's daughter, Liz Cheney, who was the principal deputy assistant secretary of state, demanded the right for the United States and other countries to provide financial assistance to civil society and nongovernmental organizations in the Islamic countries regardless of the domestic laws of these countries, as long as the assistance did not promote terrorism. The Arab ministers naturally became angry. While preparing for the meeting in the days before it was held, I made it clear to the Americans that we would not accept any indication of contempt for the laws of our countries. Egypt was obviously uncompromising in this matter and the Arab ministers asked for our help to face this attack. We threatened that if the final communiqué of the meeting included such preposterous, illegal wording that ignored the domestic laws of the countries, we would announce our withdrawal from the meeting and reject the statement. Our delegation firmly confronted Cheney's daughter, who led the U.S. position even though Condoleezza Rice was present as the head of the U.S. delegation in Manama. To the disappointment of the Americans, the conference failed to issue a statement at the end because of the Egyptian opposition. The Egyptian Ministry of Foreign Affairs and its minister were attacked by many of the Egyptian civil society organizations and the local media. The fact was completely ignored that no one, Egyptian or non-Egyptian, could spend any money in the United States or a European country without legal authorization and full observance of the laws of the country.

When the issue of the U.S. NGOs and their attempts to work in Egypt without taking Egyptian law into consideration came up after the January 25 Revolution, I recalled this confrontation. My speeches before Prime Minister Ahmed Shafiq's cabinet after the revolution returned to my memory. I presented a full report on the information I had received from Egyptian security authorities about the expenditures concerned, and the ways in which Egyptian groups, under the guise of Egyptian civil works organizations, obtained money from different sources. The minister of culture at the time, who resigned two days after his appointment, violated the recognized ethical and moral standards by publicly criticizing me for informing the Cabinet about a secret statement on money received from foreign entities. As time proved I was right, I hoped this person came to realize how mistaken he had been. Whoever read Condoleezza Rice's memoir of her years in office could deduce the reasons for the substantial American funding of Egyptian civil society organizations, and the goals set for the Broader Middle East initiative and the Forum for the Future. I should point out that I do not object to the existence of Egyptian civil society or nongovernmental organizations as long as they actively work to provide services to Egyptian society as stated in Egyptian law.

When I returned to Cairo from Manama, the president wished to hear my report on the night of my arrival. He was satisfied with our achievements and our ability to hold back the U.S. plan without causing an Egyptian–U.S. clash, since he was greatly concerned about a possible confrontation. The Americans, however, continued to exert pressure on us regarding our internal affairs, while encouraging us to continue our cooperation with them on matters that were vital for them. We planned to restrict their attempts to influence our internal conditions, while at the same time doing our best to maintain a degree of close cooperation between the two sides, in spite of the advice given by influential Americans that in the absence of major political reform in Egypt, Egyptian–U.S. relations were doomed to deteriorate. With the Bush administration coming to an end, the president looked forward to a change in attitudes. Thus he approved Egypt's obligation to cooperate with the United States at the regional level.

There was a general impression that things were getting better until Ayman Nour's verdict provided the spark for an explosion and, despite all efforts, relations became tense. The Americans, the Congress, and the administration took steps to impose restrictions on Egypt. The U.S. politicians who had witnessed the Camp David Accords had long since exited the political scene, and only a very limited number of senators who had known the president for two decades or more remained, which gradually weakened the positive effect of the peace treaty on Congress.

The restrictions included the suspension of discussion on a possible free trade agreement, a demand we had longed to fulfill. In practical terms, Egypt was not affected by this suspension. The minister of trade assured me that the QIZ signed by Egypt, the United States, and Israel had already increased Egyptian exports to U.S. markets and accomplished more than the free trade agreement would have done. This could be seen in the figures for Egyptian exports to the USA via the QIZ, which rose to $744 million in 2008, accounting for 33 percent of Egyptian exports, compared to $288 million in 2005.

The Americans suspended any talks about the increase of military support, even a limited increase to strengthen control of the border. Many congressmen, including Tom Lantos, argued against the military support and suggested transferring amounts of up to $400 million from military support to economic aid. Others asked to eliminate the economic aid completely in order to encourage growth of the Egyptian economy without any external support. Another opinion, backed by Israel, indicated that economic support had maintained the Egyptian–Israeli peace up until then.

The Egyptians thought, and still do, that the military support was very important for achieving stability in the Middle East, in which Egypt had a role to play. Economic aid, on the other hand, in spite of its importance in supporting the Egyptian economy in 1978–79 when the Egyptian–Israeli peace treaty was newly signed, no longer had the same effect, in view of Egypt's increased development and economic potential thirty years later. At the beginning of this period, the economic aid was about $815 million per year, gradually decreasing to about $415 million in 1999. Then, as an act of punishment, the Bush administration decided to reduce it to approximately $200 million annually from 2008 to 2013, or one billion dollars over five years. Some Egyptians eagerly asked the United States to set conditions for both economic and military aid. We were concerned about maintaining a sufficiently high level of military support. However, over the following years the Bush administration obviously did not intend to maintain the previous balance in the military support provided to Egypt and Israel. In 2008 the United States even decided to present Israel with support that amounted to three billion dollars for ten years—$30 billion—compared to $13 billion for Egypt over the same period. They attempted to restrict the Egyptian program to focusing on fighting terrorism, protecting border security, and supporting international peacekeeping operations. Egypt resisted.

John Negroponte, the U.S. deputy secretary of state, former director of national intelligence, and U.S. permanent representative to the UN from 2001 to 2003 during my tenure there, called in August 2007 to inform me of the U.S. decisions regarding the reduction of economic support and their attitude toward military aid. I refrained from stating the issues that the two sides should discuss in order to find a way out of the situation. Meetings were held by the relevant Egyptian agencies where many ideas were suggested, one of which was to open a joint account into which both the United States and Egypt would deposit an agreed-upon, equal amount to be spent on specified needs in Egypt. We informed the Americans at all levels that it was unreasonable to ask Egypt, a developing country that received about $200 million in U.S. aid annually, to pay at the same time the amount of $350 million per year to cover economic and trade debts. We pointed out that Egypt would be financing the U.S. economy to the tune of about $150 million annually. The Ministry of Foreign Affairs and the Ministry of International Cooperation worked persistently against this situation for years, but in vain.

Egypt decided not to jeopardize its relations with the United States and continue to play its key role in the region with the cooperation of the United States by holding major conferences on Iraq and Palestine and their future in Egypt, and by acting jointly on issues concerning Sudan, Lebanon, and other countries. Of course, our aim was to defend Egypt's interests and maintain its influence in the area, which became especially important during the period of increased tension from 2005 to 2011 as President Mubarak's rule declined.

With Rice's interest shifting to the Palestinian cause, she made several trips to the region, and to Egypt in particular. We were responsive to her concerns about the Palestinians and the peace efforts she made, which will be discussed in detail in a separate chapter. The relations between me and Rice gradually improved, strengthened by the need of the Gulf countries to counter the Iranian political attack, which was not confined to the Gulf area but also extended to Lebanon, Iraq, and finally Gaza. The views of the Egyptians and the Americans were converging, and the Americans agreed to hold meetings more than once a year, attended by Rice, the Gulf ministers, the Egyptian foreign minister, and his Jordanian counterpart; the Iraqi foreign minister would be included at a later period.

We informed the United States of our firm stand when talks began on arrangements for the security of the Gulf to reach a possible settlement with Iran. We told them that we would not be excluded, since we represented the strategic depth of the region, and we enjoyed a certain amount of influence in discussions of the Iranian nuclear issue with the International Atomic Energy Agency (IAEA). The Americans had to be aware of that.

In spite of the Egyptian decision to maintain constructive cooperation with the United States at the regional level in order to secure our role, we quietly studied the specific procedures to adopt in case the United States reduced its military support to Egypt. I will not address this matter in this book due to its sensitivity.

By the end of 2006, it was agreed to resume the Egyptian–U.S. strategic dialogue at the level of the foreign ministers, senior officials, and other agencies. The growing mutual understanding between myself and Secretary Rice and the improved relations between the other government agencies of both nations, and the fact that at least some of the difficulties regarding economic support and U.S. interference in Egyptian internal affairs had relatively subsided, undoubtedly supported this dialogue. The U.S. messages often seemed contradictory. For example, in his State of the Union address in 2005, Bush spoke about reform in both Egypt and Saudi Arabia on the one hand, while emphasizing the need to be cautious with every step taken on this long road in order not to be disappointed, on the other. During the visit of the Egyptian prime minister to Washington in May 2005, Bush again expressed the need for the United States to proceed cautiously in dealing with the Muslim Brotherhood and their long history of secret terrorist acts. On one occasion, U.S. officials stated that they approved of the openness Egypt was experiencing in 2005, which would discourage the Muslim Brotherhood, while on another occasion they stated that this same openness would enable the Muslim Brotherhood to publicly engage in political work, leading to stability in Egypt, and thus it was important to allow the group to engage in politics. The United States reiterated its belief that the fight against Islamist terrorism required the dissemination of democracy and education in Middle Eastern societies, while it held an official public dialogue with the members of the Muslim Brotherhood who were elected to the Egyptian Parliament in 2005.

The United States continued to put pressure on Egypt. In his State of the Union address in 2006, Bush never mentioned Egypt in the context of U.S. foreign relations, even though he did refer to several other Middle Eastern countries that had made progress. In February 2006 Rice visited Egypt again, and discussed the internal situation and the Americans' request to set up a complete program of political reform. She indirectly correlated the need for political reform with the economic support given to Egypt. We maintained the status quo; they talked about the need for reform, while threatening to withdraw aid; then they promoted our joint regional cooperation and sought to benefit from our capabilities and influence. The president made it clear that Egypt's internal affairs were to be managed without creating any problems externally, in spite of the intense domestic pressure which required us to return to aggressive foreign-policy practices that had last been used decades ago.

I never supported a foreign-policy confrontation with the Americans, because I believed that it would be harmful to our international position unless we were clearly forced into it; such a confrontation would also affect our image both domestically and internationally. I was convinced that stable relations with the United States and the other western powers were crucial to maintaining international confidence, and therefore international investment, in Egypt's development. Thus General Omar Suleiman and I worked on promoting our relationship with the United States and tried to relieve U.S. pressure on us internally by reaching out to them externally. I would say that Rice's relationship, as we experienced it in 2005 and the first half of 2006, lacked warmth and understanding, even though we met several times at international meetings and during her visits to Cairo. Our relations gradually improved, however, as she had to try to build bridges between us in order to deal with the deteriorating situation in Iraq, the Israeli invasion of Lebanon, the unyielding Iranian attitude toward the nuclear issue and its policies in the Gulf, and the Hamas victory in Gaza and the consequent end of the peace efforts.

A large Egyptian delegation that included the ministers of foreign affairs, international cooperation, and trade, and General Omar Suleiman, visited Washington from July 17 to 21, 2006 to participate in the launching of the Egyptian–U.S. strategic dialogue. This took place in the middle of the crisis of the Israeli invasion of Lebanon. We were well received by the Americans. Rice became more amiable and I less unfriendly, and we started to cooperate, especially when we discovered that we had interests in common other than the relations between the two countries or the situation in the Middle East. Rice's area of specialization in U.S. foreign policy was the Soviet Union. She held the post of director of Soviet and East

European affairs with the National Security Council in the administration of President George H.W. Bush for years. In spite of my now broader responsibilities, I was still interested in Soviet affairs. We discussed Soviet personalities and their influences, and the history of the rise and fall of the Soviet Union and the role the United States played in it. We became closer and our relationship gradually improved over the years, so that I would say that when she left office, we were on good terms. I perceived her as sharp-witted, strong-willed, and self-confident in spite of her difficult upbringing, to which she always referred as an example of the formidable challenges that she faced and embraced. Rice came to understand our viewpoints and interests from my frequent talks about the characteristics of the Egyptian personality. She even once said that she knew that our unyielding attitude was as hard as the granite of Aswan, referring to a statement I made in her presence during a press conference at the Cataract Hotel in Aswan in connection with a small meeting of Arab foreign ministers: "The Egyptian personality is like the granite you see from the hotel window overlooking the Nile." The president treated her discreetly. He appreciated her intelligence and straightforwardness, and often explained to her in detail the Egyptian domestic situation, the conditions Egypt faced, and its complications. He always repeated that Rice stood helpless as Bush, Dick Cheney, and even Liz Cheney were the ones who incited a clash with Egypt.

In this meeting in July 2006, Rice mentioned that the U.S. political system was complicated. However, because of Egypt's importance for the United States, they were eager to support us in every possible way. She pointed out that she had written to the House of Representatives in support of the aid programs to Egypt, and had brought the U.S. ambassador to Egypt to Washington to meet with members of Congress to urge them to keep the aid program for Egypt intact. She added that at the same time the administration required Egypt's help with this matter by adopting reform policies, which would make it easier for them to defend the aid program.

This visit also revealed to the delegation that in spite of the leverage Egypt had in Congress because of its efforts to settle the Middle East problems, many members of Congress expressed their disapproval of Ayman Nour's verdict. Some of them had requested a reduction of $200 million in Egypt's economic aid. In the remaining years until the end of Bush's presidency in January 2009, I paid several visits to Washington, alone or with General Omar Suleiman. After a trip to the United States on February 6 and 7, 2007, I presented to President Mubarak an assessment of the situation in which I mentioned that the officials I had met stressed the importance of Egyptian–U.S. relations, the vital role Egypt played in the region, and its status as the "island of stability" and the primary friend whom the United States could count on. I stated that the majority of the officials and members of Congress I had met admitted that they had adopted a wrong policy in Iraq and the region as a whole, and they needed to listen more and consult their friends in the future. I also added that Rice, Hadley, and Negroponte were all focused on the regional issues and were less concerned with the internal situation in Egypt.

In July 2007, I went back to the United States, accompanied by Omar Suleiman. During our visit an extensive round of consultations on the regional situation took place. The Egyptian–U.S. understanding was obviously developing and the Americans became more inclined to listen attentively to our point of view. Our meeting with the U.S. secretary of defense Robert Gates was the most positive one we had, during which he firmly defended the military assistance program for Egypt. He also told us that he had coordinated with Rice to continue trying to convince Congress not to reduce this aid in any way. It was clear that he paid less attention to the civilian economic-aid program, which was in fact going to be reduced. The administration was obviously about to make an unfavorable decision. During our meeting with Rice and Hadley, they inquired about the ten years included in our 1999 agreement with the Clinton administration, which were coming to an end soon; they believed that a further reduction from $415 million to only $200 million would be necessary due to the high military costs in Iraq and Afghanistan. We did not respond. We reached a deadlock. However, I sent a message to the prime minister telling him that I thought we should continue to try to talk the Americans into negotiating the issues we were concerned about. I told him that we could not finance the U.S. economy, and that I would assure the new U.S. administration that economic support to Egypt should be regarded as part of the strategic framework of the relationship for sustaining stability in the Middle East. I suggested that we should offer the new administration two options; either to resume negotiating the proposals we had presented to the Bush administration, which included the establishment of a fund or a deposit to be financed from the installments of the debt transferred instead of repaying it to the United States, or to agree to have us pay off our debts out of the annual support of $200 million at the price of 20 cents on the dollar. I emphasized the fact that we had to make a prompt decision in case the new administration followed in the footsteps of the old one, and also to decide whether we would respond by refusing to receive any economic assistance starting from fiscal year 2009, but without openly announcing it in order to avoid starting off our relationship with the new administration with a clash that could be used against us by the media. I received no reply. Still, I continued to work constructively in collaboration with the Ministry of International Cooperation.

As the U.S. decision became apparent, the U.S. ambassador to Cairo came to say that she had attended discussions in Washington that dealt with the issue of economic assistance to Egypt, and that some people were talking about how important it was to satisfy the Egyptians one way or another. I suggested to the prime minister that we should consider accepting the ambassador's offer by studying the possibility of using $200 million of the approximately $800 million in U.S. aid already allocated to Egypt but not yet used, together with the funds of 2009, which amounted to $200 million, meaning a total of $400 million to be spent on the slum cities from 2009 onward. I received no reply. Another proposal I made was to end the program and consider transferring the annual economic assistance assigned for the coming five years to the military support program. I received no reply about this, either.

During this important visit, the Americans suggested holding a meeting of the ministers of foreign affairs and the ministers of defense of the United States, the Gulf Cooperation Council countries, Egypt, and Jordan. I objected, pointing out that this proposal would have harmful effects, would further irritate the already provoked Iran, and would be useless. When the Americans tried to convince us otherwise, we insisted, and they gave in. I immediately informed Cairo of the situation so that our officials would not be deceived by their devious attempts.

In Washington, Rice referred to my discussions with Negroponte about the military assistance for both Egypt and Israel when I criticized the U.S. attitude, emphasizing the importance of this assistance and the necessity of continuing it according to the Camp David formula. Rice commented that it would be difficult to continue connecting the aid programs for both Egypt and Israel with the Camp David Accords thirty years after they had been signed, and that she would prefer to have the military aid program in particular as the basis for the Egyptian–U.S. relationship. I remarked that over the years the aid programs for both countries had been considered a special case precisely because they were linked to the accords, and the comprehensive peace that was the ultimate goal of the accords had not yet been reached. Rice certainly supported the existence of competent and efficient Egyptian Armed Forces in order to deliver a strong message to Iran, which was seeking to aggressively interfere in many countries of the region. She therefore expressed her commitment to support the Egyptian military.

As the Bush administration was about to depart, I felt that President Mubarak was eager to see this administration leave the political scene. We had maintained our vital relations with the United States only with great effort, whether at the regional level or at the level of bilateral relations, at the cost of dozens of visits of deputies of the foreign minister and other officials to Washington. Yet the United States saw fit to put a hold on $200 million of the aid for the year 2008 on the condition that Egypt fulfill certain requirements, including judicial reform, modernizing the police forces, and stopping the smuggling of arms and other objects into Gaza across the Egyptian border. President Bush visited Egypt twice during his last year in office, in January and May 2008. Despite his talk about political reform in Egypt and the region, he expressed his concern about the Islamist movements and wanted to support the secular and liberal forces. He seemed to be heavily influenced by the book by Soviet Israeli Jewish writer Natan Sharansky's book, as revealed in his ideas about the danger of political Islam in the countries neighboring Israel, by which he meant Egypt, Jordan, and the Palestinian territories, where groups with strong Islamist political tendencies were present.

I always appreciated the value of Egypt's having additional political options. Although I was fully aware that the United States and the broader western world would continue to have a decisive influence on international relations and on the Middle East for decades to come, especially after the dissolution of the Soviet Union, I also saw China as a rising power to which Egypt should open up, widely but cautiously. Russia was another alternative to the almost total U.S. dominance. Having decided to resist the west in its vicinity, which included the former Soviet republics, Russia sought to restore its relations with countries like Egypt. The relationship with Russia would certainly not be identical to that which had existed between Egypt and the Soviet Union due to the fundamentally different political and historical circumstances. However, the Russians presented interesting offers to Egypt in many fields. I favored reasonable interaction, but since caution was the watchword for the Egyptian political process, my expectations were not completely fulfilled.

Our movements in these two directions—China and Russia—were scrutinized by the United States and the rest of the west, especially when it came to the issues of security, nuclear cooperation, arms purchases, and the related advanced weapons systems.

The American election campaign ended and Obama won. As soon as he was elected, he called the Egyptian president, and then called him again when he entered the White House on January 20, 2009. President Mubarak called me at my home in the Delta near to the city of Qaha, and informed me with great satisfaction that the U.S. president-elect had talked to him, that he sounded well, and that they had agreed to meet as soon as possible. In the following weeks, Mubarak unleashed severe criticism of President Bush.

With the arrival of the Democrats in the White House, the appointment of Hillary Clinton as secretary of state, the retaining of Bob Gates at the Department of Defense, and the return of Leon Panetta, who had served as Bill Clinton's chief of staff, to hold the post of director of CIA director, President Mubarak felt relieved and saw no need for any tension between the Egyptian regime and the U.S. administration despite the legacy the Bush administration left behind, which included the reduction of economic assistance to Egypt by one half, to $200 million annually for five years.

I felt we needed to make a proper start with the new administration, especially since our previous relations with the newly appointed officials had been good. As soon as they were appointed, they gave statements in which they expressed their wish to redirect the relations to serve the interests of both sides. They were certainly aware of the disagreement we had with the Bush administration throughout its second term. At the Ministry of Foreign Affairs, we began to develop plans of actions with the new administration and seek means to protect our interests.

One day during November 2008 while I was at the Ittihadiya Presidential Palace taking part in the welcoming ceremony for a visiting foreign president, the president asked to see me in the reception room in order to discuss some foreign policy issues. The meeting lasted for about ten minutes, during which I referred to the importance of clearing the air with the new administration and therefore requested that he seriously consider releasing Ayman Nour. He rejected this proposal and explained that he could not interfere with a judge's verdict. I calmly said that he could be released on medical grounds, for which he was actually eligible, without the President's involvement. He looked calm. Before leaving the hall, I explained that I felt it was my responsibility to discuss these issues to preserve positive Egyptian–U.S. relations, and to ensure that Egypt maintained a level of influence and presence on the international scene that was commensurate with our status. As soon as I left, I met with General Omar Suleiman and told him about what I did. I also informed the chief of the presidential staff and the secretary of information to the president. Thank God I did. The president summoned Ambassador Suleiman Awad and exclaimed, "The foreign minister asked to release Ayman Nour!" Suleiman Awad answered, "Good idea." He was immediately dismissed from the room. I followed the situation from my place in the grand hall of the palace. The president's secretary came and told me what happened. Suddenly the president asked for his chief of staff. The same thing happened. The chief of staff backed my idea, and I left feeling that there was a chance the president would give in. In the evening the General Intelligence chief phoned and said that he strongly supported the idea of releasing Ayman Nour and thought that the president might consent. At the time, I believed that, considering his reaction, the president was actually thinking of the matter, and even though he had a legal way out, he did not wish to take the initiative. He had to wait for someone to bring it up. That someone was me.

When the new secretary of state Hillary Clinton came into office, I called her, as is customary, to welcome the cooperation with her. I also sent a farewell cable to Condoleezza Rice. The new secretary and I agreed on the importance of meeting soon. Hours later, the U.S. ambassador to Cairo called to say that they suggested that I travel to Washington, to meet Clinton on February 12. At the ministry, we prepared the files for the visit and the points that needed to be discussed with the Americans. I was accompanying the president on a visit to Rome on February 10, and that evening, before leaving for Washington the next morning, I reviewed with him the main points I was going to discuss with Clinton, and I asked his permission to arrange a meeting for him with President Obama in Washington. The president had not been there in five years. I also said that I would ask them to have Obama choose Cairo as the place from which to address the Islamic and Arab world in the statement which, according to all the U.S. media sources, Obama wished to give during his first months at the White House. There was a misunderstanding when Obama visited Turkey and addressed its parliament, for some mistook this statement for the other one.

We were aware of all that in Egypt. The president accepted at once and offered to have a hall with a capacity of thousands available for Obama. On February 12 I went to Washington and met with Secretary of State Clinton before noon. Our discussion included my invitation to Clinton to visit Egypt and participate in the conference we had been arranging for March 2 on the reconstruction of Gaza after it was destroyed during the Israeli invasion at the end of December 2008. She promised to think about it. I told her that her participation would send a strong message that the new administration was committed to helping the Palestinians. I even offered to name the United States as a co-sponsor along with Egypt, which would signal their intention to play a central role in the regional issues. To persuade her to accept the invitation, I suggested that we take the opportunity to hold political consultations to be attended by the United States, the Gulf Cooperation Council countries, Egypt, Jordan, and Iraq. This was the same group we had recommended to the Americans to work with in early 2006, and we had made progress with it during Rice's tenure. I explained that the role of the group was to show Iran that the Arab countries stood together in the face of its attempt to dominate the Gulf. I also suggested arranging another meeting for the group with the permanent members of the Security Council and Germany, who were negotiating with Iran on its nuclear program. Clinton interrupted, saying that she was convinced and would be attending the conference. She added that she had met with President Obama half an hour earlier, and when she told him that she would be meeting with me in a few minutes, he asked her to inform me of his real wish to strengthen U.S.–Egyptian relations, and his agreement to have his administration give a clear message that expressed their recognition of their friends in the region, with Egypt certainly at the forefront. I referred to the several difficulties that our relationship had encountered during the previous administration, and assured Clinton that in spite of this, Egypt was eager to maintain the essence of the Egyptian–U.S. relationship, since our country was convinced of its strategic nature and looked forward to starting a new period of constructive relations. Clinton reassured me that she and Obama were convinced of the importance of our relations, and that she planned to act upon this belief.

I then expressed President Mubarak's wish to meet the U.S. president, and said that it would be up to them to schedule a meeting. I also made it clear that we would welcome Obama in Cairo to address the Arab and Islamic world from Egypt, mentioning all the reasons that Cairo would be the most suitable place for this message. Clinton promised to pass this offer, as well as my view of the situation in detail, to President Obama.

I discussed the issue of economic assistance to Egypt and our wish to restore the program to the level it had been before the one-sided decision by the United States, and expressed our readiness to work together to decide on the future of the program. She understood the situation and was willing to consider the best possible way to deal with it.

We had an extensive discussion on Iran and America's attempt to keep it from becoming a military nuclear power. When we spoke about the Gulf, I criticized some of the policies of the Qataris, who often seemed to vacillate between their loyalty to Iran and their interest in maintaining active Gulf and Arab relations. When we talked about the status of the peace process in the Middle East, she expressed her intention to implement an active policy for this issue, and her belief that if Israel continued its current policy of prevarication, any chance of establishing peace would be eliminated. I alluded to the fact that the previous administration had opposed the candidacy of Mr. Farouk Hosni for the post of director general of the United Nations Educational, Scientific and Cultural Organization (UNESCO), and hoped that the matter could be reconsidered. She said that she intended neither to challenge the attitude of the U.S. opposition toward Farouk Hosni due to his hostile statements to Israel, nor to risk losing Israel's confidence in the coming period so that the country could be asked to make hard decisions in response to the settlement efforts. When I insisted, she promised to reconsider the U.S. stance provided that an Egyptian–U.S. understanding was reached.

The next time the Israeli prime minister was in Cairo, I seized the opportunity to mention to him that we hoped they would not oppose the Egyptian candidate for director general of UNESCO, who, I believed, would be willing to include Israel among the first group of countries he would visit. I added that there had been another Egyptian director general, Mohamed ElBaradei, who had done exactly that. Nonetheless, no positive response was obtained from the Israeli side.

I returned to Cairo and informed the president of my discussions with Clinton, describing how open she and the entire administration appeared to be to Egypt's concerns. He seemed satisfied. He commented that she was a special lady and would be more influential than Rice, who was held back from taking action in the Middle East by the conservative Republicans.

Clinton was a magnetic, self-confident person. The discussions and communications we had for two years up until March 2011 revealed that she carefully studied her files and read out her responses from papers and cards prepared beforehand—unlike Rice, who depended on her years of teaching experience at Stanford University in California and her work at the White House during both Bush administrations.

I was keen to maintain a very good relationship with Clinton as I did with Rice during her last years in office, and I believe that by doing so I achieved a lot of understanding that served our relations. Clinton arrived in Sharm al-Sheikh to participate in the Conference on Reconstructing Gaza and I kept my promises. She met with the president, who was interested in showing courtesy. In keeping with the importance of revitalizing the relations, Omar Suleiman and I paid the next visit to Washington to hold political discussions from May 25 to 27. The U.S. ambassador to Egypt called and said that Clinton wished to phone. I gladly received her call. She told me that President Obama welcomed the Egyptian offer to make his statement on the U.S. relationship with Islam in Cairo, and the date they suggested was June 5, 2009. When I informed the president, he seemed completely satisfied.

The meetings we held in Washington were of the utmost importance, for we had the opportunity to meet all the administration figures, unlike my first visit in February, which only lasted for about twenty-four hours. Together we met with Clinton at a working lunch, and discussed extensively the need to reinvigorate the Palestinian settlement dossier. This is a topic that I will deal with in a separate chapter. We also tackled the issues of the Gulf and Sudan in detail, as well as the upcoming visit of President Obama to Cairo. Clinton said that Obama's decision to address the Islamic world from Cairo had outraged many people, especially because of the perceived human rights problems in Egypt. Thus, the administration expected President Mubarak to take steps to alleviate the pressure before Obama's visit. Clinton highlighted the fact that the Egyptian–U.S. relationship not only had its bilateral strategic regional dimensions, but also its democratic and human rights aspects. I mentioned the Egyptian prime minister's order to have a governmental committee formed to look into the report of the National Council for Human Rights, and reassured her that there were developments in this field in Egypt. I briefed President Mubarak so that he would be aware of the U.S. stance regarding this matter.

We met with the U.S. officials in charge of Afghanistan, Iran, and Sudan. The Obama administration's special representative for Afghanistan and Pakistan, Richard Holbrooke, told us that Egypt would be invited to participate in the G8 Foreign Ministers' Meeting in Trieste together with other countries concerned with the Afghan crisis. (We did attend, and made an effective contribution.) We asked Holbrooke whether it would be useful to open a dialogue with the moderate members of Taliban. He did not give us a clear answer. I criticized what I called the blind air strikes by the American remotely piloted Predator drones, which had angered the Pakistanis and Muslims around the world. Holbrooke said that they were seeking to control those strikes so as not to kill innocent civilians, but, at the same time, the strikes managed to eliminate many opponents of the U.S. presence in Afghanistan inside Pakistani territory. When General Omar Suleiman asked again whether the United States thought it would be worthwhile for Egypt to reach out to the moderate members of the Taliban, Holbrooke replied that, although the administration was in no way ready to take part in a dialogue with the Taliban, the special relationship and coordination between our two countries made him think that we might be successful in inducing the Taliban to engage politically with the government in Afghanistan. I noticed that Holbrooke did not mention any concessions that the United States might be willing to make, directly or through the Afghan government, as an act of leniency in order to attract those members. He asked for our help with media guidance for the Afghans in Pashto via radio or television. We answered that we had the necessary experience and religious centers, but lacked funding. He said that he had recently been to the Kingdom of Saudi Arabia and the Emirates to explore ways for them to assist in Pakistan and Afghanistan, implying that he would try to obtain the necessary funds from these sources. We did not comment, and I actually completely disregarded it.

I had first met Holbrooke at the airport in New York in July 1999 while I was seeing off my friend, Ambassador Ahmed Maher. Holbrooke was standing in line for a taxi to take him into the city. I recognized him from his photographs in the media as a candidate for the post of U.S. permanent representative to the UN. I offered him a ride to downtown. We remained friends until his sad death in 2010. We cooperated closely to achieve the interests of our respective countries in the UN despite our many arguments and contradictory attitudes toward Israel. However, he was aware of Egypt's capabilities and influence within the international organization. I kept an eye on him for years, for the possibility of his becoming secretary of state in a Democratic administration could not be ruled out.

Omar Suleiman and I also met with Dennis Ross, the special advisor for the Gulf and Southwest Asia, who had a political interest in Iran. The Americans had obviously noticed that in its negotiations with the P5+1 (the UN Security Council's five permanent members plus Germany), Iran was in no rush and intended to procrastinate and waste time. The U.S. offer to cooperate with Iran was an element of the overall U.S. strategy. If Iran did not respond to the proposals of the west and the United States, their recalcitrance would mobilize international public opinion to deal with the country in a different way. My knowledge of the U.S. attitude led me to conclude that they would attempt to isolate Iran. Ross assured us that they intended to continue to consult with us on the Iranian nuclear issue, adding that the most important factor in changing Iran's policies and practices in the region was to make the country feel that its strategies in the region—in Afghanistan, Lebanon, Iraq, and Palestine—were destined to fail. Ross gave the impression that there was unlikely to be any military operation against Iran in 2009. I emphasized that it was important for the administration to speed up the Palestinian settlement so that Iran would be unable to use it to stir up tension in the region.

When we returned to Cairo on May 28, I found that the Egyptian president's office and many of the national security agencies were busy preparing for Obama's upcoming visit to Cairo. The president instructed these agencies to focus in particular on the security measures. During my visit to Washington, I had tried to find out the content of Obama's speech, but the Americans kept it secret. Since I had no indication of how far Obama would go in his speech, I thought we should consider having the Egyptian president also speak at the occasion, so that Obama's statement would be preceded or followed by a few powerful words from the Egyptian president on Islam, the region, Egypt's responsibilities toward the Arabs, and its humanitarian message. When I mentioned this to the president, he seemed interested, but during their consultations with the presidential staff, the Americans insisted on having Obama speak alone, which the president accepted. This would not be the first time the president had not attended a speech by an American president speaking on Egyptian territory; since he had previously boycotted a statement made by President Bush before the Davos Forum/Middle East in Sharm al-Sheikh in 2008.

The meeting between the two presidents on the morning of June 5, 2009 at the presidential palace at Qasr al-Qubba caused me some concern, despite the warm welcome and cordial farewell and the domestic, regional, and international fanfare that accompanied it. I was actually worried about the sad appearance of Mubarak when he received Obama, for only a few weeks earlier his grandson, Mohamed, had passed away. I attended their separate bilateral session, in which Mubarak was not a responsive participant, nor was he an active host at the breakfast held at the palace; Omar Suleiman and I had to keep the conversation going to make up for the president's lack of participation. Obama devoured the Egyptian flaky layered pastry, *feteer meshaltet*, made with honey. He also enjoyed the Egyptian falafel.

Obama expressed his opinion on the importance of education and the willingness of the United States to cooperate with Egypt and the Islamic world in this field. I suggested that the United States should grant one thousand scholarships per year at U.S. universities for doctoral degrees in science and other fields. I added that our resources fell short of what was required for the education of thousands of Egyptians at universities in the United States, for the annual cost per student ranged from $35,000 to $65,000 at a less prestigious university, and as much as $100,000 annually for a top university, such as Harvard, Yale, the University of Chicago, or Columbia. Obama promised to look into the matter, adding that we should examine practices of the Asian countries that provided tens of thousands of educational opportunities for its youth at U.S. universities. Silence prevailed for a moment. He seemed to be telling us that we should try to be as successful as the Asians and the Turks.

We had a discussion on the international economy and the difficulties he had been facing since he took office, dealing with the financial crisis that had shaken the world since September 2008. I seized the opportunity to urge him to facilitate the accession of Egypt to the Group of Twenty (G20). I felt optimistic when he said that he did not object to that. However, in the following months, Obama's positive response came to nothing at the hands of the international bureaucracy.

The Cairo streets that Obama passed through on his way to the presidential palace in Qasr al-Qubba, from the palace to Cairo University, and throughout his visit were empty. The windows and the balconies overlooking the streets were also empty. I felt bad because this would make us look like a totalitarian country that controlled all aspects of life, even the right of a citizen to open or close his window. I told my wife that it looked bad and reminded me of my visit to the Democratic People's Republic of Korea with President Mubarak when I was a member of Dr. Esmat Abdel Meguid's office in May 1990. All the way from the airport to Pyongyang no sign of life was seen. It was a dead city. Suddenly, as we turned to enter a large square, we were received by hundreds of thousands of people who were overjoyed to see the guest! That was a good example of a totalitarian country. Well, in 2009 Egypt was far beyond all that. So why did we do this to ourselves?

Obama talked briefly about his commitment to support the Palestinian cause and to try to deal positively with the other regional issues. Obama and Mubarak decided to meet in Washington in mid-August 2009. I was hoping that the president would have overcome his grief and regained his strength by then. I carefully prepared all the files and the agenda needed for the visit.

That August, the two presidents met two days after the arrival of Mubarak, who always used to arrive two or three days before the date of an official visit so that he could recover from jet lag. His age was also a factor in this. The meeting was divided into two parts: one with the two presidents meeting individually and the other including the members of both delegations. I heard from the president during the following days, and after our return to Cairo, that Obama spoke strongly about the importance of internal political reform in Egypt, and his confidence that we would do our best on this issue. Mubarak told Obama that he wanted to carry out this reform cautiously, so that things would not get out of hand and threaten the stability of the country.

During the meeting, both sides discussed the regional problems in much the same way that they had been addressed in similar meetings over the past years. The main objective was to announce the revival of Egyptian–U.S. relations and the mutual cooperation. I believe that this objective was achieved. Yet there was a particular incident that made me feel exasperated. The hall adjoining the Oval Office contained a large table, comfortable chairs, and many flags carrying the names and the battles of the U.S. military units whose personnel were lined up outside the White House and along the path through the garden to the presidential residence. I noticed that Mubarak was not admitted into the Oval Office immediately upon his arrival, but was left standing with us outside the door to the U.S. president's office. He was kept waiting for some minutes while Omar Suleiman, Trade Minister Rashid Mohamed Rashid, and I chatted with him to keep him occupied. I felt that he was trying very hard to stay calm. He had often visited the U.S. presidential residence since his appointment as vice-president in 1975 and as president in 1981, but since this was the first time I had accompanied him to the White House, I had no idea whether he had been in such a situation before. Finally the door opened, the U.S. chief of protocol asked the president to come in, and Obama received him a step away from the door. Fortunately, Obama did accompany Mubarak to his car in the garden of the White House after the meeting.

I mentioned this incident to the U.S. ambassador to Egypt, who was participating in the larger meeting, and expressed my surprise. She explained that President Mubarak had met Hillary Clinton and Senator Mitchell before coming to the White House. Obama and the vice-president needed to get a report from them, but they had just arrived shortly before President Mubarak's arrival.

A similar incident had occurred with Dmitry Medvedev during the president's visit to Moscow at the end of 2007, when President Putin was about to hand over power to him. The Egyptian president was to meet the Russian president-elect. We arrived with the president at the door in front of which Medvedev would receive him and accompany him to the meeting hall. We were kept waiting for minutes. This made me quite angry. When I told the Russian ambassador in Cairo about it, he said that he too was annoyed, putting the blame on the inexperienced staff of the next Russian president. I believed, however, that it was the doing of the arrogant presidents of the major powers, or that perhaps the Egyptian protocol team had not properly coordinated the arrangements with the Americans or the Russians. I asked the chief of the presidential staff to do the same thing when Medvedev visited Egypt in 2009, but the Egyptian sense of hospitality forbade it. In 2010 the president was invited to Washington again to attend the launching of the Israeli–Palestinian negotiations. A meeting between the two presidents was to take place at the White House. I contacted the U.S. ambassador in Cairo and the Egyptian ambassador in Washington, and warned the president's staff that it was important not to keep him waiting in front of "Emperor Augustus's door" again! The meeting ended peacefully.

I met Secretary Clinton on several occasions, and I felt that we had a healthy and positive relationship. In January and April 2010, Omar Suleiman and I paid two more visits to Washington to address the stalled Palestinian–Israeli negotiations and look for ways to move them forward. During our visit in January we met with a large number of senior administration officials, among whom was the secretary of defense. He was interested in discussing Iranian affairs and suggested that the legitimacy of the Iranian regime was debatable after its recent presidential election, making it clear once more that they had neither close knowledge of the situation in Iran nor an integrated plan for dealing with Iran and its nuclear capacity.

As for Sudan, we expressed our great concern to General Scott Gration, who was in charge of the Sudan dossier in Washington about stability in Sudan in the event of the secession of southern Sudan without adequate international guarantees. There would be major issues to be resolved, such as the nature of the relationship between northern and southern Sudan, water, oil, currency, debts, borders, and a unified vision for the southern leadership that would enable them to run the country and secure its borders. In spite of their insistence on having the Sudanese referendum held on time, the Americans obviously shared our concerns, but they had no specific plan for dealing with these challenges, which was surprising, considering that these discussions had been taking place a year before the referendum in southern Sudan was to be held. We stressed the need for the United States to convince the southern leadership to start considering the post-secession issues then, twelve months before the referendum and eighteen months before the implementation of its result, since if they remained unresolved, the secession would inevitably lead to new outbreaks of violence. We therefore suggested that southern Sudan enter a transition stage following the referendum, to allow time for these crucial issues to be resolved. The U.S. envoy asked how Egypt would address the Nile issue in the event of secession. We explained our vision of the negotiations for the framework agreement of the Nile Basin initiative, adding that the status of Egypt and Sudan was legally stable under the Convention of 1959, and that in the case of secession, the two Sudanese parties would need to agree on the best way to meet the needs of the southern part, taking into account the fact that Egypt depended entirely on the Nile for its water supply while southern Sudan had an abundance of rainwater.

We also met with Richard Holbrooke, who was interested in talking with the Egyptian intelligence chief. He, in turn, warned Holbrooke about the extent of Iran's involvement in Afghan affairs: thousands of Afghans visited Tehran (fifty-five thousand in the previous year).

At the White House Omar Suleiman and I passed through the security gate without being stopped or having our papers or bags examined. We arrived at the lounge adjoining the office of the national security advisor, who, we were told, was on his way after a meeting with President Obama. While we were talking with our ambassador, Sameh Shoukry, a secretary entered, accompanied by a marine. They both looked alarmed and asked us to accompany them. I thought that perhaps the place of our meeting with the national security advisor, General James Jones, and his staff had changed, but they took us back to the security gate. One of the experts asked if one of us had had chemotherapy. I looked at Omar Suleiman in surprise and answered that, as far as I knew, no one had. Omar Suleiman said he had not had an illness that required such treatment. The Americans looked worried and suspicious. I suddenly remembered that while I was having my routine checkup at the International Medical Center in Cairo on January 4, I had an examination in which radioactive lithium was used to check the efficiency of cardiac muscles during a treadmill test. I described to them what had happened in Cairo four days before, and told them that the physicians said that substance would disappear within two or three days, and that it should be gone by now. The marines rigidly asked for my name and papers. I surprised myself with how calm I was, cooly saying that I was the Egyptian foreign minister and had been invited by General

Jones. I added that if they continued to treat me like this, I would leave at once, and the consequences would certainly not be good. A staff member in the office of the national security advisor finally settled the matter. In the meeting, General Jones apologized and explained that the marines were well known for not following protocol! I found the U.S. procedures and equipment very interesting. It had never crossed my mind that their security equipment could detect not only bombs and solid substances but also radioactive substances.

I must admit that the U.S. security procedures for the U.S. president, vice-president, and secretary of state were the most thorough and the most ridiculous. During my meetings with U.S. officials at the White House or the State Department in Washington, I always endured these procedures patiently, but at the same time, while I was working with the Egyptian foreign ministers, I insisted that their U.S. counterparts should respect the Egyptian procedures and follow them at the meetings held on Egyptian territory, especially since the U.S. security officers were always inclined to impose their views on their host. We treated them firmly and stated that we were the only ones responsible for the security measures for our guests. There were many incidents when U.S. security officers forcefully tried to suppress Egyptian security measures within Egyptian territory, but they were firmly confronted.

Going back to my discussion of the relations between Egypt and the United States, I thought that they had greatly improved, taking into account the several high-level meetings that had been held and President Mubarak's four meetings with the U.S. president in 2009 and 2010: once in Cairo, once in L'Aquila, Italy, and twice in Washington. In 2009 President Obama signed a bill for assistance to Egypt. It provided $200 million in economic aid, including $20 million for "promoting democracy" (according to the official announcement) and $35 million for education. The special conditions that the Bush administration had insisted upon, and Egypt had refused, were dropped. In July 2010, the State Department announced the rejection of the idea of a deposit account. The $200 million appeared in the 2011 budget.

On another occasion while we were visiting Washington, in January 2010, I accompanied the Egyptian intelligence chief to his meeting with the director of the CIA, Leon Panetta, in Langley, Virginia, outside Washington. During the session, I asked to go to the restroom, and Panetta let me use the one attached to his office. As soon as I came back, I told him that he should sweep the restroom for the listening devices I had installed there. At first he looked a bit surprised, but as I was smiling, he knew that I was joking, and we laughed. He and General Omar Suleiman shared stories about the methods used by some intelligence agencies to plant listening devices to spy on their opponents, and about the successes each had enjoyed in this field.

Whenever I discussed the matter of U.S. assistance to Egypt, I came to the conclusion that the United States and Egypt should exclude it from their conversations in order to protect their relationship, which had so often been affected by financial considerations. In Egypt, we came to believe that this economic support, which had gradually been reduced from $815 million in 1980 to between $200 and $250 million in 2011, no longer represented a significant value to the Egyptian economy. Egypt could simply disregard it. I always thought that a successful visit by an Egyptian official to the Gulf would secure Arab aid far exceeding the American sum, but we were mainly concerned with the military assistance, the importance of which for the efficiency of the Egyptian Armed Forces I appreciated highly. In fact, the military aid has become the heart of the matter, the target that we have to defend against all attacks—both internal ones, regrettably, from Egyptians, and external ones, from Israel and the pro-Israel lobby in Washington. The military aid includes not only purchases of new arms and equipment, but also the spare parts needed to maintain them.

The relationship between two parties such as Egypt and the United States should be built on continuously increasing mutual understanding, as long as it serves their common interests. If one party is seeking to sustain the relationship while the other is jeopardizing it, the result will be a rupture the moment one party loses its grip.

# 5

# CHALLENGE AND CONFRONTATION: AN ATTEMPT TO EXPAND THE SECURITY COUNCIL

The attempt to expand the Security Council, begun in 1993, posed a serious challenge to all the members of the UN. In light of international developments that encouraged some of the African powers to act only in their own direct interests regardless of the international community as a whole, Egypt became aware, as did I, of the dangers threatening its international, regional, and African status if the council was expanded without taking African and Asian interests into account. In this chapter I will describe all the maneuvers that took place among the various countries in the service of their own interests.

The Charter of the United Nations provided for a Security Council of eleven members who represented the full membership of the UN and were responsible for achieving international peace and security. Five of these countries were granted permanent seats on the council. They were the founding members of the UN and the powers that had won the Second World War: the United States, the Soviet Union, Britain, France, and China. The UN Charter allows any of these permanent members, who are known as the P5, to object to any resolution presented to the council—in other words, each of them has veto power. The other six members of the council are elected for a two-year term and selected from different geographical regions. Many people do not know that Egypt was the first Arab, African, and Islamic country to be elected as a non-permanent member of the Security Council in 1946.

At the time the number of Security Council members was proportionate to the full membership, which was fifty-one states.

With the increase in membership as a result of the process of decolonization, during which many African and Asian states gained independence during the 1950s and 1960s, there were increasing demands for the expansion of non-permanent membership of the Security Council. After due deliberation, it was agreed in 1965 to increase the number of the non-permanent seats from six to ten. Each region would have a certain number of seats, and the entire UN membership would elect the representatives for those seats. For example, Africa had three non-permanent seats, South America and the Caribbean two seats, Asia two seats, and the remaining three were designated for Eastern and western Europe and others, bringing the total to fifteen.

No further increase had been made since 1965, despite the increasing number of member states. In the 1990s the Soviet Union broke up into a number of independent republics that all became members of the UN. The Socialist Federal Republic of Yugoslavia disintegrated as well, and many other countries joined the organization, which now has 193 members. As a result, there were demands to consider increasing the Security Council membership so as to have the same proportion to the full membership as had been the case in 1946 or 1965.

After the Cold War, armed conflicts broke out in some of the former Soviet republics and in the former Yugoslavia. Iraq invaded Kuwait and the so-called Second Gulf War erupted. The deliberations of the Security Council with respect to these issues were closely followed. The permanent members of the council clustered together in an attempt to dominate not just the council itself but the full UN membership. The influence of the General Assembly gradually diminished as the role of the Security Council and the collaboration among its permanent members increased. In 1992, Secretary General Boutros Boutros-Ghali presented his important report, "Agenda for Peace." Pressure to expand the Security Council increased for a number of reasons. One of these was to restore the proportion between the membership of the council and that of the UN as a whole. Another was that several countries had regained the international influence that they had lost during the Second World War, and felt that they had the right to a permanent seat on the Council. Among these powers were Japan and Germany, which had recovered economically to an extent that gave them major international influence. Their contributions to the budget of the UN and its agencies had grown to be far more than those of some of the permanent members: the Russian Federation now contributed only about 1.5 percent of the budget, whereas Japan donated 18 to 20 percent, and Germany 12 percent. Italy also felt entitled to a permanent seat; like Japan and Germany, it had been defeated in the Second World War but was now one of the seven major industrialized countries.

Other notable international powers, such as India, Brazil, and more recently Mexico, also felt that their strong economic and regional presence entitled them to demand a new status.

Africa protested against the historical injustice it had suffered from the nineteenth century until the 1960s. The Latin American countries followed suit, and both continents requested permanent seats. Although there was almost a consensus for the expansion, the members could not agree on what the expansion should look like. Some thought that both the permanent and non-permanent seats should be increased equally, while others insisted on expanding the non-permanent membership only. Each side had its reasons.

All the countries that hoped to obtain a permanent seat on the council, especially Japan, Germany, India, and Brazil, supported the expansion. So did Africa, as a matter of historical justice. It endorsed the expansion of the non-permanent seats hoping to add to its share, which was currently only three seats, or just 20 percent of the total membership of the council, even though the African countries represented one-third of the UN membership. Besides, Africa had only non-permanent seats, which were of far less importance than the permanent seats.

On the other side of the argument, other influential countries objected to the expansion of the permanent membership and thought that only the non-permanent seats should be expanded. These countries adopted different tactics. All the permanent members, except China, claimed that they approved the inclusion of new permanent members, while they had actually been politically and strategically maneuvering to defend the status they had enjoyed since the Second World War. The United States believed that it was necessary to respond positively to other countries' demands for change, but it only approved of an expansion that would not exceed five countries, which made it difficult to reach a settlement. Its attitude proved that perhaps it was supporting Japan only in order to irritate China and Russia, the most influential powers in the Pacific Ocean. Britain and France supported Germany's request for a permanent seat. Italy at once proposed the idea of a unified European representation. Although Russia claimed that it generally supported the expansion of the permanent seats for the sake of its economic and trade interests with Germany, Moscow certainly would not be happy to have Japan and Germany, whose economic and financial abilities then exceeded its own, added to the permanent member states. China was the only permanent member who definitely did not wish to see a historical adversary like Japan return to play an enhanced role in Asian and global affairs through this membership.

Another group of countries opposed the expansion of the permanent membership for complicated considerations of their own. They feared that if their traditional competitors had permanent seats, the imbalance of power among them would be increased. While India was aspiring to have a permanent seat, Pakistan was totally against the expansion of Security Council membership. Indonesia, Malaysia, and Singapore felt the same way as Pakistan. Argentina and Mexico were against Brazil, Italy and Spain against Germany, and the two Koreas against Japan.

The third and final group of countries that objected to the expansion of permanent seats on the Security Council felt that it would only increase the imbalance of power between the Security Council and the general members because every single one of the Security Council members would hold veto power. They foresaw that this would create new international centers of power, especially since the veto power had been used on many occasions to support a country's self-interest regardless of the international peace and security issues.

Egypt was an integral part of the developing countries' attitude toward this issue, within both the African group and the Non-Aligned Movement.

Both groups supported the expansion of both permanent and non-permanent memberships in order to improve the representation of the developing countries in the enlarged council. The only difference between them was that Africa insisted that the expansion should include both types of membership, while the Non-Aligned Movement was inclined to accept the expansion of the non-permanent seats only. Egypt took as its starting point the importance of maintaining African rights, at the same time seeking to preserve the unity of the African continent and avoiding splits between countries. Hence, we believed it was important to give all the countries of the continent the chance of having a permanent seat. We therefore supported two Security Council seats for Africa, one for the Islamic Arab north and the other for the sub-Saharan countries. During the period from 2004 until President Mubarak stepped down, there was much discussion about Egypt's diminished role and influence, the weakness of Egyptian foreign policy, and the country's inability to defend its various geographical and political interests. This was not actually the case: Egyptian diplomacy at the UN successfully defended the interests of Egypt and the African and Islamic regions against other African and international groups that sought to shut Egypt out. In the long run, however, it must be admitted that as the Security Council expanded and new countries, including African countries other than Egypt, obtained permanent seats, Egypt's lack of a permanent seat represents a possibly fatal blow from which it may take decades to recover. Both South Africa and Nigeria fought for permanent seats, at the expense of Egypt and the Arabs, in spite of our attempts to reach an understanding with them, as will be mentioned hereafter. We refused to submit to them, and were forced instead to challenge and confront.

In 1993, after "An Agenda for Peace" was issued, an open-ended working group was formed that included representatives of all the member states. Since then, this committee has been studying the expansion of the Security Council and reforms to its working methods, without any real progress. This is due not only to the conflicting interests of the various countries, but also the inherent complexity of the situation. The major factor is the veto power, which would be affected by both an expansion of membership and any procedural reform. Ways in which veto power is used, and ways of limiting the absolute freedom that this power gives to the permanent members to protect their own interests, have been studied. Consideration has been given to eliminating the veto completely, even for the current permanent members, which I do not believe is possible under any circumstances. As for expansion, the question now is whether or not to grant veto power to new permanent members, with the pros and cons each having its supporters.

As the Permanent Representative of Egypt to the UN (1999–2004), I observed the working of this group in a special way, for I was aware of the great harm that might be done to Egypt and its prestige if things turned out against our interests. I instructed the representatives of the Egyptian delegation working with the group to support Africa and the Non-Aligned Movement, and not to accept a compromise that might end up giving a permanent seat to a developing country without providing Egypt with an equal opportunity to obtain the same position. I kept the Ministry of Foreign Affairs accurately informed of the situation, but I noticed that they did not pay much attention to the issue, as if they thought it would not jeopardize our interests. I thought we were capable of dealing with the situation within the UN itself, completely forgetting that questions of this nature were mainly decided in terms of the status of the countries, their international and regional influence, and their ability to form coalitions and neutralize their opposition, aspects which Cairo should have taken into consideration over the years. To be honest, sometimes the Egyptian foreign policy establishment did play this game with great enthusiasm, but at other times it totally neglected it.

Without waiting for instructions from Cairo, I took the responsibility of cooperating with the ambassadors from South Africa and Nigeria, since they were most often mentioned as candidates for permanent seats in case of expansion.

The western powers of course favored South Africa, a racially diverse country that had close ties to the United States and the British Commonwealth, and a Gross National Product double or triple that of Egypt. Both South Africa and Nigeria had good reputations for their democracies, which the west approved of. Geographically, they were distant from the regions of serious disputes in the Middle East. This meant that influential regional powers would not be disturbed if these countries were assigned seats on an expanded Security Council. Israel, for example, would certainly not be happy if Egypt were to have a permanent seat; nor would Turkey, whose economic potential was three or four times that of Egypt; nor would Iran, which was aggressively competing for power and hegemony in the region.

I therefore met with the South African and Nigerian ambassadors and offered solutions. For example, we might agree to share the seats among the three of us, or with a fourth African country, on a rotation basis for the two seats assigned to Africa. Diplomats from the other two or three countries would be included in the delegations representing them in the council, so that, for example, if Egypt was granted a seat for several years, diplomats from the other countries would be seated with its delegation; they would exchange places when one of the other countries held the seat, and so on. No positive response was received from either Nigeria or South Africa.

By the spring of 2004, while I was representing Egypt in New York, I noticed some active movement on this issue in the communications among the ambassadors of the major countries and the UN secretary general. I had to alert Cairo. In March 2004, I sent a comprehensive report on this matter to the foreign minister in Cairo, which I concluded by saying, "The importance of the topic, and its impact on Egypt's regional and international standing in the future and for decades to come, requires us to continue to closely follow any development, or bilateral or multilateral communications, concerning this issue; to evaluate its impact on us; and to have a general idea of the possible avenues for action whether in Egypt, in New York, or in Addis Ababa." Paradoxically, in this report I referred to Addis Ababa in its capacity as the headquarters of the African Union, whose role, I believed then, would be merely to adopt the African position that was decided on in New York. I did not know that in the following years the file was to be completely transferred from New York to Addis Ababa, and that the entire world would be anxiously waiting for the African Union to speak for Africa.

I was correct in believing that the issue would be tackled soon. In his attempt to find a way out of this vicious circle, especially because he was to leave office soon, Kofi Annan appointed a group of senior diplomats to study the reform of the UN as a whole, not just the Security Council, and to present a report, including their suggestions, to the General Assembly. They delivered this report at the end of 2004. Although the report was more than ninety pages in length, only the three pages that contained suggestions for the expansion of the Security Council received international attention.

Without going into many technical details, I will briefly say that the suggestions in the report were limited to two options: either expand both the permanent and the non-permanent seats, or increase the number of non-permanent seats only. Both options would increase the number of seats on the council to twenty-four, an increase of nine. The first option allotted six of the new seats to permanent members (two of which would be assigned to Africa) and the other three to non-permanent ones (Africa receiving one of these, bringing the total number of non-permanent seats allotted to Africa to four). The second option had the expansion confined to the non-permanent seats. Of the nine new seats, just one seat would be added to the existing category of ten non-permanent seats (the extra seat to be given to Africa), for a total of eleven seats. The remaining eight new seats were allocated to a proposed new category of non-permanent membership. These eight seats would be elected for a four-year term, and a country could be reelected for consecutive terms, unlike the existing category of non-permanent membership, which has a two-year term and consecutive terms are not permitted.

The report disappointed both sides, those who supported the expansion and those who did not, because the working group had failed to propose a single plan. Both sides began to search the report for support for their respective positions.

The report also sharpened the differences between the two sides. The first camp, which supported the expansion of permanent seats and was larger in number, included the aspirants for the permanent seats, along with a large number of the developing countries. The second camp consisted of the countries who opposed the expansion of the permanent seats and wanted it restricted to the non-permanent ones.

The dispute spread all over the world, each side trying to attract as many supporters as possible in case the UN General Assembly needed to decide the question by voting. The second camp had the easier job. Passing a resolution in the General Assembly to expand the Security Council required 128 votes, whereas only half this number (64) was required to defeat the resolution and thus maintain the status quo. For members of the second camp, obstructing any expansion of the Security Council was preferable to allowing for the possibility that countries like Japan and Germany could become permanent members of the Security Council.

Regardless of the number of supporters each camp had, they were helpless without the support of the African group in the UN, not only because of its significant voting power (53 votes; Asia had 54 votes), but also because it was the only continent with a common position that could decisively tilt the balance in favor of the side it supported. This placed Africa at the center of the action, and moved the fight from the UN headquarters in New York to the African Union headquarters in Addis Ababa.

Meanwhile, I returned to Cairo in July 2004 to become the foreign minister. Since I knew that the report of the committee was about to be issued, one of my early decisions was to form a special unit concerned with the expansion of the Security Council. My office would be its headquarters and it would report directly to me.

When the report came out, I became aware of the conflicting pressures we would be facing: on one side, many of our friends would prompt us to support the expansion of both permanent and non-permanent seats, and on the other side, other countries, that were also our friends, would ask for our support in favor of limiting the expansion of the Security Council to non-permanent seats. And first and foremost, of course, there were the self-imposed pressures dictated by our national interests. I therefore asked to have the issue included on the agenda of the Cabinet in order to mobilize the necessary domestic support. I explained to my fellow ministers the great importance of this issue and its potential effects on our national interests, and emphasized the need to win both African and international support. In November 2004, I managed to have the Cabinet issue a resolution adopting the memorandum I presented on the subject. The resolution called for the mobilization of all efforts to support the Ministry of Foreign Affairs in its attempts to have Egypt win a permanent seat on the Security Council.

I wish to remind the reader that during the years I had been away, Egypt lost ground at the African level. We have to admit that Egypt's role in supporting the African liberation movements had placed Egypt in high regard in Africa. It maintained this status until the end of the 1980s or, perhaps, the mid-1990s, but it started to weaken as a result of the absence of the Egyptian president from the major activities held in Africa after the attempt on his life in Addis Ababa in 1995.

From my observation of our situation at the African level and what our experts in African affairs predicted about the diminishment of our role if our policies did not change, I felt the need to act forcefully, which I did as soon as I became foreign minister. I traveled to South Africa and Sudan a few days after I came to office, and visited Uganda, Kenya, and Tanzania before the end of 2004. All the African leaders I met asked where Egypt had been and why we had stayed away. It was paradoxical that this came to the surface at the beginning of 2005 when we were most in need of African support. As previously mentioned, Boutros-Ghali had been appointed as UN secretary general at the beginning of January 1992. When he left Cairo, Amr Moussa tried to cover all of Boutros-Ghali's job responsibilities, including Africa, without appointing a new state minister, as did Ahmed Maher later on.

As state minister for foreign affairs from October 2001 to July 2004, Fayza Abul-Naga tried to extend Egyptian activity across Africa. Unfortunately, her efforts were not enough to secure Egyptian interests. Once again, President Mubarak's absence from the African summits and activities went against our favor.

The paradox was clearly illustrated at the African Summit held in the capital of Nigeria, Abuja, in January 2005. It was the first summit I attended as the Egyptian foreign minister. I, as well as other members of the Egyptian delegation, sensed a feeling of acrimony toward us from the day of our arrival. However, I made it clear to the Egyptian delegates that our primary mission during the conference was to mingle with the African delegations and work on communicating with all the delegations present so as to preserve our common interests. I made every effort to meet with as many African foreign ministers as possible. I also invited them to visit Egypt, and promised to visit them as well, to discuss ways to develop our cooperation.

The South African and Nigerian foreign ministers were quite unfriendly. I was not surprised, since both countries were hoping for a permanent Security Council seat and they were aware that Egypt was their natural competitor, of whom they should be wary when voting time came around. The strength of Egypt's international relationships and its broad network of representation across five continents gave it a considerable edge. We kept all of our diplomatic missions around the world informed of all details of this issue. The Ministry of Foreign Affairs exchanged thousands of cables, recommendations, and letters with its missions abroad for the purpose of promoting our chances for a permanent seat.

Although Nigeria and South Africa exerted pressure on the rest of the African countries to support the expansion of both the permanent and the non-permanent seats on the Security Council, it was decided at the summit to form a committee that would evaluate the topic and meet by the end of the following February in Swaziland.

The committee did eventually meet to set out the criteria for the African candidate for the permanent seat. In the reports of the delegation I sent to attend the meeting, two points in particular seemed to reflect how disconnected the Egyptian–African relationship, and regretfully the Egyptian–Arab relationship too, had become. First, there was obviously coordination between Libya and Algeria on the one hand, and Nigeria and South Africa on the other. Second, the secretariat of the African Union presented a report in which it suggested that one of the qualifications should be that the candidate had played a prominent role in supporting the African liberation movements. Egypt undoubtedly met this criterion more than any other African country. It was expected that Nigeria and South Africa would reject this requirement, but what was really incomprehensible, and sad too, was that the Sudanese foreign minister supported them and asked to have this particular criterion deleted. He wondered what crime an African country had committed when it was unable to assist the African liberation movements because it suffered from racial segregation. Sudan's attitude made me realize the size of the challenges and difficulties we would be facing in defending our interests.

The Swaziland meeting ended with the adoption of a document which was later called the "Ezulwini Consensus," after the name of the city where it was held. This document did not include anything that would harm our interests, merely indicated the approval of the option which allowed the expansion of the permanent and non-permanent seats, demanded that Africa have two permanent seats with veto power and five other non-permanent seats, and postponed the discussion of the criteria for candidacy until later. During this period, we maintained constant contact with many African governments to support the Egyptian vision.

The Swaziland meeting was the starting point for a fierce election battle between the African parties who sought to stand as candidates on either of the two African permanent seats. It was clear from the very beginning that this battle was essentially for satisfying the voters rather than assessing the efficacy of the candidate. Frankly speaking, I knew that in order for Egypt to obtain the African support it needed to win a permanent seat, it would have to please every voter individually. Since the voters were not individuals but sovereign, independent countries, one had to think about what kind of "satisfaction" would suit each one. It could be cooperative programs in whatever commercial, economic, agricultural, and cultural fields they regarded as essential for them. The Ministry of Foreign Affairs was not the ministry that could provide these things; it would need to request assistance from the other government departments.

Although the Cabinet resolution held all the Egyptian ministries responsible for assisting the Ministry of Foreign Affairs in this matter, and I continued to send reports to all the political leadership and ministers informing them of the urgency of the situation and our need for their support to the African countries, I am very sorry to admit that we did not receive any real support from most of the Egyptian agencies. Some of them even refused to coordinate with the Ministry of Foreign Affairs on bilateral programs they were already implementing with a number of African countries. I could find no explanation for this other than lack of financial resources.

However, the Ministry of Foreign Affairs continued to promote Egypt's suitability for one of the two permanent seats allotted for Africa, as suggested in the senior diplomats' report, and to attempt to win African support in order to get onto one of the two African ballots before heading to the UN General Assembly for the nomination process.

During the period from 2005 to 2007, the management of this dossier and the restoration of Egyptian–African relations required a lot of time and a huge effort from me personally and from all the departments of the Ministry of Foreign Affairs. This period witnessed an unprecedented number of reciprocal visits between African foreign ministers. I was also eager to participate in all the ministerial meetings and the subsequent African summits. I seized every opportunity to strengthen our relationship with any African country, either through the Egyptian Fund for Technical Cooperation with Africa (EFTCA), which is part of the Ministry of Foreign Affairs, with its limited resources, or through the cooperation programs managed by the other Egyptian ministries. We tried to seek the help of our friends and brothers in the Gulf countries to convince various African countries to support the Egyptian position. Kuwait, the United Arab Emirates, and Oman were the first countries to offer their help.

Once I became aware of our weak position while in Abuja in January 2005, I estimated that the Ministry of Foreign Affairs would need at least four more years to overcome this period of weakness and to establish a new position that would make us reasonably competitive.

At the Arab level, I introduced a draft resolution at the Arab Summit held in Algeria in March 2005 calling on the other Arab countries to support Egypt in its attempt to obtain a permanent seat on the Security Council. The resolution was unanimously adopted as resolution no. B/307 on March 23, 2005. Although Algeria hosted the summit, it launched a fierce diplomatic campaign to discourage Arab support for the Egyptian endeavor. They even tried to suppress the resolution. I believe that Algeria was aware that it could not compete with Egypt within North Africa or the UN, and therefore tried to obstruct the African quest for permanent seats and preferred to restrict the expansion to the non-permanent seats. In this, it agreed with many medium-sized powers, such as Spain, Italy, Malaysia, Indonesia, Pakistan, and Argentina, which focused on this option for their own protection. Objectively speaking, I must admit that I preferred this option, because it was the best option in a world that did not need any more unrestricted powers.

As Algeria was obviously against the expansion of the permanent membership and would certainly object if Egypt happened to get a permanent seat, I decided to engage in Egyptian–Algerian cooperation and to make use of the broad Algerian presence across Africa to achieve our objectives for the time being. No need to cross the permanent-membership bridge until we came to it.

Many Egyptian foreign affairs experts sought a confrontation with the Algerians, whose motives they did not trust. Yet I insisted on cooperating with them in order to discourage the other Africans' aspirations and force them to recognize the rights of the Arabs, who did not have a permanent seat although as a group they contributed about 50 percent of the budget of the African Union.

Egypt's African rivals, Nigeria in particular, noticeably adopted unusual diplomatic methods to win international support for their nomination, either by coordinating with major countries, such as Japan and Germany, or by renouncing the African interests in order to satisfy the expectations of other countries. For example, the decision adopted at the Ezulwini meeting on February 22, 2005 stated that the African permanent members should have veto power, but, to our surprise, the Nigerian embassy in Beijing sent a memo to the Chinese Ministry of Foreign Affairs the day after the meeting, asking for China's support for the Nigerian candidacy and expressing their willingness to give up the veto power in return. It was shocking that Nigeria would compromise on the African demands in this manner while it was presiding over the African Union.

Although I received a copy of the memo from our embassy in Beijing, I ignored my staff's recommendations and did not disclose its contents to the other African countries, to ensure that we led a nomination campaign reflecting Egyptian values and ethics.

However, when Nigeria began attacking Egypt, I had to think about changing this approach. For instance, I was surprised by a fierce Nigerian media campaign against Egypt, which reached its peak when the Nigerian president himself attacked Egypt in an interview and said that it should not be considered an African country. The Nigerian foreign minister followed his president's example at the Sirte Conference in Libya in July 2005. I had no choice but to interrupt him, and wave the memo from the Nigerian Embassy in Beijing at the foreign ministers who were present. While I was telling the story to the African foreign ministers, who were appalled at the Nigerian misconduct, my Egyptian colleagues distributed copies of the memo among the other delegations to verify my story.

The Nigerian was at his wits' end. He kept screaming, trying to interrupt me, and claimed that the memo was a mistake on the part of their ambassador to China. It was clear that the other ministers did not believe him. The meeting ended with a new African resolution that reiterated all the elements of the African position, and neither Nigeria nor South Africa got what they hoped for: African support for their nomination for the permanent seats.

South Africa launched its nomination campaign that ran until at least mid-2005, promoting its suitability for the seat without attacking the other candidates, and Egypt did the same. It was Nigeria that was aggressive toward Egypt. I believed from the beginning that South Africa persuaded Nigeria to confront the other countries and draw their hostility, while South Africa put its own efforts into winning the race. The final step took place—or rather, South Africa thought it did—when four other countries who were seeking permanent membership—Japan, Germany, India, and Brazil—invited the African countries to a joint meeting for coordination as soon as the Sirte Conference ended.

The meeting was held in New York on July 19, 2005. In spite of the efforts of Nigeria and South Africa to soften the stance of the other African countries, the meeting did not reach a conclusion. The African delegations upheld their demand for two permanent seats and five non-permanent ones, and refused to waive the veto power. It was impossible to reach an agreement since the four non-African countries were ready to support Africa's request for two permanent seats, but refused to support the five non-permanent seats for fear of angering the other geographical groups. They could not agree to support veto power for the new permanent members, because they were fully aware that the countries that currently had permanent membership would not accept it at all, and in fact would rather block the expansion completely than grant this power to the new countries.

The failure of the meeting did not discourage the four non-African countries. They agreed, along with the African Union chair, Nigeria, to hold a second meeting the very next week. This meeting was held in London on July 25, 2005. It was quite amusing that the foreign ministers of Brazil, Germany, India, and Japan were seated in the lounge outside the meeting hall for four or five hours waiting for the African group to reach an agreement among themselves concerning their demands. This was a stormy meeting, in which Egypt led a number of the African countries that absolutely refused to give up any of the African demands (including veto power). They finally agreed to simply listen to what the four foreign ministers would offer without responding positively or negatively before reporting to the African heads of state at the Addis Ababa summit in January 2006. However, the African delegations were taken by surprise by the German foreign minister's request to meet individually with his Nigerian counterpart in a side room adjacent to the meeting hall. While the German minister kept coming back occasionally to coordinate with the other three foreign ministers, the Nigerian minister remained inside and left the other African delegations uninformed. As soon as the bilateral meeting ended, the Nigerian minister returned to his seat and refused to answer any of the other African ministers' queries. He only spoke when the official meeting between the four countries and the African delegations started. The four countries stated the elements of the agreement, which included a fifth non-permanent seat on the condition that it would not be exclusively allotted to Africa, but rotated among all the geographical groups. The South African foreign minister thought that the moment had finally come and immediately agreed without consulting the other African delegations. Her Nigerian counterpart even voluntarily announced that Africa waived the veto power. Many African delegations, with Egypt at the forefront, objected so furiously that the Nigerian minister had to adjourn the meeting.

It is worth noting here that on July 18, 2005, when the coordination between Nigeria and South Africa was apparently at its height, we received a Nigerian presidential envoy in Cairo. He delivered a message seeking our mutual support to obtain membership on the Security Council. He added that South Africa could not represent the continent, since it had only recently been recognized as an African country and was not yet fully informed on African affairs. The Nigerian national security advisor also met with our ambassador in Abuja and passed along the same message. There is no need to comment on this situation, which uncovered the methods adopted by our rivals in this matter.

The African attitude toward the demands of the four countries remained ambiguous. Hoping to settle the matter, Nigeria called for an emergency African summit in Addis Ababa on August 4, 2005. Most African countries were so unhappy with the Nigerian approach that they ignored this invitation. The secretariat of the African Union even circulated a note indicating that the summit would not be held due to the lack of the required quorum, but surprisingly, we received another note stating exactly the opposite from the African Union chair, Nigeria, indicating that the summit was to be held in spite of the note sent from the secretariat of the union. This was an unprecedented violation of the procedural rules of the African Union.

I would like to share here the following sequence of events. The sole Nigerian aim for holding this summit was obviously to force the African countries to give up their demands and comply with the propositions of the four countries, regardless of their relevance to African interests. Nigeria clearly took advantage of the fact that it held the presidency of the union and therefore controlled the African meetings to ignore any opposition to the president's suggestions and to impose the opinion that best served its own interests. My staff, who were working on this file, handed me a memo that included all the considerations, and suggested that we refuse to participate in the emergency summit or commit to its resolutions. I gathered them to hear the opinions of each one of them. They all agreed that it was necessary to boycott the summit, but I promised only to think it over. I spent the night thinking about the situation and its possible consequences. I finally decided that we should attend the summit and strongly defend our interests. I could not imagine Egypt being absent from such a crucial African summit. The next day I informed my staff of my decision to attend. We immediately set to work on our plan. I called several African foreign ministers to warn them of the dangers of the Nigerian approach for African interests. We also sent an official note to all the African countries exposing Nigeria's violation of the legal norms.

We had messages ready from President Mubarak to all the African presidents in which we urged them to sustain the African position in all respects. We felt that the veto power should not be waived and that Africa should be granted two permanent seats—demands that would hardly be accepted by the current permanent members, who were refusing to give the new members veto power or to add more than five seats, whereas we wanted to add six seats (two for Africa, and one each for Japan, India, Germany, and Brazil).

I was convinced that Japan, Indian, Germany, and Brazil were making serious efforts toward permanent membership. I did not trust the current permanent members or their real motivations, even though I was certain they would reject any expansion. I also feared that something might happen that would affect Egyptian interests for decades to come. I therefore phoned President Mubarak, who had not been informed of the situation before, and explained the whole thing to him. I prepared a detailed written presentation and enlisted the help of the competent secretary of information to the president, Suleiman Awad, whose extended service as deputy permanent representative of Egypt to the UN in New York did much to convince the president of the importance of the issue and its impact on Egypt's international standing. The president started to show signs of interest and, like me, was inclined to support the expansion of the non-permanent seats only because he was certain that there would be no expansion of the permanent seats. He often repeated what the U.S. deputy secretary of state had mentioned in a consultation regarding America's refusal of the suggested African expansion. The president, however, was eager to sign the letters to the African presidents, which were promptly sent to all the African leaders to study before the exceptional summit was held.

We arrived in Addis Ababa the day before the summit. Since we were running short of time, I met with the African foreign ministers to prompt them to uphold the legitimate African demands. While many African heads of state were representing their countries, the Egyptian delegation was headed by the foreign minister. Yet I managed to meet with a number of African heads of state and explain the situation to them.

The emergency summit began at ten o'clock on the morning of August 4. It consisted of one session that lasted for seven continuous hours of heated debate, which forced all the attendees to remain seated and not leave even for a few minutes. The session began with the Nigerian foreign minister giving an account of the London meeting from his point of view. I had to interrupt him more than once to point out the inaccuracy of his story, especially when he claimed that it was agreed in London to amend the African demands. While the chairperson of the meeting, the Nigerian president, was trying to have his foreign minister's report approved, the Zambian president interrupted him to express his dissatisfaction with the way the session was being managed, backed by a number of other delegates who shared the same feelings. In spite of the South African president's quiet attempts to help his Nigerian ally, it was obvious that the African attendees had had quite enough. The summit ended with the rejection of the amendments to the African demands and the reaffirmation of their support for the original demands. This was a victory for us and for the efforts of the Egyptian Ministry of Foreign Affairs over the previous months to maintain African cohesion. Our trip back home was one of the happiest moments my colleagues and I ever had.

From Addis Ababa Airport, I called the secretary of information to the president, who had been trying all day to find out how things were going. I informed him of the situation, and told him in English, "We defeated our opponents," while the Nigerian foreign minister was passing in front of me. Ambassador Suleiman Awad called the president, who was at Borg al-Arab, to brief him on the situation. All during the flight from Addis Ababa to Cairo, the president kept asking whether we had arrived yet, and gave me instructions to call him as soon as we reached Cairo. We arrived at 11:00 p.m. When I got home, I called the president on the secure line, but his secretary said that he would not wake him up unless it was urgent. I decided to wait until the following day. I was surprised to hear the presidential telephone ring in my bedroom on Friday morning at 7:00 a.m. The president was calling to ask for a full report, and kept inquiring about the details of my statement.

Nigeria did not abandon its attempts to change the African attitude. As the head of the African Union, it tried to call for a second emergency summit in November 2005. It could not achieve its goals this time either, and the summit ended with the adoption of a new resolution that reaffirmed the African position.

I would claim that the failure of the two Addis Ababa summits, in August and November 2005, to alter the African attitude was the turning point at which the issue of expanding the Security Council began to subside entirely at the international level. The four non-African countries were convinced that their African allies were unable to bring the other Africans around, and consequently, they would not mobilize enough votes to adopt a draft resolution concerning the expansion of the Security Council in the General Assembly. International interest in the issue began to wane, especially when Egypt succeeded once again at thwarting further attempts to amend the African demands at the summits held in Khartoum in January 2006, Banjul (Gambia) in July 2006, and all other subsequent summits up until now. The passage of a resolution to maintain the African demands first mentioned in the Ezulwini Consensus has become a routine process.

China was fighting ferociously against Japan and India, fearing that they would obtain permanent seats. Thus we worked together closely. I cooperated with China to benefit from its great influence on the African scene. China was providing billions of dollars of economic assistance to African countries. The Egyptian economic cooperation program with Africa did not exceed ten million dollars in 2004 (although it was gradually increased as a result of my pressure on the prime minister, reaching $23 million in 2011). The Chinese support, therefore, was greatly needed to achieve our common objective. We did not object to other countries, such as Japan and Germany, obtaining permanent membership as long as it would not have any harmful effects on us. I always informed the foreign ministers of both countries in all our meetings of our vision regarding this matter. I also had a discussion with the Japanese foreign minister in connection with the meeting of the foreign ministers of the countries concerned with Iraqi affairs in Sharm al-Sheikh in November 2004. I told him that while Egypt understood Japan's ambitions and was ready to support them, Japan was likewise obliged to support Egypt in obtaining a seat if the expansion was agreed upon. If Japan refused to help Egypt, Egypt would not help Japan and might even seek to thwart it. The Japanese minister was astonished at the words of this "reckless" Egyptian minister who made threats far beyond his country's abilities. I was truly confident, however, that we could gather the Africans around us. During the visit of the Indian foreign minister to Cairo, I tried again to convince him to join forces with us, but the Indians did not accept our offer.

I was worried about Libya's position under the leadership of Qadhafi, whose sole idea was to have one permanent seat for the representative of the African Union, not an individual African country. He came up with ideas that I knew the international community would reject. What really worried me was that things might turn out so that Qadhafi would believe that Libya could have the permanent seat assigned to Africa, and then, when another African country took it, the Arabs would be unseated as a result of the Libyan confusion. The Senegalese president, Abdoulaye Wade, who was competing with the South African and Nigerian presidents, supported Qadhafi's view. This pro-Qadhafi opportunism bothered me a great deal, because Qadhafi was trying to convince President Mubarak of his good intentions during their meetings and asked him to change the Egyptian position, which I defended.

I remember that I severely criticized the Nigerian foreign minister in front of Mubarak and Qadhafi, calling him an "imprudent, ignorant" minister. I noticed that President Mubarak was displeased. He even asked Ambassador Suleiman Awad to tell me that he was surprised at my harsh attitude and did not like to offend officials of other countries, especially in the presence of a third party.

The Nigerians played against us. They were rough and outrageous. I made a statement in which I criticized some of their public attitudes toward Egypt and their conversations about it. The president expressed his concern and said that it was not appropriate to clash with African parties. I explained that I was normally quite considerate but that the Nigerians had overstepped the bounds in this fierce battle against us.

At the Khartoum summit the Nigerian president claimed that Sudan could not preside over the African Union because of the charges of the International Criminal Court (ICC) against al-Bashir. As a result, he said, the Union should consider extending the Nigerian presidency to a third term. We refused, and mobilized efforts to support a third party. We succeeded, and Nigeria left the presidency, to be replaced by Gambia.

The battle over the expansion of the Security Council forced us to work hard to maximize our leverage and try to strengthen our international position in preparation for another possible African or international struggle for the voting at the UN.

I had been working for a long time to reach an understanding with Brazil and India. I assured them that Egypt was the key to Africa, not any other country, by which I meant Nigeria. I convinced Mubarak that it was important to build strong relationships with Brazil and South Africa, and to restore ties with India. Mubarak traveled to India and then to South Africa. At my insistence, he planned more than once to travel to Brazil, with side trips to Argentina and possibly Mexico, but his grandson's death and his own deteriorating health kept him from going on such a long trip. My great hopes for his greater participation in international affairs were confounded by his limited physical abilities and his inner circle's concern about him.

According to a report I handed to the president, he was to discuss with the Indian prime minister and the South African president Egypt's desire to join the IBSA. I personally visited Brazil twice and received positive reactions, but these countries were maneuvering, keeping in mind the expansion of the Security Council. I urged the Egyptian government to open up to them. Many ministers took the initiative, but they considered trade to be the only key to dealing with these countries. We also had, and still have, a good relationship with the BRIC countries (Brazil, Russia, India, and China), who have emerging economic capabilities and great potential to influence international trade. I was certain that South Africa would try to join this group. In an attempt to get Egypt in first, I corresponded with the foreign ministers of these countries and they seemed to support the idea. Our vital political role was greatly appreciated. It was this status that I used to compensate for our vulnerable economy in our dealings with them, as well as on the global economic level. I should admit once more that the economies of these countries greatly surpassed ours, but it was worth a try. I wanted to avoid a recurrence of what had happened in 2000 and thereafter, when we neglected to reply to the invitation of India and Brazil to join them; they included South Africa instead, forming the IBSA.

We were not happy when the G8 invited a group of countries with rising economies, including Mexico, Brazil, India, South Africa, and China, without extending the invitation to any of us whose economic capabilities fell short of the requirements needed for attendance. Egypt was only invited as a member of the New Partnership for Africa's Development (NEPAD), which included Nigeria, Algeria, South Africa, and Senegal besides Egypt. The G8 invitees met with them for no more than one hour. We made great efforts to convince the G8 of the importance of having Egypt join them. Italy, our Mediterranean partner, invited us to attend L'Aquila Summit, and the president went, after a long absence from these kinds of meetings. France, which co-chaired the Union for the Mediterranean (UFM) with Egypt, invited us to their major economies summit, and the president attended it as well. Things started to move ahead. In his attempt to strengthen French–German cooperation at the European and international levels, President Sarkozy of France asked to revive the issue of the expansion of the Security Council, and in 2007 and later he called for the expansion of the permanent membership to include Brazil, India, Japan, Germany, and an African country, perhaps South Africa. We were infuriated but held back our anger. We did not criticize the French openly but had serious talks with them in closed meetings. Sarkozy then had a change of heart and said that an Arab country representing the Arab and Islamic civilization should also be included. Our position was restored.

Sarkozy suggested adding more countries to the G8 to reach twelve or thirteen. We considered this as a threat to us and insisted that France should reconsider this suggestion. Sarkozy then talked about adding Egypt, along with China, Brazil, South Africa, Mexico, and India, to the group of rising economies, which would comprise fourteen countries.

When Germany hosted a summit of industrialized countries in the city of Heiligendamm on the Baltic Sea, we tried to convince them to invite us along with South Africa, Mexico, India, Brazil, and China, but our request was turned down. The Germans explained that they were not the only ones authorized to issue invitations. We did not accept this explanation, especially since Italy and France later revealed that the host was free to choose the guest countries. Consequently, we decided that Mubarak, who had been invited as a member of NEPAD, would not participate. Chancellor Angela Merkel was displeased and her relationship with the Egyptian president remained frosty for a while. I told the German foreign minister that they needed to understand how vital this matter was to us, and that everything was a matter of give and take. Nothing was for free.

Much to our surprise, a British minister put forward South Africa as the occupant of the permanent seat assigned to Africa, if there was ever to be one. We had to explain to the British the responsibilities of the members of the Security Council to pursue international security and peace. Such responsibilities were not determined solely according to the economic capacity of the countries or their influence in a marginal geographical region, by which we meant the South African region, but according to their military capacity, their contribution to international security and peace, their participation in UN peacekeeping operations, or their international diplomatic impact. After that, the British became more cautious in dealing with this issue. At the same time, we coordinated with the Ministry of Defense to reinforce the Egyptian presence within the UN peacekeeping forces in Africa and internationally. With the cooperation of the Ministry of Defense, the Egyptian contribution to the UN forces increased dramatically.

Sarkozy returned to the African scene, and in an African–French summit he attempted to impose changes in the African position. The co-chairs of the Union for the Mediterranean, Egypt and France, competed and fought a silent battle, until Egypt prevailed. French meddling in African affairs ended. The French president learned his lesson, and decided to try to win the Egyptians over by suggesting a strategic alliance among Egypt, Brazil, India, and France, and to hold a four-way summit in the summer of 2009. The idea was never realized, although we were ready to endorse it. When we saw that Mexico was not ready to acknowledge the expectations of the other rising powers, we talked to them, helped the Mexican foreign minister make the Mexico climate summit a success, and asked them to consider our demands regarding the issue of cooperation with the emerging powers.

To counter the deterioration of the international economy in 2008, the western powers, at the invitation of Britain, reactivated the G20, which consisted of twenty major economies that had been brought together for the first time in 1998. At that time Egypt had been invited to join, but because it ignored the invitation, it was not granted membership. The revived G20 was to replace the G8 in cooperating with the emerging economies. This meant that the efforts we had made over the years to join the G8 were wasted, and now the only choice we had was to join the G20. We asked the British, the French, and all the other members of the G20 for permissions to join them, but they avoided the topic. Some even admitted that Egypt was not as economically qualified as Turkey, Spain, Malaysia, Saudi Arabia, Indonesia, and other emerging economies.

The World Bank president proposed to form a steering committee to address the international economic situation. Saudi Arabia and South Africa were named as members. I wrote to him insisting that he should consider Egypt for membership. He explained that the Gross Domestic Product (GDP) of these countries was very high compared to Egypt's. The U.S. convened a G20 summit in Pittsburgh and the U.S. president disregarded our demands. I talked to Rice and wrote to her to protest, but all in vain. Things were not developing the way we would have liked. Our absence from groups that were determined by economic standards was bound to have political consequences. I decided not to ignore these major summits, held in London, Pittsburgh, Seoul, and Toronto, which we did not attend, but took every opportunity to criticize the countries which sought to dominate the world while excluding everyone else.

We kept on working. We expanded our diplomatic relations to include the island countries of the Pacific Ocean and the Caribbean, and some small European principalities. Our goal was to collect votes in the UN General Assembly, especially since we observed that both Nigeria and South Africa were developing their relations with South America and the Caribbean islands and attending conferences in those places in an attempt to strengthen their relationship with what is known as "African Diaspora."

I never ceased repeating the elements of Egyptian power: the largest armed forces in Africa, able to contribute to peacekeeping operations and always ready to provide more; the largest number of diplomatic missions, both inside and outside of Africa, of any African countries, allowing it to exert an international influence for peace and security; considerable soft power, both cultural and economic, in many forms: Arab, Islamic, Christian, African, Asian, and Mediterranean. These are matters that the international community takes into consideration, or it should, in making decisions about the Security Council.

Coming to the end of this chapter, I wish to emphasize that Egypt did not seek to hamper the expansion of the Security Council, but it could not stand still while others were pursuing their own interests at the expense of Egypt's. If we have to impede the interests of others in order to maintain ours, we will not hesitate for a second; in this case, however, the Egyptian interests are identical to the legitimate African aspirations. Thus, we could not consent to renounce the rights of all Africans in order to satisfy the ambitions of a few.

# 6

# THE NILE RIVER: CHALLENGES AND ATTEMPTS TO REACH AN UNDERSTANDING

One of my chief concerns as foreign minister, and the most critical for our national security, is the Nile River. I have to admit that throughout my working years in diplomacy and foreign policy I did not have a real chance to focus seriously on this matter, especially since the Egyptian Ministry of Irrigation was totally responsible for this issue and had reputable experts who were fully acquainted with the river, its resources, and the rules governing its historical legal agreements. Still, the Nile was regarded as a priority for all the Egyptian national security agencies, notably the Ministry of Defense and the General Intelligence Service. Egypt was making serious efforts to interact with Nile basin riparian states. The Nile actually consists of two rivers: the Blue Nile, which originates in the northern Ethiopian highlands, flows into Sudan, and supplies almost 86 percent of the Nile water that enters Egyptian territory at latitude 22°, and the White Nile, which flows from the Tropical African Plateau and joins the Blue Nile in Khartoum, forming the Nile River as it is known in Egypt.

During the years when I served at the UN, I always had the impression that the countries of the river basin were always complaining of our negligence, in spite of our continuous concern with their affairs. I wish to mention that all points discussed herein in connection with the Nile express my own point of view as an Egyptian foreign minister who sought to support Egypt's vital interests and protect its legitimate share of the water; to educate the coming generations about the situation; and to keep everyone informed for the nearly seven years during which I served as foreign minister. Hence, one of my priorities was to visit the Nile Basin countries and become acquainted with the many aspects of the situation, so that I could deal with a complex situation that had begun in the last decades of the nineteenth century and persisted into the twenty-first. Egypt has had a presence in Sudan since the campaign of Tosson Pasha, Muhammad Ali's son, at the beginning of the nineteenth century. It has also experienced friendships, hostilities, and clashes with Ethiopia and the various peoples of Sudan.

As soon as I took office, I asked the officials in the African affairs and legal departments to provide me with a detailed report on the development of the Nile dossier, particularly the basin countries and the negotiations on the legal and institutional frameworks of the Nile Basin Initiative (NBI). I began to learn some of the details of this initiative from a letter I received from the minister of irrigation, Dr. Mahmoud Abu-Zeid, in which he mentioned that the negotiations were entering a more sensitive stage, and were becoming more political than technical. This important letter made me realize that although we had a small department at the ministry which monitored the water issue in general and the Nile water in particular, this department was not taken care of as it should, either by recruiting efficient staff or participating actively in all related fields. I asked to have a permanent working group formed that would support the Ministry of Irrigation in the negotiations on the Comprehensive Framework Agreement.

In August 2004, I went on an African tour, visiting Kenya, Uganda, and Sudan. Although the officials and the media in Kenya and Uganda were concerned with the role of Egypt in Africa and its relations with their countries, it was surprising and sad to see their bitterness toward anything to do with the Arabs, and for reasons I believe we had nothing to do with. In Kenya I met with the entire leadership, who accused the Sudanese regime of complicating their relationship with Egypt and the Arabs. They called on Egypt to give special attention to their economic problems. I told them that we all suffered from the disturbing developments in Sudan, and we should help the country find a way out, not complicate things further by taking sides in their internal disputes. As for our bilateral relations, I explained that we worked with them according to the Common Market for Eastern and Southern Africa Agreement (COMESA), which promoted bilateral trade so that we could benefit from the customs exemptions that the agreement provided. As a result, we bought most of our tea from Kenya instead of India and Sri Lanka, which made the latter two countries unhappy. In response to a complaint from some representatives in the Kenyan Parliament that their regions could not obtain drinking water despite their closeness to the shores of Lake Victoria, I told them that at that time Egypt was digging a hundred wells in Kenya to supply water. With the help of the minister of irrigation, I managed to increase this to 120 wells in the following years, which were dug by the Egyptian engineers and technicians at the General Company for Research and Ground Water (REGWA). We both took part in the inauguration of one of the wells in July 2006.

This visit opened my eyes to the feelings of suspicion and cautiousness the Kenyans had toward us. At the end of this visit, I held a press conference and had separate meetings with people from the media in Kenya, who were highly aggressive, saying accusingly, "You take our water and enjoy it without giving us anything in return. We need development, electricity, and energy." I explained that we were not depriving them of anything because the rain kept falling; they could use as much of it as they wished and there would still be plenty left for everyone else. I assured them that Egypt benefited from only 4 percent or 5 percent of the rainwater, that Egypt received only 55 billion cubic meters of a total of 1.6 trillion cubic meters of the rain which fell on the river basin, and that we could all work together to increase the usable amount. But all my words fell on deaf ears.

I left for Uganda. I arrived in the evening and met with President Yoweri Museveni at 11:00 p.m. As I handed him a written message from President Mubarak, he said, "You know? No Egyptian pharaoh has ever visited us, even though your origins go back to us here in Uganda and the Upper Nile!" When I returned to Cairo, I told the president what Museveni had said. He remarked that Museveni forgot that he had visited him during an African tour when he was vice-president. At the African Union Summit in Abuja in January 2005, I made a point of seeking out Museveni and telling him what President Mubarak had said. He replied, "I wish the president would pay me a visit, and not the vice-president who had become a president." I promised that I would bring him to Uganda. In the following years, I managed to convince the president to travel to South Africa and to stop for a few hours at Entebbe Airport on the shores of Lake Victoria in Uganda. The Egyptian security agencies resisted the idea of stopping in Uganda, worried that his plane might be vulnerable to attacks from the bushes and swamps near the airport. The road from the airport to Kampala was also a security concern—it is very narrow, with high-density housing on both sides. I talked the president into going and asserted that there would certainly be serious consequences if we did not make a point of having the Egyptian head of state visit them. In the end, I convinced him to make a visit for a few hours. The president did not visit Kenya, Tanzania, or any of the other basin countries during my tenure as foreign minister.

I was received by Museveni at a humble African residence but with a warm welcome and great respect for the visiting Egyptian minister. The Ugandan president said, "Couldn't you make your brothers with the large white turbans stop their brutal clash with the tribes in southern Sudan? They are causing damage to everyone." I then surmised that what I had heard in Kenya was not an isolated matter, that there was indeed a problem, whether real or fabricated, and that these countries were strongly opposed to the actions of the Sudanese government. Museveni accused al-Bashir of meddling in Ugandan affairs, and assisting and financing Ugandan groups that led armed resistance against his rule in Kampala. Then he mentioned the difficulties his country faced in meeting its energy needs, pointing to the fact that the water level of Lake Victoria was decreasing sharply as a result of the low rainfall in all the provinces of the equatorial plateau. They needed electricity so that the inhabitants of this area would not use the wood from the forests to produce energy. The loss of forests led to reduced rainfall and consequently the loss of renewable swamps. In Nairobi, I had heard many Kenyans accuse Uganda of reducing the lake's water level. They did not believe that lack of rainfall, or of water reaching the lake, was causing the low levels, but that Uganda was diverting large amounts of water through the Owen Dam to produce electricity, to the detriment of Tanzania and Kenya.

I did not wish to argue about Sudan with President Museveni. I just said that we were trying to help it as much as possible to overcome its current difficulties. I then mentioned that Egypt was interested in building good relations with Uganda, and was trying to help them by increasing water flows in the small rivers that drained into the White Nile. Egypt was putting a lot of money and effort into this project. Museveni agreed, and confirmed that we were financing many projects including ones to uproot weeds and water hyacinth from the beds of the small rivers in Uganda. I held a press conference and had interviews with several newspapers and television channels in Uganda. Once again I encountered aggressive questions: "You take the water and don't give anything in return." I explained repeatedly that the rain nature bestowed upon them provided them with many benefits, and that the topographic features of the area pushed the water from the plateau down into the riverbed. Without the river, we could not survive. Their problem, I believe, was that they faced difficulties in developing their economy while they watched Egypt develop and prosper. Museveni spoke enthusiastically about the new group he was trying to form in Eastern Africa for the purpose of developing political and economic cooperation in the region. This group was to include Kenya, Uganda, Tanzania, Rwanda, and Burundi. He thought that this group would have leverage over the continent. When I returned to Cairo, I asked the Department of African Affairs at the ministry to follow closely the latest developments of the formation of this group, its institutions, capacities, regulations, and impacts on the African policies and on the economies of the COMESA countries, and our bilateral relations with these countries. When Museveni talked about the historical relations between his area and Egypt, he referred to the drawings of animals and birds he had seen in the temples and cemeteries of the Egyptian pharaohs; the cows, in particular, were similar to the ones they had in Eastern Africa in general and in Uganda in particular. He said again that we shared the same origin. He also said that all this should make us cooperate for our common interests, and Egypt should seek to help them and build bridges between the different countries. Neither in Kenya nor Uganda were the negotiations on the Nile River Basin Initiative (NBI) discussed in detail.

On my way back from Uganda, I passed through Khartoum, where I met Foreign Minister Mustafa Osman Ismail and other state ministers. I recounted my impressions of my visits to Kenya and Uganda. I sensed a hint of criticism when they spoke about Museveni and the Ugandan policies in the region. They criticized the Ugandan intrusion over the years to provoke southern Sudan, and believed that Uganda sought hegemony over eastern Africa and southern Sudan. Although I was eager to hear their opinions, I was careful not to fall prey to old hostilities and disagreements that would complicate matters for me.

We had embassies in all of the eastern African countries. I decided that we should give more attention to this region, to have our embassies and missions work more effectively, and to recommend the best-qualified people for these positions, which required special abilities and loyalty to the priorities of our country. This was not an easy task because our ambassadors tried to avoid being appointed to these African countries. The lower-ranking staff also wished to serve in more lively, comfortable places. To combat this reluctance, we provided them with better facilities and medical care, gave them special prices on holiday trips, and significantly raised the state's contribution to school fees. Nevertheless, many of these difficulties still existed at the end of my tenure. Many of our diplomats talked about the importance of Africa and the need to give it diplomatic priority, but when the time came for annual transfers, they often turned down African appointments. For years, I sorrowfully watched Egyptian diplomats, especially the higher-ranking staff, persistently refuse to serve in Africa. I supplied the department concerned with the Nile River with personnel and facilities and asked the African department to strengthen cooperation and work more closely with the Ministry of Irrigation and the Egyptian national security agencies.

In the weeks after my return from my first African tour, I started to plan a visit to Ethiopia and Tanzania. By the time I left office in 2011, I had visited Ethiopia about ten times, and Kenya and Tanzania several times each. The long journeys and the condition of the planes made these visits difficult for me. In Ethiopia, I met with Prime Minister Meles Zenawi, who received me at the state palace. The shrewd foreign minister, Seyoum

Mesfin, was also present. Zenawi discussed the historical tensions between Egypt and Ethiopia and added that it was time for Egypt to be aware of the importance of Ethiopia and our bilateral cooperation. The Ethiopian prime minister severely criticized Eritrea and its president, Isaias Afwerki, and accused Egypt of being against Ethiopia in the past, as if he meant to say that we helped Eritrea become independent by supporting the revolutionary organizations which were fighting against Emperor Haile Selassie or during the rule of Mengistu Haile Mariam. I told him that Egypt sought to have strong relations with Ethiopia and did not back Eritrea against them, although I had to admit that there were voices in Egypt that sought to cause trouble for Ethiopia by working with Eritrea to pressure Ethiopia over the Nile. By saying this I meant to imply that he should seek an agreement with us concerning the water issue in particular, and not to push us away in the direction of other parties. I did not wish to argue with him about his relationship with Isaias Awerki, their alliance against Mengistu Haile Mariam, and their cooperation with Mengistu, which had lasted for years until they fell into disagreement. I did assure him that we wished to develop our relations in all fields, especially our trade relations and the subject of meat imports, to which they paid great attention. I told him that Egypt imported hundreds of millions of dollars' worth of meat every year, and we could gradually switch to Ethiopia, but they had to help us by carefully inspecting their exported meat, this being a delicate matter for the Egyptian people. I felt that he was anxious to enter the Egyptian market. When I returned to Cairo, I mentioned to the Cabinet that there was a wide range of issues on which we could communicate with Ethiopia, overcome all the difficulties we had for decades, and settle many of our chronic disagreements, especially the water issue.

Egypt's imports of meat and cattle was the primary topic of our discussions with the Africans. The Ethiopians gave it special priority, the Kenyans displayed the livestock they had available to export to us, and the Tanzanian president offered large areas for us to use for breeding the required livestock, as well as the possibility of setting up slaughterhouses for us at their ports, where our veterinary inspectors would be present. I brought the matter before the Cabinet, which decided to look into the Tanzanian offers, and the relevant ministries and agencies were asked to follow up. As for Ethiopia, we had a real intention to buy its meat and to promote our bilateral relations, but, unfortunately, little was achieved in this area, because the meat import mafia in Egypt fought for its own interests. This led to the disruption of our relations with Ethiopia, Uganda, Kenya, Tanzania, and South Sudan, all of which felt embittered toward Egypt for breaking its promise in this area.

We approached Ethiopia and sought to restore the tripartite cooperation initiative among the foreign ministers of Egypt, Sudan, and Ethiopia. We held trilateral meetings to promote cooperation in many fields, mainly the issue of the Nile waters. We encouraged the Ethiopian prime minister to come to Egypt to visit the president. He did come to attend the New Partnership for Africa's Development (NEPAD) summit in May 2005, which improved the relations between the two countries. When Ethiopian troops entered Somalia, Egypt did not express any objection. We only told the Ethiopian foreign minister, Seyoum Mesfin, that although we understood the need for Ethiopia to intervene in Somalia in order to resist the armed groups that controlled it, we hoped that their troops would stay only long enough to accomplish their mission and leave. Otherwise, they would find themselves entangled in a potentially harmful situation. Seyoum Mesfin felt Egypt's desire to reassure Ethiopia and that we were not looking for conflict with Ethiopia or Eritrea. Nonetheless, because the Nile negotiations were becoming complicated, as will be discussed later, the Ethiopian prime minister mentioned to me on at least two occasions—once in 2009 and again in July 2010 during my visit accompanied by Minister Fayza Abul-Naga—that they monitored our communications with groups opposed to the regime in Addis Ababa. He added that they understood our wish to put pressure on them concerning the Nile dossier, but that it would be useless. He advised us to stop these acts because they were detrimental to our relations. When I briefed General Omar Suleiman, he denied completely that we were trying to damage Ethiopia any way, and explained that our cooperation with Eritrea would not threaten our relations with Ethiopia. I have to admit that Egyptian–Ethiopian relations, which had a history of unpleasant experiences, were unstable. Nevertheless, Egypt had certainly decided during the first years of the twenty-first century to sustain a positive relationship with Ethiopia. In spite of our efforts, the suspicions of the Ethiopians made it difficult to develop our relationship as well as we had hoped.

I will now discuss the negotiations concerning the Nile, which are the main topic of this chapter. First, I will review the historical background and the methods Egypt adopted over the past century to maintain its water rights with respect to the other basin countries.

The Nile has always played an important role in Egypt's relationship with the external world. In the first years of the twentieth century, Britain, which was occupying Egypt and Sudan, tried to exploit the river to threaten and pressure the Egyptian government. For example, in 1913 Britain conducted studies for building the Sennar Dam on the Blue Nile in order to indicate to the internal powers in Egypt, which were growing increasingly discontent, that their actions could cause them trouble. On another occasion, Field Marshal Edmund Allenby warned Saad Zaghloul that Britain planned to increase the cultivated land in Sudan by diverting Nile water. After the British sirdar's assassination, Britain grew cotton in the Gezira area in Sudan, and allotted 4.5 billion cubic meters of water for this purpose, as a punishment for the Egyptians.

Throughout the twentieth century Egypt has faced difficulties in its relations with the other basin parties. In 1958, before signing the 1959 Nile Waters Agreement that established quotas for Egypt and Sudan, Sudan announced that it would not comply with the 1929 Agreement, which it had not signed. This situation was related to the crisis of the Gezira irrigation project in Sudan. The other upstream countries followed suit. Upon its independence, Tanzania insisted that it would not sign an agreement with Britain on its succession to treaties concluded on its behalf by Britain, and President Julius Nyerere declared the Nyerere Doctrine, which did not recognize the agreements signed by Britain on behalf of Tanzania, including the 1929 Agreement, in spite of his good relations with Egyptian President Nasser at the time. Uganda, Kenya, and Burundi did the same upon their independence in the early 1960s.

During this period there were several attempts to promote cooperation among the basin countries. First there was the Hydromet project for conducting studies in the equatorial lakes in 1964, followed by the UNDUGU group, formed in 1983 to undertake development projects in the basin countries. In 1995 the Tecconile project was founded, from which the idea of an agreement to govern the cooperation among the basin countries was born. Finally the Nile Basin Initiative (NBI) was proposed by the World Bank to promote the cooperation among the basin countries by reaching an agreement on the regulations for the use of the Nile waters, and the establishment of an institutional framework—a ministerial council assisted by a technical advisory committee and a permanent secretariat based in Entebbe, Uganda.

I believe that the persistence of the upstream countries in refusing to engage in cooperation in accordance with the existing agreements from the time of their independence to 1999 hampered all attempts to establish the principle of collective benefit. Each party maintained its position, so that, at the UN Conference on Water held in Mar del Plata, Argentina in 1977, Ethiopia presented a paper in which it asserted its authority to use the Nile water without any restrictions. In 1997 it reiterated the same position during a General Assembly session to adopt a convention for non-navigational uses of international watercourses. With the introduction of the NBI in 1999, a new opportunity was provided to study and implement joint projects for the benefit of the peoples of the basin countries in a way that would serve the interests of all without prejudice.

Although the NBI aimed from the very beginning to support cooperation among the basin countries, create development projects, and control water loss, to the benefit of all, there was a shift in focus over the years. The parties became preoccupied with arguments over the Draft Framework Agreement, which was concerned with the recognition of rights, current usages, and prior notification of any future projects that upstream countries are planning to implement. The upstream countries rejected this draft, claiming that the existing agreements were connected to the colonial period, and thus no longer applicable. These claims could be refuted because all international agreements dealing with rivers recognized existing agreements, including the Helsinki Rules in 1966, the 1997 UN Convention, and the Berlin Rules, as well as the regional agreements, such as the agreements made within various African, European, and Latin American groupings.

Hoping to end the continuous arguments over the conditions of the Framework Agreement, the basin countries formed a negotiating committee at the beginning of 2004 to resume work on the Draft Framework Agreement and to reach a compromise. The committee failed to find an agreement. This was the situation when I took office in 2004: a deadlock over the relationship between the new Draft Framework Agreement and the existing agreements. Egypt demanded that the new Draft Framework Agreement should not affect the existing agreements, which preserved Egypt's rights and its designated quota, while the upstream countries refused to recognize these agreements. Furthermore, Egypt insisted that the agreement must include a clear provision on the prior notification and the procedures required for any projects that any country intended to implement on the river.

In this complicated situation at the beginning of 2005, the Ministry of Foreign Affairs also had to deal with a looming political situation concerning the Nile waters. Although it was not clear yet how things would turn out, it would certainly result in a crisis with technical, legal, and political elements that would require a comprehensive approach on the part of Egypt. The Higher Committee of Nile Water was formed, presided over by the prime minister and comprising a large number of ministers and other government officials. The committee was charged with conducting periodical followups of the negotiations, identifying the benchmarks, determining when to be resilient or inflexible, and supporting Egyptian negotiators by proposing projects that would connect the basin countries with Egypt and encourage them to cooperate with Egypt rather than clash with it.

The Ministry of Irrigation was responsible for establishing the limits for negotiation, and providing the practical alternatives according to the available data on the water resources. It pointed out that the Egyptian water quota, set at 55.5 billion cubic meters annually by the 1959 Agreement, was fixed, while the population had steadily increased to more than 83 million people. The resulting per-capita amount was less than 700 cubic meters annually, which was below the water poverty limit. Nuclear desalination plants were too expensive for Egypt to afford. The ministry also stated that the existing agreements prohibited the upstream countries from launching any project that would affect Egypt's quota without the consent of the Egyptian government, and that Egypt would definitely reject any agreement that would decrease its quota, especially since the upstream countries had other abundant water resources. Ethiopia, for example, had eleven river basins, providing 1.023 trillion cubic meters of water per year, and an average annual rainfall of 923 billion cubic meters. Uganda was so rich in water resources that 17 percent of its territory was submerged lands and wetlands. In Tanzania there were two hundred rivers, and 1.6 trillion cubic meters flowed in the Congo River annually, most of which ended up in the ocean. According to this technical evaluation, the objectives were set as follows: to preserve Egypt's water quota without any concessions; to seek to increase the available water by controlling water loss; to set up joint development projects with the upstream countries, support our bilateral relations, and avoid escalation; and to benefit from international grants and assistance.

In view of this stressful situation, in February 2006 Dr. Mahmoud Abu-Zeid and I decided to travel to Tanzania, Kenya, Uganda, Burundi, and Rwanda, and to include Ethiopia on a later trip. During this tour the influence of the Egyptian minister of irrigation and water resources became clear. He had been negotiating for five years to defend Egypt's historical rights to the river water. When the other basin countries rejected the colonial-era agreements, he agreed to replace them with a new concept suggested by World Bank experts, Water Security for All. This meant that any new framework agreement reached in the negotiations for the NBI was to have no negative effects on the water security of the basin countries, their current usage, or their present or future rights. During our tour, we tried to convince the leaderships of the five countries to accept the international and Egyptian proposals. We assured them that Egypt intended to work with them to meet the demands of development in their countries. We received positive reactions, but no agreement was reached. Without going into the many technical and legal details, there were two points of contention that dominated the discussion. One was reconciling the new framework agreement, which was being negotiated, with the previous water agreements.

The other was setting up notification procedures to ensure that projects in upstream countries would not damage the countries farther downstream. When the negotiating committees failed to reach a consensus, creating a crisis, they brought the matter before the ministers of water resources. During 2007 and 2008, these ministers held several rounds of negotiation in Bujumbura (Burundi), Entebbe, and Cairo, but failed to reach an agreement. Dr. Mahmoud Abu-Zeid told me that it was agreed that the Uganda meeting would adopt the provision of water security, within the Draft Framework Agreement, with Egypt and Sudan expressing reservations, and that the dispute would be referred to the heads of state and government of the basin countries. In July 2008, the ministers of water resources met again in Kinshasa, where they agreed to give the Congolese minister of irrigation and water resources, who was presiding over the meeting, a period of three months to reach a consensual solution on water security.

Once the water issue was passed along to the political leaders of the Nile riparian states countries, the foreign ministers assumed secondary roles. It quickly became clear that Ethiopia had assumed the leading role, which it was using for its own ends without any consideration for Egypt or Sudan. We felt that we needed to talk the Ethiopians into changing their attitude.

Because of the involvement of the countries' heads of state, we had to proceed with caution. To be honest, I was worried that the Egyptian president would not grasp many of the technical or legal details, especially when he attended a closed meeting with the other presidents on his own, this being a feature of the African methodology. Mubarak's personality prevented him from going into complicated details. I had to protect our position against any risk. On the other hand, I believed that escalating the issue in such a manner without any real indication of flexibility from the others would result in the failure of the presidential meeting, which in turn would lead to confrontation.

On the evening of September 9, 2008, while I was attending al-Azhar's celebration of the Islamic New Year, during which the president was to give a short speech before a large gathering of government and religious officials, I met with Dr. Mahmoud Abu-Zeid, who had full knowledge of the water case and its difficulties, and we discussed the latest developments of the situation. The next morning I was surprised to hear that he had been replaced by a new minister of irrigation and water resources, Dr. Mohamed Nasr Eldin Allam. When I asked the president's secretary of information about it, he explained that Dr. Abu-Zeid had disagreed with the prime minister and some of the other ministers. I was frustrated. I went and talked to the General Intelligence chief, who had no knowledge of the matter and seemed upset at this turn of events. I could not understand how the chief negotiator on a vital issue could be replaced while we were in a middle of a battle of which he knew all the subtleties and details. I felt that it indicated a lack of clear understanding of the conditions of the negotiations, and would weaken the Egyptian negotiating capacity, not because the Egyptian position was inherently weak, but because of the new minister's unfamiliarity with the issue and the personalities. When the new minister asked to meet me, I greeted him in my office and assured him that the Ministry of Foreign Affairs would support him in all respects, and that we had an active staff working in harmony and full coordination. In the end, it took three years of internal work as well as work with other state agencies, Egyptian universities, nongovernmental organizations, and experts on this and other closely related issues to arrive at a water agreement.

To return to the 2008 negotiations, the Congolese minister tried to implement the mandate he had received at the Kinshasa meeting, but failed. At the urgent request of the basin countries, the Congo called for an exceptional meeting in Kinshasa. This meeting brought discord and divisiveness. It was the first meeting to be held after the appointment of the new Egyptian minister of irrigation and water resources. I was surprised by a call I received from Dr. Mohamed Nasr Eldin Allam in Kinshasa. He told me that the seven upstream countries—Ethiopia, Kenya, Tanzania, Uganda, Rwanda, Burundi, and Democratic Republic of the Congo—had agreed to sign the Draft Framework Agreement separately. They claimed that it had been more than ten years since the negotiations had started, and they would not wait for the approval of Egypt and Sudan. The minister added that Sudan had withdrawn from the meeting, and asked what he should do in this situation. I told him that withdrawal was not an option for Egypt and that it was necessary to keep working until the situation was thoroughly studied. He had to return to the meeting and calmly report Egypt's reservations about the attitude of the other countries, especially the fact that all decisions were to be made by consensus, which meant that the majority could not overrule the minority. Egypt insisted on including an article in the Agreement that ensured water security, existing rights, and present and future usage, and another article about the need for prior notification of any new project. Egypt also insisted that any future amendments to the articles of the Framework should be by full consensus. Following the meeting, Sudan and Egypt agreed to send a joint memorandum to the chairman of the Council of the Ministers of the Democratic Republic of the Congo stating their rejection of the resolutions of the Kinshasa exceptional meeting.

Four weeks later, on July 27, 2009, a meeting of the water ministers of the basin countries was held in Alexandria. After a hard struggle, it was agreed that all of the riparian countries needed to act in a coordinated manner. Both the technical and negotiating committees were to convene three meetings in six months to resolve the points of disagreement, so that all the Nile countries could act in unison. These meetings failed to achieve their goals because each country held so strongly to its opinion.

I took great interest in the work of the minister of irrigation and water resources, because he had taken over the Nile Basin dossier at a critical time that required both technical knowledge of the issue and demonstration of statesmanship in order to balance Egypt's requirements with the need for good relations with the upstream countries. It was a difficult task that required an awareness of the African nature along with the technical requirements. The new minister did have the necessary technical qualifications. He was a hard worker, and eager to preserve Egypt's water rights. I also knew that his academic and scientific background had not given him any political experience. As the meetings progressed, a number of our ambassadors to the basin countries remarked on the nervousness of the Egyptian delegation, by which they meant the head of the delegation, and his continuous attempts to override the upstream countries. I spoke with the minister of irrigation and the prime minister about this; they both cited the difficult circumstances of the negotiations. With the countries in open disagreement, and the press statements being given by the Egyptian minister, I became aware of the profound differences among the ministers of irrigation, which could only complicate the situation and would not serve our cause. I discussed the situation with the president, who seemed annoyed and spoke with the prime minister and the minister of irrigation and water resources. In view of the president's age, and his incomplete knowledge of the issues, I did not think that he should become further involved. I believed that the prime minister, who also presided over the Higher Committee for Water which had been formed years ago and had been working regularly, could carry out the duties perfectly. Yet it would not be easy to exclude the president if a meeting of the heads of state were held in Cairo, while if the meeting were held in another basin country and he did not attend, it would give the wrong impression to the other participants.

I suggested to the president that he invite some of the other presidents for individual discussions on the water initiative in connection with the Forum on China–Africa Cooperation in November 2009, hoping that this might change the situation or at least clear the air. We extended an invitation to the presidents of Kenya, Tanzania, and Rwanda, and the prime minister of Ethiopia, to visit Cairo. The presidents of Tanzania and Rwanda did come and displayed a lot of flexibility, and we decided to promote Egyptian assistance programs for both countries. We also used the occasion of the Forum on China–Africa Cooperation, and the participation of the Ugandan president and the Ethiopian prime minister in that event, for further attempts to promote our views. They met with the Egyptian prime minister, who expressed our point of view in detail. The Ethiopian prime minister stated that they would not change their attitude regarding the historical agreements.

We felt it was important for us to try to avoid divisiveness. It was decided to hold a meeting for the ministers of irrigation in February 2010, at the end of the agreed-upon six months, in Sharm al-Sheikh to reconsider the situation, when the rest of the basin countries were still threatening to sign the proposed Framework Agreement despite the Egyptian and Sudanese objections. I also spoke with many foreign ministers and officials in the Gulf, urging them to use their influence over the basin countries, where they had large investments, to persuade them to change their attitude toward us, and many promised they would.

Some of the basin countries flatly refused the proposed Egyptian draft on water security. Uganda reiterated what I had repeatedly heard from President Museveni, that with due respect to the needs of Egypt and Sudan for water considering their desert nature, the economic development of the upstream countries and the effects of climate change demanded the use of Nile water. This would decrease the amount of water reaching Egypt and Sudan, and it was important to guarantee that it would not greatly affect the water security of those two countries. The Ugandans stressed the necessity of fair usage without causing damage to other countries sharing the Nile water. They also strongly recommended establishing a commission to monitor the execution of the Framework Agreement and the commitment of the countries to the rule of international law.

In accordance with the decision of the Higher Committee for Water to provide substantial assistance to the basin countries in order to influence their attitudes, the Ministry of Foreign Affairs presented to the prime minister a list of their requirements and recommendations. I had been expressing my fear all along to the prime minister and the other members of the Higher Committee that we would be faced with extortion attempts, and that our financial means would fall short of supplying the assistance the upstream Nile Basin states were expecting. I preferred to focus on building a relationship of common interest by enhancing trade relations and using them to influence the other parties.

The World Bank sources and the other donors were not optimistic about a breakthrough, and suggested that we should look for new negotiating methods. Although donor partners were eager to reach consent on the Draft Framework Agreement, they realized too much haste could be fatal, due to the extreme sensitivity of the controversial points. This is in fact what happened, as will be seen later.

I followed the negotiations and meetings that were held during the last months of 2009 closely and reached some conclusions, which I sent to the prime minister, who presided over the Higher Committee for Water, and to the other members of the committee. I informed them that Egypt was facing a bloc of seven countries that were insisting on signing the Draft Framework Agreement without the consent of Egypt and Sudan, and without the article on water security, the most important article for Egypt. The last rounds of negotiations had proved the difficulty of changing the attitudes of the seven countries, which were becoming increasingly inflexible. I added that proposals advanced by the upstream countries were not acceptable to Egypt even if they did not represent a direct threat to Egyptian water rights and usage in the short term, because Egyptian public opinion would never tolerate it. I warned them that the signing of the Framework Agreement without Egypt and Sudan would be disastrous, because the upstream countries might later try to redistribute the water quotas among themselves with no input from us. I also believed that Egyptian diplomacy had the necessary tools to influence the countries in question and the donor partners, so as to block any project in the upstream countries which might jeopardize Egypt's water security. I recommended that we look for alternatives, one of which was the signing of a memorandum of understanding for project implementation in which the basin countries would agree on a package of projects to be executed in the long term (ten to twenty-five years) with international financing, to support economic development and enhance the river resources. Another alternative was a proposal from the World Bank for a simplified agreement to form a commission of the basin countries, which would regulate the relations among these countries and implement development projects involving the river resources. The third and last alternative was a mix of the first two, which would avoid legal complications and not make the upstream countries feel that the ten years of negotiations had been wasted. A commission would be established to supervise the memorandum of understanding for executing projects, as provided in the first alternative, while negotiations on the Framework Agreement continued.

I suggested that we discuss the matter first with Sudan after all the internal authorities approved, and then with the donors, who would have a major influence. I reminded everyone about the prime minister's meeting with Meles Zenawi in Sharm al-Sheikh in connection with the Forum on China–Africa Cooperation, when Zenawi called for trilateral cooperation among Egypt, Sudan, and Ethiopia and consultation on the Eastern (or

Blue) Nile. I asked the prime minister to follow up on this matter with Zenawi on his upcoming visit to Addis Ababa, since the suggestions Zenawi had made could be the key to getting things moving. At the end of December 2009, the Higher Committee approved the proposition for a simplified agreement on the formation of a commission of the basin countries that would supervise development projects. Upon its approval, I provided the Higher Committee with a paper including the main elements of the proposition and the ways to execute it in coordination with the donors and the basin countries. The Egyptian and Sudanese sides discussed methods of implementation during intensive consultations, which also revealed points of disagreement between them that needed more time for discussion.

At the end of December 2009, the Egyptian prime minister, at the head of a large delegation of Egyptian businessmen, visited Ethiopia. I followed the situation with great concern because I was convinced that Ethiopia was the key to dealing with the situation, and that it was seeking any possible advantages for itself. My advice was to be careful that Ethiopia, or any other basin country, did not make demands that were beyond our capabilities. In fact, Meles Zenawi stressed that the economic relationship should necessarily be separated from the negotiations on the Framework Agreement. This was an additional indication of Ethiopia's intention to move forward with the signing of the Agreement in spite of our objection. Again I warned the prime minister and the other state agencies, including the minister of irrigation. I also proposed a set of additional procedures for dealing with the situation, including putting gradual pressure on the upstream countries and embarrassing them in a way that would secure the support of the donor countries and the international donor community for the Egyptian demands, especially the idea of establishing a simplified institutional agreement. I also proposed promoting these ideas with the donor states, the foremost of which was the United States, and continued efforts to promote our relationship with each individual country without succumbing to extortion. I suggested assembling the legal defenses for the Egyptian position with the assistance of an international expert. These procedures were to be conducted simultaneously. I stressed that it was important to send a peaceful media message that would make us appear calm and composed.

I then suggested that a delegation of all the Egyptian agencies presided over by the officials of the Ministry of Foreign Affairs should travel to Washington to hold talks with the Americans and the World Bank concerning the establishment of the simplified commission, and to explain the Egyptian position regarding the proposed Framework Agreement. Our delegation received a positive reaction to their visit, and the U.S. officials were totally aware of the difficulty of reaching a consensus on the Framework Agreement. They agreed on the importance of proceeding directly with the formation of the commission. They would help with regard to the African countries. They mentioned the environmental challenges facing eastern Africa, including food shortages and climate change, as well as the political challenges in Sudan. They also expressed their wish to bring Egypt and Ethiopia closer together. Finally, they proposed an Egyptian–Ethiopian political declaration in support of the commission. I felt that the U.S. reaction was encouraging and would help to the situation.

While the debate between the upstream and downstream countries was going on, I read an important report by a senior international lawyer who had done a lot of work for Egypt. He mentioned that if Egypt acceded to the Draft Framework Agreement as agreed upon by the upstream countries, the Agreement should explicitly stipulate that the new Framework Agreement would not affect the existing agreements, especially since the Agreement in its current form did not address the existing principles of usage and rights. This was a clear warning to the upstream countries.

As the ministerial meeting in Sharm al-Sheikh approached and the probability that the upstream countries would sign the Framework Agreement without taking Egypt into account, I asked the president's office to prepare letters to be sent to the heads of state of the upstream countries, urging them to agree to the simplified commission and not sign the more complex Agreement. Furthermore, the minister of irrigation suggested that Egypt offer generous gifts to the upstream countries, to the value of $100 million, without demanding anything in particular in return. I strongly objected to this suggestion, which would open the way for long-term extortion by those countries. This was indicated by the demands of Burundi and some of the other basin countries, which amounted to hundreds of millions of dollars. The president's letters were delivered by Egyptian representatives at the ministerial level. The Egyptian ministers of foreign affairs and international cooperation visited Addis Ababa to discuss the Egyptian president's letter and its implementation, and the Ethiopians promised to respond to our suggestions.

I received a suggestion from Dr. Nabil al-Arabi, from whose legal expertise we had benefited, in which he referred to the importance of making one last attempt to introduce amendments to the provisions of the Framework Agreement. The amendments would provide for the use of the same formulations given in the 1966 Helsinki rules, which included the primary rules for regulating river management on an international level. They also included compliance with the existing agreements and the necessity of prior notification for new river projects, and provided for a dispute mechanism in case of disagreement. I referred the suggestion to the chairman of the Higher Committee for study, even though I knew that Ethiopia had refused to comply with it when it was first proposed in 1997. I also asked the legal department at the Ministry of Foreign Affairs to form a committee that included international law experts specializing in these kinds of amendments. This committee produced a draft that upheld the rights and the current usages that were being rejected by the upstream countries.

Sudan was coming under increasing pressure from its neighbors to abandon Egypt. We convinced the Sudanese that their endorsement was vital to Egypt because the internal Sudanese situation was exerting pressure on both of us.

The majority of the basin countries, including Ethiopia, expressed their willingness to move forward with the formation of the commission while, at the same time, they refused to abandon the Draft Framework Agreement. It seemed inevitable that we were heading for a crisis.

At the Sharm al-Sheikh meeting on April 13, which was held under Egyptian chairmanship, the attendees examined the outcomes of the technical meetings, which had failed to reach an agreement, and the upstream countries insisted on having the Framework Agreement open for signature as it stood, to take effect on May 14, 2010. Egypt responded with the legal arguments it had assembled and its historical rights as confirmed by international law. The Ministry of Foreign Affairs formulated the Egyptian positions for the minutes of the meetings, which emphasized our refusal of the procedure in form and substance, and our adherence to the existing agreements, which ensured our water rights.

I suggested to the prime minister that Egypt, together with the donors, should object publicly and legally to the establishment of any project on the river by the countries supporting the initiative that would affect Egypt and Sudan, since the old agreements were not being complied with and Egypt would not recognize the Framework Agreement. We held a meeting at the Ministry of Foreign Affairs with all the ambassadors and donor representatives to Cairo to inform them of the development of the situation and our objections. We also sent a message to the president of the World Bank, to the donors, and to the foreign ministers and other officials of the donor countries, setting forth our position, warning of the possible implications, and asking the World Bank and the international donors to convince the upstream countries that it was necessary to maintain the Basin Initiative and not ignore it by signing the new Framework Agreement. I also registered Egypt's position with the UN by sending a detailed letter to the UN secretary general.

We received positive responses from the World Bank to the letter I sent to its president, Robert Zoellick. In her talks with our ambassador in Washington, the vice-president of the bank indicated that the bank's rules about international rivers were very clear. They set out specific steps to be followed for the prior notification of projects that would negatively affect other countries, and stated that the consent of the affected countries was required before the projects could be financed or executed through the bank.

It had been a month since the Framework Agreement was opened for signature. Four countries—Uganda, Ethiopia, Tanzania, and Rwanda—signed it on May 14. I knew it was just a matter of time before these countries achieved their goal of having six countries sign the agreement. They would then claim that the agreement had come into force, ignoring the fact that the agreement of nine countries had been needed to open it for signature in the first place, and that the signatures of all the basin countries were required in order for the agreement to come into force. Both of these prerequisites were stipulated by the Framework Agreement itself.

I suggested to the president that Egypt suspend its participation in all the activities of the Nile Basin Initiative as a sign of protest against the signatories and the international partners, and request a meeting of the basin countries, the donor countries, and the other donors to resolve the situation. This did not mean that we would totally withdraw from the Initiative or let the upstream countries have the upper hand. The president preferred not to start a confrontation, but to continue trying to reach an understanding among all parties, which I believed to be impossible in view of my talks with many officials of these countries. A diplomatic confrontation was a must. We tried to persuade the remaining countries to defer their signing. Kenya refused outright, while Burundi and the Democratic Republic of the Congo were clearly trying to get from us whatever they could by holding us over a barrel, and we sent them millions of dollars' worth of aid. In the light of these developments, I wrote to the UN secretary general informing him that the countries that had signed the draft had overstepped the rules governing the Nile Basin Initiative.

On May 26, 2010, the Supreme Committee on Water Resources met to discuss the situation. Following the president's instructions, it was decided to continue the dialogues and projects that had begun in the context of the meetings of the Initiative. Hence, the Egyptian delegations and the minister of irrigation and water resources were assigned to attend the meetings, monitor the situation, and hamper any attempts by the upstream countries to implement the agreement and establish the commission. Since Meles Zenawi and the Ethiopian foreign minister were talking about the development of an Eastern Nile (Blue Nile) project, we decided to look for ways to cooperate with Ethiopia to develop this basin. In order for Egypt to maintain its bilateral relationships with the upstream countries, we considered it preferable to continue as usual with the Egyptian projects in these countries, except for the well-drilling projects in Uganda and Tanzania. We were aware of the recent developments in southern Sudan and the inevitability of its secession. Consequently, we decided to intensify our presence in southern Sudan and support the Egyptian projects there. Since the agreement still needed one more signature in order to become official, Egypt planned to persuade both Burundi and the Democratic Republic of the Congo not to sign it and to have them stand with us, or at least remain neutral if they felt they could not support Egypt and Sudan. We therefore increased their development assistance to $50 million for each of them for a period of five years. I felt this was blackmail, especially in the case of Burundi.

Joseph Kabila, the president of the Congo, came to Egypt at Mubarak's invitation. During his visit, he was eager to reiterate his support to Egypt. He had some requests for us, of course, and we discussed the development programs and assistance that Egypt could provide the Congo in different areas, taking into account the Congo's abundant mineral resources. I suggested that we would respond according to our capabilities and the things at which we were most proficient, such as military and security training, agriculture, and medicine. Kabila's visit was very important and we gave him a hearty, hospitable Egyptian reception. Mubarak knew about Kabila's obsession with motorcycles and decided to give him as a present an old motorcycle from the Nasser era, which he greatly appreciated.

As for Burundi, we accepted its incessant demands which lasted from the day of the first signatures on May 14, 2010 until Burundi itself signed it at the end of February 2011. During these eight months, we sent different kinds of assistance and millions of pounds. It seemed our efforts were never enough.

I had asked our ambassador in Paris to ask the French, who maintained good relations with Burundi and were influential there, to do their best to keep Burundi from signing the Framework Agreement. I also addressed the matter myself during one of my periodic meetings with the French foreign minister, Bernard Kouchner, who promised to do what he thought was necessary to accomplish this goal.

I always knew that neither Egyptian economic assistance nor bribery, regardless of its size and influence, would completely solve the problem. It would have a short-term effect, and then things would go back to the way they had been before. The real alternative was the establishment of long-term mutual interests. Trade, I believed, was the cornerstone. We could engage these countries in trade and economic interests that would offer direct, tangible advantages for their people as well as for us.

Ethiopia, Tanzania, Kenya, Uganda, and South Sudan were offering their meat and cattle for sale to the Egyptian and Arab market when we were, and still are, influenced by our own short-sighted interests. They offered us vast lands for growing what we needed and developing our own livestock resources in our own markets. We expressed our enthusiasm for their cattle proposals verbally without taking any action. Our businessmen showed interest, but their passion for the idea was short-lived, and they rarely kept their promises. We held monthly briefing sessions for Egyptian companies that wished to work in Africa, to inform them of the circumstances and opportunities in these countries and the laws governing foreign investments. We also provided the opportunity for all African officials visiting Egypt upon the invitation of our different agencies to visit our industrial cities, companies, and factories. Unfortunately, many of these companies did not try very hard to penetrate African markets, despite all the encouragement they received. There was some talk of the Nasr Company, which had operated in Africa during the revolutionary tide in the 1960s, resuming its business, but nobody mentioned that the company was still working at a low level in some African countries. No one wanted to admit that the governments and their companies did a great deal of promoting, but did not actually enter the trade market, invest, or promote development, while in the 1960s an Egyptian company had worked as an undercover agent for Egyptian intelligence operations in the liberation struggle in Africa, a kind of struggle that does not exist any more. Consequently, companies had lost their luster.

After the initial signatures of the Framework Agreement on May 14, there was an increased demand for intervention and assistance. The Europeans publicly admitted that although the Nile Basin Initiative was facing a serious problem because of the inability of the basin countries to reach a consensus concerning the Agreement, the donor countries and the other donors did not want to give up so easily and continued to work on it. The European sources also added that the six equatorial upstream countries could not technically affect Egypt's water quota; in particular, Uganda could not stop the water from flowing out of the northern end of Lake Victoria or from the dam area in southern Sudan. Nor could Ethiopia greatly affect Egypt's water quota, with its heavy rains and its primary concern with hydroelectric projects that represented no danger to Egypt.

The European sources, including the British sources, which had full knowledge of the issue, also suggested that the Nile Basin be divided into two sections so that we would have one river with two systems. The first system would encompass the equatorial plateau countries, where the donors' financed projects would not have any harmful effects at all on the two downstream countries. The second system, which included Egypt, Sudan, and Ethiopia, would execute joint projects in the Eastern Nile Basin, which would focus on Ethiopia, and projects for decreasing water loss, from which all of the Eastern Nile Basin countries would benefit. These European studies concluded that this arrangement could replace the Nile Basin Initiative, which had never achieved its objective of reaching an agreement that included all the basin countries. We carefully studied all these suggestions and their potential effects on us. I always insisted that, under any circumstances, Egypt should insist on its right to be notified ahead of any plans or projects. Nothing should be done without ensuring the preservation of Egypt's agreed-upon water quota.

In parallel with these European suggestions, Ethiopia had also been providing ideas, which had been suggested by U.S. universities and other American experts since 1964. Ethiopia suggested that Egypt should consider storing water in huge reservoirs in the Ethiopian highlands in order to avoid the evaporation to which the dam exposed the river within the Egyptian borders. This idea naturally appealed to Ethiopia because it would provide water reservoirs and produce electricity, as well as bringing Egypt under its control. These ideas were completely rejected; Egypt should store its water reserves within its own territory. We had to keep in mind that these U.S. ideas were brought up when Egypt was working with the Soviet Union in building the High Dam, and the United States was probably trying to cause trouble. Plans were drawn up for thirty-three small dams in the Ethiopian Highlands, but the lack of safety and stability shattered those dreams.

I did ask our agencies to study these suggestions, bearing in mind that our main concern at the time was to block the Framework Agreement. After that, we could consider any creative idea that would enable all the countries to protect their interests.

During the period from June 22 to 28, 2010, the countries of the Nile Basin Initiative held another ministerial meeting in which both Egypt and Sudan participated. Sudan announced that it would suspend its participation until a Comprehensive Framework Agreement on the whole situation was reached. We then concluded that the Eastern Nile project would be dropped, thus putting pressure on Ethiopia. I asked the Egyptian minister of irrigation and water resources to be careful not to make any decision that would upset Egyptian–Sudanese unity. The vice-president of the World Bank, representing the donors, also participated in the meeting. I asked the Egyptian delegation to state that Egypt would be willing to accept a mediator or a facilitator in the negotiations. Some of the names I suggested were former U.S. secretary of state James Baker, former British prime minister Tony Blair, former South African president Thabo Mbeki, and the former UN secretary general Kofi Annan. President Zoellick of the World Bank had in fact previously suggested the possibility of having James Baker as mediator. We did not really support this idea because we did not want to invite international interference that could be difficult to control and might harm our interests.

During the summer of 2008, Baker attempted to get Mubarak on the phone to discuss the possibility of mediation. The president called me to get the background of the situation before he agreed to talk to Baker. I must admit that the president could not possibly be fully aware of all the affairs of the country, even though he always insisted on having the final word. Thus, one always had to be prepared to offer an accurate summary of whatever issue was at hand. I briefly explained all the details of the water negotiations to him and advised him not to accept mediation at this stage, because it would weaken our position and might irritate the World Bank and the donors if we refused their propositions. The president asked me to call Baker, apologize that the president could not receive his call, and explain the Egyptian vision fully. I did, and Baker was responsive.

Meanwhile, the Egyptian delegation in the negotiations noticed that the Nile Basin Initiative Secretariat, to which Egypt made financial contributions, was distorting the minutes of the meetings and writing what other countries dictated rather than what had actually taken place. Our protests did nothing to stop this.

Ever since we had rejected the Framework Agreement, we had been trying especially hard to build bridges between Egypt and the other countries. I asked the legal staff at the Ministry of Foreign Affairs to secretly and quietly consider the possibility of finding a new formulation for the articles in dispute, which Egypt could accept with Sudan's consent. This would allow the negotiations to get back onto a more fruitful path, either directly or through a mediator.

In the same period during 2010, the Israeli foreign minister visited some African countries. The Egyptian media began screaming that Israel had displaced Egypt in favor of other African countries, and was now stirring up trouble within the Nile Basin Initiative. These media reports, which I found very upsetting, revealed a complete lack of knowledge and research. I asked for a report on the Israeli penetration into the basin countries in particular. I received it in less than twenty-four hours. It stated that there were Israeli resident diplomatic representations in only a limited number of basin countries; the Israeli resident ambassador in Addis Ababa also represented his country as an accredited but nonresident ambassador to Rwanda and Burundi; and the resident ambassador in Nairobi represented Israel in Tanzania, Uganda, and the Seychelles Islands. The honorary Israeli consul in Tanzania also represented his country as chargé d'affaires in Eritrea. The report mentioned that Israel's purposes in strengthening its relationship with the Arab and African countries were to curb Iran's ambitions, find new markets for its exports, especially weapons, and obtain strategic minerals. There were inconsistencies in Israel's relationships with the basin countries for it had no official diplomatic representation in the Democratic Republic of Congo even though Israeli companies monopolized the diamond trade. It had old relations with Uganda that dated back to the 1960s; the military, intelligence, irrigation, and agriculture were their major areas of cooperation. Israel also had good relations with Rwanda, where they focused on military matters. It had strong relations with Ethiopia, cooperating on arms and agriculture. It also provided assistance for Kenya and Tanzania in agriculture, irrigation, and water. Egypt's relationship with these countries and the programs it provided for them went far beyond what Israel was offering.

On May 30, 2010, I met with the Ethiopian foreign minister, Seyoum Mesfin, in Nice in connection with the Africa–France Summit, where we discussed the problems of the Nile Basin Initiative. He explained that their signing of the Comprehensive Framework Agreement did not terminate the negotiations on the controversial sections. These would be included as supplements, under discussion for an extended period of time that would come to an end when a new understanding was reached, or else the agreement would remain as it was without reaching a settlement. I commented that this process would ignore Egypt's interests. He replied that the idea of the supplements was still under discussion, and that no date had been set for the annulment of the existing agreements. I replied that I might accept his proposal if he agreed to produce a written declaration that the old historical agreements would remain in effect until a complete consensus was reached. He smiled but did not comment, revealing his intention to try to weaken the Egyptian attitude.

I emphasized the importance of revitalizing the discussions on the Eastern Nile among Egypt, Sudan, and Ethiopia. By doing so, we hoped to remove the Framework Agreement from the spotlight and focus instead on specific projects, this being the objective of the Egyptian proposal for a simplified commission. Mesfin welcomed the proposal, mentioning that Meles Zenawi, the Ethiopian prime minister, had suggested the same idea to the Egyptian prime minister during the latter's visit to Addis Ababa.

I also met with Zenawi in Nice and briefed him on my talks with the Ethiopian foreign minister. He said that he was aware of the situation and expressed his approval. He referred again to the fact that he had confirmed information about attempts by the Egyptian General Intelligence to stir up occasional disturbances in certain regions of Ethiopia. I refuted this information based on my discussion with the director of General Intelligence, adding that we had no designs or feelings of hostility against them at all. However, there was a certain amount of internal hostility against his government; the people behind it sought to contact all the foreign agencies in several capitals, and we could not refuse to receive any information. I assured him that we were not working against them, directly or indirectly. We agreed that I would visit Ethiopia to consider the possibility of repairing some of the difficulties resulting from their signing of the Framework Agreement, and to discuss Egyptian development investment in Ethiopia. The president approved this course of action. I recounted my conversation with Zenawi to the General Intelligence chief, and he also agreed.

Egyptian diplomacy did not sit idle while the other countries signed the Draft Framework Agreement. Besides our ongoing communication with them, as well as our participation in the ministerial sessions of the Initiative countries (which I recommended discontinuing but the president refused), we had active communication with the donors, either through letters or in person. I sent assistant ministers with messages to India, China, Malaysia, Singapore, all the European countries, and the United States, asking the donors not to make any decision about projects in upstream countries before discussing them with us, so that we would not be negatively affected by them. They listened attentively and confirmed their desire to help all parties and harm no one. It became apparent that these communications and visits opened the eyes of the officials and experts in these countries and made them aware of all the facts.

I had met Robert Zoellick at the Nice summit. I explained our point of view and asked him to make sure the World Bank abided by the rules for financing any water project in the upstream countries. He was responsive, and again offered the bank as a facilitator for the negotiations.

We reviewed many of the confidential written reports and delegates' comments from the upstream countries. The Ugandans and Tanzanians were the most adamant in their attitude toward us, although they seemed flexible when actually dealing with us. Burundi, did not sign the Agreement in the first wave but did so in February 2011 after it had received a great deal of aid from Egypt. Indeed, they had assured the Europeans in June 2010 that they intended to sign the agreement but that their upcoming elections necessitated some delay in taking this step. Some Sudanese sources claimed that they could not let the Egyptians stand alone in spite of the Egyptians' stubbornness about adhering to the 1929 and 1959 Agreements, the right of prior notification, and the cancellation of any project that would endanger their interests.

Ethiopia repeatedly informed the donors that Egypt was negotiating in bad faith in order to sustain its monopolization of the Nile waters and to stop the projects of the upstream countries. It was also spreading false information, as stated by the Ethiopian minister of irrigation to a European source.

We continued to intensify our contacts with the upstream states. This was in light of the assurances of those countries, including Ethiopia, that they were hoping to reach an understanding with us on the situation and to settle the differences on the Comprehensive Framework Agreement. Therefore, in light of the decision of the Higher Committee to continue our dialogue with the upstream countries, Fayza Abul-Naga visited Burundi, Tanzania, and Uganda to explain the Egyptian vision to their leaders. She had a very positive meeting with the Burundian president, who assured her that he would not adopt any situation that would cause any harm to Egypt and advised us to intensify our communications with Uganda and Tanzania. In Tanzania, the president emphasized that the problem was not water scarcity but water management, and that the issue should be dealt with at the highest political level, meaning that it should be forwarded to the ministers of foreign affairs, who had diplomatic expertise that the technical ministers did not necessarily have. The Tanzanian president suggested that the foreign ministers of the basin countries should organize a summit for their heads of state to try to reach a consensus. He suggested that this take place following the upcoming presidential elections in Burundi, Rwanda, and Tanzania. In Uganda, Museveni spoke again about the right to development and the necessity of having a reserve of water resources that would provide some level of water security for all the basin countries, most of which depended on rainwater, which was not always reliable. He added that the construction of dams for producing electricity did not affect the natural flow of the river or represent a threat to the downstream countries. He agreed to hold a summit to discuss the matter. He also referred to the dangers of collecting water from the swamps of South Sudan, because the draining of the water decreased the rate of evaporation, which reduced the rainfall in Uganda. Museveni often mentioned such ideas in my presence. I always replied that such matters should be examined scientifically and we should not let unfounded fears control us. I wanted to assure him that the rain does not mainly come from the swamps of South Sudan, but reaches the equatorial plateau from the Indian Ocean. However, I preferred not to argue the point with him right then.

I accompanied Fayza Abul-Naga on a visit to Ethiopia, as agreed with Meles Zenawi and Seyoum Mesfin, and the Egyptian–Ethiopian joint committee returned to work after years of inaction.

The Ethiopians greeted us warmly in spite of our frankness. We told them that the Nile Basin Initiative had been derailed from its original objective, which was to support the development of water resources and energy projects, and turned instead into legal disputes over river water quotas. As previously explained, the 84 billion cubic meters of river water at issue represent a very small fraction of the total water resources available to the basin countries—about 1.66 trillion cubic meters. We reminded them that Egypt had never objected to any projects in the basin countries, and was ready to support water and energy projects in the upstream countries on the condition that Egypt's usage of the Nile, its only source of life, would be left intact. We both explained the importance of focusing on projects for collecting lost water and the Eastern Nile Basin projects for the benefit of all. At the same time we would continue negotiating the unresolved articles of the Framework Agreement, for which we were then considering a new formulation that would be acceptable to all and would not negatively affect our interests.

Meles Zenawi commented that the relations between Ethiopia and Egypt were eternal, similar to Catholic marriage in which divorce is prohibited. He mentioned that Ethiopia regarded the 1959 Agreement between Egypt and Sudan as unfair because it addressed the rights of only those two countries, while both of them considered the Framework Agreement harmful to their interests. He added that Ethiopia was not demanding the cessation of the 1959 Agreement, unlike Egypt's and Sudan's attitude toward the Framework Agreement, although they did harbor a feeling of injustice because the agreement seemed to assign all of the Nile waters to Egypt and Sudan and keep the upstream countries from getting their share. He also indicated that the Entebbe Agreement, by which he meant the Framework Agreement, made the upstream countries feel that they had acquired their rights. He thought that the best solution was for all the basin countries to admit that there were two groups of countries: the first consisting of Egypt and Sudan under the umbrella of the 1959 Agreement, and the second consisting of the upstream countries under the umbrella of the 2010 Agreement. This needed to be done in such a way that neither group would try to impose its will on the other. A new agreement would be made within the framework of the Nile Basin Initiative, which would focus on the commonalities and the points of agreement, and would allow the implementation of projects from which all would benefit. He pointed to the agreement of the Eastern Nile Basin countries as an example to follow.

Zenawi also said that the Ethiopian people falsely believed that the river water is their private property and that they were entitled to the lion's share. They did not realize that they did not need it at all, except for producing electricity. He then said that he knew that the Egyptian Ministry of Foreign Affairs, and I personally, had communicated with many countries and parties to stop them from financing energy projects in Ethiopia, and he had documents proving that Egypt contacted Italy and urged it to pressure Ethiopia on the issue of the Nile water. I acknowledge that we had done this, and would continue to do so if it served our interests; Egypt recognized the right of all countries to development and that we had no objection to projects that would not threaten our interests. Hence, according to the rules of prior notification, we should be informed of any future projects. If Ethiopia, or any other country, notified us so that we could assess the situation, we would be responsive and would not stand in their way; but if we were ignored, as Ethiopia was doing in its attempts to build dams on the river, we would have no choice but to talk with the donors, with whom we had strong communications and whom we could influence. In this context, we did in fact have contacts with Italy and other parties. I assured him that we did look forward to further understanding and cooperation with them, but that, with all due respect, no Egyptian official could tolerate risks to Egypt's interests when projects about which he knew nothing were being implemented on the course of the river.

We then discussed a particularly important point with Meles Zenawi. He admitted that he was surprised that Egypt had invited the Eritrean president after the first five countries had signed the Framework Agreement, and that he had conclusive evidence that the Egyptian General Intelligence, with the assistance of Eritrea, was supporting rebel movements in Somalia, notably al-Shabab. This was an example of the old method of making sure that Ethiopia was too occupied with internal problems to try to cause trouble for Egypt over the Nile waters. He said that such an approach was no longer useful. I explained to him the circumstances surrounding the Eritrean president's visit, and that he had come to see the Egyptian president, who had recently had major surgery. I denied that we had interfered in Somalia. On the contrary, we had informed the Ethiopian foreign minister when we received him, which was at the time the Ethiopian army was entering Somalia, that we understood their position on the matter but that they had to get out of Somalia as soon as possible. I had also informed my Ethiopian counterpart, Mesfin, in writing about the circumstances and the outcomes of the meetings Omar Suleiman and I had with the Eritrean President during our short visit to the Eritrean capital.

I felt that the Ethiopian prime minister was dredging up Ethiopia's long-held doubts about Egypt as a result of Egypt's active resistance to the signing of the Draft Framework Agreement. He did not seem to understand the transformations that had taken place in Egypt's foreign policy since the Eritrean–Ethiopian war, when it maintained its neutrality. Egypt was now eager to work with Ethiopia, as was demonstrated by the Egyptian–Sudanese–Ethiopian dialogue and the regular meetings of the foreign ministers. He did not recall that Egypt was not happy about the conditions in Somalia under the al-Shabab groups, but, like all the other regional and international forces, it tried to collect as much information as possible before taking action. If the Ethiopians found us communicating with one side or another, it did not mean that we were seeking to jeopardize Ethiopia's interests, or those of any other country.

I presented the outcomes of this visit to the president and all the other top Egyptian officials, including Zenawi's suggestion to reorganize the management of the Nile Basin into two sub-groups, one for the Blue Nile and another for the White Nile. This was a new idea that had actually been picked up in some quarters in Europe that might open the door to dialogue and negotiations, but it also had implications that could endanger the legal status of the existing agreements, which Egypt would not agree to change unless our interests were protected in any new agreement.

All the proposals generated in these meetings required further communication and study with the basin countries or the donors. I asked the water rights and legal working group at the ministry to continue studying all the information available. I was concerned about the aggressive attack on the minister of irrigation and water resources from his colleagues in the basin countries, and which he himself might have brought on himself, as his colleagues believed. This prompted us to ask Fayza Abul-Naga to participate, in light of her political and diplomatic abilities, to help handle confrontations resulting from technical differences among the water ministers. I discovered that some of our information about lost water, increasing the water flow, and similar matters was inaccurate and contradictory, especially in questions about the effects of upstream projects on Egypt's water quota. One person would say that this dam or that would definitely have harmful effects, while someone else would make it look less dangerous. In many cases, I did not have verified facts, which put us at a disadvantage. I also heard that certain Arab countries had major agricultural investments in Sudan, that India had agricultural projects in Ethiopia, and that Brazil was studying the possibility of investing in the production of biofuels (ethanol) in Ethiopia, Sudan, and the other basin countries. It was terribly frustrating that, although I persistently requested the documented scientific details of all these issues, neither the water resources administration, the Ministry of Foreign Affairs, the General Intelligence, nor the Egyptian scientific research agencies were able to provide precise information. I regarded this as a major deficiency in our scientific abilities. I had a great deal of documented information and plenty of interesting details on the land areas, the working companies, and their products, but no one could inform me about the effects of these activities on the water usage or our water quota.

The African Union Summit in Kampala at the end of July 2010 provided a good opportunity for the Ugandan president and the Egyptian prime minister to meet. Museveni said much the same things as before. He said that we should be aware in Egypt that our quotas would be decreased because of the development needs of the riparian countries. We replied that we all had to try to maximize the use of the river resources and stop losing water. He repeated his speech about the dangers of draining the swamps in southern Sudan. We explained that we did not wish to drain any area, and that we couldn't even do that, but we were trying to benefit more from the excess water, especially the Jonglei Canal. He then objected to the digging of the canal because it threatened the environmental balance of the region. He continued to open up. He talked about development and his wish to have Egypt provide economic and investment assistance for Uganda, and accused some Egyptian companies and businessmen of failing for years to keep their promises to invest in Uganda. The discussions revealed that many leaders of the region blamed Egypt for enjoying water and development while their hands were tied because of the Egyptian restraints. We rejected these accusations and tried to make them understand the real situation, but they turned a deaf ear. Their views and attitudes dated from the early years of their independence, as previously mentioned.

I was checking all the foreign cables early in the morning, as usual, when I read in one of them that President Museveni would be visiting Libya to hold consultations with Qadhafi. I immediately suggested to President Mubarak to write to Qadhafi or call him to ask him to use his influence to try to soften Museveni a bit on the issue of Nile water. The president asked me to talk with the Libyan foreign minister on his behalf and express his wish to have the colonel intervene with Museveni.

Qadhafi called President Mubarak following Museveni's visit to Tripoli to tell him that he had talked with Museveni, who promised to send Qadhafi a letter fully explaining his perspective, and when he received the letter, he wished to have the Egyptian foreign minister come to discuss the matter. The president decided to dispatch both me and Fayza

Abul-Naga, who was gradually replacing the minister of irrigation and water resources, to meet with Qadhafi in Tripoli. Qadhafi received us in his tent in al-Mazraa outside Tripoli. He handed us a copy of Museveni's letter, listed the threats and risks facing the Nile River that Egypt was unaware of, notably the eradication of forest timber, which was used by the inhabitants of the equatorial plateau to produce energy in the absence of electricity. He added that the preservation of the river would require enormous electricity production to upgrade the industrial capacity of the basin countries. He mentioned the fluctuation in the volume of the river from year to year, and the need for an irrigation system to deal with it, so they would not have to depend on rain or glacial melting from the Rwenzori Mountains. He also highlighted how important it was to develop a capacity to desalinate sea water using solar or nuclear energy, and that Egypt should focus on this, instead of claiming that the upstream countries had no right to produce electricity or develop agriculture and industrialization. The letter revealed that the Ugandans, like the Ethiopians, were intent on increasing their use of the river water to produce electricity, and were paying no attention to our concerns.

I informed President Mubarak and the prime minister of the content of the letter and Qadhafi's conversation with us. I asked to have the Egyptian minister of electricity travel to Uganda and Ethiopia to discuss how we could cooperate in the matter of electricity to meet the needs of these countries. As soon as I returned to Cairo, I told the president that Qadhafi was continuing to drive a wedge between the Gulf countries and Egypt. He accused the Gulf countries of working against Egypt's interests in the ways in which they invested their money—mainly in agriculture and water exploitation in Sudan, Ethiopia, and other basin countries. To prove his point, he handed us several papers and studies that he had got hold of. We told our brothers in the Gulf countries again that it was important that they take Egypt's concerns into consideration when they decided on their investments or projects in the basin countries. When Qadhafi provided us with this information about the Gulf countries, much of which we already knew, we were aware that he was trying to sour our relations with them, but we had to raise the matter with them anyway.

At the end of 2003, Qadhafi asked for the approval of Egypt and Sudan to extend a branch of the Nile from southern Egypt to Libya to increase the capacity of the Great River, a network of pipelines bringing water from aquifers in the Western Desert to Libya's Mediterranean. Both Egypt and Ethiopia refused the idea, but Qadhafi kept insisting.

Our communications with the Arab and Asian countries that were investing in Egypt caused some trouble for us with our brothers in Sudan, but we dealt with it in a straightforward manner. In connection with the Arab–African Summit in the Libyan city of Sirte in October 2010, I met with the Sudanese presidential advisor Mustafa Osman Ismail. I said that Libya had received information from some Gulf countries and China indicating that Egypt had asked them not to finance any water or agricultural projects in the Nile Basin countries, including Sudan. I explained that it was important to have full coordination between our countries on the use of water resources according to the assigned quotas. I added that we had information confirming that Sudan used its full quota designated by the 1959 Agreement; thus, the agricultural and water projects under discussion entailed giving Sudan additional water above its quota, which required reducing Egypt's allotment. I pointed out that they should consult with us regarding these projects, as well as the dam projects they intended to build on the Atbarah River, and reminded him that they had previously filled the lake behind Merowe Dam in a short period of time, in violation of their agreement with Egypt, thus decreasing the amount of water reaching Egypt during that time. Ismail then indicated that it was important for the ministers of water resources to openly discuss these issues together. I agreed, and went on to discuss the matter with the Egyptian minister of irrigation. As a result, a consultative meeting between the Egyptian and Sudanese ministers of foreign affairs and irrigation was held in Cairo in November 2010. On January 29, 2011, I met with the Tanzanian foreign minister in Addis Ababa for further discussions of water issues. He suggested that the ministers of foreign affairs should meet to discuss the points of disagreement. I had no objection, but warned him that the inflexibility shown by the upstream countries would put the outcome of this meeting at risk, and might further complicate the situation rather than settle it. I was aware that they were maneuvering for the sake of their own national advantage, while they continued to sweet-talk us without making any concessions or providing reasonable solutions.

This was the situation at the end of 2010. It remained almost unchanged until I left office on March 5, 2011.

During my nearly seven years in office, I continually thought about the reasons that made us agree to the World Bank initiative to join the Nile Basin countries in one institutional framework and to move beyond the conditions that prevailed during the second half of the twentieth century. Why did we do this? The answer to this legitimate question is the wish to strengthen cooperation and to establish an institutional framework that would permit comprehensive development of the river's resources to the benefit of all concerned. I have commented many times that we could have achieved these goals solely by focusing on bilateral cooperation with individual countries. As the extent of the problems have become more obvious now, I believe that we should have taken protective measures by obtaining predetermined guarantees from the World Bank, the initiator of the whole idea, that our participation would not affect our interests as historically recognized by international law, instead of stepping into the unknown and then dealing with our recalcitrant basin partners after ten years of deliberations.

In 1993 Meles Zenawi, on behalf of Ethiopia, signed a declaration with Egypt in Cairo, in which he agreed to everything that he was rejecting now. When he was asked why he did this, he replied that the country had been internally weak at the beginning of his government's rule, and it was in their best interests at the time to sign something they were not convinced of. This strange answer revealed an opportunism that should make us cautious when dealing with these partners. Their plans for megadams storing hundreds of billions of cubic meters of water should make us concerned about their management, as well as their security and environmental impacts on Egypt, Sudan, and even Ethiopia itself. In Egypt, we certainly did not object to any measures that would help Ethiopia develop, or meet its energy needs, or supply the rest of the basin countries with electricity. For us, the vital point is that none of these projects will have negative impacts on Egypt and its annual water quota, and that the projects themselves should be technically sound.

I followed the handling of the water issue in the Egyptian media over the years, and felt that many journalists who tackled this issue, along with the performance of the Egyptian government in general and that of the Ministry of Foreign Affairs in particular, did not make enough of an effort to inform themselves about all the aspects of the extremely sensitive topic. They should have been more professional when dealing with this matter. I was particularly shocked at the nonchalant and hasty manner in which the issue was treated after January 25, 2011; it was not only disgraceful, but harmful to our national interests.

As I wrote these pages at the beginning of 2012, I thought that by exerting our best efforts, being alert, continuously analyzing situations, and intensifying the cooperation with our partners inside and outside the Nile Basin, we could undoubtedly reach a satisfactory settlement that protected everyone's interests. It is essential that we should not take, or agree to take, any action that might freeze or decrease Egypt's water quota in the future. We should now be aware of our need for desalination projects and for the use of all available types of energy. We also need to plan for rationalizing the usage of river water and recycling it, because the pressures of development and a growing population will only continue to increase.

Finally, we should not, under any circumstances, allow internal Egyptian policy to distract us from this national issue, which all of us have to defend. There is no Egyptian alive today, or yet to be born, who would approve of anything that might cause harm to us in the realm of water. It is our life, and we will do anything to keep it safe.

My father, the pilot Ali Ahmed Aboul Gheit, 1941.    My mother, Fatma al-Messiri, 1941.

With my parents, 1942.

With my mother on a street in Cairo, 1948.

Aged ten on the beach at Alexandria, 1952.

During my studies at Military
Technical College, 1960.

Wedding photograph of my wife,
Laila Kamal al-Din Salah, 1968.

Delivering my report as rapporteur to the UN Administrative and Financial Committee of the UN General Assembly, 1975.

With Esmat Abdel Meguid, Egypt's permanent representative to the UN (center), and PLO leader, Yasser Arafat, 1975.

At the UN General Assembly with Foreign Minister Kamal Hassan Ali, 1983.

With Foreign Minister Esmat Abdel Meguid at the seat of the Egyptian Cabinet, 1984.

With my wife at the
Egyptian embassy in
Rome, 1995.

On a plane bound for Tel Aviv with Foreign Minister Amr Moussa, May 1999.

At the UN with PLO leader, Yasser Arafat, 1999.

# 7

# CHALLENGES OF SUSTAINING STATUS: EGYPT AND AFRICA

D
r. Esmat Abdel Meguid, who was Egypt's permanent representative
to the UN from March 1972 to March 1983, used to tell us something I have never forgotten. He told us that with the signing of the
peace treaty with Israel in May 1979, most of the Arab countries, supported
by the Soviet Union and its partners and followers, started maneuvering in
an attempt to stir up trouble for Egypt wherever they could. At the UN,
Egypt had too much leverage to be affected by this kind of thing, while in
other organizations, the majority of which opposed the Egyptian–Israeli
peace treaty, it was in fact possible to have Egypt penalized. These groups
included the Non-Aligned Movement (NAM), the Organization of the
Islamic Conference (OIC), and the Arab League, as well as some Asian–
African forums. Several attempts were made to expel Egypt from these
forums, or at least to suspend its membership. At the Non-Aligned Movement summit in Cuba in September 1979, a number of countries were
ready to attack, but the Egyptian delegation was aware of their plot and
was well prepared for the confrontation. The UN African Group had been
convened by Dr. Esmat Abdel Meguid before his departure for Havana, the
capital of Cuba, the revolutionary country that was the Soviet Union's ally.

He explained the situation to the UN ambassadors of the African countries who would be accompanying him to the conference in Havana. He
said that Egypt, their brother African country, was currently under attack

from some of its Arab brothers supported by the Soviet Union. As Egypt's representative and vice-chairman of the Egyptian delegation to Havana, he asked them to support Egypt and refuse to suspend its membership in the NAM, of which Egypt had been a founding member in 1961. The ambassadors immediately expressed their support of Egypt and promised to discuss the matter with their heads of state and their foreign ministers. One of the ambassadors present at the meeting told Abdel Meguid, "You have always been present at our meetings and done your best to protect the interests of our countries at the UN. Egypt has long been supporting us in our fight against the colonial powers, such as Britain, France, Belgium, Holland, Spain, and Portugal." Dr. Abdel Meguid admitted that this African attitude was a beacon for him for the rest of the years he worked in New York and for the seven years he served as foreign minister. Attempts to expel Egypt from the NAM in Havana failed as a result of the African countries' support of Egypt. These countries also had Egypt readmitted to the OIC in Rabat in 1984, when President Ahmed Sékou Touré of Guinea led an initiative by Guinea and Morocco to reactivate Egypt's membership. These acts revealed the kind of relationship Egypt had with the African countries, which were ready to protect any other African country in need. In fact, any decision-maker in Egyptian foreign policy must bear in mind that Africa is considered vital to Egypt's political life, and it is essential to continue to develop our relationship with its countries.

During the years from 1977 to 1992, while I was serving under the Egyptian foreign ministers Mohamed Ibrahim Kamel, Kamal Hassan Ali, Esmat Abdel Meguid, and finally Amr Moussa, Dr. Boutros Boutros-Ghali worked hard to maintain an active Egyptian–African relationship. He visited the continent several times every year and was eager to have strong personal relationships with the heads of the countries and their top officials. He even encouraged President Mubarak to visit these countries and receive their heads of state or government in Cairo regularly. The Egyptian Fund for Technical Cooperation with Africa (EFTCA) was established in 1981, during Boutros-Ghali's tenure as state minister, with the help of Kamal Hassan Ali. His focus on Latin America and Africa, in coordination with the foreign minister, provided Egypt with an opportunity to build relations with these parties, particularly the African countries. Nonetheless, it must be admitted that in spite of the friendliness and warmth of the relations, our efforts were limited to exchanging visits and to Egypt's offers of gifts, which included weapons, equipment, military training, and other military support. This situation persisted from the difficult period following the 1967 defeat, when Egypt was focused on liberating its occupied territories, until Boutros-Ghali's departure from the Ministry of Foreign Affairs to become the UN secretary general.

Throughout these years, Egyptian trade with African countries did not reflect the political dimension and the mutual respect Egypt enjoyed with these countries. There had been no Egyptian companies capable of entering the African markets, which would have promoted common interests. As I have previously mentioned, there was the Nasr Company for trading with Africa, but it focused on Egypt's political and security role rather than trade, investment, and economic opportunities for the Egyptian market. Egypt maintained its special African status all these years due to its well-known support for the African liberation movements against colonialism. Some competitive African powers emerged from these struggles, such as Nigeria in western Africa, Algeria prior to its internal disturbances beginning in 1992, and South Africa after the apartheid policy ended and the black majority began to rule in 1994.

Foreign Minister Amr Moussa gave considerable attention to the Egyptian position in Africa and made several tours. He succeeded in making Egypt a member of the Common Market for Eastern and Southern Africa (COMESA) in 1998, which would have provided Egypt with commercial opportunities in Africa at a time when some Egyptian businessmen and companies were ready to move the Egyptian economy into a new, dynamic phase. At the same time, the Ministry of Foreign Affairs countered some views within COMESA, which harbored unfounded concerns about Egypt's membership.

The foreign minister paid several visits to the continent, either alone or accompanied by a large number of businessmen. There was an indication that Egypt intended to take advantage of its warm political ties and develop them into mutually beneficial economic relations.

When I assumed my duties as Egypt's permanent representative to the UN, I noticed that many African powers, such as South Africa, Nigeria, Ghana, Senegal, Ethiopia, and Algeria, had begun to compete with Egypt's special status at the African and international levels. Some African ambassadors, who were friends of mine, admitted that they were dismayed at Egypt's apparent lack of interest in African affairs, compared to historical relations between Egypt and the continent.

While I was in New York, I continued to monitor Egypt's performance at the African level. I came to the conclusion that we had in fact lost some prestige and influence, mainly because the Egyptian president had stopped attending any African summit or other activity since the assassination attempt in Addis Ababa in June 1995, even though all the relevant Egyptian agencies continued to monitor African activities. As a result, an impression had emerged that Egypt had lost interest in Africa and that it had recentered its focus on places other than Africa. This belief, which was, perhaps, shared by both Egyptians and their African brothers, was due to Egypt's recent interest in the emerging economies group, including Brazil, India, China, South Africa, Malaysia, Indonesia, Singapore, and others. In fact, Egypt had tried to join this group in addition to its traditional economic and trade relations with the northern Mediterranean countries and the United States. Nonetheless, Middle East issues remained an Egyptian priority.

This was the situation that I had inherited from my predecessor as foreign minister, my colleague Ahmed Maher, and from State Minister for Foreign Affairs Fayza Abul-Naga, when I became foreign minister in July 2004. From the moment of my appointment, I noticed that President Mubarak seemed to feel that our position in Africa was inappropriate to our status as the oldest country on the continent, with a diplomatic presence as old as any of the other African countries. Perhaps he picked up this impression from the information that reached him from the UN, from the African leaders he met in Cairo, or from one of the few international conferences he briefly attended.

As soon as I arrived in Cairo, I asked for all the available information on Egypt and Africa so that we could form a sound new plan that would reflect the current conditions and interests of Egypt and the African countries, rather than those of a bygone past. Egypt had stood with the African brothers in their long struggle for independence, and had helped them to build up a capable governing class. Now it was time to determine what new efforts should be undertaken that would allow Egypt to be as visible as possible on the African scene.

The studies I received in 2004 showed that Egypt has had a large number of diplomatic missions in Africa since the early 1960s. In 2004 there were thirty-five missions in sub-Saharan Africa, with nonresident representations in ten more countries. This amounts to about one-quarter of Egypt's total diplomatic representation worldwide, including Ministry of Foreign Affairs staff, security and intelligence agencies, military personnel, and trade representatives. However, the same studies indicated that Egypt had no significant trade with Africa. If Egypt had not joined the COMESA, its trade with Africa would not have developed to the extent that it did.

Until 2004, the EFTCA had trained about six thousand African workers in various fields, in cooperation with most of the Egyptian government ministries. Since the Fund was established, Egypt had dispatched about seven thousand experts, including university professors, football and other sports coaches, physicians, and pharmacists to many African countries, and diplomats from all the African countries received training at the Egyptian Institute of Diplomatic Studies. Because the Fund's activities were spread over so many countries, they were not as effective as they would have been if they had been concentrated in certain high-priority countries. Thus it was decided that the Fund's priorities should be adjusted so that the Nile Basin countries, including Eritrea, would receive about 40 percent of its expenditures, with another 40 percent to the African Islamic countries surrounding the Arab countries, from Senegal in northwestern Africa to Eritrea on the Red Sea and Somalia on the Indian Ocean. The remaining 20 percent would be spent on other African countries. I discovered that we were offering assistance to South Africa and the group of southern countries that were under its full control. This seemed unreasonable for a country like South Africa, whose GDP was triple that of Egypt in 2004 with about half the population. Therefore, we decided to decrease the resources designated for southern Africa. We started to implement these priorities in 2004.

It bothered me that Egypt was constantly highlighting the role of the EFTCA, which was a fund with a budget that did not exceed ten million dollars annually. Comparisons were being drawn at the time between the influence of Egypt and China. At the Forum on China–Africa Cooperation in 2006, China announced that it intended to spend five billion dollars on assistance to the African countries from 2006 to 2009, while Egypt planned to spend about $30 million during the same period. I presented the problem of our inadequate assistance to Africa to the Cabinet. I also recommended that the ministers and other senior officials should make more visits to African countries and attend as many African events and conferences as possible. I stressed the importance of regaining our influence at the African level, and set our quest for increased recognition in the framework of possibly obtaining a permanent seat on the UN Security Council if the council ever expanded.

The prime minister commented, "We do need to reinvigorate our interests on the continent and build economic and trade relationships with its countries, which provide potential markets for our industry and trade. The Egyptian ministers should open up to the continent, especially in the fields of trade, communication, aviation, health, and agriculture." He then approved an increase of three million dollars in the Fund, amounting to a total of $13 million in 2006. In a private conversation I told the prime minister that, even though this represented a 30 percent increase in the Fund, it was very small in absolute terms and would not make much difference in terms of expenditures. He then promised to increase the amount gradually. He did keep this promise, for by the end of 2010 the budget of the Fund amounted to about $23 million, an increase of 65 percent since I had taken office.

The reports on Egypt's efforts in Africa indicated that it was the only African country that had held the presidency of the Organization of African Union three times—in 1964, 1989, and 1993—and it had organized two conferences, in 1964 and 1993. We had discontinued our joint meetings with African countries ten years before, and I felt that we should start inviting Africa again to attend conferences in Egypt, so as to revitalize our role on the continent. The hard work began. By the end of 2010, Egypt had hosted an African summit and a Non-Aligned (NAM) summit, and had agreed with the Organization of the Islamic Conference (OIC) to hold its 2011 conference in Egypt. Several major African ministerial conferences were also held in Egypt, including two on communication, two on trade, and one each on scientific research, oil and energy, industry, finance, and economics. Egyptian trade with the COMESA increased, reaching a total of almost one billion dollars with a large surplus on the Egyptian side. We hosted the headquarters of the COMESA Regional Investment Agency. Egypt was also a founding member of the New Partnership for Africa's Development (NEPAD).

In addition we participated in the activities of other African agencies and organizations, in which Egypt was not a member due to the geographical division of Africa into five regions. For example, Egypt sat as an observer country for the Intergovernmental Authority on Development (IGAD) and was a co-opted member of the International Conference on the Great Lakes Region (ICGLR).

In coordination with the Ministries of Defense and Interior, and because of our active presence at the UN, by the end of 2010 Egypt was taking part in most of the peacekeeping operations in Africa. About five thousand members of the Armed Forces and the Ministry of Interior were stationed in Darfur, southern Sudan, Ivory Coast, the Democratic Republic of Congo, Central African Republic, and Chad.

The number of African trainees in Egypt reached 7,700, about 250 Egyptian experts were working across the continent, and almost 500 African diplomats were trained in Egypt during the period from 2007 to 2010. The Egyptian Diplomatic Institute offered special courses for specific regions, such as southern Sudan, which was on its way to independence. I myself, as well as several Egyptian delegations, traveled to a number of African capitals. Nineteen meetings of joint committees between Egypt and various African countries were also held in Cairo or in the capitals of those countries over a period of five years. As previously mentioned, these committees had completely ceased to meet.

Egypt paid considerable attention to southern Sudan and Ethiopia. In 2010 Egypt was the major supplier for southern Sudan; it constructed two power stations at a cost that exceeded $25 million; Alexandria University opened a new campus in Tonj; and a hospital was built in Juba. As for Ethiopia, by the end of 2010 Egypt had sent 121 experts there over a period of four years, and currently has about twenty-six experts in the country, most of whom are professors at Addis Ababa University and Jimma University. Egypt also provided food assistance for Ethiopia in some drought-stricken regions at a cost that exceeded three million Egyptian pounds during the period from 2007 to 2010. I always regarded this assistance as a symbolic effort, since Ethiopia also received hundreds of millions of dollars in development aid from the western countries and China.

Egypt, represented by the Ministry of Foreign Affairs, al-Azhar University, and the Ministry of Religious Endowments, dispatched large numbers of imams and preachers during the holy month of Ramadan to the Islamic countries of Africa, in addition to the permanent presence of 637 al-Azhar envoys throughout Islamic Africa by the end of 2010. In Nigeria, there were two Egyptian schools known as the Egyptian–Nigerian School, which were staffed by Egyptian teachers. The Ministry of Foreign Affairs helped to send dozens of Egyptian physicians to western Africa, contracting directly with the hospitals involved. All over the continent, Egypt provided relief assistance, university staff, religious assistance from al-Azhar, President Mubarak's scholarships for advanced education, three integrated medical centers, and thirty-seven physicians in distant areas. The ministry helped major Egyptian companies such as Arab Contractors, Orascom, and Elsewedy Electric enter the African market.

In spite of all this work, I observed over the years that the Egyptian media severely criticized our efforts and claimed that Egypt was not present on the African scene. The public had to be made aware of Egypt's contributions. We distributed brochures and prepared press releases. We invited Egyptian companies to meet with the African ambassadors to Egypt, and to offer tours of the Egyptian industrial centers and the Smart Village. Yet the media ignored all these efforts. Instead, they compared the hard work Egypt was doing with the efforts made by foreign powers, such as China,

Japan, India, and Malaysia, but such criticisms neglected to mention the fact that these foreign powers had established long-term assistance programs in these African countries. In comparing Egypt and China, it must be pointed out that Egyptian trade with Africa in 2010 never exceeded a billion dollars, while China's trade amounted to $110 billion, more than a hundred times that of Egypt.

According to the reports I had, the fund had previously planned to establish plantations of about ten thousand feddans to produce crops to be shared between Egypt and the partner country. The first one was in Zambia and the result was far from satisfactory. The government failed in farming. I wanted to stop this activity and instead encourage Egyptian companies to invest in agriculture with their money at their own risk. Between 2004 and January 2011, I seized every opportunity available to travel to Africa, and asked the assistant foreign ministers for African affairs, who were numerous at the time, and the directors of the fund to follow suit. They made thirty-six visits to different African countries.

My first trip to Africa, other than the previously mentioned one-day visits to Libya and Sudan, was to South Africa to attend the ministerial meeting for the Non-Aligned Movement in 2004. We had always paid close attention to South Africa because it was the largest economy in Africa, and could easily achieve gains at the expense of Egypt. One might ask why the two countries wouldn't work together for their own benefit as well as the good of the continent. One explanation is that our competition over a permanent seat on the Security Council tended to complicate matters. The Egyptian ambassador to South Africa said that we had neglected South Africa and they knew it, and that we were trying to compete with them while they were out of our league. I disagreed. I explained that it was an influential country because of its very large financial and economic resources compared to those of Egypt, and that our countries should cooperate intensively, if they wished, especially in trade, investment, and scientific research—fields in which they were more advanced than we were. Our ambassador said that the South Africans were upset because they believed that the Egyptian president ignored President Mandela during his presidency and had not visited. I did not say what I was really thinking.

I had known since the mid-1990s that South Africa held a grudge against Egypt after it had been forced to give up the African seat at the International Atomic Energy Agency in Vienna because of its apartheid policy, and was temporarily replaced by Egypt.

In my meeting with President Mbeki, he expressed his gratitude to Egypt for its support during the sufferings of the apartheid period and throughout the 1970s and 1980s, and for its sustained support since then. My meeting with the foreign minister, Nkosazana Clarice Dlamini-Zuma, did not run so smoothly. She said, "You're competing with us for no good reason. We feel neglected, and so do the other African countries."

I explained that we worked in several directions and were greatly concerned with our relations with Europe, the United States, and the various Asian powers. I told her that I appreciated her frankness but had to admit that I thought that South Africa was focused on the rest of the continent merely as a springboard for their international ambitions, hinting at their aspiration to obtain the permanent seat on the Security Council, an issue that had not been included in our discussions. Egypt had many interests, and they had to understand that. I left knowing that we had a problem with them. They used their large resources and financial abilities unsparingly as a means to extend their influence in the southern region, which was largely under their control: ten countries that fully supported them. They insinuated themselves into African disputes, providing financial support and spending extravagantly in order to consolidate their presence on the continent. Their foreign minister always flew in private planes with an annual budget equal to decades' worth of travel for the Egyptian foreign ministers. Their president traveled all over the continent and attended everything, whereas the Egyptian president was often absent. Nigeria could also have been their rival, but they did not want to clash with more than one powerful African country at a time.

I compared their prestigious position in southern Africa with the difficulties we faced in our relationships with our neighbors in northern Africa: Libya acting irrationally under Qadhafi's leadership, Algeria competing with Egypt, the Polisario Front being under Algeria's control, and finally, Tunisia and Mauritania, neither of which were concerned about

Egypt's standing despite our attempts to improve understanding among our three countries.

We attended the Abuja Summit, as previously mentioned, in an attempt to arrange to host an African summit in Egypt as a way to help our re-emergence. The earliest possible date for a summit was the summer of 2011. Several other countries had hosted summits in 2003 and 2004 before I came to office. Since the founding of the African Union, the African summits had been held twice a year, one at the headquarters in Addis Ababa in January and the other in another member country by the end of June. I tried for two or three years to have an African summit held in Egypt. In its attempt to avoid the sanctions imposed following the Lockerbie incident, which were to be settled by the payment of a large sum, Libya sought to hold a summit in Sirte, ignoring Egypt's attempts to secure a summit. Finally, we managed to reach an agreement with the head of the AU Secretariat Oumar Konare to hold an African summit in the summer of 2009. I was not pleased to have the summit in Egypt presided over by Tanzania, but it was eastern Africa's turn to preside. I accepted this situation to avoid clashing with Libya, knowing that otherwise Mubarak would concede the hosting and the presidency of the summit to Qadhafi because then Mubarak would not have to travel so far. Not only did we host an African summit, the most recent of which had been the Africa–Europe Summit held in Cairo in 2000, but we also sought to hold a number of important ministerial meetings in Egypt during the period from 2006 to 2010, including the Africa–Europe Ministerial Meeting for foreign ministers, the Ministerial Meeting of the Forum on China–Africa Cooperation, and the Preparatory Ministerial Meeting of the Arab–Africa Summit.

The NEPAD Summit was held in Sharm al-Sheikh in 2005, attended by a large number of African participants. I felt then that although the president was trying to cut costs, he was willing to host other conferences in Egypt, preferably the African summits, because of his unwillingness to travel abroad. He was so tight with money that we had a quarrel with the presidential staff over a shortage of refreshments for the participating delegations in spite of the outstanding organization for which the president's office was generally known. We often had to spend from the ministry budget to cover some of the expenses for the summits held in 2008 and 2009, for which the president's office was actually responsible.

I estimated that it would take us several years to restore our position at the African level. Some ministers were eager to help and offered to travel to the African countries as necessary, while others wanted to avoid the conferences held in African countries. I was really annoyed and discussed this with them several times, but my efforts were in vain.

Aware that his absence from conferences had bad effects on us, and responding to my persistence, the president agreed to travel to Abuja in Nigeria, where he stayed for only a day and a half. He did not attend the next AU or OIC conferences, which were held in sub-Saharan African countries: Banjul in Gambia, Dakar in Senegal, Kampala in Uganda, and Bamako in Mali.

During my visit to Ghana, the Ghanaian president insisted that the Egyptian president attend the African summit which was held to celebrate the fiftieth anniversary of Ghana's independence from Britain. He recalled the strong relations between Gamal Abd al-Nasser and the first Ghanaian president, Kwame Nkrumah. I told him frankly that I would try to help him but could promise nothing. I suggested that, in order to get President Mubarak to accept, he should visit Mubarak in Cairo and personally invite him to come to Ghana. He did ask to visit Egypt. When I noticed that there was no immediate response, I explained my strategy to the president. He said smilingly, "We'll receive him and I'll think about it." The Ghanaian president came and the president accepted his invitation. When it was time to keep his promise, concerns about the security and health conditions in western Africa and complaints about the long flights and uncomfortable accommodations emerged. I pressured the president into keeping his promise. I left before he did, worrying that things would not turn out as I hoped, but he came. He arrived at noon on the opening day of the summit in Accra and left before two o'clock in the afternoon, without attending the luncheon for the leaders. He spent just two hours in the conference hall. I was sorry that the president had taken off from Cairo at dawn only to return in the evening—two flights totaling thirteen hours—without meeting all the African presidents who looked up to Egypt and its president.

Similarly, Sudan was looking forward to holding a conference in Khartoum in 2006 on their fiftieth anniversary of independence. The president made another promise. A rumor was then circulated by a Sudanese woman that he would be assassinated. He decided not to go, and another opportunity for the president to appear on the African scene was lost. I planned to compensate for the president's absence by relying on the prime minister, despite all the trouble it might cause for both of us. Between 2008 and 2011 I had to ask for the president's approval to have the prime minister attend the African summits held in Addis Ababa and Kampala when the negotiations on the Comprehensive Framework Agreement for the Nile were being conducted.

The AU conferences gave us an opportunity to strengthen our relationship with the host countries by offering them our expertise in organizational and technical fields. We offered our support to the foreign ministers. We assisted most of the countries that hosted conferences from 2006 to 2011 by providing protocol services, guidance and training for the private security of VIPs, simultaneous and written translation services, and suggestions about accommodations and administrative services.

Many leaders and foreign ministers appreciated our costly contributions, which helped to portray Egypt as an advanced country capable of helping them organize successful conferences. Nonetheless, I had to admit that being from northern Africa, or rather Arabs, affects the way the Africans regard us. During my visit to the capital of Rwanda in 2006, I happened to watch Egypt play a football match against the Ivory Coast in the African Nations Championship tournament in the hotel lobby. I saw hundreds of Rwandans and other Africans who strongly supported the Ivory Coast team. I kept going to my room to watch the match alone to relieve some of the stress I felt, and then returning to the lobby to be shocked at the Africans' support of the African team in its match against, I regret to say, an Arab team.

I had been closely following the situation in Somalia during my first years as foreign minister. The warlords sought Egypt's support to unify their country, but we at the Ministry of Foreign Affairs and the General Intelligence did not trust the warlords, who were later defeated by an organized group of Islamist militants.

I personally had an unpleasant experience with the leaderships of these fighting groups. Foreign Minister Amr Moussa and the General Intelligence chief held a major conference for these leaders in Cairo in 1998 to reach an agreement on unity and the restoration of the central government. Efforts were to be made to improve living conditions and infrastructure, and Egypt provided assistance. The leaders signed a joint agreement in Cairo. We were optimistic, but a few days after they went back, disputes erupted again and the situation returned to what it was before. After all the efforts we had made and expenses we had borne, we were misled by these leaders. They enjoyed their stay in Cairo and had a good time at the hotel, but nothing was achieved. One of them even sent for his girlfriend in the United States to come and stay with him after the others had left. We were annoyed at his behavior, but were advised by experts in Somali affairs not to object because he was an influential person.

This bad experience made me more careful as foreign minister not to be deceived by certain Somali dignitaries who tried to take advantage of the suffering in Somalia. I tirelessly sought to help the Somalis to restore peace and agree on a government acceptable to all by encouraging them to hold meetings in Somalia in coordination with other international powers who were eager to achieve peace there. I felt that the unified Somalia of Mohamed Siad Barre's era, as we knew it, would not be easily restored, if at all. It would be difficult to unite Puntland, Somaliland, the government of Mogadishu, and the government of the youth groups in southern Somalia. Nevertheless, we were willing to help the government of Sharif Ahmed to regain control over the center of the country and Mogadishu by providing the necessary resources. We believed that the conditions in Puntland and Somaliland would persist for a long time, so we decided to provide them with aid through the EFTCA. For years, this fund had been offering food assistance to the Somali regions that were suffering from severe conditions, despite the threat this might represent to the unity of Somalia.

Some in Egypt accused us of neglecting Somalia and allowing the situation to deteriorate to the point that the Ethiopians had an opportunity to enter. I believe that the Somalis themselves were the ones responsible for this tragedy. For years Egypt had been doing everything within its power to help, but the narrow interests of the warlords and the different tribes got in the way.

The deteriorating situation led to the emergence of piracy on the coasts of Somalia, which threatened international shipping in many areas in the Gulf of Aden and the Indian Ocean. As the conditions were worsening and the merchant vessels entering the Red Sea on their way to the Suez Canal were under threat of attack, I suggested that one or more Egyptian naval units be sent to participate in the international maritime efforts to control the situation. (Egypt did participate in all the international meetings to deal with the piracy.) My suggestion was not accepted due to its high cost. Matters were taken over by the more influential countries, and Egypt was absent from these efforts. I made other attempts, but there was no response. Our main concern was to maintain the effectiveness of our naval units within our territorial waters and deal with our own immediate priorities. Naval units from Turkey, Iran, Korea, India, and China, as well as warships of the North Atlantic Treaty Organization (NATO), were seen in the Indian Ocean and the entrance to the Red Sea, where we had long been resisting the involvement of foreign countries.

Not only were we concerned with the affairs of Somalia and Sudan, but we also sought to build relations of understanding with Eritrea. We needed to maintain mutual cooperation with it because of its strategic location on the Red Sea, while simultaneously sustaining a good relationship with Ethiopia. We often had to walk a tightrope in our relations with both Eritrea and Ethiopia, whose mutual hostility was well known, but they were both strategically important for us. I must also admit that the leaders of the two countries had difficult personalities and such high self-esteem that they had to be treated with special care.

During these years, the Ministry of Foreign Affairs had been active at the continental level, as indicated by my own tours in western, central, and eastern Africa and by the travels of my assistants. These trips enabled us to get acquainted with the conditions of the vast continent. What bothered me the most about these trips was the long flights on planes that sometimes were not totally safe, and the lengthy stays at the ministerial conferences and the AU summits in the various African capitals. We often had to stay for eight full hours in Addis Ababa or another capital. I often felt cut off from my responsibilities back in Cairo, in spite of the modern electronic communications that enabled us to follow all the international developments and Egypt's reaction to them. I almost felt that the African Union intentionally prolonged these meetings.

Upon my recommendation to the president, the prime minister traveled to Addis Ababa to attend the Summit of the African Union for a couple of days and returned immediately to Cairo, while I stayed in Addis Ababa to follow the deliberations, which were a repeat of previous years. I used to urge the president and the secretariat of the African Union to take steps to either reduce these meetings or increase their effectiveness. Throughout these years, Egypt repeatedly presented proposals or draft resolutions that would enhance its status on the continent. South Africa and Algeria were trying to do the same. The competition among the delegations of Nigeria, South Africa, and Egypt was quite obvious. The heads of state also vied for taking the floor; when the Senegalese president spoke before the summit for hours, the Ethiopian prime minister would try to compete with him on every occasion and on all topics. Muammar Qadhafi also attended these summits and tried to talk the other heads of state into establishing a United States of Africa. Although his vague ideas were reservedly approved, it was known that none of these immature concepts would be executed. Libya spent its money on extravagances while its poor infrastructure was visible to all.

In its attempt to embarrass the other competitors, including Egypt, Algeria, Libya, and Nigeria, South Africa offered to contribute about 25 percent of the AU budget. After discussing the matter with some of the other foreign ministers, I got them to agree that it was unwise to have one country responsible for a quarter of the budget, which would probably end up in a limited number of countries. At the Sirte summit in Libya in July 2005, South Africa insisted that Pretoria would provide not less than 20 percent of the AU budget. I then had to pick up this gauntlet that was thrown down before Egypt, which was regarded as South Africa's counterweight in northern Africa. I called President Mubarak to discuss the situation and to ask him to act promptly. Although I told him that we would end up contributing about $20 million to the African Union annually and an equal amount to the Arab League, he unhesitatingly agreed. When I returned to the meeting, I found that the Libyan foreign minister had suggested that each of the major countries pay 15 percent of the AU budget. I immediately agreed. Thereafter, Egypt made an annual contribution of about $18 million to the AU budget.

As my mission came to an end, I believed that we had succeeded to a great extent in developing our abilities in Africa. Yet there are certain points I wish to mention, the most important of which is the need to increase the budget of the EFTCA. The fund needs about $150 million or $200 million annually, instead of the current, much smaller budget, in order for Egypt to play the role it deserves at the continental level. The contributions made by al-Azhar and the Ministry of Higher Education are also insufficient.

Any Egyptian decision-maker has to think carefully about the balance between the benefits of a strong Egyptian presence at the African level and the development needs of the Egyptians, which are huge and require all available resources. This aspect has not been raised before when Egyptian foreign policy and its priorities were criticized.

It is essential to have a coordination committee presided over by the Ministry of Foreign Affairs and encompassing all the Egyptian agencies working in the African field, in order to coordinate efforts, optimize the use of resources, and set priorities in a way that will serve Egyptian interests in the long run. We should increase the capacities of our embassies in Africa and provide them with all necessary resources. As I have mentioned before, our diplomats refuse to work in Africa and our ambassadors only reluctantly accept assignments there. Change is needed, especially to ensure fair distribution of aid in all areas where our missions are located. Egyptian companies that wish to enter African markets will have to take the initiative in establishing permanent connections for Egypt with the African countries. We will then be able to say that Egypt has reclaimed its status in a new setting that does not just depend on providing assistance, but connects Egypt with other African countries on the bases of two-way mutual interests.

# 8

# CHALLENGES OF DIVISION: SUDAN

I barely managed to enter the Naivasha Stadium in Kenya before noon on January 9, 2005, representing Egypt, which had been invited to witness the signing of the Comprehensive Peace Agreement (CPA) between the government of Sudan in Khartoum and the Sudan Peoples' Liberation Movement (SPLM) in southern Sudan after a civil war that had lasted for almost twenty-one years. Among the attendees were the leaders of the Intergovernmental Authority on Development (IGAD), U.S. Secretary of State Colin Powell, representatives of the permanent members of the UN Security Council, and the Norwegian foreign minister, whose country had played a major role in supporting John Garang, the southern Sudanese political leader and head of the SPLM, in brokering a comprehensive agreement, and in fact had spent large amounts of money in order to achieve this aim. The Comprehensive Agreement, which was several volumes long, had been negotiated by Sudanese Vice-President Ali Osman Taha and Garang.

The Comprehensive Agreement declared a cease-fire between the Sudanese army and the Liberation Movement troops; set a six-year transitional period during which the northern and southern sides would jointly rule the country with Garang serving as Sudanese vice-president; and with southern politicians appointed to leading positions in the central government in Khartoum. The agreement stipulated the right of the Liberation

Movement and its southern alliances to form a government in southern Sudan to fully manage the affairs there for a period of six years, at the end of which a referendum would be held for the people of southern Sudan to decide whether to continue within the federal state of the Sudan, or become completely independent from the northern part. The agreement set the date for that referendum on January 9, 2011; if the referendum was in favor of secession and independence, this would take place after six more months, on July 9, 2011.

A feeling of joy and cheerfulness prevailed that afternoon during the ceremony. The celebration of the southern people indicated how things might develop in the following years. I spoke briefly with the secretary general of the Arab League, Amr Moussa, who was participating in the ceremony. I confidently told him, "Unfortunately, this situation will end with the disintegration of Sudan." He answered, "Indeed."

The representatives of the two sides of the dispute signed the Comprehensive Agreement. President Museveni also signed it, since Uganda held the presidency of the IGAD that year. I signed it on behalf of Egypt, because Egypt's role in dealing with this crisis could not be overlooked. For several years Egypt had opposed the negotiations supported by African and western powers, whose real motives and desires we distrusted. We also suspected the role played by western churches.

I accompanied the first deputy chief of the General Intelligence, Mohsen al-Nu'mani, to meet John Garang at the hotel in Nairobi where he was staying. I met Colin Powell as he was leaving Garang's suite. He seemed happy and satisfied with the outcome of the day. We talked briefly. He said that we should provide all the elements of success for this agreement and not let anyone ruin it, because it represented the real future for the Sudan. I answered that we should bring harmony back to all the disputed parties, and give peace a chance to prevail; then Sudan could move forward with real development.

Garang had the same charisma I had seen in him in a meeting at the Ministry of Foreign Affairs in Cairo in 1998 at the invitation of the General Intelligence which was delivered by Mohsen al-Nu'mani. At that time, I had admired his personality and his conversation with Amr Moussa. He appeared as a revolutionary with a philosophical depth. I remember saying to the foreign minister after his departure, "It is natural that he would have that depth and philosophical vision. I think he's spent all the years of rebellion since his dissent from al-Nimeiry's government in 1984 reading and looking for ways to achieve the objectives of the revolution."

Garang and his senior assistants gave Mohsen al-Nu'mani a warm welcome. I also noticed that Garang's wife seemed to know al-Nu'mani well. During the meeting, which lasted for about thirty minutes I felt that I was in the company of a group of Sudanese revolutionaries who spoke fluent English, were dressed in western style, and had very strong ties with western philosophy and concepts, which differed completely from the Arab concepts.

Garang said that he hoped that Egypt would assist in implementing the Comprehensive Agreement, focusing on the development of the destitute southern regions. I promised him that Egypt would do its best, and that we hoped that peace would be achieved while maintaining the unity of the Sudan. He emphasized that his goal was not secession, for he even saw himself as the elected president of the unified Sudan one day, and that the rebellion was a means to build a new, unified Sudan.

We left Nairobi that evening. I told Mohsen al-Nu'mani that I feared that this agreement would cause the disintegration of Sudan, in spite of all the constructive ideas that Garang had talked about. Al-Nu'mani commented that the government in Khartoum should be asked how things turned out this way, and why the western and regional powers had been allowed to achieve their goals in the south. I was disappointed that we had let the situation deteriorate to this point. He said that the northern leadership did not listen to any advice.

Our ambassador in Khartoum, Assem Ibrahim, who had also served as ambassador to Nairobi and Addis Ababa, was my friend. We met on the North Coast each year during the summer vacation—he coming from Khartoum and I from New York. He usually briefed me about developments in Sudan and provided detailed answers to my many questions about the situation and the possibilities for Sudan, a country of vital importance to Egypt. We also discussed the attitudes of the neighboring countries. In summer 2003 our ambassador said that the central government in Khartoum and the Sudanese army could not do anything further. It might be possible for Garang, whose People's Movement was supported by the rebels in Darfur, to defeat the Sudanese army and enter Khartoum, which would have serious consequences for the north. He added that the Sudanese army was exhausted and needed time to rest after a continuous period of armed clashes in different parts of the country. The Khartoum government did not have a very high opinion of southern Sudan. Ibrahim thought that Sudan might finally be able to live in peace if the southern part disappeared. When I returned to Cairo, I told the president my impression of the situation in Kenya, and added that Sudan was facing a critical period. The north needed continuous advice in order to make peace with the south and put hostility aside. Development was also essential to keep Sudan unified. Egypt should provide as much support to southern Sudan as possible, although I had my doubts about the feasibility of a unified Sudan in the long term.

I discussed the situation with General Omar Suleiman. His staff had in-depth knowledge of the situation in Sudan, and their communications with Juba, the capital of southern Sudan, and the SPLM and its leadership were extremely effective. We both believed that it was important to design Egyptian programs for supporting and cooperating with southern Sudan so as to strengthen the option of unity by the time of the referendum. If the majority chose to secede, contrary to our desire, we would have at least maintained relations of cooperation and understanding with this new country. We could not forget the efforts Egypt made over the years in providing the youth of southern Sudan with opportunities to study at Egyptian universities, particularly at Alexandria University, from which dozens of the officials who would be qualified to rule in southern Sudan had graduated. Accordingly, the General Intelligence and the Ministry of Foreign Affairs implemented detailed programs in southern Sudan with the full support of the Egyptian government and Cabinet. Nonetheless, all the evaluation reports presented to the president, and all of the discussions with his officials, indicated that secession would most probably take place at the end of the six-year transitional period. Then John Garang exited the political stage in a fatal helicopter crash in southern Uganda. The gravity of this development and its possible consequences were immediately felt. We continued to build strong relations with Salva Kiir, the new leader of the SPLM and the new first vice-president of Sudan.

At this time, in 2004 and 2005, I was concerned with two main issues in Sudanese affairs. The first was how to deal with southern Sudan in the wake of the Comprehensive Agreement. The second was Darfur and the threat it posed to Sudan.

Since 2002, during my time at the UN, the international community had been following the military operations of the Sudanese army in the Darfur region, which is the same size as France. It had spoken out against the attacks on the Sudanese civilians in the region, and pointed to the violations of international humanitarian law. The reports of the various human rights organizations were made public and discussed by all. Throughout 2003 and 2004, it was clear that the conditions in Sudan were terrible, and that Cairo and Khartoum should be made aware of the consequences of possible foreign interference. Thus it was necessary for the Sudanese government not to allow any acts that could be considered crimes under international law.

Perhaps the reader will remember that I traveled to Khartoum to meet with President al-Bashir a week after I was appointed as foreign minister. I candidly discussed the gravity of the situation in Sudan and the possibility of his being personally indicted, as had happened to the Serbian president Slobodan Milosevic. In all our subsequent communications with the Sudanese, we asked them not to underestimate the increasing accusations of human rights violations. On the other hand, I noticed that, while the Security Council and the western powers issued repeated statements and resolutions against the Sudanese government and demanded the cessation of their military operations, they did not ask the rebels in Darfur to do the same.

It seemed to me that this lopsided international attitude would prompt the rebels to continue their attacks. If this happened, the government would have to retaliate, and thus face growing international criticism. Hence I brought the matter up with all the foreign ministers, especially those from countries who were permanent members of the Security Council, during the General Assembly in September 2004. I asked them all to stop issuing these statements and resolutions, which only encouraged the rebels to carry on their attacks, and try instead to arrive at a settlement. I tried to explain to the ministers that it was important to understand the real situation in Sudan, the culture of desert life, and the effects of periodic droughts on the movements of the inhabitants, the conflicts among the tribes, and other matters. I also assured them that Egypt was asking the central government to cease any acts that could be considered a violation of human rights.

At the end of July 2004, I spent a whole morning in the city of al-Fashir in Darfur. I witnessed at first hand the deteriorating conditions of the people in Darfur, who were forced to live in tents after their villages had been burned down. They lacked food, schools, and healthcare. Before President Mubarak went on a long vacation to Ras al-Hikma on the North Coast, General Omar Suleiman and I talked to him, and he agreed to send a large number of Egyptian C130 planes to carry, food, medications, tents, and other kinds of aid to add to the international relief efforts. The Egyptian Armed Forces set up a large field hospital with a capacity of sixty to one hundred beds to provide medical services for the refugees and the displaced in Darfur. Although the Egyptian president was conscious of the financial cost to Egypt, he was aware of the dangers besetting Sudan: dissolution and civil wars in the southern, western, and eastern parts of the country.

In the statement I made before the General Assembly on September 24, 2004, I said, "There is a pressing humanitarian problem in Darfur, and a real humanitarian tragedy that needs urgent international efforts to avoid its exacerbation, but we should also try to understand the conditions in Sudan with its ethnic composition, and cultural and ideological legacies. The Sudanese issue is complex by nature and is faced by extremely intricate problems, and we have to help solve them, not further complicate the situation. We call on the international community to not only criticize this side or that, or to lay the blame on policies of one party or another, but what will be more useful than all that is to take prompt action to provide humanitarian assistance to the Darfurians who are in desperate need of it." This criticism of the international community was an Egyptian protest against all attempts of interference in Sudanese affairs and against the threats of the west to launch international military operations against Sudan to stop the massacre in Darfur. We had talks at the same time with several influential international parties—France, the United States, Britain, and Russia—on the importance of getting Sudan's neighbors to stop meddling in its affairs, particularly in Darfur. News was spreading about Eritrean activity in eastern and western Sudan, and about Chad allowing the rebels and opposition movements to use its territories. Libya had also insisted on intruding. The situation in Sudan was disastrous. The central government was aware of the international and regional pressure, which was to some extent provoked by its own attitudes and actions over the years. In the midst of this situation, the Security Council adopted a resolution in March 2005 referring the crimes against humanity committed by the regime in Sudan to the International Criminal Court.

Dr. Mustafa Osman Ismail arrived in Cairo at the beginning of 2005, before the resolution was issued. Dr. Ismail had been required to give up his position as Sudan's foreign minister in accordance with the Naivasha Agreement, which assigned it instead to a southerner, Lam Akol. We discussed the situation and I introduced him to some Egyptian legal experts, notably Dr. Mufeed Shehab, Dr. Nabil al-Arabi, and others. He was advised to have the regime in Sudan hold serious trials to consider the charges of war crimes and crimes against humanity brought by the international community against some individuals in Sudan. Dr. Ismail promised to inform President al-Bashir of our views and the importance of taking the matter seriously, or the Sudanese president and his men would face charges of their own. We worked toward peace in Sudan by encouraging the government to execute the Naivasha Agreement with integrity; by trying to stop the fighting in eastern Sudan; and by improving the relations between Chad and Sudan in order to stop the rebels from crossing the borders or receiving support from either government. As previously mentioned, we discussed this issue with Libya, France, the United States, and Eritrea, and attended meetings in Cairo, Tripoli, and elsewhere in an attempt to achieve these objectives. We also held meetings specifically for the countries neighboring Sudan—Chad, Libya, Egypt, and Eritrea—for continuous assessment of the situation.

The situation in Sudan forced thousands of refugees into Egypt, either to stay or to migrate to Europe or North America through the office of the United Nations High Commissioner for Refugees (UNHCR). The southern Sudanese refugees staged a sit-in in front of the UNHCR office in Cairo. Fights broke out with the residents of the area, and the Egyptian media talked about the difficult situation the commissioner was in. The Egyptian authorities tried to transfer the refugees to camps until their legal status was considered, but they refused to go. The subject was raised in the Egyptian Cabinet, where some members felt it was important to disperse the sit-in and transfer the refugees to a safe area. Unfortunately, dozens were killed while evacuating the square. I was concerned about the consequences of this incident, which revealed the aggressiveness of the people in charge of this operation.

Southern Sudan revolted. The inhabitants attacked the Egyptian irrigation sites. The attack left a scar that would need time to heal, especially since our aim was to build strong relations with southern Sudan. We immediately provided more technical cooperation programs in an attempt to repair our relationship. We agreed to open a representative office for the government of southern Sudan in Cairo in accordance with the Naivasha Agreement, which provided for representation in foreign countries. The government in Khartoum was displeased; we explained that the name of the southern official was included in the list of members of the Sudanese Embassy in Cairo. More, and larger, southern delegations were visiting Cairo and needed someone to tend to them while they were in Egypt. This southern official also served as a liaison between Egypt and the southern Sudanese authorities to facilitate the delivery of Egyptian assistance to southern Sudan.

Active attempts were made to settle the situation in Darfur. As the head of the African Union in 2005–2006, Nigeria offered to host negotiations in Abuja between the government and the rebels in Darfur. Egypt was invited as an observer. We were represented by Ahmed Haggag, who followed the discussions for weeks and cabled the news to us back home. An agreement was reached but was rejected by the main elements of the rebellion, the Sudan Liberation Movement (SLM) led by Abdul Wahid al-Nour and the

Judgment and Equality Movement (JEM) headed by Khalil Ibrahim. It was decided to send observers and peace forces from the African Union. The secretariat of the African Union procrastinated over Egypt's offer to send a large number of observers and troops. I emphasized to the secretary general of the African Union, Oumar Konare, that Egypt was very much concerned about the conditions in Sudan and that we should be present wherever Sudanese affairs were involved. I also complained to the UN secretary general, who was trying to organize African troops in Darfur, in accordance with a resolution of the African Union and financed by the western powers, which provided significant logistic capabilities. We received an answer, or rather an allegation: it was Sudan that refused to have Egyptian troops included. I contacted President al-Bashir's advisor Mustafa Osman Ismail and Foreign Minister Lam Akol, both of whom completely denied it. We found out that there were factions within the Sudanese government that opposed any significant Egyptian military presence in Darfur, but they were obliged to accept us. The same situation recurred when international peacekeeping forces were required to separate the northern and southern troops. When we asked to participate, the UN secretariat claimed that the southerners did not wish to have Egyptian forces inside southern Sudan. I spoke with Sudanese Vice-President Salva Kiir, who denied it completely. It was agreed to place Egyptian forces in the Nuba Mountains.

Sudan resisted the presence of UN-sponsored international forces in Darfur. They feared the impact of internationalization on the regime in Khartoum, especially considering the charges against President al-Bashir and some of his senior assistants and the possibility of their indictment by the International Criminal Court.

There was increasing pressure from the international community and the UN. A meeting was held in Addis Ababa to discuss the situation, in which I participated along with a number of western foreign ministers, notably Condoleezza Rice, the UN secretary general Kofi Annan, and the secretary general of the Arab League. We had an extended discussion in which Lam Akol defended his country's perspective, but it was agreed at the end to form a hybrid force of international and African troops. I should here clearly point out the right of Sudan to protect its territories against foreign interference and to have the mission and responsibilities of the international hybrid forces precisely determined. Egypt asked to participate. I always referred, at every opportunity, to the capabilities of the Egyptian Armed Forces. I noticed that the administration at the secretariat of the African Union did not have enough military experience to help the UN with the dispatch of experts and troops. I offered a number of operations planning officers from our forces, and the attendees in Addis Ababa approved. Egypt—not the international community—paid their salaries and covered all their expenses. The Egyptian troops in Sudan were increased to include two mechanized infantry battalions, military engineers, ground transportation, mine removal, and other forces in Darfur, and another two mechanized infantry battalions and other forces in the Nuba Mountains on the border between northern and southern Sudan. We continued to offer even more troops, ranking highly among the contributors to the international peacekeeping operations.

In accordance with the resolution of the Higher Committee of Nile Water, we started to build a power station in Wau, in southern Sudan, in 2007, which was inaugurated in February 2009. Three more plants were built: in Bor, the capital of Jonglei State; in Bambu, the capital of Western Equatorial State, and in Rumbek, the capital of Lakes State, with an overall budget of 158 million pounds.

An Egyptian–southern Sudanese company for electricity was established. Efforts continued to open a southern campus of Alexandria University in Tonj and Warab. In 2006 the General Intelligence, Ministry of Foreign Affairs, and Ministry of Health set up the famous Egyptian clinic in Juba, where an Egyptian general consulate had been opened earlier. Two integrated clinics were opened in Bor and Gogrial. Juba Primary and Secondary School was built, and in 2006 we started building an Egyptian school compound for primary, agricultural, polytechnic, and vocational education in Jonglei State.

Egypt also offered scholarships for the southerners: three hundred bachelor-level scholarships, twenty-five master's scholarships, and five doctoral scholarships. Places were provided at Egyptian specialized institutes in the fields of banking, agriculture, irrigation, media, and communications, as well as at the Police Academy. During 2007 major projects were implemented to purify stream water in the Bahr al-Ghazal basin; set up marinas; establish a central laboratory for analyzing water quality in Juba; drill groundwater wells; set up processing facilities for pure drinking water; train and build capacities in Malakal; establish two sites for the irrigation department in Juba and Wau; set up a hundred-acre model farm in Wau; drill forty wells in Darfur; send medical convoys to southern Sudan and Darfur; buy kits to set up four workshops for metalwork, lathe turning, carpentry, and mechanics at the Juba educational compound; and offer a three-million-dollar program of medical and food aid for a period of four years.

During 2006 and 2007, efforts to reach a settlement in Darfur continued, because the Abuja Agreement could not end the fighting. At the same time there was tension on the Sudan–Chad border in spite of attempts, by Egypt and others, to calm down both sides.

At the end of 2007, while I was attending a ministerial meeting at the Arab League, I noticed that the Sudanese state minister, Ali Karti, who was representing Sudan, had long conversations with the Qatari prime minister and foreign minister, Sheikh Hamad bin Jassem bin Jaber al-Thani, who remained throughout the entire session, which ran late into the evening. I asked the sheikh, "What is so interesting that keeps Sheikh Hamad seated all through a routine ministerial meeting?" He answered, "I am concerned with the League affairs and its work." When the meeting was about to end, the Sudanese delegation presented a draft agreement concerning the situation in Darfur. It stated that the Arab ministers were assigning Qatar as mediator between the parties in Darfur. The Qatari representative was to work toward a cease-fire and a permanent settlement under the supervision of the African–Arab Ministerial Committee, the Arab League, the African Union, and the UN, all of which had already been working on a settlement for a year. The resolution presented by Sudan was approved and adopted. I told Sheikh Hamad, "Now I know why you stayed," and asked the Sudanese state minister, "Why did you keep this a secret? We've known for hours about this arrangement. We wouldn't have opposed the mandate, but will be glad if Qatar, or any other country, manages to arrange a cease-fire." I told him, with a hint of reproach, that relations between Egypt's and Sudan's diplomats should be conducted with greater candor and that his approach in assigning Qatar a role as mediator revealed misconceptions that he, or perhaps the leadership in Khartoum, had about Egypt. I affirmed that we were working hard to defend Sudan against a ferocious attack. President al-Bashir and the emir of Qatar had had reciprocal visits during which they decided to have Qatar act as a mediator, to which we would have agreed.

Libya, meanwhile, was annoyed at what they regarded as Qatar's interference in Sudanese affairs, which they considered part of their sphere of influence, in particular as regards Sudanese–Chadian relations and the situation in Darfur. We made serious efforts to calm Libya down. We also summoned some of the southern Sudanese rebels to Cairo and tried to talk them into agreeing to pacify the region. I explained to General Omar Suleiman that we were already familiar with the situation and would not have objected to any course of action that would serve Sudan's interests. What really bothered me was that Ali Karti kept it secret. Omar Suleiman discussed the matter with the director of the Sudanese Intelligence Services. I also mildly criticized the Sudanese president, as President Mubarak had instructed me. This maneuver on the part of Sudan was incomprehensible to us. Perhaps they believed that Egypt would not be pleased if Qatar became involved in Sudan, or perhaps the Sudanese had their doubts about the Egyptian contacts with southern Sudan and the rebels in Darfur, with whom we, like others, had been in constant touch, trying to convince them to accept a cease-fire. In his conversation with Mubarak in Doha in October 2010, the emir of Qatar mentioned that Qatar could never be a rival of Egypt in terms of regional influence, but that it was making efforts to serve what it believed to be Arab interests. Mubarak commented that a country as great as Egypt could not be threatened by a younger brother.

The Sudanese affirmed that they did not mean to offend Egypt at all. Nonetheless, Mustafa Osman Ismail and Ali Karti expressed their concern about our contacts with the rebels in Darfur. As for our intensive activities in southern Sudan, at which they hinted, we explained that Egypt was trying to help the Sudanese people in both the north and the south, in order to promote the option of unity. Thus, Khartoum should feel grateful, not disturbed at Egypt's significant efforts in southern Sudan.

At the beginning of the Doha negotiations in October 2010, I met with the Qatari minister of state. I informed him of our perspective, and wished him success in his future endeavors. The negotiations took place, papers and agreements were signed, and the war was still in progress when I left office in March 2011.

All these years, we had been working in coordination with many other countries, including Libya, Chad, France, and Saudi Arabia, to end the conflict in Darfur. Sudan was under more and more pressure. The prosecutor of the International Criminal Court, Luis Moreno Ocampo, urged Sudan to take legal steps against two Sudanese officials who were charged with crimes committed during the conflict in Darfur. On orders from the president, I advised the Sudanese to take credible legal measures to prove to the ICC and its prosecutor that their charges were being taken seriously. I asked them to consider passing Sudanese legislation that would meet the requirements of the ICC. I received Ocampo in Cairo to discuss the many legal, political, and social considerations that had to be taken into account when dealing with Darfur and Sudan. We continued to pass on Ocampo's comments to President al-Bashir. Omar Suleiman and I paid several visits to Khartoum and Juba in order to discuss the Sudanese situation in general and the ICC case in particular, and to monitor the implementation of the Naivasha Agreement. I felt that Ocampo would not hesitate to take action against the Sudanese officials, in spite of my warnings of the danger of any developments that would lead to charges against President al-Bashir. Nonetheless, I must admit that horrendous violations were committed in Darfur against Sudanese citizens in a war between the army and rebel groups. In my opinion, the focus should have been on ending the war and restoring stability in accordance with the agreement and with the history and culture of the region.

In case Ocampo should proceed to file an indictment in the ICC against President al-Bashir, despite our warnings, I asked the legal department at the ministry and some other Egyptian legal experts to come up with a suitable Egyptian response. It was decided that since Egypt was not a party to the Rome Statute of the ICC, it was not obliged to cooperate with the prosecutor, and we would instead work within the context of the African Union and the Arab League to address the situation. We informed the Sudanese of this decision in advance. In July 2008 Ocampo issued an arrest warrant for President al-Bashir. Following our previous decision, we proceeded to work within the framework of the Arab League, the African Union, and the Non-Aligned Movement to ask the Security Council to stay the proceedings against the Sudanese President, in accordance with Article 16 of the Rome Statute. Since the western powers disliked this option, which was against their interests, the charges were never dropped or delayed.

I had studied the methods of the ICC over the years, and noticed that, besides the legal considerations that guided its performance, it was definitely driven by the viewpoints of the parties who were in control of the Security Council, and western interests in general. Hence, I always doubted its motives and tried to be aware of the political objectives that the ICC or its prosecutor might have in view.

I kept the president informed of all the developments. He even complained of receiving too many written political and legal reports, which I often summarized orally in our phone calls. He always replied that it was necessary to do our best to stabilize Sudan and to secure its territorial integrity even if southern Sudan were to secede, because the weakening of the central government in Khartoum would affect Egyptian national security.

As soon as Ocampo presented his report to the ICC demanding the arrest of the Sudanese president, we tried to ease the pressure on the Sudanese and to find a way out of this difficult position. Mustafa Osman Ismail came to Cairo and we discussed the situation. I asked him not to escalate against the humanitarian organizations working in Darfur, many of which the government had decided to expel. I warned him that the deteriorating humanitarian situation in the camps might lead to a humanitarian crisis that could encourage those who wished to interfere in Sudan to carry out their plans. After we had studied the situation fully, both internally and externally, we decided to make a suggestion, which was approved by the Arab ministers. We proposed convening a high-level international conference to outline a comprehensive deal among the major powers and Sudan that would pave the way for the Security Council to intervene to delay the court proceedings, either temporarily or permanently. What I was really worried about was the Sudanese president's apparent stubbornness and his tendency to challenge the court.

At this same time, in early 2009, a new military confrontation was predicted on the Chad–Sudan border, because each country was allowing the other's rebels to work from within its territories. We tried to calm both parties down. The French asked to join our efforts in dealing with this issue, but we believed that French involvement would lead to adverse Libyan movements that would damage our individual efforts. Yet both Egypt and France continued to cooperate closely on Darfur and its relationship with Chad, Egypt, Libya, and Sudan. I expressed my surprise to Bernard Kouchner, the French foreign minister, that Abdul Wahid al-Nour, the leader of one of Darfur's anti-government movements, was living in France and seemed untouched by French demands to end the conflict. As if he had been waiting for this moment, Kouchner immediately suggested that France hand Abdul Wahid al-Nour over to us and have him stay in Egypt. I told him we would have to think about it, since it would have its implications for several regional actors, including Sudan and Libya. General Omar Suleiman was inclined to approve, on the condition that Nour would not be politically active.

The role of Libya in the Sudanese conflict raises many questions. It suggests either that Libya had no desire for stability on the Libyan–Chadian–Sudanese borders, or that it sought to control the whole situation regardless of the harmful effects on all three countries as well as Egypt.

With the advent of President Obama's administration, the situation improved slightly. A new U.S. envoy to Sudan was appointed who had strong relations with Obama himself, which helped to reduce the U.S. pressure on President al-Bashir. We observed in mid-2009 that there was considerable western concern about the situation in southern Sudan and an increasing fear of the collapse of the Comprehensive Peace Agreement due to the failure of the parties to abide by their commitments. In my opinion, these concerns would help to ease the ICC pressure on Sudan and encourage the government to move forward with the implementation of Naivasha Agreement in return. The reaction from Sudan was promising. The new U.S. envoy to Sudan visited Cairo, and the recent fresh impetus in Egyptian–U.S. relations helped to promote cooperation between Cairo and Washington on Sudan. The U.S. envoy, Scott Gration, told me that they were thinking of inviting all the countries that had either signed or witnessed the Comprehensive Peace Agreement, which was now at risk, to an international conference to be held in Egypt in June 2009 under joint U.S.–Egyptian chairmanship to emphasize the importance of the peace agreement and encourage all parties to implement the remaining stages until 2011. I welcomed the idea on the condition that both the northern and the southern sides approved.

The implementation of the agreement exposed weaknesses in the commitment of both sides. I repeatedly told President al-Bashir, Vice-President Ali Osman Taha, and other Sudanese officials that the government had to make serious efforts to support the option of unity. The government was not doing this, and we were worried that secession was inevitable, as I had expected, when the referendum took place in January 2011.

The Sudanese first vice-president, Salva Kiir, a southerner, visited Cairo in 2009, one of a series of meetings with us in Cairo, Juba, and New York. When President Mubarak urged him to work in favor of the unity option, he openly complained of the way the Sudanese government acted toward the south: "Mr. President, they're pushing us toward separation. They don't want us to stay united." I must mention here that in spite of the apparent reluctance of the Sudanese government to support the unity option, and all the time it wasted before it began to take the issue seriously, President al-Bashir certainly intended to invest time and money in encouraging the southerners to remain in Sudan. Our communications with many northern officials showed that they were conscious of the terrible consequences of secession. There were even suggestions to postpone the referendum for a while or to delay the implementation of the referendum results for several years. During his visit to Cairo at the end of May 2009, the Sudanese presidential advisor Mustafa Osman Ismail asked us to approach the Americans about postponing the referendum. This was a delicate matter for us, because we knew that Salva Kiir and the southern leadership would insist on holding the referendum as scheduled. We discussed the situation at the General Intelligence and the Ministry of Foreign

Affairs, and between General Omar Suleiman and myself. It was logical to try to delay the referendum in order to avoid the severe intertribal clashes that many of the southern tribes were threatening. We visited southern Sudan again to review the situation. The southerners insisted on holding the referendum on time, and we wanted to win their trust at any cost, even at the expense of the displeasure of the northerners.

Egypt worked tirelessly to achieve the stability of its neighbor, which is of immense strategic importance to Egyptian national security. While continuing to engage in dialogue with the Khartoum government, we maintained good relations with the actors in Darfur and invited them to visit Cairo, which irritated the government in Khartoum. We also developed strong relations with Gration in order to keep ourselves informed about U.S. thinking on Sudan, taking into account the fact that the United States and the west had always been in favor of the breakup of Sudan.

In the midst of these critical developments regarding the future of Sudan, U.S. sources, supported by Israeli reports obtained by our embassies in Washington and Tel Aviv, revealed that an outside party launched air raids, probably by drones, on one or more convoys carrying weapons inside eastern Sudanese territories south of Egypt on the Red Sea shore. The vehicles, weapons, and ammunition in the convoy were destroyed. General Omar Suleiman and I paid another visit to Khartoum, where we discussed this alarming development with President al-Bashir and his senior aides. The president confirmed the reports and added that many passing vessels stopped in bays on the Sudanese Red Sea coast in order to unload cargoes of smuggled goods—arms as well as other things. Sudan was trying to control these coastal areas and its territorial waters, but the length of the coastline made the task extremely difficult.

Once we were back in Cairo, Egypt worked on enhancing its security measures against weapons smuggling. President al-Bashir thought the contraband was coming from Yemen or Iran. The U.S. sources further complicated the situation by suggesting that the weapons were sent by air from Iran to Syria to Sudan, from which point they entered Egyptian territory. The dangerous conditions in Sudan in general, and in Darfur in particular, made it even more important for Egypt to control its southern border. The abduction of a group of Italian tourists in Egypt's Western Desert on the Sudanese border in September 2008 was just one of the problems Egypt faced as a result of the conflict in Darfur. I was personally criticized by the Egyptian press for mistakenly announcing from New York that the tourists had been rescued. It was not accurate at the time, but it did happen later. I neither responded to that criticism nor mentioned that I had received my information from a reliable source.

As Egypt continued to assist Sudan, Mustafa Osman Ismail asked that Egypt host a pledging conference to support development in Darfur, which was agreed upon by Khartoum and the Organization of the Islamic Conference (OIC) in association with Turkey. The conference was held in March 2010. We received contributions of about $800 million, which the participating countries pledged to send to Sudan for the benefit of Darfur.

Egypt went to great lengths to support Sudan. The following unclassified cable, which the Ministry of Foreign Affairs sent to all its embassies abroad, clearly illustrates the Egyptian concern with Sudanese affairs at the end of 2009 and the beginning of 2010.

*UNCLASSIFIED CIRCULAR TO ALL EGYPTIAN MISSIONS*

1. The ministry is eager to convey the message to the various international and regional parties that Sudan is passing through a decisive stage in its history, and the challenges it faces threaten the future of its peace and stability as well as those of the whole region. In spite of their internal nature, their impacts would be felt regionally and internationally.

2. We emphasize the role of Egypt and the international community in providing the necessary support to Sudan to overcome this crisis in its history, whose repercussions will undoubtedly be felt beyond the Sudanese borders to the vulnerable neighboring area.

3. The ministry recommends that the cases of southern Sudan and Darfur should be considered in tandem, since they will together affect the future of Sudan. Sudan is on the verge of two important developments, the first of which is the elections by April 2010, and the second one is the referendum for self-determination by January 2011.

4.  In spite of the slight progress in the peace process in southern Sudan with respect to the implementation of the Comprehensive Peace Agreement, several challenges still exist; an agreement has to be reached concerning the division of oil revenue, the demarcation of the border, the integration of the Armed Forces and disarmament, the debatable result of the census, and the law of the referendum, as well as the insecurity of southern Sudan, which greatly hinders the preservation of its security and stability. In this context, the Ministry of Foreign Affairs wishes to encourage a sense of joint responsibility in the two partners governing Sudan to reach an agreement on these unresolved points in order to support the security and stability of the region.

5.  We undertake active communications to highlight Egypt's support for the unity of Sudan and its eagerness to encourage all possible international and regional efforts to present unity as an attractive option for all the Sudanese. The ministry has sought to promote the idea that voting for secession at this time will have its several negative impacts on the Sudanese people as well as their neighbors. This Egyptian vision is shared by many international parties who believe that there are real risks threatening the security and stability of the region if secession takes place.

6.  The Ministry of Foreign Affairs is making substantial efforts to provide Egyptian assistance to the government of southern Sudan in anticipation of the possible secession. In this regard, the ministry is coordinating Egypt's contributions to southern Sudan in the area of infrastructure, including electricity, medical centers, and schools, in addition to training courses on capacity-building for the southerners.

7.  We are aware that the relationship between northern and southern Sudan is crucial at this time. Thus, relying on Egypt's good relationship with both parties to the Comprehensive Peace Agreement, Egyptian diplomacy is making efforts to encourage both sides to improve their relations, which will, in turn, lead to improved conditions not only in Sudan but in the region as a whole. In all our communications with the Sudanese parties we are determined to

promote a stable, united Sudan as an example to be followed by the peoples of the African areas that have suffered from the effects of war and internal conflicts for years.

8. Since the crisis in Darfur attracts the full attention of Egypt and the international community, the various Sudanese issues are interrelated, and the paths of peace for Darfur and southern Sudan are physically related, we have sought in our communications with all the concerned international parties to explain that the political developments in Darfur and the arrest warrant issued by the ICC against President Omar al-Bashir have had a negative effect on the implementation of the Comprehensive Peace Agreement. Egyptian diplomacy acknowledges that the situation in Darfur has added a new negative factor in the relationship between the northern and southern parties, and also in the relations between Sudan and the international community, which have been greatly affected by the decision of the ICC. In general, the conditions in Darfur do not help the parties to the Peace Agreement—the government and the People's Movements—to overcome their mutual mistrust. Thus, we are currently focusing on designing a comprehensive method to guarantee that progress in one respect will not negatively affect the other.

9. Egypt plays a vital role in rebuilding trust between the two partners in governance and achieving peace in Darfur. In so doing we depend on our ability to maintain an equal distance from all the Sudanese parties, so that we can work effectively to realize these objectives. Egypt supports the efforts made by the common mediator Djibril Bassole, who represents both the international and the regional will. We are focusing on coordinating all the efforts made to achieve peace in Darfur in order to avoid duplication and contradiction.

10. Egypt recommends that the international community take a stand against the rebels in Darfur, since this will have a positive effect on the political process there and make it possible to reach a peace agreement in Darfur, on the condition that the international community shows its commitment to assist in the reconstruction and development of Darfur in coordination with the international

obligations to spread peace, security, and stability throughout all of Sudan indiscriminately.

11. This diplomatic response to the situation in Sudan is based on various paths that include the different Sudanese parties, the two partners in governance in particular, and the regional countries, including Libya, Chad, and Eritrea, in addition to continuous communications with the influential international powers—the United States, Britain, France, and China—and the international and regional organizations. The aim of this movement is to highlight the Egyptian viewpoint on the issues of southern Sudan and Darfur in a way that may provide stability and security in Sudan in the end, this being the main objective which the international community seeks to achieve in Sudan in the near future.

*END OF CIRCULAR*

The increasingly complex domestic situation in Sudan affected the ongoing discussion between Nile riparian states on the Comprehensive Framework Agreement on the management of the Nile waters. Maintaining close coordination between Egypt and Sudan on these matters was essential, and was a controlling factor in our posture toward political developments within Sudan. As it became apparent that negotiations on the Comprehensive Framework Agreement would not be successful and that the upstream countries would persist in their attempts to impose their views on Egypt and Sudan, it was necessary for Egypt to become more active diplomatically to maintain the coherence of the Egyptian–Sudanese position, by intensifying the communications, visits, and consultations between both sides. I also seized the opportunity of the ministerial meeting of the Forum on China–Africa Cooperation and the Chinese prime minister's visit to Cairo to ask the Chinese to study the establishment of an Egyptian–Chinese mechanism for a joint study of water projects set up in the upstream countries so that China would not launch any project that might have harmful effects on the downstream countries.

The Egyptian and Sudanese sides also discussed the engineering projects that Ethiopia was establishing without prior notification, especially

Tekeze and Tanables Dams, and whether it would be useful for Egypt and Sudan to object or not, especially that both projects were associated with the irrigated agriculture. The Sudanese stated that their source did not refer to any activity concerning the irrigated agriculture in these two projects so far, and they would not protest unless there was evidence to the contrary.

In 2009 and 2010, as the referendum in southern Sudan approached, there was much talk about what would happen to the Nile water quotas if southern Sudan seceded. In Egypt, we were counting on the fact that southern Sudan had abundant water resources which could be developed by major projects for managing the water of the swamps and canals. According to the 1959 Agreement, the Sudanese quota applied to the entire country, north and south. We needed to find out what the southern authorities had in mind about the water quota before taking an official stance. The Egyptian consul general in Juba met with the Sudanese first vice-president and with the president of the government of southern Sudan, Salva Kiir, about the Jonglei Canal project, which Egypt had been trying to launch in southern Sudan since 1980. The project would add about 5.3 billion cubic meters of water to the White Nile in southern Khartoum. Salva Kiir said that he was in favor of resuming the canal project, which had halted at the outbreak of the civil war in 1983, but that he did not want to announce it publicly, for fear of the dissenters who would intentionally use the occasion to damage southern Sudan's friendly relationship with Egypt.

Salva Kiir added that Khartoum wished to keep control of the project, since the agreement to construct the canal was made between Cairo and Khartoum. The southerners would not accept this because it marginalized their role. (This had actually been another factor, besides the outbreak of the rebellion, that had delayed the project in the first place.) He wanted to resume the project as soon as possible, on the condition that the remaining path of the 320-kilometer canal could be adjusted to protect the communities and the wildlife living in the area surrounding the canal. He pointed out that attractive development projects were needed in order to encourage settled communities so as to reduce the absolute independence on grazing and cattle raiding in Jonglei State, the most volatile area of southern Sudan because of historical tribal disputes. He suggested building several bridges over the canal, an idea that dated back to 1982. Finally, he proposed updating the Egyptian–Sudanese memorandum of understanding for the project, turning it into an agreement between Cairo and Juba.

During this period, many of the southern officials' statements revealed an openness to Egypt and expressed good intentions toward the water issue. I believe that this was a maneuver to gain time and neutralize the role of Egypt when they declared their independence.

We needed to show our gratitude for the cooperative attitude of the southerners, so we were eager to set up large projects and programs. On a short visit to Juba in October 2009 that lasted for several hours, President Mubarak consulted with the southern leadership. Although the visit expressed Egyptian concern with the affairs of southern Sudan, it did not include any specific project that the Egyptian president could announce. One of the problems I always faced when preparing for Mubarak's visits was that, for security reasons, they were unannounced. We were only informed the evening before the visit, and then only because General Omar Suleiman and I were key players. For this visit to Juba in particular, I could not obtain even a brief report on the technical cooperation or specific recommendations from the relevant department since this required extensive coordination among all the Egyptian agencies dealing with Sudan, for which there was not enough time. In spite of this, I tried to convince the president to offer some sort of special gift during this visit. During my meeting with Salva Kiir and General Omar Suleiman two years earlier, I had noticed that the building the southern government used was in bad condition and needed to be renovated. I passed a note to the president suggesting that he offer to reconstruct the building in three months as a gift from Egypt. He read the note and returned it to me. He did not support the idea. I believe this was because he preferred to take time to think about a decision, especially when money was involved. We thus missed an occasion for an Egyptian presence that would not reoccur for years to come.

We received reports on the Israeli activities within southern Sudan from the Egyptian embassies in Khartoum, Juba, Tel Aviv, and other cities in Africa and Europe. The Israelis were strengthening their relationship with the southern dignitaries and were making use of the southern diplomatic offices in some capitals, notably Washington, to promote their relations with southern Sudan.

Through Kenya and Uganda, Israel offered scholarships to southern Sudanese students in the fields of agriculture, irrigation, and tourism. Israel also bought land through businessmen to support its activities there. I requested a study comparing the Israeli and Egyptian aid programs. The results were in favor of Israel with regard to the size of the programs, their monetary value, and their value at the grassroots level.

For years, I tried to bring to the Arabs' attention the new conditions that might emerge in southern Sudan. I wrote several letters to the foreign ministers of the Gulf Cooperation Council countries urging them to consider increasing their investment in southern Sudan. I suggested not only direct assistance, important as that was, but economic projects from which their own countries would benefit as well. Such acts might encourage the eventual government of Juba to join the Arab League, in which the southerners had so far been noticeably uninterested. During the Arab Summit in Sirte, the head of one Gulf country asked to hold a special meeting for all the countries of the Arab League to discuss the possibility of the secession of southern Sudan. I attended the meeting on behalf of the president of Egypt. The head of the Gulf country stated that the latest developments indicated that Sudan was about to disintegrate. He stated that his country would allot a billion dollars for capacity-building in northern Sudan to resist the secession. He hinted that the west supported the breakup, and that the Arabs had to resist and show support for the northern military potential. I believed that this suggestion would bring the situation back to square one and cause Sudan to return to armed confrontation. There were even rumors that Sudan be divided into three countries: Bahr al-Ghazal, Upper Nile, and Equatorial. It seemed to me that the person who suggested this idea was unaware of the actual conditions in Sudan. On behalf of Egypt, I stated that we supported any ideas that would achieve peace and stability in Sudan, north and south, under the current circumstances. I added that we welcomed the development and investment assistance, which Egypt had long been concerned with, but if military aid was increased, we would be at the risk of further deterioration. I then discussed all the dangers surrounding Sudan and the threats of the foreign intervention, especially if the Arabs chose the option now under discussion. The suggestion was dismissed. None of the ministers who were present approved of it, and the person who proposed it did not defend it either.

The Sudanese president visited the Egyptian president two hours after the Arab meeting ended. He asked me in front of Mubarak, "Why do you oppose a proposal for helping the Sudan?" I defended my opinion and I think that President al-Bashir accepted it.

During the last week of May 2010, the International Criminal Court notified the Security Council that Sudan was not cooperating in its criminal proceedings against Ahmed Haroun, the governor of South Kordofan and a former minister in the Sudanese government, and Ali Kushayb, the commander of a militia in Darfur. The timing of this announcement was revealing. There was an inclination to heighten pressure on the Sudanese regime, especially because it was obvious that the United States was concerned with the relationship of the Sudanese government to southern Sudan in view of the upcoming referendum. I noticed that the ICC notification sent to the Security Council did not include President al-Bashir, only his assistants. The ICC—or, more precisely, the western powers that stood behind it—did not wish to take action against the Sudanese president. I believed that, in this matter, all roads led to southern Sudan and the west's preference for secession. If al-Bashir was willing to accept this, the western powers would not seek to prosecute him.

With the approach of both the referendum in southern Sudan and the Sudanese presidential election in 2010, I noticed that the Sudanese were more willing to express their dissatisfaction with the Egyptian attitude. For our part, our analysis indicated that Sudan was on its way to disintegration, and thus we had to maintain good relations with both northern and southern Sudan. Omar Suleiman and I accordingly paid visits to both Khartoum and Juba.

An outlandish statement was attributed to the Sudanese foreign minister, Ali Karti, in which he purportedly said that he hoped that Egypt would play a more positive role in Sudan and that the Sudanese people expected Egypt to support the country's unity. I asked our ambassador to inquire about the authenticity of this statement from the Sudanese minister himself. The minister said that his statement had been distorted and that the Egyptian ambassador could make an announcement to the media to this effect. Ali Karti demanded that Egypt make serious efforts to convince the southern Sudanese leaders who had studied in Egypt that unity was the more viable option.

As the January 2011 referendum approached, the leadership in Khartoum asked for Egypt's assistance. Ali Osman Taha said that they would make sincere efforts to have southern Sudan vote against separation and hoped that Egypt would help them with this matter. We confirmed that we already had. Yet we could not afford to lose the trust of the southern leadership, which we gained over years of persistent effort. We pointed out that the Egyptian investments in all of Sudan amounted to about $2.5 billion.

In his presidential election campaign, President al-Bashir claimed that Halayeb—an area in southeastern Egypt that is under Egyptian sovereignty—was Sudanese land and that he believed in the concept of an economic integration zone. I commented that in Egypt we agreed about the concept of establishing an integration area, as long as it extended both north and south of the international boundary between Egypt and Sudan which was the 22nd parallel north. In this case I could not choose to remain quiet as I normally would on such a controversial topic with our twin country. I noticed that in his press conference with Ali Karti, my successor fell into a trap set by the shrewd Sudanese minister, who stated that Halayeb represented an "integration zone" between Egypt and Sudan, a description which our minister accepted without asking for further explanation. It seemed that we were giving up our sovereignty over the area north of the 22nd parallel to Sudan. Our clever legal expert should not have made such a mistake.

As the sixty-fifth session of the UN General Assembly was about to be held in September 2010, the U.S. president suggested a meeting on Sudan to garner international support for the upcoming referendum on January 9, which the United States strongly supported. We agreed to participate in this meeting, and declared that Egypt would seek to convince the two parties to agree on a post-referendum transitional period to implement the result of the referendum, whatever it might be, while avoiding conflict within southern Sudan, between the south and the north, or with neighboring countries.

An agreement should also be reached on a method to resolve the tribal conflicts in southern Sudan—on the borders in particular—by following the
existing procedures for disarmament and for reintegration of the militias into
the community. We expressed our eagerness to maintain peace and stability
between northern and southern Sudan, taking into account all the possible
post-referendum scenarios, most of which were not promising.

Before my departure to New York for the General Assembly and the
conference on Sudan, Sudanese Foreign Minister Ali Karti arrived in Cairo
on September 16 to convey a verbal message from his president to President Mubarak. The Sudanese president promised that his government
would abide by the result of the referendum, on the condition that all
parties would guarantee a free and fair referendum. Sudan was looking forward to Egypt's assistance in emphasizing the importance of choosing the
unity option. The Sudanese also hoped that Egypt would encourage the
United States to support the positions of the Sudanese government, taking
into consideration the sensitive relations between northern and southern
Sudan, their common interests, and the large tribal overlap on the border, which would require allowing the tribes freedom of movement across
the border in the dry season. They sought our help with the Darfur issue
and against any attempts to disintegrate the northern half of the country. I
passed on the verbal message to the president, pointing out that it reflected
a deep concern about the possible repercussions of secession on the unity
of northern Sudan. I confirmed that we were seeking to help Khartoum
and warn the United States and the other western powers about the possibility of violence, either between or within the northern and southern
areas. I promised to bring up these issues during the New York meeting.

In Egypt, we studied all the possible results of the Sudanese referendum and their consequences. During the second half of September
2010, all the Egyptian agencies concerned held a series of meetings to
determine the Egyptian position regarding the political, security, military, legal, and economic issues of the possible secession: recognition of
the country of southern Sudan, its timing, the status of our diplomatic
representation, and the ways to maintain positive relations with both
countries. Other problems to be considered were the potential influx of a

large number of southern refugees into Egypt, the status of the Egyptian troops under UN command in southern Sudan, and the water treaties. In case of secession, which was the most likely outcome, it was suggested that an association called the Nile Valley Grouping, to include Egypt and northern and southern Sudan, might be formed.

I participated in the High-Level Meeting on Sudan at the UN on September 24, 2010, which received considerable international attention, partly because President Obama attended part some of the proceedings, and partly because the international community was becoming aware of the potential dangers as the referendum drew closer. The well-known western powers stressed the importance of holding the referendum as scheduled since any delay without the consent of southern Sudan would prompt a return to conflict. They warned the Khartoum government against complicating the situation. Egypt, along with Ethiopia, took a more cautious approach. We emphasized the importance of resolving the outstanding issues, including the demarcation of the border and the implementation of the Abyei referendum (a separate referendum on the status of the Abyei region), and pointed out that the referendum was a means to achieve peace and stability and not an end in itself. Thus its timing should not be regarded as a sacred cow; on the contrary, it could be adjusted in order to guarantee its integrity.

While I was getting ready to leave New York September 29, I received a phone call from U.S. Secretary of State Hillary Clinton, who expressed her deep concern about the conditions in Sudan, since there had been reports of attempts to hinder the referendum, which could cause a new civil war. Clinton asked us to urge the Sudanese to implement the Comprehensive Agreement in full and to the letter. I shared her concern and added that the parties who had promoted the right of self-determination for the southerners and were now urging them to secede, whether out of ideology or idealism, might come to regret it if the situation in Sudan became worse. I told her that we had been warning about these dangers for a long time, and had always tried to promote the more peaceful views of the National Congress Party, which was the ruling party in Khartoum, and the SPLM. I told her that we would continue our efforts to maintain the peace and stability of Sudan, pointing out that for years Egypt had been providing more humanitarian, service, and development aid for the southerners than any other country.

After I had returned to Cairo, there were reports of the deterioration of the relationship between the parties that had concluded the peace agreement in southern Sudan that would further complicate the situation. Not only did the southerners support secession, but they also refused to form a confederation. I informed President Mubarak, who was quite concerned about the situation, that Salva Kiir had told me in New York that the confederation option was out of the question.

During my meetings in New York I informed the Americans about the Sudanese messages to Egypt, the most important of which was the one that had been conveyed from President al-Bashir to President Mubarak by Ali Karti on September 16, namely that Sudan would abide by the result of the referendum on condition that all parties would guarantee a free and fair referendum. Over the next few days, we tried to reconcile the Sudanese and American views, on the one hand, and on the other, urged both Sudanese factions not to make any premature announcement of their intentions. To this end, we sought to arrange a meeting between the U.S. envoy, Gration, and Bashir's close advisor Ghazi Salah al-Din, in either Cairo or New York.

Suddenly we received information via the Egyptian General Intelligence network that Sudanese Vice-President Ali Osman Taha had expressed his displeasure, personally rather than officially, at my departure from the UN meeting on Sudan before he made his statement, although I had listened to Salva Kiir's speech.

At that time Omar Suleiman and I were preparing for another visit to Khartoum, to try to head off any escalation of hostilities. Foreign Minister Ali Karti wanted us to come promptly so as to have a strategic and political influence on the current situation, not a visit for public relations purposes; to stay for at least one night; and to pay separate visits to Khartoum and Juba.

I was really surprised at Karti's words and at Sudan's sensitivity, in spite of our hard work to bring together the Sudanese government and the western powers. We had even refused to abandon President al-Bashir when France tried to prevent his participation in the Africa–France

Summit in Egypt in May 2010, and we refused to host it. It was held in Nice instead of Sharm al-Sheikh because we would not let an Arab African president be humiliated in our country. We did not react negatively to any of the Sudanese criticism of our attitude toward the south, which we knew was probably going to secede. We had strategic interests with southern Sudan as well as our old, vital interests with Khartoum, for both of them were our twins in the Nile Valley. I apprised President Mubarak of the situation, discussed it with General Omar Suleiman, and mentioned that Ali Osman Taha's objection to the fact that I had left New York before hearing his speech was unfounded. I told the president that I had spoken with both Salva Kiir and Ali Osman Taha individually and had in fact stayed to listen to both of their statements until the main session ended, after which I had to attend other important meetings. I added that we could not totally back northern Sudan but had to maintain a balance between north and south. The positions of the two sides portended future difficulties. While addressing the Sudanese Parliament in mid-October, President al-Bashir stressed that the only option for the National Congress Party was the unity of Sudan. In his talks with us, the U.S. envoy Gration expressed his doubts that Sudan seriously intended to hold the referendum; in return, we asked them to consider the Sudanese concern about the U.S. intentions toward them, a concern that we felt during our visit to Khartoum at the time.

Omar Suleiman and I traveled to Khartoum to try to conciliate the two sides, and to consolidate our relations with northern Sudan. I talked openly with Vice-President Ali Osman Taha, who mistakenly thought I had left before he made his statement at the meeting in New York. I explained that it was not unusual to have to leave a meeting for a few minutes and then return. He said he understood. While I was talking to him, I looked at him closely and remembered that President Mubarak had for a long time mistaken Taha, who had been foreign minister in the 1990s, for Mustafa Osman Ismail, who was the Sudanese foreign minister in 2000 and then became President al-Bashir's advisor. Whenever the president was informed that Mustafa Osman Ismail wished to see him in Cairo, he would receive him, saying, "Come here you murderer," in reference to the assassination attempt on Mubarak in Addis Ababa in 1995, in which Ali Osman Taha had been mentioned as one of the masterminds. They always laughed at this confusion.

Several parties made attempts to settle the disputes between northern and southern Sudan ahead of the referendum. Thabo Mbeki, the former South African president who presided over an African Union committee on Sudan, held meetings to solve the problems of the demarcation of the border, the implementation of the results of Abyei referendum, the division of oil revenue, the citizenship issue, and the status of more than one and a half million southerners living in northern Sudan. Colonel Qadhafi suggested a Libya–Egypt–Sudan summit in Khartoum with Salva Kiir in attendance, in order to convince him to give priority to the unity option. In Egypt we did our best to promote the unity option, but we knew that we were swimming against the tide. We had to be cautious in every step we took since we were walking a tightrope.

On December 21, 2010, President Mubarak attended a meeting in Khartoum that was also attended by Muammar Qadhafi, Sheikh Hamad bin Khalifa of Qatar, al-Bashir, and Salva Kiir. The objective of the meeting was to begin to define the post-referendum relationship between north and south, to strengthen their ties in the political, economic, and social fields, and to pledge to establish a full economic partnership regardless of the result of the referendum. Unfortunately, Qadhafi's interference made it difficult for the parties to agree on a statement that would allay the fears of both sides or lay out a path for the post-referendum period.

It was clear that Salva Kiir had deep suspicions of the intentions of the northern side before this meeting was held. He attended anyway, all the while bearing in mind that the future would bring forth an independent country in southern Sudan.

The referendum was held on January 9, 2011 as scheduled, and the result was what had been expected for years. I myself exited the political scene a few weeks later.

I would like to add few words concerning the Egyptian–Sudanese relationship. Northern Sudan demanded that Egypt stand with it during the civil war. Egypt sought to unite the two parts of Sudan and ease the tension between them. Even though the southerners had been long suspicious of our intentions, we were trying to win their trust so that we could talk them into accepting what was best for all the Nile Valley partners.

It is surely obvious by now that Egypt's actions with respect to Sudan were very crucial and required complicated calculations. Making it even more difficult was the belief, in some of the riparian countries, that anyone who disagrees with their policies and objectives is by necessity a potential enemy, if not an actual one; there was a dismaying lack of mutual trust among them.

# 9

# EGYPT AND THE CHALLENGES OF THE ARAB WORLD

**B**y the time I became foreign minister in July 2004, the Middle East was enmeshed in situations that could only guarantee future tensions. The Israeli–Palestinian conflict and clashes between the two sides during the Second Intifada had put an end to the peace processes due to Israel's ill-treatment of the Palestinians. Iraq came under U.S. occupation, and the threat of civil war loomed over this easternmost wing of the Arab world. Syria was receiving threats from the U.S. secretary of state and was being accused of meddling in Iraqi affairs and allowing Arab and Islamic militants to cross its territory to join the war in Iraq. The situation in Sudan had become internationalized and it was being held to account by the international community through several UN Security Council resolutions on Darfur.

Meanwhile, Iran's threats to Bahrain and the United Arab Emirates had escalated in the aftermath of the fall of Iraq. The country's nuclear program also started to attract the attention of the west, resulting in strained Iranian–western relations, with implications for the region as a whole.

Yemen was suffering from internal division, as signs of al-Qa'ida's presence appeared on its soil, paving the way for instability, opening the door to more foreign interventions, and raising questions about the situation in the Arab Peninsula, and Saudi Arabia in particular. Finally, Somalia was splintering into several autonomous areas, making the idea of restoring unity under a central government in Mogadishu seem even less likely.

Egypt maintained relatively good relations with everyone, though we were not in frequent contact with the Iraqis because of our discontent over the U.S. occupation. However, we kept our diplomatic mission to Baghdad, in case we were able to resume more active relations at a later stage, and also to stay abreast of the developments in Iraq's difficult internal situation. Motivated by its responsibilities toward the Arab region, Egypt did not want to abandon Iraq to its fate, but it had to beware of the actions of the angry American superpower.

From the very beginning I was aware of the importance of maintaining the Cairo–Damascus–Riyadh axis, and of ensuring ongoing coordination with Farouk al-Sharaa, Syria's foreign minister, and Prince Sa'ud al-Faisal, Saudi Arabia's foreign minister. My connection to them dated back to the Second Gulf War in 1990–91. On the other hand, some voices within the Egyptian Ministry of Foreign Affairs argued that we were not showing sufficient interest in the Gulf Cooperation Council, especially in light of the escalating Iranian threats after the fall of Iraq. Hence, reinvigorating Egypt's engagement with this Arab grouping became among our top priorities.

To implement my views regarding deepening our communication and coordination with Syria, which had strategic importance for Egypt within the Arab region, I provided the Syrians with an important report we received from our mission in New York on the French and American intentions against Syria under the terms of UN Security Council Resolution 1559 on the situation in Lebanon. Then I met with the Syrian foreign minister to discuss the situation in Lebanon, sharing our respective assessments of the situation and stressing the need for Syria to be careful not to stir up any trouble for itself in Lebanon or on its border with Iraq because of its pro-Iranian stances on Iraq. The goal was to alert and advise the Syrians, not to threaten them or work against them. In September 2004, I met with Lebanese Prime Minister Rafik Hariri, who naturally supported all the requirements of Resolution 1559, including Syria's withdrawal from Lebanon and the handling of Hezbollah's weapons. Hariri voiced sharp criticism of Syria, despite his efforts to maintain a productive relationship with Damascus.

Hariri appreciated the affinity that President Mubarak held for him. The president was well acquainted with the situation in Lebanon and, despite his appreciation of Hariri, was also aware of the importance of Syria and its influences in the region's policies. Hariri was in constant contact with the Egyptian president in order to secure Egypt's support for himself. Needless to say, he never missed an event in Cairo, no matter how relevant or irrelevant it was to Lebanon, without calling me to get the whole picture of the situation. I responded to him as honestly as possible, though within the limits of Egypt's own interests.

As the year 2004 came to an end, I made my first trip to the Gulf, which included meetings of joint Egyptian committees with a number of GCC countries, which had been stalled for many years. I went to Oman, Bahrain, Qatar, Kuwait, and Abu Dhabi. The Gulf's interest in these talks was apparent from the perspective of their traditional interest in Egypt; they also viewed them as a message of Egyptian support in the face of Iran.

In Qatar, I was set to meet with the Emir, Sheikh Hamad bin Khalifa, and Foreign Minister Hamad bin Jassem. But while I was in Bahrain, before leaving to Qatar, I suddenly received a message from the Egyptian ambassador in Qatar, just one day ahead of my visit, informing me that the Emir had traveled to Morocco on an emergency, accompanied by the Qatari foreign minister. He explained that the crown prince and prime minister of Qatar would welcome Egypt's foreign minister, and that the consultations would be conducted with the Qatari minister of state for foreign affairs, Abdullah Al-Mahmoud.

I hesitated in Bahrain for a while, contemplating the situation and considering whether to continue with the visit despite the apparent reduction in the level of Qatari interest, especially since its foreign minister did not even bother to make the gesture of a courtesy call to apologize for not being there. Should I resume the mission as if nothing has happened in order to keep up appearances and not expose the relationship to misunderstandings from the beginning? I decided to continue, and the Qatari hospitality was obvious when I arrived. As soon as I returned home, I reported the incident to the president, elaborating that I did not want to cause new problems with the Qataris at the beginning of my work, especially since I had witnessed the media war with them when I was working as an assistant to Amr Moussa in 1997 not long after the attempted coup against the emir of Qatar. Qatar accused Egypt and Saudi Arabia of plotting to overthrow the emir, leading to a heated exchange of media attacks between Doha and Cairo.

As Egyptian–Syrian communications picked up speed, I went to Damascus in early February 2005 and I met with President Bashar al-Assad. Because there had been so much talk about the return of Syria and Israel to the negotiations, stalled since 2000, I inquired about Syria's stance in this regard. Assad told me that he would inform all the parties of his willingness to return to negotiations. However, he expected that the negotiations would pick up from the point where they had ended in the past, with respect to what Syria had already obtained from Israel regarding the border and withdrawal from the Golan Heights.

He added that there were four themes on the agenda of these negotiations: security, water, the nature of the relations between the parties, and land and borders. During the meeting, President Assad further referred to the joint Arab action and its impact on supporting Syria, proposing to hold a five-way meeting between Syria, Egypt, Saudi Arabia, Jordan, and Palestine to move the peace process forward.

The Syrian proposal, according to my analysis of the situation, was a bid to avoid the growing western pressure on Damascus to withdraw from Lebanon, and to use the negotiations with Israel to calm the U.S. actions against Syria because of the Iraqi situation. The Americans, I believed, held many grudges against Syria, because of the difficulties they were having in Iraq. They would not facilitate any negotiations between Israel and Syria unless Damascus adjusted its policy in Iraq.

Rafik Hariri was assassinated on February 13, 2005, while I was in Washington. I was certain that this crime would be an opportunity for the United States and its allies to put additional pressure on Syria.

A few minutes prior to my meeting with U.S. Secretary of State Condoleezza Rice, I received a telephone call from Farouk al-Sharaa, asking me to convey to her a Syrian request not to rush into hasty reactions, insisting that Syria had nothing to do with this assassination. I delivered the message to her, and her reply was as I have reported in the fourth chapter of this book:

rejecting the Syrian position and doubting its credibility. Farouk al-Sharaa came to Egypt a few days after my return from Washington; I told him that Syria had to continue to implement Resolution 1559, and that the reactions in Washington were not positive toward Syria. Needless to say, I added, failing to follow the resolution would put Syria in trouble with the western world, and the assassination of Hariri would be used as a pretext to attack it. Al-Sharaa responded that they would respect the resolution, but they did not intend to withdraw from all of Lebanon. They would remain in the Bekaa Valley inside Lebanon until a settlement for the Arab–Israeli or the Syrian–Israeli conflict was reached, since the withdrawal of Syria from this region would make it easier for Israel to carry out military operations that threaten Syria from these areas. I reminded al-Sharaa that the Americans wanted the resolution implemented immediately, whereas France was showing more flexibility, talking about gradual implementation. Nonetheless, al-Sharaa insisted on his point of view, which he conveyed to President Mubarak in a later meeting.

On my part, I informed the president that I knew about Washington's bad intentions toward Syria, and that the U.S. presence in Iraq was an important factor that the Syrians needed to keep in mind. The president ridiculed Syria's insistence that staying in Bekaa was vital to Syria's defense. If Israel wanted to attack Syria, he said, it would not use ground forces, seek to enter Damascus, or further occupy Syrian territory with the intent of forcing a peace treaty. Rather, it would carry out aerial operations against vital targets in Syria to weaken the regime.

The presidents of Syria and Egypt were scheduled to meet at the Arab summit in Algeria, where President Mubarak talked to Assad, in my presence and the presence of Syria's foreign minister, strongly urging him to withdraw from Lebanon in accordance with Resolution 1559. Assad said he would need months to find a place inside Syria for the withdrawing forces. Mubarak replied that the U.S. intentions toward the Syrians were bad and advised him to move, adding that Egypt would help him find a secure solution. Then Mubarak and I headed to an Egyptian–French presidential meeting in Paris, where we asked the French not to put severe pressure on Syria. We believed that Syria would implement the resolution, as well as all the elements of the 1989 Taif Agreement.

I visited Damascus again in June 2005, for further reassurance and coordination with Syria. I could sense a certain amount of tension from the Syrian side as they confirmed their intention to withdraw from Lebanon in accordance with Resolution 1559.

Several Iraqi parties, especially the Sunnis, were demanding that Egypt pay more attention to Iraq. I had my reservations during my first months as foreign minister because of my distress over the U.S. occupation. However, at the request of both the Sunni and Shi'i Iraqi leaderships, I managed to convince President Mubarak that we could increase the number of Egyptian employees in the mission in Baghdad, bearing in mind that the head of the Egyptian mission was due to return home soon, and a replacement was to be dispatched in June 2005.

The Americans were asking Egypt to send troops, which we would not do under any circumstances. We had made this clear to the Americans on a previous occasion, stating that the most we could do to help was to agree to hold a conference on Iraq in Sharm al-Sheikh to show that the Arab countries and the rest of the world were paying attention to developments in Iraq. This conference was held in November 2004. The United States and the European Union likewise called for an international conference in Brussels in support of Iraq on June 21, 2005. There was nothing new in these conferences; whether the big international conferences, such as the ones in Sharm al-Sheikh or Brussels, or the smaller ones, which were called Iraq's Neighboring Countries and Egypt, they were mere repetitions of one another. When I mentioned at the Brussels conference that Egypt had sent a new head to its mission in Baghdad, some were under the impression that we were sending an ambassador to Baghdad for the first time, even though we had had a mission there for years. It had left for a few weeks during the U.S. invasion, and returned immediately thereafter, in April 2004.

At the Sharm al-Sheikh conference, held in November 2004, the United States attempted to launch a dialogue with Iran about Iraq, on the level of the foreign ministries. Egypt was willing to help break the ice between the Iranians and Americans by having them sit close to one another at a rectangular table among a large number of ministers. Colin Powell attempted to get the Iranian minister to open up, but the latter was careful not to give the Americans or their media outlets an opportunity to claim that Iran had entered into a dialogue with the 'Great Satan.' The same thing was repeated with Condoleezza Rice years later, to no avail.

I met with a large number of foreign ministers, in both Sharm al-Sheikh and Brussels, and presented the Egyptian perspective of rejecting—and even resisting—any attempt by any party to divide Iraq into three successor states. Some conservative U.S. voices in Washington had been suggesting this, ignoring the negative effects on the whole region. I believed they were acting in Israel's interests, seeking to divide Iraq so as to weaken the whole Arab body.

Egypt believed it was necessary to address the dangers of potential civil war in Iraq and prevent the fall of Iraq to Iran's ambitions. The problem was how to resist Iranian influence without a strong presence on the ground in Iraq. Civil war was clearly on the verge of breaking out, and Iraq was about to be torn by Sunni–Shia conflicts, which were bound to involve the neighboring Arab states and Iran.

Early in July 2005, I was in Sirte, Libya, attending an important African summit, to which I dedicated my full attention because South Africa and Nigeria were trying to obtain the support of the other African states to be nominated for the possible two permanent African seats on the UN Security Council. I received a telephone call from the deputy director of my office in Cairo informing me that the head of our mission in Baghdad had been abducted by an Iraqi group in protest against Egypt's sending an ambassador to Baghdad. I returned to Cairo immediately after being assured that the African summit would not permit South Africa and Nigeria to achieve their goal.

Minister Plenipotentiary Ihab al-Sherif, God rest his soul, had arrived in Baghdad only a few days before being abducted. He had previously served as deputy assistant minister of Arab affairs at the Ministry of Foreign Affairs, with specific responsibilities for the Arab Mashriq—Iraq, Syria, and Lebanon. He was therefore the best person to head the Egyptian mission in Baghdad, where full diplomatic relations had still not been restored despite the fall of Saddam Hussein, to succeed the outgoing ambassador, whose term had ended and who was due to return home for retirement.

Having met this Egyptian diplomat during the preparation for the Sharm al-Sheikh conference on Iraq, as well as in the meetings of Iraq's neighboring countries, I knew that he was closely acquainted with the case and with internal developments in Iraq. During the meeting of Iraq's neighboring countries in March 2005 in Istanbul, I had a long conversation with him. He agreed quite enthusiastically to go to Baghdad, pointing out that he would expect to stay there for two years at most before being transferred to another location. I agreed to this if I was still in office by then.

Another Egyptian diplomat, the chief of the General Intelligence Bureau in Baghdad, had been abducted as well shortly after I took office in July 2004—one year prior to the abduction of Ihab al-Sherif. We managed to free him through active contacts conducted by our intelligence, helped by his own knowledge of the situation in Iraq. Therefore, I had high hopes that our intelligence would also succeed in negotiating Sherif's release, or else that either the Iraqis or the Americans would learn his whereabouts and free him. The days passed heavily, and I was in constant contact with Major General Omar Suleiman, to whom I entrusted the entire issue.

News of the abduction swept all over the Egyptian media outlets, along with commentaries criticizing the Foreign Ministry for not providing enough information to satisfy public opinion. However, we were in no position to talk about anything, as the issue was being handled at a very rapid pace by the Egyptian Intelligence Service, which was being careful not to reveal anything that might end up serving the interests of the abductors, the usual approach in such cases.

During the annual ceremony of the Egyptian Armed Forces commemorating the July 23 revolution, I met with Major General Omar Suleiman, who had telephoned a few minutes ahead of the ceremony, asking to talk to me privately. He said that he had received a call from the CIA informing us that they had located our abducted ambassador, and that they were willing to carry out a military operation to release him. But they could not guarantee the results; he might end up being killed by his abductors or in any exchange of fire.

Omar Suleiman asked for my opinion, and I asked him to let me think it over. The ceremony lasted for a whole hour, which I spent mulling over my response. I thought about how vital the release of our ambassador would be to us. On the other hand, it was hard to figure out what the kidnappers might end up doing with him, for a military operation might lead to the death of some of the abductors, which in turn might incite an act of revenge on their part against other Egyptian diplomats or any Egyptian who might fall into their hands in the future. Meanwhile, it seemed to me that since the intelligence bureau chief had been released before, the head of our mission might be peacefully released as well, especially since we were willing to pay whatever sum of money might be requested as a ransom. I finally reached the conclusion that we should take the risk and tell the Americans to carry out the operation immediately, that very night, since we had been informed that the abductors were constantly moving from one place to another.

As soon as the music performance was over and just before the official dinner began, I informed Omar Suleiman of my approval for the operation to be carried out immediately. He replied that this was his opinion as well, and that he would inform the president that night about the situation and our agreement on the suggested approach. That was one of the hardest nights of my life, hardly sleeping, anticipating the news of the release at any time. Nothing happened. I called Omar Suleiman first thing in the morning, and he said that the Americans had let us down and that their information was neither sufficient nor accurate. The very next day, the abductors announced that they had killed our martyr, Ihab al-Sherif.

The president telephoned—I could hear the extreme exasperation and distress in his voice—to inquire about the number of our diplomats and employees in Baghdad, and I gave him a full report on the situation. He ordered that everyone should depart immediately, especially since the announcement of the martyrdom of our ambassador was accompanied by the shooting of the second in command at the embassy of the United Arab Emirates, along with a Russian diplomat and a Pakistani. I told him that we had a lot of property in Baghdad that should not be left like that, or else it would all be stolen, not to mention the large-scale communications networks, barcodes, and computers. He reluctantly agreed to leave one staff member and a group of Egyptian military guards.

The incident had a disturbing psychological effect on me and my family. I gradually got the whole story from the returning diplomats and intelligence men. Our ambassador had two residences. One was located inside the Egyptian mission itself, where he stayed for several days upon his arrival, under heavy Egyptian and Iraqi guard. The second residence was an apartment far from the mission's building. I was told that al-Sherif had, unfortunately, decided to spend the night in the apartment, insisting on moving to it. Turning a deaf ear to the objections of the intelligence chief, he moved in without his assigned guards, six members of the Egyptian army. He was abducted while making a short tour on a Friday morning in the neighborhood where the apartment was located. In Egypt, we were all deeply saddened by what happened to our ambassador, for we were not yet accustomed to the level of violence that existed in Baghdad.

The president was also deeply saddened by the incident, and for weeks he refused to talk about Iraq. He did not want to present a medal in honor of the memory of our martyr, for reasons that I was not aware of, despite my repeated requests. In the meantime, the Ministry of Foreign Affairs named the Arab sector's meeting room in the Maspero building after him: "Ihab al-Sherif Hall." His picture is on one of the walls of Tahrir Palace—the old building of the Ministry of Foreign Affairs—along with pictures of the ministry's other martyrs. I felt deep sorrow for al-Sherif's family, especially since my wife had lost her father, Ambassador Kamal al-Din Salah, who was assassinated in Somalia in April 1957 when she was still a child. There was also a great deal of public distress over the incident. I was fully aware, however, that withdrawing completely from Iraq would put us at a considerable disadvantage, especially in light of the information we were receiving on the Iranian activities in Iraq. Some at the Foreign Ministry were even saying that Iran was swallowing Iraq up. My response, however, was that it was difficult for any regional party—Iran, Turkey, or anyone else—to swallow up a country the size of Iraq. It was vital for us to continue to remain present and work quietly in Iraq in one way or another. So we began to return to Iraq and rebuild our presence there, with a great deal of alertness and caution.

In the weeks after that tragic incident, I convinced the president to coordinate with the Arab League to chair a meeting for the leaders of all the Iraqi factions at the headquarters of the Arab League, and then to host them at the Ittihadiya Palace, all at Egypt's expense. He agreed to do this, although he believed that the conference should be the responsibility of the Arab League and all its member states, not just the host country. Thereby, we issued strict instructions for this hospitability, in coordination with all the hotels. I also suggested that we offer to treat one thousand wounded Iraqis in Egyptian hospitals. But he disagreed, saying that we would be opening a door that would be hard to close. He felt that our offer to train Iraqis in our military, intelligence, and diplomatic institutes was sufficient, as some Iraqis had already begun to enroll in courses in many branches of administration and government in Cairo.

The president, along with the Interior Ministry and the rest of the Egyptian security services, were worried about the presence of the thousands of the Iraqis who would be coming to Cairo as family members of the conference attendees, fearing a threat to Egyptian national security. The political position, however, was in favor of allowing them all to come to Egypt, which is a sanctuary for every Arab.

The conference resulted in an agreement for internal reconciliation. Even so, a long period of suffering and internal debate followed, during which Iraq was subjected to unprecedented shocks, assassinations, and bombings. As the year drew to a close, the United States was running out of patience with Syria and its alleged meddling in Iraq. The Syrians were being accused of the assassination of Rafik Hariri, as the international investigators' information indicated that certain figures in the Syrian government circle had had a hand in his death.

Stephen Hadley, the U.S. national security advisor who succeeded Rice when she moved to the State Department, said at the end of September 2005 that the United States hoped for the fall of Assad, who had allowed the infiltration of Arab and Islamic insurgents across the borders into Iraq; he believed that these people were responsible for the ongoing killings. I was in Washington at the time, and I warned Hadley against the dangers of targeting Syria, which would bring the whole region to boiling point. The U.S. campaign against the Syrian stance on Lebanon was escalated, with the Europeans following suit, despite the full Syrian withdrawal from Lebanon in implementation of the Taif Agreement, which had been suspended since 1989 with respect to the section on Syrian forces. In our contacts with Syria, whether during the visits of the Syrian or Egyptian presidents to Cairo or Damascus or in meetings between foreign ministers, we kept the Syrians apprised of our analyses regarding the possible measures that could be taken against them by western powers. We also highlighted the necessity of Syria's complete withdrawal from Lebanon without leaving behind any intelligence or other presence, because that would get them into even more trouble. At the same time, we emphasized the significance of America's negative opinion of them as the situation in Iraq continued to deteriorate, as well as the necessity of removing some the officials who were specifically being accused by the Americans of interfering in Iraq or Lebanon. Needless to say, it was no secret that claims that Syria was responsible for the assassination of Hariri, which has not been proven, were made mainly for the purpose of pressuring Syria. It was therefore in Syria's best interests to be flexible. Damascus listened to some of our advice, and discussions began between the United States and Syria on the status of the country's border with Iraq. The Syrians also agreed to tighten their control over their own troops on these borders. The Syrian forces were supplied with large numbers of British night-vision devices to prevent cross-border infiltration.

As I continued to monitor the situation, I was certain that U.S. pressure against Syria would never cross a certain threshold beyond which the status quo in the Golan Heights would be affected. Since the cease-fire agreement between Israel and Syria in 1974, Tel Aviv had been totally satisfied with Syria's behavior in the Golan, and the United States was careful not to take any measures that would threaten the situation on that front.

As 2006 began, the situation in Iraq dramatically deteriorated, and the United States asked Egypt to consider sending ground troops into Iraq or Afghanistan. We flatly rejected this request. Another request was made, either from Saudi Arabia or from the United States, that the violent conflict in Iraq made it incumbent upon Muslims to consider sending Islamic and Arab forces to Iraq. The talk was specifically about troops from Pakistan, the Gulf States, and Egypt. The idea did not appeal at all to Egypt or Iran. Furthermore, my conversations with the Iraqi foreign minister, Hoshyar

Zebari, with whom I enjoyed a relationship of cooperation and increasing trust, revealed that Iraq had deep suspicions that Syria and Iran were conspiring to fan the flames in Iraq, so that the United States would remain preoccupied with it and pay less attention to the other two countries.

Egypt set several goals for itself during this period. First and foremost was the importance of securing Syria against any U.S. action that would endanger its stability. Otherwise, the result would be a greatly increased Israeli presence in the Arab Mashriq region once Iraq and Syria had fallen. We had been observing for years the U.S. objection to any attempts by Syria to obtain weapons from any source, and we had quietly resisted these attempts to destabilize Syria. The second Egyptian goal was to try to restore Iraq's balance and offer whatever help we could, short of sending armed forces into Iraqi territory. Along with Saudi Arabia, we kept advising the Sunnis in Iraq of the importance of engaging in the political process underway in Iraq. The third Egyptian goal remained unchanged for years, namely, maintaining an active Egyptian–Saudi relationship and a supportive Egyptian stance for the GCC countries in case of any political confrontation with Iran, as well as assuring them that Egypt was their strategic depth, regardless of their strong relations with the United States and other western powers. In this context, we closely followed Iran's relationship with Hamas in the Palestinian arena, especially in Gaza, and the Lebanese organization Hezbollah, which had close ties to the Iranians and Syrians.

I was attending an Egyptian cabinet meeting on July 12, 2006, when the minister of information showed me a text message on his mobile phone to say that Israel had announced that a military operation had been launched against it, killing some Israeli troops and wounding others. Israel accused Hezbollah of carrying out the attack against this Israeli patrol. Within a minute or two, I received a message from my office with the same information. The assistant foreign minister who managed my office contacted me to discuss how to proceed. I asked her to form an immediate task force to craft a response that would prevent the situation from erupting in a way that would harm our interests. I had barely finished my telephone conversation when of the Cabinet employees told me that the president wanted to speak to me. I went to the office of the prime minister to use the secure telephone device that was connected directly to the president's office. The president said, "Have you seen what happened? The situation will become heated and Israel will strike back hard. I am afraid that Syria will be affected by Israel's sharp actions." I had to agree with him. He continued, "I want you to travel immediately to Damascus to meet with President Bashar. Talk to him and warn him not fall into a trap that might be set for him by Israel." I called Walid al-Muallem, the Syrian foreign minister, on his cell phone, asking for an immediate visit to Syria. He promised to call back in a few minutes. When he did, he said that the president would receive me when I arrived. I replied that I would leave Cairo in less than thirty minutes. I had already spoken with the Egyptian defense minister, who was at the Cabinet meeting, and requested an airplane immediately, assuring him that the expense would be covered by the president's office since this was the president's directive, not the foreign minister's initiative.

The expenses of the private airplanes we used in such missions have always been a subject of debate among the Foreign Ministry, Defense Ministry, and intelligence services. I argued that these were state missions, but they insisted that if we did not pay, no planes would be available. Meanwhile the president's office would refuse to interfere, so the Ministry of Foreign Affairs had to pay these high expenses for trips related to Egyptian national security.

The Syrian president welcomed me immediately upon my arrival at around 2:00 p.m. I told him that the president sent his regards, and did not want to talk to him over the phone for fear of surveillance. I said that the president was concerned about the plan, for which Hezbollah had already claimed responsibility, to hold prisoners in order to exchange them for Lebanese mujahideen. I stated that, based on our decades-long experience, we were concerned that the Israeli reaction would be sharp, adding that I personally felt the current Israeli prime minister, Ehud Olmert, and his defense minister, Amir Peretz, were not very competent. The Israeli media reported that neither of them had any experience in military affairs, which meant that one or both of them would need to be replaced, and therefore they were both under pressure. Hence, my utmost fear was that the two of them would exaggerate Israel's military reaction so as to ward off the charges against themselves. I added that we were afraid that Syria would be dragged into a confrontation with Israel. We believed Syria could quickly intervene to urge Hezbollah to restrain itself, and that Damascus should demand the release of the two missing soldiers, whose names had been announced by Israel.

This was not my first time to visit the Syrian president in his office, for I had met him in Damascus at least twice before. One of them was when I was dispatched by President Mubarak to talk to the Syrian president about how Syria should deal with the UN and the investigations into the assassination of Rafik Hariri, asking them to be cautious. I had been familiar with the building, at the center of the Syrian capital, ever since I accompanied Dr. Esmat Abdel Meguid and Amr Moussa during the consultations on drafting the Damascus Declaration in 1991–92, and during the Israeli–Syrian negotiations in 1996–99.

President Assad was clearly interested in the views I conveyed to him. I would even say that he seemed concerned and apprehensive about the possibility of a confrontation between Hezbollah and Israel. Therefore, I advised Syria to adopt a quiet media approach, which he promised to do. He also promised to call Hassan Nasrallah, the secretary general of Hezbollah, and persuade him of the need for restraint. I knew it might take some time to reach Nasrallah, who must surely have been on the run by then. I added that we would contact the Israelis and ask them to restrain their reaction, and would ask the UN secretary general to put his weight on the side of non-escalation. Finally, I would talk with Condoleezza Rice to get the United States to intervene in controlling the Israeli reaction.

As I left the presidential headquarters, Walid al-Muallem said he wanted to invite me to lunch at a Syrian luxury restaurant, but I was determined to leave immediately and start doing what we had agreed upon. Later, as I thought over my conversation with the Syrian president, I realized that he had sounded as if he had been taken unpleasantly by surprise when told about this issue. Also, a brief statement by Walid al-Muallem prompted me to think further; he said that he did not rule out the possibility that Iran had had a hand in that attack. This statement made me reconsider my evaluation of the situation, for it was not actually unlikely that Iran had pushed

Hezbollah to carry out the operation as a message to Israel not to target Iran, or else Hezbollah would be used against the Israeli territories. It was also meant as a message to the Americans and the other western powers, which were trying to tighten the screws on Iran and its nuclear capacities, to show that Iran was capable of a strong response. I arrived in Cairo in the evening and informed the president of my conversation, and of my belief that Syria had not been aware of the attack ahead of time, and that I would contact Israel, the United States, and the UN.

I immediately contacted the Israeli foreign minister, Tzipi Livni, whose office informed mine that she was in a meeting with the prime minister and would contact us as soon as it was over. Then I had a long conversation with the secretary general of the UN, who was genuinely concerned about the deterioration of the situation and promised to speak to the Israelis and the permanent members of the Security Council. After that, I was about to contact the U.S. secretary of state, when my secretary informed me that Tzipi Livni was on the line. I talked to her about the purpose and the outcome of my visit to Damascus, saying that we should control the situation and not let it explode, and that the Syrians would help manage Hezbollah. Livni replied that she could not remain silent about this provocation; they believed that Iran and perhaps Syria as well were behind it. I assured her that Syria had nothing to do with it, but she insisted that it was too late, and that Israel would execute painful military action against Hezbollah that night. I informed the president, the minister of defense, and General Omar Suleiman of what was going on so as to prepare ourselves for further deterioration of the situation. Then I went on to contact Rice, who appeared to understand the Israeli reaction and did not want to hinder it in any way.

I was briefed on the first report from the work group I had set up that afternoon. It referred to a visit to Lebanon by Iran's foreign minister, as well as another by Nasrallah to Tehran. In conclusion, the report hinted that the visits were part of the preparation for a confrontation in Lebanon that summer. I felt deeply upset by the consequences of the upcoming Israeli military operation. We had been arranging a meeting between Fouad Siniora, the Lebanese prime minister, and President Assad, but by then I was sure that the meeting was unlikely to take place. President Mubarak had been talking to Assad since the latter's visit to Sharm al-Sheikh on June 18, 2006 about how to strengthen the Syrian–Lebanese relationship, and to confirm the border between the two countries.

I asked the president for permission to brief the Saudis on the situation, and told him that we should expect a difficult period as a result of what we regarded as a hasty Israeli military action. Upon his approval, I contacted Prince Sa'ud al-Faisal and asked to meet him the next afternoon. He replied that he would be happy to receive me in Jeddah and we agreed on a time.

My relationship with Prince Sa'ud was strengthened during my term as foreign minister, and I have always believed that he was one of the smartest and most experienced ministers I ever worked with. He relied not only on the experience he had gained since his appointment as the foreign minister of Saudi Arabia in 1975, but he was also armed with a great deal of philosophical knowledge thanks to his in-depth readings of everything that was essential to the formation of the foreign minister of such an important country as Saudi Arabia. We often exchanged views about various books we read, including books I had recommended to him.

Sa'ud al-Faisal surrounded himself with a small circle of friends, with whom he maintained a decades-long relationship. I have always seen them as an example of wisdom, knowledge, and loyalty to friendship; they were not after fame or wealth through their relationship with him. I was received by him in the military airport of Jeddah, and he drove the car himself to his home overlooking one of the beaches of Jeddah. The view was breathtaking. I informed him of the outcomes of my visit to Damascus the previous day, of our view in Egypt of the Israeli military action against Lebanon as extremely violent, and of our warning to the Syrians against drifting into a confrontation with Israel. I also assured him that such a confrontation, if it occurred, would put considerable pressure on Egypt, and therefore we did not want Syria to act in a way that would inflict damage on itself and on us. I asked Prince Sa'ud to attempt, on his part, to persuade the Americans to contain the Israeli reaction and to warn Syrians against making the wrong decision. I mentioned Walid al-Muallem's statement about not ruling out Iran's responsibility in encouraging Hezbollah to carry out that operation—an operation which I believed, at the time, was meaningless and completely harmful to Lebanon, and perhaps to Syria as well.

The reactions of the Saudi prince showed that he was not pleased with Syria's positions, and that Damascus's relations with Tehran were putting unwelcome pressure on the Saudi relationship with Syria, not to mention the fact that the Saudis viewed the assassination of Rafik Hariri as an unforgivable insult. The military operation carried out by Hezbollah was characterized by a lack of responsibility and disregard for its gravity. Al Faisal said he would contact the Americans to try to influence Israel.

By the time I returned to Cairo in the evening, the Israeli air operations and border shelling had begun. An urgent meeting of the Arab foreign ministers was called for July 15. It produced a sharp clash between Saudi Arabia and Syria. The Saudis criticized the position of those who spoke of the right of resistance from southern Lebanon, yet at the same time banned it from Golan. Meanwhile, some GCC states criticized the resistance and Hezbollah's movements in southern Syria for taking place without coordination with any of the internal forces in Lebanon or with the Arab countries. Walid al-Muallem, the foreign minister of Syria, could only condemn the Israeli attack without defending what Hezbollah had done in any way. Until then, Syria had kept a clear distance between itself and the Hezbollah military operation. Qatar, on the other hand, supported Syria in its cautious stance and expressed understanding for the operation that occurred on the Lebanese border, which was a position perhaps intended to provoke Saudi Arabia.

The Egyptian delegation had prepared a draft resolution to be presented at the ministerial meeting. However, I modified it by proposing several points that were adopted by the Arab ministers and were formulated into a resolution that could be adopted by the meeting.

Of course I called for a condemnation of the Israeli military operations, which were extremely severe and violent, and of the targeting of civilians on both sides. I also called for requesting the UN Security Council for an immediate intervention to put an end to the fighting, referring to the importance of restoring the search for a peaceful settlement of the Arab–Israeli conflict.

The responses of the Arab ministers revealed a lack of confidence in the motives of Hezbollah and its objectives behind their operation. I traveled to Washington for a previously scheduled round of strategic dialogue between Egypt and the United States. Some of the elements of this meeting have been reported in the fourth chapter of the book, on Egypt's relationship with the United States. The meetings in Washington revealed that the Americans were in no hurry to intervene to call for a cease-fire. I spoke at length with Condoleezza Rice, asking her to call for the UN Security Council to act and not allow any more of the killing and destruction that we had already seen on television. I knew that in Washington they were looking at the Hezbollah operation as a proxy war with Iran, and that it was Iran that should be asked about the operation and its underlying objectives. Therefore, the Americans would not mind if Hezbollah were defeated. I told them that Israel would not accomplish its goals with this military offensive, and that giving it time would only lead to more loss of lives and deep Arab–Muslim anger.

It became clear that the Americans were taking a completely opposite view to Egypt's. Upon my return to Cairo from Washington, I composed a draft of the Egyptian position, which called for a cease-fire and the immediate withdrawal of the Israeli troops from Lebanon, along with an exchange of Lebanese prisoners in return for the two Israeli soldiers. Our position also included a request for an increase of the international peace-keeping forces that had been in southern Lebanon since 1978, allowing the Lebanese army to be stationed along the Lebanese–Israeli border, and that all parties should respect the Blue Line (the international frontier between Israel and Lebanon). Our position, which we publicized fully, also dealt with the importance of Arab and international intervention to implement Resolution 1559 and secure internal reconciliation among the Lebanese political factions after Hariri's assassination. In the following days, in all of our meetings with European and other ministers, I took it upon myself to criticize the American position, which was prolonging the war, while asking all countries to pressure the United States, which was in a position to threaten Israel by asking the UN Security Council to issue a strong resolution demanding an immediate cease-fire. Since Cairo was receiving a large number of foreign ministers, European officials, and others at that time, I explained to everyone that the Americans were trying to give more time to Israel, and that the latter would certainly not achieve the goal behind its operations. President Mubarak was informing everyone he met that Israel was fighting a losing battle, and that a regular, formally trained army was committing a grave mistake by entering into a war with irregular, poorly trained groups.

Several groups in Egypt and the Arab world were talking about the importance and even the need for Egypt to escalate the political position against Israel. Meanwhile, we in Cairo believed that the battle waged by Hezbollah was only serving Iranian interests, and that Egypt had no interest in escalating the confrontation with Israel.

In light of the expansion of the armed clash and Israel's failure to destroy the infrastructure of Hezbollah, I noticed that the Syrian state's political discourse began to engage in the ongoing confrontation. It began to create a linkage between ending the fighting between Israel and Hezbollah and Syria's regional situation and reviving the negotiations for the return of the Golan and easing Syria's international isolation since Hariri's assassination.

I noticed that the United States, under international pressure, was attempting to formulate a position that could be supported by the UN Security Council, but this would surely require more time, thus allowing Israel more time to accomplish what it could not have achieved had the UN acted more quickly. A large number of ministers met in Rome to draw up a suggested cease-fire. The American and Israeli statements seemed to support the use of NATO directly on the ground in Lebanon, or to establish an international force operating on Lebanese territory under NATO supervision. Personally, I believed that it was an excuse for western forces to return to Lebanese soil, as had happened in 1982 when the United States, France, Italy, and Britain sent troops to Beirut following the Israeli invasion of Lebanon. I could easily predict the consequences of that act, especially since some parties believed that the mission of these NATO troops in 2006 should be to disarm Hezbollah in accordance with Resolution 1559 and monitor the Lebanese–Syrian border. These ideas could in no way be accepted without exacerbating the internal situation in Lebanon and implicating Syria even more seriously in Lebanese affairs. Of course, the stated aim of sending NATO troops was to support the Lebanese army and enable it to reach the Lebanese–Israeli border.

I spoke with many people about the irrationality of the Israeli and U.S. proposals. I thought that, instead, we should develop the capabilities of the UN peacekeeping forces, UNIFIL, and increase their numbers significantly, a suggestion that we had been making for some time.

This period was characterized by severe pressures. Some Egyptians, without sufficient knowledge of the situation, were demanding that Egypt take some kind of action against Israel. I was not unaware of the anger that was caused by Egypt's refusal to act decisively. I had the same feelings of anger, but I understood that we were facing a much larger battle than a mere confrontation between Israel and Hezbollah on Lebanese territory. I was keeping an eye on the Iranian nuclear program as one of the factors in this confrontation. The Shi'i influence in the region was also included in my calculations. Israel's position seemed to be designed for a confrontation that would go beyond Lebanon and Syria, and we were concerned about possible escalation.

I felt that the foreign minister of Egypt should pay a visit to Lebanon and show support for the Lebanese in this unequal confrontation. I spoke with the president upon my return from the United States on July 20 and then from Rome on July 25, but he refused to let me go to Lebanon, citing the dangers of the situation. I told him, "Mr. President, it is important to show up there." He replied that the aid and the field hospital we had sent to Beirut were enough. I felt disappointed. At this point, I must admit that President Mubarak's decisions and actions have almost always been governed by caution and nothing but caution. Still, we felt the suffering of the Lebanese people. I asked my working group to study a set of proposals for showing practical Egyptian support for the Lebanese. Many proposals were made, including the hospital that the president referred to, as well as the dispatch of Egyptian military ships to one of the southern Lebanese ports carrying large quantities of fresh water for the southern population, in addition to shipments of medicine and tents for the inhabitants of southern Lebanon who had been displaced toward Beirut and other parts of the country.

Omar Suleiman continued to make contacts with the Israeli security forces, expressing Egypt's anger and warning against the continuation of military operations. Our ambassador to Israel also spoke with Israeli politicians about the negative effects of this process on the chances of building trust between the Arab peoples and Israel.

I noted that Israel's frustration at not defeating Hezbollah led to some intemperate remarks about Syria by Israelis in many international capitals, where the Israelis were facing criticism for the threatening tone they were taking against Syria. In more than one conversation with Omar Suleiman, I pointed out the dangers of this attitude and the importance of warning Israel not to make any more inaccurate and inflammatory statements. I asked the Foreign Ministry's crisis work group to prepare some ideas in case the scope of the war expanded and involved Syria.

I presented all of the many ideas to the president as options to choose from, should the situation become more complicated. Among them were: calling for an international summit or an international meeting of foreign ministers to demand a cessation of fighting, especially since we no longer expected the Security Council would take measures contrary to U.S. policy, which harbored considerable antipathy toward Syria, as we all knew; considering recalling the Egyptian ambassador to Israel for an open-ended consultation; expelling the Israeli ambassador; calling for an emergency Arab summit; seeking the involvement of the UN Security Council or the General Assembly; freezing some aspects of our relations with Israel; suspending the Qualified Industrial Zone (QIZ) system, despite its extreme benefits for Egypt; taking other kinds of action against Israel, such as the cancellations of visits and participation in seminars; reducing the issuance of visas; closing the Israeli Academic Center in Cairo; and intensifying high-level contacts with Syria.

Correspondence between Cairo and Damascus increased sharply during this period. When I returned to Cairo from Damascus on the evening of July 12, I notified Walid al-Muallem through our embassy of the intensity of my conversations with the Israeli side, warning them against their military operation planned for the evening of July 12. I also maintained intensive communications with the UN secretary general to assess the situation on a constant basis and to present the Egyptian view, and at the same time to learn from him what was going on behind the scenes, away from the eyes of our ambassadors in the various capitals. Our embassies were ordered to intensify their efforts to find out what was being plotted in the western capitals.

In the interest of improving Egyptian–Saudi coordination, I visited Prince Sa'ud again on July 31 to find out what he thought of the situation so far. We had met and exchanged views a week earlier in Rome, and I noted his deep knowledge of the Lebanese issue. I tried to find out from him the outcome of President Assad's visit to Riyadh the day before to meet with the king. The prince repeated his sharp criticism of Syria, saying that it was gradually drifting away from the Arabs and seriously approaching Iran.

Prince Sa'ud proposed a meeting of the Arab Ministerial Council in Beirut. I expressed my full support of the idea, saying that I would head for Beirut within two days, as the president had grasped the importance of my visit, especially since the Iranian foreign minister had preceded us there, giving the impression that Iran, not the Arab brethren, was the primary supporter of Lebanon. I suggested to Prince Sa'ud that all the ministers should travel from Cairo on the C130 aircraft of the Egyptian Air Force, since Israel had prohibited flying through Lebanese airspace. I agreed that I would announce this proposal, at the time he deemed appropriate, and we would allow the Arab officials to travel on Egyptian military aircraft.

Sa'ud al-Faisal said that the Syrians were claiming that Hezbollah had actually won the military confrontation with Israel. This seemed reckless; Syria really should have been acting more cautiously in order to avoid any possible retaliation by the wounded Israel. However, Prince Sa'ud added that, according to his information, the United States had informed the Syrians that Israel had no intention of attacking them. This was why Saudi Arabia was surprised by the internal Syrian mobilization. If it reflected a genuine fear of an Israeli trick, it was logical. But if Syria was preparing to take advantage of Israel's failure to destroy Hezbollah, it was likely to make mistakes. I agreed with Prince Sa'ud not to recommend that our leaders hold an extraordinary Arab summit; because it would not be able to reach an agreement on the measures to take in response to the ongoing conflict, it would be viewed by some parties as insufficient, which would deepen the rift between some of the Arab countries.

The postponed visit to Beirut was scheduled for August 2. The Egyptian Ministry of Defense informed Lebanon, through the Egyptian–Israeli liaison committee, that Egypt would be sending an aircraft carrying the Egyptian foreign minister in the morning and would return later that same evening. The Americans, too, were notified to make sure that everyone knew about this Egyptian plane. The visit came at a sensitive moment amid angry feelings in Lebanon that none of the Arabs were coming to their country, especially in view of Al Jazeera's News Channel inflammatory coverage of Egypt.

On the morning of the visit, I was surprised to find myself quoted in one of the Cairo-based newspapers that published very provocative and totally false statements on the situation in Lebanon. The paper claimed that I announced to the Foreign Affairs Committee of the Egyptian People's Assembly on August 1 that the Arabs would fight Israel until the last Egyptian soldier. I was deeply distressed by the irresponsible claim, for it put me personally at risk in any follies that might be committed by one party or another, not to mention its negative impact on the Beirut visit.

I did not notice any military measures at the airport in Beirut or in the city. There were even people—though perhaps fewer than usual—at the beaches and some swimming pools that could be seen from the air as the plane landed. I met President Élias Lahoud and Prime Minister Siniora. We talked about the importance of the cease-fire, and I agreed with them that the Egyptian delegation to the UN would move within the framework of the Arab Group to call for a session at the Security Council to consider the question of the cease-fire. I also agreed with the Lebanese leaders that there was no need to create a new international force for Lebanon, but to keep the UNIFIL forces, increasing their numbers and expanding their functions. I also made media statements that Egypt left the implementation of Resolution 1559 and the disarmament of Hezbollah to the Lebanese people to determine on their own.

During the visit, I met with the speaker of the Lebanese parliament, Nabih Berri, and a large number of parliamentarians as well. It was obvious that they appreciated the visit, especially since I was the first Arab minister to come to Beirut. Some Lebanese journalists, however, did not miss the chance to refer to the visit of the Iranian foreign minister two days before, while others spoke of Iran's attempts to involve itself in Lebanese affairs so as to appear as the defender of Hezbollah, Hamas, Syria, and Lebanon itself.

The Arab ministers gathered in Cairo to fly to Beirut on the morning of August 4. I apologized to them for the roughness of the trip, as the Egyptian military transport plane was not equipped with the usual amenities. We once again informed the Israelis and the Americans of the Egyptian military flight. We learned from them that the foreign minister of Qatar would also arrive alone in Beirut in his Airbus 330, which provoked some elbow-nudging and eye-winking from the ministers. In a meeting of the Arab League Council, held in Beirut to affirm Arab solidarity with Lebanon, Prince Sa'ud al-Faisal announced that the king of Saudi Arabia had donated one billion dollars to help rebuild and rehabilitate southern Lebanon. This announcement was regarded as particularly significant because the prime minister of Lebanon, in thanking the Kingdom of the Saudi Arabia for this gesture, referred to the kingdom as "Big Sister." The foreign minister of Qatar announced a major contribution as well; this was the petrodollars talking. I was silent on the issue of financial support, but did explain that I had already visited Beirut two days ago and met with Egyptian doctors and members of the Egyptian Armed Forces who worked in the Egyptian Military Hospital at the Alexandria branch of Beirut Arab University.

The increased confidence of the Syrian foreign minister was evident in his speech during the meeting and in his public statement. Syria seemed to be coming much closer to the positions of Iran and Hezbollah, especially since the Americans had reported that Israel did not intend to expand operations against it.

Under pressure and considerable uproar, the international community was moving closer to issuing a comprehensive resolution on the situation in Lebanon, the status of Hezbollah's arms, a possible cease-fire, and the withdrawal of the Israeli forces from Lebanese soil, along with the with-drawal of Hezbollah forces from all territory south of the Litani River in Lebanon. Hezbollah was talking as if it had won a great historic victory. I had to admit to them that, despite all of Israel's efforts against them, the Israelis had not succeeded in destroying the party's military potential. On the other hand, Israel did succeed in removing Hezbollah's armed person-nel away from the border and north of the Litani River. Security Council Resolution 1701 also included other measures to severely restrict the party and limit its continued attempts to acquire more arms from Iran.

The Battle of Southern Lebanon showed the intensity of the divisions among the Arab countries. It also revealed that the Israeli army that had invaded southern Beirut in 1982 was not the same army in 2006 in the face of an experienced Lebanese resistance that used land maneuvers to achieve its goal of a military confrontation, despite heavy losses in the Leb-anese infrastructure, especially in the south. I believed that Lebanon paid a heavy price in this confrontation, which was initiated by Hezbollah in coordination with Iran. In his assessment of the outcome of the confron-tation, Sheikh Hassan Nasrallah admitted that, had he known in advance the destruction and losses that the war would cause in Lebanon, he would not have launched this raid against the Israeli patrol. The subsequent years have, in fact, revealed an apparent caution on the part of Hezbollah and its leadership not to provoke Israel in any way, and even a tendency on the part of the party's spokesmen to deny any connection to any incident that might have targeted Israel from the territory of southern Lebanon.

President Assad took advantage of these developments and delivered a forceful statement in which he expressed his support for Hezbollah in its battle with Israel, especially since the war had ended without escala-tion against Syria. Assad indirectly attacked the leaders of Saudi Arabia and Egypt, describing those who did not support the war as "half-men" or "pre-tenders to wisdom." Saudi–Syrian relations were also among the losses of the war, followed by Egyptian–Syrian relations.

I listened to this speech during my stay in my chalet on Egypt's Med-iterranean coast, and fully expected it to cause problems in our relations with Syria. Only minutes passed before I received a telephone call from the president asking, "What is this talk? And how can Assad talk about the other leaders like that?" Our relations with Syrian did in fact become more complicated, and had not been resolved by the time the Egyptian president left office in February 2011.

Egypt's relations with Syria had previously been quite good. The first Egyptian–Syrian summit I had to attend after becoming foreign minister was in 2004 when I accompanied President Mubarak to the Syrian capital for consultations with President Assad over a late breakfast, urging the Syrian president to take steps to implement Resolution 1559 on Lebanon. Mubarak spoke in a gentle and sympathetic manner with the Syrian president, who shared the same sentiments. Mubarak even advised Assad in 2005, when western pressure was growing on Syria to get out of Lebanon and control the border with Iraq, about the importance of dismissing some of his senior aides whom the president believed were causing problems with the foreign countries, and going so far as to identify one of them by name: Farouk al-Sharaa, whom Mubarak did not like. Assad's response was that he stuck with al-Sharaa because of his strong loyalty to his father and to himself.

The relationship between the two presidents changed after Assad's statement in the wake of the Hezbollah attack. The Egyptian president criticized Assad's positions, his excessive egotism, and the way he lectured leaders during the Arab summits, especially at the first summit after Assad took office in 2000. Many of the other Arab leaders also ridiculed Assad's lectures.

King Abdullah bin Abdulaziz took a strong stance against Assad's statements, and Saudi Arabia boycotted Syria. I noticed that President Mubarak also kept away from Syria. However, I was careful not to rush into confrontation with Syria, and tried as much as possible to ease the confrontation and absorb it to protect the interests of both countries.

As a result of these developments, the Egyptian view and its alliances started to change in Lebanon. Egypt ceased to take much interest in defending Syria's opinion of Resolution 1559 or Resolution 1701 on dealing with the war in southern Lebanon.

As soon as I became foreign minister, I began to notice the warmth of both the Egyptian–Saudi and the Egyptian–Gulf relations. The Egyptian president's comments on Gulf leaders, whenever they came up in conversation, showed that he had good feelings and respect for all of them. He even described the emir of Qatar, Sheikh Hamad bin Khalifa, as a good-hearted, frank, and straightforward man, adding that the real problem was not the emir but the prime minister and foreign minister, who had their own agenda. I quickly discovered that the Gulf leaders felt the same way about the Egyptian president.

When U.S. pressure on Egypt was increasing in 2005, King Abdullah bin Abdulaziz told us that he intended to take advantage of his visit to the United States to discuss U.S.–Egyptian relations with President Bush and urge him to maintain a good relationship with President Mubarak and not to stir up domestic feeling against him. I also noticed that senior Egyptian officials, especially General Omar Suleiman, maintained close relations with their Gulf counterparts, especially in Saudi Arabia.

Egypt was not hesitant to ask for assistance from the oil-rich countries, which often caused me a lot of embarrassment, if not distress. Mubarak used to ask or order a senior Egyptian official to present particularly pressing Egyptian needs to the leaders in these countries—asking for locomotives, for example, from Qatar and Libya. These countries would often agree to provide direct funding for Egyptian needs. When an Egyptian ferry sank in the Red Sea, Mubarak was quick to mention to the Saudis the need for funds to purchase new ferries. A global rise in grain prices led to an Egyptian request to the UAE and Saudi Arabia to finance millions of tons of wheat purchases. The deterioration of the international economic situation in 2008 caused Egypt to move quickly to seek support for the Egyptian economy, which had just entered an economic takeoff that was apparent to all. Egypt sent some senior financial officials to request aid from the Arab sovereign funds, offering them in exchange ambitious investment projects on Egyptian soil, particularly in Sinai.

I received a proposal from our ambassador in Riyadh to establish a strategic Egyptian–Saudi partnership. I applauded the idea as useful and presented it to the president. He approved, adding that we were already doing this. We asked the Cabinet to draft an integrated Egyptian proposal to be presented to the Saudis. I noticed resistance from some ministers to the idea, but found out that it was only a maneuver to maintain their individual freedom of movement with respect to the kingdom.

On another level, Iran had stepped up its activity in the Gulf region in the face of the GCC countries. Due to their interest in the Iranian nuclear program, and eager to reach an agreement with Tehran, the European powers began to say that the west appreciated Iran's interest in the collective security of the Gulf, and that they—the western countries—were ready to enter into consultations with Iran to reach an understanding in this regard, and also to include countries such as Russia, China, and India.

In all our contacts with the GCC or western powers, I emphasized that as the largest Arab force in the region, Egypt was interested in all regional issues, and that we must participate in any collective security arrangements.

In view of the clarity of Iran's interests in the Red Sea and the strengthening of its relations with Eritrea and Djibouti, Egypt and Saudi Arabia began a series of meetings to assess the situation in the region, and in particular to evaluate information about arms-smuggling operations to Egypt, Saudi Arabia, and Sudan. Sensing the Iranian threat, Bahrain proposed a meeting—perhaps the first of periodic meetings—between Egypt and the GCC to monitor Iranian threats, but the idea was vetoed by one of the GCC states. As the situation became more complicated in 2007, I proposed the idea again, and monitored the resistance from this same state. Meanwhile, this state had agreed to a similar proposal calling for periodic meetings between the GCC and Jordan, Egypt, and the United States.

Our information indicated that the Qatar-backed Syrian position of supporting Iranian interests had led to the emergence of an opposing group composed of Egypt, Saudi Arabia, the United Arab Emirates, and Kuwait, which emphasized the importance of not allowing Iran to manipulate Arab issues in order to protect its interests in the region or in the face of the west. I believe that Syria became aware at this stage, in the late months of 2006, that President Assad's statement on the war in Lebanon had had a negative impact on Egyptian–Syrian relations, causing Egypt's attention to gradually move away from Syria. The United States had decided to confront Syria in Lebanon and use the special tribunal for the assassination of Hariri to tighten its grip on the Syrians. Consequently, Syria dispatched its deputy foreign minister, Faisal Mekdad, to meet with me in Cairo in early September 2006. Mekdad carried a message from Assad to Mubarak about the importance of a reconciliation between Egypt and Syria. I conveyed it to the president; he sounded uninterested. I urged the president to respond to the Syrian overtures; perhaps we could use it to influence the Syrian position. Still he would not agree and I sensed that he did not want to abandon Saudi Arabia, which had made the king's rejection of the actions of the Syrian president quite clear. I decided to keep in touch with Minister Walid al-Muallem; I thought that if he had attended in person, instead of his deputy, to convey Assad's message, perhaps Mubarak would have shown some interest. The talk with Faisal Mekdad revealed that Syria was feeling its distance from Egypt and Saudi Arabia, at a time when increasing American and western pressure had put it in a position of isolation and thus harmed it. Saudi Arabia and Egypt were working actively at this time to improve our cooperation with Jordan, which only added to Syria's isolation.

There has never been any question that Egypt would allow Syria to be isolated or weakened. All we wanted was for Syria not to take positions that appeared to support Iranian policies. Thus, when the new French president, Nicolas Sarkozy, suggested inviting Syria to join the Union for the Mediterranean, Mubarak did not object. And when Sarkozy suggested to Mubarak that France could try to draw Syria away from Iran via a degree of controlled openness, Mubarak encouraged him, although he did point out the importance of accurately confirming Syria's stances.

The tension between Syria and Saudi Arabia was mainly over the situation in Lebanon. I did not want Egypt to seem as if it no longer cared about Lebanon. As such, I never missed an opportunity to visit to Beirut, even if only for a few hours, so as to keep the Lebanese, especially the Sunni parties, aware of the Egyptian interest. The Egyptian General Intelligence, on the other hand, openly maintained its contacts with Hezbollah. We wanted to reach the truth about the assassination of Hariri and the forces who carried it out. Yet at the same time, we did not want to let the issue of the tribunal lead to the explosion of Lebanon.

France's transformation—from President Jacques Chirac's bitter hostility toward the Syrians over Hariri's assassination, to Sarkozy's dialogue with them—encouraged the Syrian president to make a fresh attempt to revive Syria's relations with Saudi Arabia and Egypt through positive statements and visible interest. He met with Prince Sa'ud al-Faisal and France's foreign minister in Cairo. Yet the Saudi minister continued to criticize Syria very sharply. Another meeting was held in Paris with a large number of Arab and other ministers to discuss Hariri's tribunal and its funding. Saudi Arabia's hardline stance against the Syrians continued. I maintained my positive relationship with Walid al-Muallem, who I believed had a high level of professionalism and knowledge. I conveyed to President Mubarak the Syrian attempts to open up to us through Walid al-Muallem, whom I met on several occasions, and Vice-President Farouk al-Sharaa, whom I met in Dakar in connection with the Islamic summit. Mubarak requested the restoration of the active relations between Egypt and Syria.

Mubarak met with President Assad on the last day of the Arab summit in Riyadh in 2007. The meeting was cold and did not achieve a breakthrough in the relationship because of Mubarak's concern not to appear as if he were abandoning Saudi Arabia. He was also trying to feel out the possibility of softening King Abdullah's stand against Assad, but Saudi anger against the Syrian president was still strong. So, finding no support from Saudi Arabia, Mubarak maintained his distance from Syria. At this time, it seemed to me that the president had firmly linked our position with Saudi Arabia and against Syria, but I felt we should maintain as much freedom of movement and flexibility as possible. Once again, the Syrians proposed bringing the Egyptian and Syrian leaders together to break the ice in the relationship. However, they believed that President Assad's visits to Egypt had outnumbered the Egyptian visits to Syria, which unfortunately led to a dispute. The Syrians proposed that I or General Omar Suleiman visit Damascus to invite the Syrian president and announce the invitation publicly, so that the balance would be restored and Assad could come to Cairo. We rejected the proposal. The Egyptian intelligence chief continued to maintain high-level contacts with his Syrian counterpart, hoping that this would help to restore the relationship between the Egyptian and Syrian presidents.

We received information about Syria's desire to negotiate with Israel, perhaps as a way to escape the pressures of the Special Tribunal for Lebanon.

I proposed to the president that we push in this direction by starting an initiative to open a Syrian dialogue with both Israel and the United States, in the belief that Egypt's presence would protect Syria from any adverse consequences. However, the president, who was closely following Judge Serge Brammertz's investigation of the assassination of Hariri, showed no enthusiasm for the idea. Mubarak would meet for hours with the Norwegian ambassador Terje Rød-Larsen, whom the UN Security Council had assigned to monitor the implementation of Resolution 1559, whenever he attended meetings in Cairo. I briefed the president on all the details of the developments of the special tribunal, which we were following closely, but Egypt did not volunteer any individuals and information to the investigation, so as not to completely wreck Egyptian–Syrian relations.

Since it was Saudi Arabia's turn to take leadership of the Arab summit in March 2007, the Egyptian president's instructions were to help the Saudi side and to fully coordinate with them. I held more than one meeting with Prince Sa'ud for this purpose. We agreed on the importance of continuing to adhere to the Arab Peace Initiative in all our deliberations, especially since some people were whispering at the time about dropping it because it had not achieved its goal. However, none of these whispers offered an acceptable alternative. There was also an Egyptian–Saudi–Kuwaiti consensus on an Arab economic summit, which could be held on a periodic basis. We and the Saudis looked forward to expanding the Arab national security framework, particularly in the Gulf and Red Sea regions. The Saudis, despite their traditional caution in foreign policy issues, were willing to establish a joint naval force with Egypt and other countries in the Red Sea in defense of the Arab interests in this vital region. As the piracy operations of Somali groups expanded from the Indian Ocean and the shores of Somalia to the Gulf of Aden, the Red Sea, and the Bab al-Mandeb strait, Egypt and Saudi Arabia increased their exchange of information through joint meetings of the naval forces and the foreign ministries.

In the president's meetings with the king of Saudi Arabia, the discussion always extended to Iran, its attempts to infiltrate into other countries—especially as the Lebanon war came to an end—and the need to restrict its ambitions on the Islamic and Arab stage.

The Pakistanis were upset by the Iranian pressure on them in Afghanistan and Baluchistan. President Pervez Musharraf suggested to President Mubarak and the king of Saudi Arabia the idea of a meeting of the Sunni Islamic forces to galvanize the Islamic countries to increase their cooperation in all areas. However, the Pakistani thinking, to which they had also recruited Turkey, had aimed instead at emphasizing Iran's isolation, and consequently forcing it to consider restricting its activities in the fields of nuclear armament and strategic deployment. The meeting in Islamabad was attended by the foreign ministers of the major Sunni countries: Saudi Arabia, Turkey, Malaysia, Indonesia, Pakistan, Jordan, and Egypt. We discussed the position of the Islamic world vis-à-vis the west. Iran protested that it had not been invited. I spoke with Saudi Foreign Minister Prince Sa'ud about the risk of appearing to contribute to the isolation of Iran, a division that would certainly be exploited by the western powers to serve their interests, and the prince agreed with me. This effort was limited to one meeting and was not repeated, mainly because countries like Morocco and Senegal felt ignored because they had not been invited.

As Saudi Arabia, in its capacity as leader of the Arab Summit in 2007, launched some initiatives to deal with Somalia, Sudan, Lebanon, and Palestine, the Egyptian media was talking about the loss of Egypt's role. However, in more than one conversation with the president, I got the impression that he was not comfortable with the flamboyant Saudi efforts, which appeared to be based on what Egypt had previously achieved in some of these areas, especially on the issue of Palestinian reconciliation, without giving due credit to Egypt. Yet the president continued to say that the Saudis would not go too far. His constant concern was that his relations with Colonel Qadhafi should not affect our ties with Saudi Arabia, especially since Qadhafi lost no opportunity to harshly attack Saudi Arabia and King Abdullah bin Abdulaziz, much to Mubarak's embarrassment. Mubarak would then feel obliged to speak up, hinting that Qadhafi had tried to assassinate the king, which was unacceptable in terms of the relations of Arab leaders with each other.

We were not unaware that Qadhafi was playing with the Huthis in northern Yemen, supporting their efforts and providing them with arms financing to create a hotbed of tension on Saudi Arabia's southern border.

To counteract this, Saudis moved onto Libya's borders with Sudan, Niger, and Chad to resist Libyan influence. In his attempt to weaken Saudi influence on the issue of supplying oil to India and China, Qadhafi went so far as to ask Egypt to agree to the construction of an oil pipeline between Tripoli and Port Sudan, passing through Egyptian territory. We considered this idea a product of wild imagination. Meanwhile, Qadhafi had been helping the Darfur rebels in order to maintain his influence in Sudan. This caused a serious loss of confidence between Libya and the Khartoum government. When Omar Suleiman and I met with Libyan Foreign Minister Moussa Koussa and the Libyan intelligence chief Abdullah Senussi, their sharp criticism of the Sudanese was very clear, and the mistrust between them was abundant. On the Sudanese side, there was talk about the rebel Sudanese organizations being financed by the Libyans. These organizations had raided Omdurman with hundreds of vans bought from Dubai and delivered across Libya's border with Chad. We informed the Libyans that all this tension on our southern border would distract us from other issues and thus weaken our influence. Their response, however, was always that they were working to calm everyone and reach a settlement.

From our point of view, there were no new issues in Libya's relations with Sudan, or in Qadhafi's attempts to destabilize Sudan or work against the regime in Khartoum. In this context, I recall a conversation that happened in front of me in the summer of 1983 when I was working with Foreign Minister Kamal Hassan Ali. The minister said that the Americans informed Egypt about Libyan preparations for an attempt to overthrow the regime in Sudan by arming thousands of opponents of President Gaafar Nimeiry and pushing them across the desert from Darfur to Khartoum. To support the rebels, Libya intended to use long-range bombers—obtained from the Soviet Union—to blow up the Sudanese air bases and prevent Sudanese air intervention against the rebels' lines. Ali continued that President Mubarak then held an important meeting of the foreign minister, defense minister, the general intelligence, and other officials to assess the situation. They agreed on an Egyptian approach to prevent Qadhafi from jeopardizing Sudan's stability. Qadhafi had been taking sharply aggressive positions against Cairo since the assassination of President Sadat. Hence,

Egypt decided to send an air combat group of two squadrons of Egyptian F-4 fighter jets to some airports in southern Egypt and to provide fuel supplies by air, in order to counter the Qadhafi-backed insurgent groups. The operation, however, was not carried out, for a reason that I did not know at that time. I noticed that Field Marshal Abd al-Halim Abu Ghazala, in one of his conversations with Prime Minister Kamal Hassan Ali in 1984, complained about the high cost borne by the budget of the Armed Forces to defend Egyptian foreign interests. Referring to the Qadhafi incident specifically, he said that the transfer of these two squadrons to the airports of southern Egypt cost twelve million Egyptian pounds, at that time, for the transfer alone, not for carrying out actual operations.

I have narrated this incident so that the reader will understand the complexity of the Egyptian–Libyan relations during the rule of Qadhafi. The memory of this incident helped me to understand why the Khartoum government allowed the transfer of arms through its territory into Libya to support the anti-Qadhafi rebels in 2011.

As stated earlier, Qadhafi was a complex character whose sole concerns seemed to be to defend Islam and the Arab presence on the African continent. We felt that many African countries, especially those adjacent to Libya, were seeking to benefit from Libyan funds, though they always expressed their contempt for Libya's behavior, which was offensive to us as Arabs. We often tried to leverage the Libyan influence to serve some Egyptian objectives directly, but we did not achieve much in this area. The Libyans rejected all Egyptian offers of cooperation in economic and technical work in Africa. We have often gone to huge expense, straining our resources, yet with no profit. It was just a waste of Libya's oil wealth. Qadhafi loved to participate in African summits, and I used to monitor the large number of giant planes that would fly into the host city, imagining the exorbitant sums that were being spent so recklessly.

In 2004, Libya was working hard to attract European and other western economic investment, because of Libya's oil and gas resources, which were close to Europe across the Mediterranean Sea, and other major projects that Libya wanted to launch. President Chirac and President Sarkozy, as well as the heads of the British and Italian governments, among others, visited Libya, and Qadhafi was invited to Paris, Rome, Moscow, and other capitals. However, the western leaders complained persistently and severely to President Mubarak about Qadhafi's treatment of them. They often implied he was crazy, using gestures without actually uttering the word. Qadhafi fought Sarkozy's idea of a Union for the Mediterranean, stating that it and the Barcelona project were nothing more than a European attempt at domination. I often tried, during meetings and in private conversations, to talk him out of obstructing the project. As a counteroffer, Qadhafi proposed expanding the framework of the Western Mediterranean Group "5+5," which was made up of five European countries of Western Mediterranean and five North African countries, not including Egypt, requesting that both Egypt and Greece be added to the group so as to better address the issues of Palestine, Israel, and Lebanon. We did not mind supporting this effort of Qadhafi's as long as it did not contradict the philosophy of the Barcelona process or the Union for the Mediterranean. However, we were informed by some European parties that certain Arab countries in North Africa strongly resisted the addition of Egypt to the group; some of them even named these countries to us, but of course the countries in question categorically denied it. Whenever we spoke to the Libyans about receiving this kind of information, a faint smile was the only response we got.

I followed the development of Libya's infrastructure with great interest, because it would allow Egyptian companies to participate on a large scale. I would bring up the matter with the president immediately after my return from every visit to Tripoli or Sirte or other cities in Libya, talking about Libyan projects for ports, railways, housing, tourism, and so on. He always replied that corruption and commissions were the sole focus of interest of the circle around Qadhafi.

Throughout this period, Iraq was never far from my attention, despite the harm inflicted upon us by the loss of our ambassador and the smear campaigns I had personally experienced. Some people in Egypt deplored our supposed neglect of Iraq. They felt that this should not be the Egyptian approach, even if we had lost an ambassador; Iraq had a strategic importance that must not be left prey to the United States, Iran, or both. Others thought that Egypt should not return to Iraq as long as the U.S. occupation continued. Although the strategic importance of Iraq made it important for us to return, the predominant factor that prompted me personally to start moving in the direction of Iraq was our economic interests. I believed that Egypt and its companies could find opportunities in a country that was being rebuilt or would soon be rebuilt. I discussed the issue with the president, who, in spite of his caution in matters of individual and corporate security, was in favor of the Egyptian return to Iraq. I proposed this to the Egyptian Cabinet, and sent invitations to the Iraqi vice-president, prime minister, and other influential figures, to visit Egypt and strengthen their contacts with it.

In the following years, I visited several Iraqi cities: Baghdad, Suleimaniya, and Erbil. These trips were arranged with caution and care, without informing anyone in Cairo. I would inform the Iraqi foreign minister directly, arrive in the early morning, and return to Cairo by midnight. I would make the arrangements so quietly that even my wife would not know that I was going, so she would not be frightened. Then she would get surprised and angry when someone telephoned her saying that I was in Iraq.

Our ambassador returned to Baghdad, and two Egyptian consulates were opened in the north and south. The trade and construction sector in Egypt began making overtures to the Iraqis, giving them opportunity to get acquainted with the capabilities of Egyptian oil companies in the fields of construction, pipelines, repairs, equipment, and other technical elements. We also tried to resolve all the unsettled issues left over from the era of Saddam, especially the Iraqi debt to Egypt. The Iraqis agreed to pay all wages owed to Egyptian citizens who had worked in Iraq in the 1990s, but refused at first to pay any interest on these amounts, which were estimated at half a billion dollars. They offered to negotiate and we agreed. Then the Iraqis made a proposal that halted all these efforts: they demanded that we write off the debts they owed to the Egyptian private sector and the Egyptian Armed Forces, in exchange for repaying their debts to government companies. No Egyptian official could approve this, of course, and it all came to an end.

The Turks were moving boldly into Iraq, benefiting from the proximity of their companies right across the border. Iran also created a large presence for itself on the Iraqi stage. I felt that our cooperation with the Turks, the Americans, and Saudi Arabia would allow Egypt to achieve an influential political and economic position in Iraq as well as in the Kurdish region. My two visits to the Kurdish region indicated that it was growing and thriving economically.

Once again, Iran was the main theme of many of our discussions with the Saudis. We decided that confrontation should not be the only option for us; the continuation of dialogue, debate, and exchange of views were too important to be neglected. It began to seem possible to arrange a tripartite meeting with the Saudi king, the Egyptian president, and the leader of the Iranian revolution, once certain preparations had been made. Examples of these were supporting the Shi'i groups with Arabist leanings, strengthening the Arab governments with influential Shi'i minorities, and advising the Sunnis in Iraq to participate fully in Iraq's political process. In this context, Egypt intensified its interest in and support for the positions of the Gulf states.

During the early months of 2008, there were quiet suggestions from western sources that President Assad should not be allowed to preside over the Arab summit at a time when his country was facing accusations of involvement in the assassination of Rafik Hariri. Syria made vigorous efforts to quash these rumors and defend its right to hold the summit in Damascus, accusing Saudi Arabia and Egypt of trying to move it. The fact was that neither Egypt nor any other Arab country tried to keep Syria out of the presidency. The idea persisted, however, increasing the Syrians' resentment of Egypt. The situation became even more complicated when the Egyptian president neither participated in the summit himself nor assigned me to lead the Egyptian delegation. The idea was to avoid an Egyptian–Syrian political dialogue that might irritate the Saudis when they saw that Egypt had sent a Cabinet-level minister while Riyadh was represented only by its Arab League delegate.

The situation had deteriorated in Lebanon by the beginning of May 2008, after Hezbollah staged a sudden and effective military demonstration that revealed its absolute military control in Lebanon. In Egypt, we received reports of military operations threatening the Sunnis and their leadership in Lebanon. I sensed that matters might get completely out of hand, allowing the Lebanese state to descend into chaos, or leading to Israeli intervention. I believed that the way out was to seek the immediate intervention of the Arab League. I contacted the Saudi foreign minister early on the morning following the Hezbollah action, informing him that we were about to request an immediate meeting of the Council of the Arab League and asking whether Saudi Arabia would work with us. I explained my conviction as to the seriousness of the situation and of Hezbollah's military aggression, which threatened the delicate balance in Lebanon. Prince Sa'ud agreed with me, and the other Arab countries followed. Syria was unenthusiastic, while Qatar was looking around anxiously. We would prepare a draft resolution calling for a cease-fire, condemning the offensive operations, and insisting that Hezbollah withdraw from the areas it entered. This set off a months-long confrontation with Syria, backed by Qatar and Sudan.

It was my assessment that the Arab League would be required to call upon the internal parties in Lebanon to meet and negotiate a settlement through peaceful means and with no threats of force. I spoke with President Mubarak on May 10, 2008 about a proposal that Egypt would make to invite the parties to negotiate in Cairo under the supervision of either Egypt or an Arab committee. But he did not approve the idea, saying that he knew the Lebanese well, and that the cost for such a process would be prohibitive. I believe that what he had in mind was what Saudi Arabia had spent to conclude the Taif Agreement in 1989. So I did not argue. That evening, Qatar's foreign minister offered to host the meeting under Arab supervision. This was agreed upon. Qatar exerted a serious effort and reached an agreement that would provide Hezbollah and Syria with everything they wanted with regard to Lebanon. President Mubarak expressed his surprise that all the Lebanese factions had accepted this agreement, which contained the same elements that had been previously rejected. We then knew that Qatar had spent huge amounts of money to convince all parties to accept it. Meanwhile, it was reported that Saudi Arabia had pressured Saad Hariri, Rafik Hariri's son and leader of one of the Lebanese factions, into accepting this agreement despite the intensification of the Saudi–Syrian dispute over Lebanon, which had been exacerbated by the Special Tribunal's procedures concerning the assassination of Rafik Harari.

Relations between the Syrian and Egyptian presidents were deteriorating. President Mubarak was deeply hurt by the failure of the Syrian president to offer him condolences on the death of his grandson. "He did not personally offer me condolences, even though I attended his brother's funeral. Only his wife called after ten days to express her condolences to my wife on the death of our grandson."

U.S. forces in Iraq escalated the situation with a military operation by its Special Forces to arrest Arab or Iraqi jihadists inside Syrian territories on the border with Iraq. Israel raided a Syrian facility in northwestern Syria, and it was reported that Israeli fighter bombers flew into Turkish airspace in order to reach its targets inside Syria near the Turkish border. Yet the Syrians turned a blind eye to Turkey's behavior. In the weeks following the raid, it was revealed that they were targeting a nuclear facility being built by Syria in cooperation with North Korea. The Americans provided us with all the details, on their own initiative.

In the midst of this situation, the Yemeni president came up with a proposal at the request of President Assad and presented it to us. It spoke of the importance of building bridges between Egypt and Syria and suggested that the foreign ministers and intelligence chiefs of both countries should meet to discuss how to resolve their differences. President Mubarak, however, was not enthusiastic about the proposal.

The Arab Economic Summit was held in Kuwait in February 2009. King Abdullah bin Abdulaziz unexpectedly presented an initiative to reconcile with Syria and set aside their differences in order to protect the Arab position in the face of the Israeli attack on Gaza. In his comments to me about this Saudi initiative, the Egyptian president expressed his dismay at this unilateral Saudi initiative, which was announced without prior consultation with him. He told me that he had expected Saudi Arabia to coordinate with Egypt on this matter, especially after Egypt had supported Saudi Arabia during the Israeli attack on Lebanon, and in light of the fact that, in relation to Syria's President Assad, President Mubarak had been aligned with King Abdullah, who was deeply distressed by the attitude and policies of the Syrian President, whom King Abdullah called a "reckless young man." During the summit, the president had to attend a working lunch with King Abdullah and the Syrian president. Despite his extreme displeasure at the independent Saudi initiative, he agreed to attend the meeting in order to protect Egyptian interests. Besides the president of Syria and the king of Saudi Arabia, the emir of Kuwait also attended. Unfortunately, the meeting did not result in any major breakthrough in relations between the Egyptian and Syrian presidents, although it did open the way for what appeared to be a restoration of normal Saudi–Syrian relations.

The Saudi proposal for this meeting had actually included the emir of Qatar as well, which President Mubarak firmly rejected in protest against the Qatari position and Al Jazeera's attack on Egypt during the war against Gaza in late December 2008 and the early weeks of January 2009. This will be discussed further in the chapter on the Arab–Israeli conflict and the efforts toward a Palestinian settlement. As part of my general assessment of the region, I was monitoring what I described as an ongoing attack by the so-called revolutionary forces of Iran, Syria, Hezbollah, Hamas, and Qatar against the axis of Egypt, Saudi Arabia, the UAE, and Jordan. That axis remained constantly on the defensive despite the ongoing meetings.

The Saudis tried to revive the relations between Egypt and Qatar. Prince Sa'ud and the Saudi intelligence chief, Prince Muqrin bin Abdulaziz, invited the foreign ministers and heads of intelligence of Egypt and Qatar to Riyadh to settle the Egyptian–Qatari disputes. I pointed out that Qatar had tried to hold an extraordinary Arab summit during the Israeli invasion of Gaza without consulting Egypt. We were ignored for a whole day while they were in contact with over a dozen other Arab countries before their emir spoke to President Mubarak in the evening. We therefore decided not to cooperate with them, and the summit was aborted. The Qataris pointed to old accusations that Egypt conspired against the emir of Qatar and tried to replace him in 1995, an accusation that was categorically denied by Omar Suleiman. The president became even more distressed, and he decided not to attend the Arab summit in Qatar in late March 2009.

President Mubarak was very pleased with the results of the Lebanese elections, in which Saad Hariri's coalition won the majority of votes. He advised him not to run for the post of prime minister and to leave Fouad Siniora in that position, while Saad, who was also known as Sheikh Saad, would be the one who actually controlled the situation. The Saudis agreed with us about this. Saad Hariri did try to become prime minister, but he ultimately lost to a candidate supported by Syria, Hezbollah, and Qatar.

The convening of the Arab Summit in Sirte, Libya in March 2010 complicated things even more between Egypt and Syria. The Syrian president asked to visit President Mubarak in Sharm al-Sheikh after the summit, because the president had undergone major surgery in February. We asked the Syrians to wait for the president to regain his health, at which point we could arrange a definite date and time for a visit. The Syrians got angry, considering this a summons, not a visit. After this, no progress was made in Egypt–Syria relations until President Mubarak left power.

The complicated relationship between the two presidents had an extremely negative impact on the relations between the two countries for three years or more. During this entire period, I worked to maintain contacts with the Syrians in connection with the Palestinian settlement, convinced them to attend the 2007 Annapolis conference on the Palestinian–Israeli negotiations, and offered them many tips for their relations with western powers.

Today, I would say that Egypt and Syria undoubtedly adopted contradictory policies in their relations with Iran and the United States. The intensification of competition in the Middle East at that time, the increased Iranian presence in Lebanon and the Islamic world in general, and the tension between Iran and the Arab powers over the Iranian nuclear program all had a direct effect on the orientations of the Egyptian and Syrian presidents. It ought to be said, however, that they should have maintained a minimal level of personal connection and joint Egyptian–Syrian action so as to preserve important Arab interests. The situation makes clear the tremendous influence of personal relations and sensitivities among the Arab leaders on the course of events. Of course, the differences in the national interests of each state and every regime, as well as the regional and international ties governing these positions, cannot be ignored.

Although I have never been particularly interested in sports contests between Egypt and other Arab and African countries, I have been always concerned that these rivalries would lead to an incident that might damage our relationships with them. This was exactly what happened with Algeria.

Relations between Egypt and Algeria and their presidents have been characterized by constructive joint work over the years. Egypt has found in Algeria an important economic partner, which led to the establishment of public and private Egyptian companies with significant investments in Algeria and a number of contracts of importance to both economies. This productive relationship was damaged because of a competition leading up to the 2010 FIFA World Cup in South Africa. A ridiculous tragedy took place as a result of a match in Cairo, where some fans hurled solid objects onto a bus carrying the Algerian team from the airport to their hotel, injuring some of the players. Strangely enough, Cairo denied responsibility and claimed that the wounds were self-inflicted. The president was convinced that this was indeed what had happened. I tried to correct him calmly, but he was determined to stick to the version he had heard elsewhere. Egypt won the Cairo match and agreed to hold a third match to settle the competition in Khartoum, on the basis of an Egyptian proposal. We received information from Algeria and Sudan that the Algerian fans, known for their violence, were preparing to attack the Egyptian team and fans. There was a widespread rumor that the Algerians were buying 'white weapons' (non-firearm weapons) from Khartoum. We warned the Sudanese authorities, and we were assured that the Sudanese would take strict measures to protect the two teams and their fans.

I spoke with the president while he was receiving the credentials of twenty new ambassadors in Cairo, saying that the position was sensitive and that I was afraid the reports we had received were correct. Therefore, I suggested sending two thousand soldiers in civilian clothes to protect the Egyptian fans, thousands of whom were traveling to the match. He thought about it, and then said it was very dangerous because they might end up committing a massacre if an incident occurred, no matter how trivial it was.

I let myself be convinced by his opinion. We formed a work group from all the Egyptian authorities responsible for monitoring the match. Once the match had begun, several incidents occurred in the stadium and in the streets of Khartoum and Omdurman amid false rumors that Algerians were killing Egyptians.

The reports were false, or at least inaccurate, yet they shook the relationship between the two countries and the two peoples. We committed serious mistakes, both in the performance of the Egyptian media, official and private, and on the political level, acting in a way that revealed the populism of the political positions we adopted. The crisis continued for months and we suffered serious economic losses.

On the eve of the match between the Egyptian and Algerian teams in Khartoum, and also during the Cairo match, the Egyptian performance revealed the weakness of the government's control and the power of demagoguery. The president was managing the situation on his own from home, issuing instructions directly to the Egyptian minister of information, who threatened to send Egyptian troops to Khartoum, and to the General Intelligence, which asked the Sudanese to intervene in a situation that they did not cause. Meanwhile, the Egyptian media kept hurling abuse at the Algerians, which I believe was a major factor. As the security situation deteriorated, I wrote to the president on September 21, 2009: "My assessment is that the continuation of the current media line—which is full of abuse against Algeria—does not benefit any party and impairs our diplomatic ability to contain the crisis with the Algerian officials. This will have bad effects on our citizens there and definitely causes more harm than good to Egypt's foreign image." In conclusion, I called for the Egyptian Ministry of Information to try to control the situation. Unfortunately, they produced a sad piece of media work that revealed the weak performance of the Egyptian state and populist governance.

I decided to travel with General Omar Suleiman to Khartoum at the end of November 2010 to try to salvage our relations with Sudan, which had long been attacked by absurdities in the Egyptian media.

The visit revealed Sudan's distress as a result of our actions toward them and toward Algeria. However, Khartoum worked hard to restore the Egyptian–Algerian relationship, which I thought would take years to mend. I encouraged President Mubarak to travel to Algeria at the first opportunity to improve the situation. The Algerian president's brother had passed away, giving us the opportunity we needed. President Mubarak traveled to offer his condolences and was warmly welcomed by the Algerian state, although not the Algerian people. Huge differences do exist between Egypt and Algeria, in terms of their impact in the Arab world and internationally, but we must always be careful not to insult or belittle any Arab country; the loss would be ours. This has always been my approach toward our relationships with Arab countries, except perhaps in the case of Qatar, which I believed was specifically targeting the role and effectiveness of Egypt on the Arab level. This could not be tolerated under any circumstances, and therefore we had to acknowledge it in our policies toward Qatar.

An Arab summit was held in Libya in March 2010. The Libyans submitted a proposal to establish an Arab States Union instead of the Arab League. The Qataris and Algerians were concerned about rotating the post of secretary general of the League of Arab States, so it would not be exclusive to Egypt. I asked President Mubarak to take definite action to counter these maneuvers, but he preferred to deal calmly with what I saw as a threat to our interests. The emir of Qatar was willing to consider the Libyan proposal, which was also concerned with the appointment of foreign, defense, and foreign trade ministers for the Arab Union. He also proposed to form a committee from Qatar, Libya, and Yemen to address the issue of Arab joint action and the purpose of the Arab States Union, following the example of the African Union. I was greatly surprised that a proposal of this kind did not include the name of Egypt, which hosts the Arab League. I therefore delivered a sharp message to the Libyans that we would block the idea as long as they left us out. The Egyptian prime minister, who was representing Egypt, did not want to engage in debates with the Libyans or Qataris. But under the pressure of these two parties, and on my recommendation, he was forced to take a position.

The Libyans and Qataris were thus compelled to expand the proposal to include both Egypt, the host country of the Arab League, and Iraq, host of the next summit, which was to study the recommendations of this committee. However, the 2011 meeting was not held.

Another surprise revelation at the Arab summit in March 2010 was Qadhafi's idea of launching a military confrontation with Israel in light of its continued occupation of Arab lands. He was opposed by Bashar al-Assad, who said that Syria could not engage in an armed confrontation and that it was not in the interest of the Arabs. The Palestinian delegation, led by the Palestinian president, Abu Mazen (also known as Mahmoud Abbas), gave the Syrians and everyone else some very meaningful looks.

The secretary general of the Arab League spoke about his proposal to establish the Arab League Neighborhood Project, which he had mentioned earlier in 2009. I was aware of the importance of the project for improving the effectiveness of the Arab League and extending its influence to the belt surrounding the Arab countries in Africa and Asia. Although we at the Egyptian foreign ministry were studying the idea with a relatively positive outlook, a great deal more study would be required, especially the potential impact on the Arab Legue's relations with conflict zones, as numerous as they are in the immediate neighborhood of the Arab countries.

President Mubarak rejected the idea and was close to an argument with Amr Moussa, the secretary general of the Arab League. He said that he knew that the purpose of the proposal was to add Iran to the Arab framework, not to mention how dangerous it would be to expand it to include countries such as Turkey and Pakistan. The issue was suspended, perhaps temporarily.

Returning to Qatar: In the second half of 2010, we received information about a huge Qatari project to build a gas pipeline connecting Qatar with Turkey via Saudi Arabia and the Mashriq countries, which would connect with the gas lines from Central Asia and Azerbaijan in Turkish territory to Eastern and Western Europe, either by overland routes or by sea routes under the Mediterranean or the Black Sea. We believed this idea might have a negative impact on Egypt, which was seeking its own gas and pipelines deals, including linkage with Turkey. We were quietly working with Saudi Arabia, and proposed making our approval of the project contingent on running the pipes through Egyptian lands and territorial waters. King Abdullah immediately agreed. It remained for us to approach Qatar, to which President Mubarak dispatched an Egyptian presidential envoy. The Qataris expressed their readiness to consider the issue, which encouraged President Mubarak to travel to Qatar in October 2010 to obtain the initial approval of the emir of Qatar. Since leaving office, I have been following the 2011 bombings of the Arab gas pipeline in Sinai, and I was saddened that these bombings have caused this Qatari–Saudi–Egyptian–Turkish project to be suspended. The loss was huge and will affect Egypt for decades.

We have known for decades that Egypt's relations with the Arab world represent the first circle of the strategic movement, aimed at defending the security and safety of this region, which has been under pressure for a thousand years from both Central Asia and the European continent. Egypt has sometimes carried this message successfully, and sometimes failed. But what is important, in my estimation, is that Egypt has not been aware of the tremendous changes, over the period from the 1967 defeat to the present day, which have been creeping over the Arab region from the ocean and the Gulf. These changes have affected its relations with nearby influential neighbors such as Turkey and Iran, and with the superpowers, especially the European Union and the United States, in terms of oil and gas interests. The economic growth and financial wealth of the countries of the Arabian Peninsula were unprecedented, while traditional social concepts persisted, leading to a sense that war is being waged once again between Islam and the west. From my point of view, these developments have been linked, as a result of Egypt's very complex internal pressures, with Cairo's sense that the problems it faces internally and externally place it in an uncomfortable position in relation to the rest of the region. This is especially true if some countries have ambitions to influence or dominate Arab actions, with results that could cast doubt on the strength and vitality of the Arab world.

This was the situation I faced personally, from the invasion of Lebanon in 2006 until the end of my term as foreign minister in March 2011. Yet I still believe that the elements of traditional power in Egyptian society, paired with the advantages of its location and history over the centuries as well as its culture and soft power, are all pillars to support an ongoing Egyptian role in the Arab region, in the Islamic world, and internationally.

# 10

# EGYPT AND THE CHALLENGES OF THE REGION

One can never examine the regional situation in the Middle East from an Egyptian perspective without considering a number of priorities that reflect the Egyptian concerns about the region. The Arab–Israeli conflict is, naturally, at the forefront of Egyptian priorities, including the ceaseless hundred-year-long effort to reach a settlement on the Palestinian issue, which will be handled separately in a chapter of its own. Since we have reviewed Egypt and Arab world affairs in a previous chapter, it is time to address Egypt's relations with the major regional powers in the Middle East. These countries are Turkey and Iran, which, unlike Israel, which is not part of the Arab or Islamic worlds, made important contributions throughout the history of the region, whether during the period of Islamic rule or for centuries before that.

It is also important to deal with the issues of nuclear weapons, weapons of mass destruction, and the efforts to eliminate them, especially since the Israeli nuclear project threatens the whole region and everyone in it. Naturally, different countries have different ideas about how to deal with this.

In the non-Arab Islamic Middle East, Turkey unquestionably jumps to the forefront because of its historical relations with Egypt. All Egyptians have learned in school about the battles of Ramesses II with the empire of the Hittites in Asia Minor (Anatolia). Perhaps the first written treaty in human history is the peace agreement between the pharaoh of Egypt and the king of the Hittites, which is the clearest evidence of how deep-rooted this historical relationship is between the two regions, Egypt and Asia Minor. I have often taken Egyptian guests to the UN headquarters in New York to look at a copper model of a treaty between the Hittites and Egypt, copied from a stone-cut original discovered in Anatolia and donated to the UN by Turkey. It sits in a conspicuous position in the main corridor linking the Security Council, the Economic and Social Council, the Trusteeship Council, and the UN General Assembly Hall.

Similarly, Iran has a high priority in Egypt's relations. Iran has had a major influence on the course of history and Islamic civilization. The connections between these two poles of civilization—Iran and Egypt—stretch back to their respective ancient empires; Persia (the former name of Iran) invaded Egypt in pre-Islamic times.

My diplomatic training emphasized how important it is for Egypt to maintain a triangle of active cooperation with Turkey and Iran, not only to serve the Middle East region and achieve peace, stability, and development, but also to protect this great Islamic region against foreign intervention.

Throughout my diplomatic career, I have closely followed Egypt's relations with these important parties, from the poor relationship between Cairo and Tehran in the Nasserite era, to the improvement of the Egyptian relationship with both Turkey and Iran during Sadat's years until the beginning of the Iranian revolution. President Nasser's conflicts with the United States and NATO, and the hostile relationship between the United States and the Soviet Union shaped the difficult relationship between Egypt and all three of these parties. With the shift in Egypt's foreign policy under Sadat's presidency, all of these relations gradually improved, although they were not guided by a coherent theoretical framework.

During my formative diplomatic years, I believed in the importance of establishing an Egyptian–Iranian–Turkish axis capable of standing up to Israel, especially after Egypt's defeat in 1967. I have thought about how the twin powers of Iran and Turkey could serve the confrontation with Israel through an active Islamic framework for cooperation in all fields. Regrettably, though, I tended to lose sight of the principles governing these two countries, not only in the Islamic region, but in the face of the great powers as well, whose influences and policies do govern the actions of Turkey and Iran with respect to the other Islamic countries.

Safavid Iran competed against Ottoman Turkey for power and influence in Central Asia, Iraq, and the Caucasus, but the two of them struggled together against the Russian Empire for centuries. In the twentieth century, after the end of the Second World War, the confrontations of the Cold War and the politics of alliances emerged. Iran and Turkey subsequently formed a series of close ties with the western powers, leaving little room for Egyptian–Iranian–Turkish cooperation in the sense referred to above.

The Iranian revolution broke out in 1979, coinciding with the signing of the Camp David Accords between Egypt and Israel under U.S. auspices, thus changing the alliances and strategic outlook between Egypt and Iran. Egypt turned to Turkey, resuscitating historical relations dating back to the Ottoman era with Turkey, which had been governed for years by the historical difficulties between Syria and Turkey and by Egypt's traditional caution toward anything that posed a threat to Syria.

For over two decades, I have watched Egypt and the Islamic Republic of Iran try, cautiously yet constantly, to establish a stable relationship. The closer they approached to a major breakthrough in these relations, the farther apart they ended up. Diplomatic relations between them had been severed ever since Egypt received the shah of Iran in his exile in 1980. For years, the ambassadors of the two countries to the UN, in Geneva or New York or Vienna, had been engaged in talks to restore these diplomatic relations and the commercial, economic, and investment transactions that would follow. But many obstacles stood in their way. Chief among these was the Iranian Revolution, which resisted any relationship with Egypt, the country that had signed the Camp David Accords with Israel. Egypt and Iran did approach a full restoration of diplomatic relations in 2003; the Interests Section that each government had established in the capital of the other country in 1980 was upgraded to a Legation. Finally, each legation was led by a person with the diplomatic rank of an ambassador.

In 2003, I was following from New York a draft agreement between Egypt and Iran that was about to be officially announced. However, it was abruptly suspended when the Egyptian president realized that Iran would not change its approach toward Egypt. In this context came my appointment as foreign minister in 2004, and it became my job to deal with the two important countries of Iran and Turkey. They now had to be handled within a new framework because of the U.S. invasion of Iraq, the presence of U.S. forces in Baghdad, and the threats being felt by Syria from this western presence across the Iraqi–Syrian border. The situation led to the reinforcement of Syrian–Iranian cooperation in their confrontation against the United States, which also now found itself on the borders of Iran, from Iraq on the west and from Afghanistan on the east. Meanwhile, the Iranian nuclear program emerged, further complicating the overall situation in the region. We in Egypt linked it closely with Israel's military nuclear capabilities and the tireless Egyptian efforts since 1974 to declare the Middle East a nuclear-weapon-free zone and to encourage all the region's countries to join the Nuclear Non-Proliferation Treaty (NPT).

From the beginning of my work in 2004, I maintained relations based on mutual respect with the foreign ministers of Turkey and Iran, whom I met in 2004 and 2005 several times in Cairo, Sharm al-Sheikh, Istanbul, Tehran, and Amman, during meetings of the Neighboring Countries of Iraq and Egypt Group, the Group of Eight Industrialized Nations (G8), and other European and Asian groups. My Turkish counterpart, Abdullah Gül, who later became president of the Republic of Turkey, worked with me to bring these relations to an integrated strategic framework. Turkey has a population almost as large as Egypt's, a highly advantageous location, ties with the Turkic peoples and nations in Central Asia, good relations with other Islamic countries, and the potential for European Union membership. Turkey has historically viewed Egypt as a strong and influential peer among Arab, Islamic, and Mediterranean nations. Egypt also enjoys economic ties with Europe thanks to the Egyptian–European partnership agreement, which offered an opportunity for Turkey to penetrate the European markets through Turkish–Egyptian coproduction agreements.

Turkey's economic success intensified the desire of the Turkish leadership to open up to the Arab countries as a whole. The Islamist orientation of the ruling party had, undoubtedly, led Turkey to adopt an orientation to

Israel that was different from the traditional Turkish–Israeli relationship. Turkey began to express its support for the Palestinians and their demand for an end to the Israeli occupation and the establishment of a Palestinian state. These positions were more acceptable to the Arab countries and peoples. Turkish trade increased in the region as a whole. Turkey benefited enormously, especially since its new approach did not affect its relationship with NATO and/or its cooperation with the western world in general.

Denmark's prime minister, Lars Rasmussen, had caused a crisis by his reaction to the anti–Prophet Muhammad cartoons, yet he later became secretary general of NATO. As NATO members, the Turks prevaricated. Instead of undermining Rasmussen's candidacy by formally objecting to his nomination, they limited themselves to expressing reservations that did not prevent Rasmussen's appointment. In return, Turkey received a senior position within the NATO bureaucracy. Their behavior and attitudes were comprehensible; I could not blame them. Yet unfortunately and sadly enough, many in Egypt and the Arab region held up Turkey's behavior as an example to be followed, whereas it was in fact nothing but a natural instance of states in pursuit of their interests at a particular moment in time.

I noticed at the beginning of my term as foreign minister that whenever I mentioned Turkey and its positions to President Mubarak, I would get rather restrained reactions on his part. Let us build the relationship cautiously, he would say, adding that his experience with them reflected their tendency to pursue their own interests without paying attention to anyone else's. But I also noticed that as the Egyptian–Turkish economic relationship began to have a positive effect on the rising Egyptian economy, his reservations gradually faded away in favor of full openness to Turkey.

As the relations between the two countries were being cemented, an extremely disturbing event occurred out of the blue. Turkey, through a statement issued by its Ministry of Foreign Affairs, announced that it was warning countries that had signed maritime boundary agreements with the Republic of Cyprus involving exclusive economic zones not to take advantage of these agreements. As it happened, the Egyptian Ministry of Petroleum had reached an agreement whereby it could search deep waters opposite the Egyptian coast between Egypt and Cyprus for gas and oil deposits. A Turkish diplomat spoke to our embassy in Ankara, saying that the Turkish fleet was capable of enforcing this warning. I read the cable on the subject that our embassy in Ankara sent in January 2007, and could see it only as a foolish act from a diplomat unaware of the ramifications of his statement. I wrote, and then talked to, the Turkish foreign minister, who understood the absurdity of their rhetoric and responded, "I hope we both would turn a deaf ear to such talk."

The Ministry of Petroleum resumed its work. Egypt and Turkey were both wary of an issue that could complicate the development of an important economic and political relationship. The Turks asked us to jointly delimit the maritime boundaries and exclusive economic zones between us. We agreed, although we were careful not to approach the maritime tripoint between Egypt, Greece, and Turkey so as not to allow the disagreements between Greece and Turkey to affect our interests with either nation. The relations were deepened and we continued to talk with Turkish foreign ministers about all issues that affected the strategic cooperation between the two countries. Numerous visits were exchanged at the highest levels.

Then Israel attacked Gaza in December 2008, and the Turkish president expressed his deep concern to the Egyptian president. The president dispatched me to attempt to reach an Egyptian–Turkish understanding about the necessary conditions for a cease-fire. My consultations in Ankara revealed that the Turkish president was irritated by Israel's actions, but the Turkish prime minister, Recep Tayyip Erdogan, expressed extreme anger and accused Israel of deceiving Turkey and using it as a conduit for negotiations with Syria, then attacking the Palestinians. In January 2009, his hostility to Israel became even more acute, and he started hurling criticism against Egypt as well, asking for more effort on our part. I believe he was not sufficiently informed about what we were doing, despite all attempts on our part to keep them fully informed. By the time the crisis came to an end, I could sense the distance between President Mubarak and Prime Minister Erdogan, a gap that lasted until Mubarak left office.

With the increasing Turkish influence on Middle East events, and the clear economic and trade advantages that they began to enjoy with many Arab countries, the Turks opened up to Syria and Jordan in similar ways. We had no objection to these overtures, and proceeded to prepare a document establishing full strategic relations between Egypt and Turkey. However, its signature was delayed because Mubarak was upset by Erdogan's behavior toward him personally. I was saddened by how easily the differences of personalities or orientations could disrupt the important interests of countries.

The Turks then proposed connecting the electricity grids between Egypt and Turkey to power the huge growth of their economy, which by the beginning of 2011 had become about four times as big as the Egyptian economy. They were also asking for Egyptian gas. We did not object as long as the process proceeded in accordance with the existing integrated plans for gas pipelines in the region, even though we were aware that Israel and Turkey were considering four gas, oil, water, and electricity lines between them until December 2006. In the meantime, Russia was also discussing with Israel the construction of a Russian–Azerbaijani gas pipeline that would pass through Turkey to Israel in order to diversify Israel's sources of gas, thus protecting its strategic position.

Another development further complicated Mubarak's relationship with Erdogan. Egypt called for a summit of the Alliance of Civilizations at the Bibliotheca Alexandrina in 2010. A group of leaders of Mediterranean countries, including the president of Israel, Shimon Peres, were invited. The Egyptian president insisted on inviting the Turkish president, not the prime minister, although the latter was the one who had come up with a joint initiative with the Spanish prime minister under the name Zapatero/Erdogan. The summit did not take place, due to the president's resistance to inviting Erdogan, not to mention the French and Spanish irritation over not inviting the Turkish prime minister. Once again, I say it was sad that personal feelings overruled the political interests in these relations, which I tried so hard to circumvent.

In my assessment of the Turkish policies toward the region, I would say that the activities undertaken by Turkey in the five years between 2005 to 2010 were in fact aiming to make full use of the general improvement in the Turkish economy. No Turkish initiative on any political issue led to any kind of breakthrough. Nonetheless, the Turks have been praised and admired by Arab and Egyptian observers who were inspired by the models of economic growth and political development, even as the strategic relationship between Israel and Turkey continued to flounder.

Over the years, I have continued to follow the Turkish assessment of Iranian developments. I have often noticed that Turkey has been deeply troubled by Iran's positions, either in the latter's relations with the countries of the region or in its nuclear program. I have always assumed that the Turks do not want to see another nuclear state on their borders besides Russia. They are also aware that the complexity of the relationship between Iran and the western powers puts Ankara in an unenviable position. The Turkish diplomatic efforts were aiming at calming the situation, in the realization that any success in this realm on Turkey's part would strengthen its application for EU membership.

As soon as I assumed my duties in 2004, I felt it was important to develop a viable Egyptian position with respect to Iran. I was aware that the Iranian nuclear program would lead the country to a sharp confrontation with the western powers. For the sake of our relations with the west, then, it was imperative that we not appear to be opening a door to the Iranians on such a sensitive issue. Egypt's relations with the Gulf countries also necessitated caution in dealing with Iran. But the major factor was the security dimension, and the personal experience of the president and the Egyptian intelligence agencies.

The Egyptian security services have always suspected that Iran wished to infiltrate Egypt and cultivate the same kind of revolutionary environment that existed in Iran. The Egyptian president's decades-long experience suggested that Iran's relationship with Egypt had suffered because of its own internal policies. Egypt had been trying for years, unsuccessfully, to remove from Iran certain Egyptian citizens who were wanted by the Egyptian security services. But with the U.S. invasion of Iraq, the American threats to Syria, and Iran's development of nuclear capabilities, the Iranians sought to revitalize their relationship with Egypt, as a way of obtaining an additional line of defense within the framework of the Non-Aligned Movement and the African groups. Throughout the period from 2004 to 2008, Iran's foreign ministers expressed their desire to improve relations. In October 2005 I met with Dr. Mohamed ElBaradei, who conveyed the Iranian foreign minister's willingness to discuss the extradition of the Egyptian extremist elements, the Khaled al-Islambouli mural, and the street in Tehran named after him. (Khaled al-Islambouli was the assassin of President Anwar al-Sadat.) They also wanted to renew their request to remove the flag of the shah from inside his grave in Cairo, and settle the cases of the Iranian diplomats convicted of espionage. All of these issues had come close to being settled in 2003, but eventually failed. I decided at the time that Egypt's membership on the board of governors of the International Atomic Energy Agency (IAEA) was what had prompted the Iranians to move in our direction. Dr. ElBaradei suggested that we assign someone like Dr. Mustafa al-Fiqi, formerly a senior advisor to the president, as a go-between. I conveyed this to the president, who rejected any such move.

The Iranian foreign minister Manouchehr Mottaki broached the subject with me again during a conference on national reconciliation in Iraq, which was held in Cairo in November 2005 and which was attended by several Arab and other regional foreign ministers. The Iranian minister suggested, as a start, the development of cultural and tourist connections. At that time, many Arab circles were talking about efforts to promote Shi'ism in Syria, Egypt, and the belt of African countries adjacent to Arab North Africa, including Senegal, Niger, and the Central African Republic. The president's response was: "The Iranians want to send us thousands of tourists, then infiltrate Egyptian society." He referred the question to the security services, which refused to consider it.

The Iranian president, Mahmoud Ahmadinejad, then sought a direct meeting with Mubarak in connection with the extraordinary Islamic Summit in Jeddah on December 5 and 6, 2005. The president was not in favor of this meeting in spite of my encouragement. He sent me to the summit, abruptly showed up in its final hours as a compliment to the Saudis, and then left immediately.

Despite this Egyptian caution in opening up more broadly to Iran, I personally dealt with Iranian diplomats with openness and cooperation during my service at the UN, consulting with them on many issues on which the two countries shared a common stance. Foremost among these were the Palestinian question, disarmament, and economic issues.

Iran's foreign minister spoke to me again during my visit to Tehran as part of the foreign ministers' meetings of the Neighboring Countries of Iraq and Egypt Group, during the first half of 2006, and urged us to reactivate relations. I told him I was trying to do this, but that the Egyptian and Iranian security services had not yet established the necessary conditions. The Iranian minister presented his country's stance on the issue of nuclear fuel, asserting that they had no desire to produce it but only to study the fuel cycle. I could tell he was not telling the truth, but I did not want to engage in dispute with him. I merely said that I recognized the right of all states to knowledge about nuclear power and the peaceful uses of atomic energy.

Then came Hezbollah's battle with Israel in August 2006, accompanied by Iranian accusations against Bahrain and the UAE. Iran also began to meddle in the Palestinian question and Gaza. These Iranian steps led to a change in Egypt's position toward Iran. One example of this shift was Egypt's support of a draft resolution submitted by the western countries to the IAEA in September 2006 asking to refer Iran's nuclear program to the Security Council. There was considerable evidence, at the time, that Iran possessed an integrated nuclear project whose goal was a full fuel cycle, a program which had not been approved by the IAEA and was not in compliance with any of the relevant international agreements. We succeeded in adding an introductory paragraph to the draft, stating that our concern with Iran's nuclear program was part of the process of ridding the Middle East region of weapons of mass destruction.

Egypt's position on the issue of nuclear non-proliferation in the Middle East stemmed from its conviction that Israel unquestionably possesses military nuclear capabilities, or could obtain them within a few weeks if it wanted to. Hence, since 1974, and in coordination with Iran, Egypt has been proposing a resolution to the UN General Assembly demanding the establishment of a nuclear-weapon-free zone in the Middle East. The resolution was presented annually, though without result. However, in 1981, Egypt decided to ratify the Nuclear Non-Proliferation Treaty (NPT), having signed it in 1970. There were two reasons for this. First, that it would help Egypt in its endeavors to establish a peaceful nuclear project, including research reactors and power reactors. Second, the United States has always assured Egypt that it would force Israel to sign the NPT within a short period of time, which has not happened. As a result, Israel's nuclear program has remained outside the framework of international control. I say today, as I said back then, that we should have linked Egypt's accession to the NPT with Israel's, which would have forced Israel into definite action one way or the other.

Although Egypt and Iran were unable to come to complete agreement on the nuclear issue during these years, the Egyptian position has always supported Iran's right to peaceful uses of atomic energy. Our demand was that all of its programs be subject to IAEA supervision. Our premise stemmed from two essential points. The first is that Egypt does not support the emergence of regional nuclear powers, because this is completely contrary to our desire to eliminate nuclear weapons and weapons of mass destruction from the Middle East. The second point is that the presence of nuclear weapons is very likely to lead to an armed confrontation in the region, with very harmful effects for Egypt. But if nuclear powers did emerge in the region—a frightening prospect—Egypt would feel compelled to follow suit, despite the enormous costs. This would disrupt Egyptian development programs in favor of a useless military nuclear project whose sole purpose would be to project strength and power or to defend a regime similar to that of Iran or North Korea.

I have always thought of nuclear weapons in today's world as weapons of deterrence, not of defense. However, our experience with Israel has shown that nuclear weapons do not necessarily work as deterrents. After all, Egyptian forces crossed the Suez Canal and destroyed the Bar Lev Line, undeterred by the existence of Israeli nuclear weaponry.

Egypt has always rejected the double standard of the western powers on this nuclear issue. We demanded that Israel be held to the same standards as Iran and everyone else.

In the face of these clear Egyptian positions, the United States and the Russians, among others, were presenting ideas to limit the production of nuclear fuel to a small group of countries. One of these was the initiative of the Global Partnership for Nuclear Energy, whereby the United

States or Russia was to supply the fuel for other countries' nuclear reactors. Such a proposal, we believed, would put us at the mercy of these states in the future.

Some of our brothers in the Gulf were paying attention to the Iranian nuclear program beyond its ramifications for the Israeli nuclear program or the general situation in the Middle East. Egypt was determined not to separate the security of the Gulf from that of the rest of the Middle East with regard to the issues of nuclear disarmament and weapons of mass destruction. In July 2007, I learned about a conversation of a prominent Syrian figure with our ambassador to Damascus, criticizing our position on Iran's nuclear capabilities and our determination to remove nuclear weapons and weapons of mass destruction from the Middle East. He told us that Iran was in fact developing a military nuclear capability, solely in order to preserve the strategic balance with Israel, with no intention of harm to the Arabs. This Syrian source did not bother to think the situation through. It plainly meant that Iran would be nuclear-capable and that its nuclear weapons, like those of Pakistan, will serve only the interests of their respective countries, not the Arab or Islamic ones.

Therefore, it came as no surprise when I learned in 2008 from U.S. intelligence sources that Israel had attacked a Syrian military facility that was in fact a nuclear reactor, built with North Korean assistance to produce plutonium with the aim of developing a Syrian nuclear weapon. We immediately urged the United States to compel Israel to sign the NPT and completely abandon its nuclear weapons. Nuclear capabilities on the part of one country inevitably encourage others to acquire the same. We were particularly concerned about Libya, which had revealed a comprehensive nuclear project in 2003 that had been frozen years before. Those countries might then try to acquire a nuclear weapon, to balance the Israeli threat to the entire region. The United States has always insisted that we must not consider escalating like this.

Iran continued to seek to develop its relations with Egypt. As a major regional player, Iran sought to deepen its contacts with Egypt as a way to overcome its international isolation and its inability to achieve diplomatic success at the global level. Indeed, it was no secret that the Iranians had failed miserably in their candidacy for a seat on the Security Council, receiving only thirty-two votes out of the necessary 108. They had also been forced, along with Syria, to discontinue their bid for membership on the Human Rights Council. In the face of these disappointments, in June 2007 they began to express their desire to restore normal relations with Egypt. We agreed to do so, although it took me a lot of effort to persuade the president to agree. I pointed out that it would always be up to us to decide whether to move their direction or not.

The deputy foreign minister of Iran came to Cairo in February 2008 and held a round of discussions, followed by frank consultations between the security services of the two countries. Months later, the assistant foreign minister of Egypt visited Tehran to continue the dialogue, and the situation returned to what it had been in 2005–2006. Egypt's main concern was security agreements between the two countries, while Iran was talking about the Iranian flag on the shrine of the last shah of Iran, which was located in Cairo. They wanted to separate the political agenda from the security agenda—to restore diplomatic relations, start cooperating, and gradually consider the security issues. The Egyptian delegation, which had visited Iran in December 2007, had reached the conclusion that developing political relations first would offer advantages to Iran without their having to make any security concessions, and Egypt would not benefit at all. The Iranians hinted at sending Egypt a gift of two hundred thousand tons of grain as a goodwill gesture. I did not favor this idea.

In 2007–2008, however, the Iranian vice-president visited Egypt to participate in Islamic conferences along with former president Mohamed Khatami, the secretary general of the Iranian National Security Council, the Iranian foreign minister, and the chairman of the Foreign Relations Committee of the Shura Council. Ali Larijani, the speaker of the Iranian parliament, participated personally in the conference of the Supreme Council for Islamic Affairs. The Egyptian president received many of the Iranian officials, but did not modify his attitude in light of Iran's unwillingness to change its approach.

In addition to its security cooperation with us, Iran was required to change its regional approach by ceasing to use its Arab connections to seek support from the western powers for its nuclear program. Despite my knowledge of his firm position on the subject, I wrote a detailed report for President Mubarak that included a thorough analysis of the Iranian position and Egypt's relation to it, noting that for many years these relations had been unequal. Even though its regional actions bother us from time to time, the memo stated, we needed to maintain a dialogue with them in order to explain our positions and try to understand theirs. The memorandum also pointed out the common denominators in Egyptian and Iranian policies: rejection of American hegemony, resistance to the imposition of foreign agendas, rejection of double standards in the matter of nuclear power, and the prevention of wars between religious sects. The memo reiterated Egypt's demands to change the name of Islambouli Street in Tehran and remove the mural bearing his image from one of Tehran's buildings, emphasized the importance of Iran's cooperation on security issues, insisted on an end to Iran's support for groups that oppose peace between Israel and the Palestinians; and requested that Iran not impede Egypt's role in any future arrangements for Gulf security.

In the conclusion of the report, I stressed how important it was to continue making positive statements about Iran and its relations with Egypt. Other proposals contained in the report included the continuation of the security and political dialogue whenever possible, the opening of telephone connections between the two countries, and the facilitation of Iran's participation in international exhibitions and symposiums in Egypt. The Iranians, for their part, wanted an Egyptian–Saudi–Iranian summit to address any lingering problems. I still believed that Iran's real underlying objective was to strengthen its position with the western powers on the nuclear issue. Nevertheless, I wrote to the president again in May 2008 about the importance of considering the Iranian proposal positively. The president informed me that King Abdullah would not accept the idea, so it was futile to promote it.

In the midst of all these attempts to improve Egyptian–Iranian relations, our security services received definite information about an Iranian plot to smuggle large quantities of drugs into Saudi Arabia. We passed the details on to the Saudis. Then several sources within the North Atlantic alliance informed us that Iran had plans to smuggle weapons in containers through the Suez Canal to Lebanon and Hezbollah. We monitored the situation extremely closely, examining whatever entered our territories in Sinai or covertly through Sudan. However, we continued to deal with Iran as if nothing threatening were happening, and cooperating with them within the framework of the Non-Aligned Movement.

Throughout these years I followed closely the developments of the Iranian nuclear program and the western and Israeli attitudes toward it. The Israelis were trying hard to direct international attention to it in order both to antagonize Iran and to distract attention from the Palestinian settlement, which we had been neglecting for some time. After long study of Iran's nuclear program, the Europeans and Americans confirmed in 2005, 2006, and 2007 that Iran was not close to the nuclear-weapon threshold. Later, however, at the end of 2008, some British intelligence reports claimed that Iran was making significant progress in its nuclear weapons development, raising serious risks of Israeli or U.S. military action against Iran. Iran was bound to respond, which would ignite the Middle East. U.S. sources also reported progress in Iran's uranium enrichment capabilities, and estimated that Tehran could produce a nuclear bomb within several years, but that it was still developing missiles that could carry a nuclear device.

Meanwhile, Israel demanded, and obtained, from the United States bunker buster munitions that are capable of penetrating deep underground facilities.

Finally, the United States became more and more aware that Israel would not accept an Iranian nuclear capability. It insisted that Israel not target the Iranians except in coordination with Washington.

Throughout these five years, I suspected Israel's intentions, but doubted its ability to carry out a unilateral airborne military action against Iran, either because of geographical restraints or because the Israelis lacked the capabilities. If any Iranian military installations or nuclear plants were to be destroyed, it would require the involvement of the United States, and perhaps also of the European powers. I often discussed this with the president in telephone conversations and written memos. The president remained convinced that Israel was in fact capable of carrying out unilateral action against Iran, and that it would certainly do so if it believed that Tehran was developing a military nuclear capability. When I mentioned the problems of geography and distance, the president would reply that the Israelis would not hesitate to use the airspace of third parties. Yet whenever I tried to explain the consequences of Israel flying in Jordanian airspace, in terms of avoiding provocation to Jordan or to the Americans in Iraq, he would reply that the Israelis would try to use the airspace of Azerbaijan. The likelihood of Russia permitting this maneuver was extremely low. Israel would also have to seek Turkey's permission to use its airspace, which the Turks would never grant. Besides, there are also an estimated 20 million Azerbaijanis living in northern Iran. In the event of military operations against Iran, they would no doubt flee to Azerbaijan, causing many problems there.

The Russian foreign minister, Sergey Lavrov, had called me more than once, as threats of war against Iran were mounting, saying that Russia was aware of the serious ramifications of such an act and could not agree to it. Lavrov said he expected large-scale migrations from Iran to Russia were Iran to be attacked. I assigned a group at the Foreign Ministry to study all aspects of the situation. This effort was eventually expanded to include all other state agencies, to determine how Egypt could be protected in the event of such an unacceptable incident. We reassessed the situation every year until my departure from the ministry in March 2011.

The foundation of our assumptions at the beginning of 2010 was that there would be no Israeli or U.S. action that year, but that the danger would increase by early 2011. The analysis went on to say that the presence of the United States in Iraq, and in Afghanistan in lesser numbers, hampered U.S. action against Iran. If the United States took any action at all, it would be to delay Iran's access to full nuclear potential and then use a carrot-and-stick policy to encourage them to change their approach. In all of these scenarios, we could see grave consequences for our interests: the displacement of Egyptians from the Gulf; tension in Egyptian society; Israeli attempts to cross the border with Gaza; Iran responding by hitting the Suez Canal areas with missiles, especially if there were U.S. naval vessels in the area; energy price hikes that would affect the Egyptian economy; a decline in tourism to Egypt; reduced traffic in the Suez Canal; reduced foreign investment in Egypt. There were many recommendations to deal with all these dangers, but the clear conclusion was that Egyptian interests would be best served by avoiding any attack on Iran, which could only increase tension between Islam and the western world. The best solution would be to get the international community to agree to Iran's right to peaceful uses of nuclear energy, including uranium enrichment and full scientific research, but governed by the NPT and under full supervision and control of the international community. In return, Israel would be expected to sign the NPT, fully disclose its nuclear program, and dismantle its nuclear military capabilities, all of which would be monitored by the international community. Finally, a zone free of nuclear weapons and weapons of mass destruction would be declared in the Middle East just as Egypt had been calling for over the previous decade.

Many countries in the Middle East are at the threshold of some level of nuclear capability. The region is in need of a clear system that secures the interests of all parties. This cannot wait for a comprehensive settlement of the Middle East conflict.

In 2008, Egypt objected to some of the proposals made by large nuclear powers in what was then called the Nuclear Supply Guarantee Initiative before the IAEA. Egypt joined with like-minded countries in opposing these plans, which gave certain countries a monopoly on nuclear knowledge and the right to produce nuclear fuel. It also strongly opposed the proposal made by the U.S. secretary of state in May 2008, and repeated in many American documents, that the United States should provide a nuclear guarantee for both Israel and the Arab countries and protect them against Iran. The Egyptian viewpoint was then, and I think is still, that the defense of the Middle East and its countries should stem from the region itself. The goal of eliminating nuclear weapons and weapons of mass destruction from the region must be met by abandoning all of these weapons, and obtaining a commitment from the nuclear powers not to introduce them into the Middle East.

Moreover, the defense of the region should be achieved mainly by settling the political problems in the Middle East, and then establishing security and cooperation systems among its countries that forbid the use of force to settle disputes, thereby securing stability and maintaining balance between the principal regional powers.

Egypt strongly supported the proposal of the Arab summit in Riyadh in March 2006 to build Arab nuclear capabilities for generating energy. It 2008, it announced its definite intention to start producing electric power from nuclear plants. It was, and still is, my belief that it is imperative for the Arab countries to work together through a clear program of cooperation to protect themselves against extortion and conflict among themselves. Examples of problems in this area are numerous. For decades, Egypt insisted on its right to enjoy the full potential of the nuclear fuel cycle. It refused to sign any nuclear protocols with advanced nuclear countries that did not include guarantees of this right. On the other hand, some Arab states have agreed, as part of their preparation for constructing nuclear plants, to waive the right to a fuel cycle. This puts pressure on Egypt to do the same, to which it certainly should not yield.

Between 2004 and 2010, the IAEA attempted to weaken Egypt's position by claiming that Egypt had violated the programs of cooperation it had set up with the IAEA since 1970. We assured everybody that Egypt did not have a military nuclear program, or programs to produce highly enriched uranium, and continued to deny the accusations. We simply provided the facts until the agency finally desisted, thanks to the Egyptian clarity in handling the issue. In our assessment, the object of this harassment was to make us sign the Additional Protocol, which provides the IAEA with broader access to the country's territory and more information about its programs.

Egypt has consistently linked its position to Israel's, calling for it to ratify the NPT. We have made firm decisions in recent decades not to ratify the Biological Weapons Convention, or sign the Chemical Weapons Convention, or sign anything to do with the Nuclear Test Ban Treaty as long as Israel has not signed the NPT and renounced its nuclear weapons.

For years, Egypt has resisted the attempts of the United States and the other western powers to protect Israel's nuclear program at all of the five-year Periodic Review Conferences of the NPT. We constantly demanded that Israel join, and hosted an international conference on how to remove nuclear weapons and weapons of mass destruction from the Middle East. Remarkably, the Egyptian pressure resulted in U.S. action, albeit limited. The U.S. assistant secretary of state made a statement in favor of preventing proliferation, calling on all nuclear powers to sign on to the NPT, including India, Pakistan, Israel, and North Korea. We were concerned that this statement might constitute an implicit international recognition of Israel as a nuclear power, despite the fact that Israel had not conducted nuclear tests or explosions on its territory so far, which would have damaged Egypt severely. In addition, the United States and the European countries have tried to force unacceptable conditions on other countries by using the procedures of the NPT Review Conference. They sought to restrict the right to withdraw from the treaty, as guaranteed by its terms, as well as make the Additional Protocol mandatory for all treaty members and require them to accept the nuclear supply and nuclear fuel initiatives proposed by the west. Once again, Egypt resisted.

On the last day of the Review Conference in May 2010, I was closely following from Cairo our attempt to include in the conference proceedings a call for Israel to accede to the NPT, and to hold an international conference in 2012 to discuss the main Egyptian demand for a Nuclear Free Zone (NFZ). The president called me to say that the U.S. vice-president, Joe Biden, had called to ask us to remove Israel's name from the conference proceedings, and that he had agreed. I told the president that this would undermine years of extended efforts, and that this situation was extremely threatening to our position. He replied that the telephone connection had been bad, and he had imagined that Biden was talking about something else. Yet, now that he understood the situation, he agreed that we should stick to our previous position. Within a few minutes, our ambassador to the UN, Maged Abdel Fattah, who was fighting our battle nobly at the conference, telephoned saying that the Americans had informed him that the Egyptian president had taken a new position, and that he was being asked to inform the president of the Review Conference of this change. I told him that there was absolutely no change to our position, and asked him to continue to support the Egyptian vision that had been agreed upon for months, supported by all of Egypt's military and diplomatic experts on disarmament.

For many months, I had been briefing the president on the Egyptian strategy on disarmament issues in general, and on the affairs of the NPT Review Conference and the IAEA in particular. That was why I was so taken aback when he informed me that he had agreed to remove Israel from the conference proceedings. I forced myself to explain the situation patiently, not angrily. The president accepted my explanation very calmly and agreed without hesitation to inform the Americans that he had had a misunderstanding with the U.S. vice-president.

The conference concluded with a huge gain for Egypt. Actually, one of my reasons for keeping the president informed in such detail was my fear that the United States would attempts to circumvent us by using the U.S. president or his deputy to contact the Egyptian president, presuming that the latter would not be familiar with the details. It turned out I was absolutely right.

The U.S. attempts to weaken the Egyptian position were at their height during the Review Conference in May 2010. The American cables released by WikiLeaks revealed attempt to circumvent the position of the Egyptian foreign ministry and weaken the influence of the Egyptian foreign minister within the Egyptian regime, but the solidity of the Egyptian position was decisive in defeating these maneuvers. I, myself, lost no opportunity to weaken the U.S. position, which was blindly defending Israel, a country that was damaging all their efforts to free the world from nuclear weapons. I recall having a long argument with Hillary Clinton, the U.S. secretary of state, on this topic during the Nuclear Security Summit in Washington in April 2010. The United States had indirectly attempted to use this nuclear summit to expand the basic concepts governing the Non-proliferation Treaty (NPT). These three concepts were a fair balance of the interests of all countries, the right to peaceful uses of atomic energy, and progress toward the elimination of nuclear weapons. The United States was trying to add a fourth dimension, to make nuclear security and counterterrorism a new pillar of the treaty. We were not willing to add anything to the NPT as long as Israel refused to sign it as it stood. We agreed to construct nuclear power plants, in the hope that international nuclear conventions can be strengthened, and that a balance can be struck between security and cooperation in the peaceful use of nuclear energy.

A report was issued by the IAEA under the leadership of Yukiya Amano, the director general of the IAEA and a Japanese national, alleging that Iran's nuclear program includes a military dimension. Amano then visited Egypt in June 2010 and talked about imposing economic sanctions on Iran. We told him we could not agree to impose sanctions on countries in a bid to affect their political positions or actions. History has shown that sanctions are ineffective when a country is determined to follow its own path. In our opinion, the optimal way to deal with Iran is for all the countries in the region to reach a comprehensive agreement compelling everyone to renounce the military nuclear option, but above all, to require Israel to sign the NPT.

European and western voices rushed to threaten Iran with military action. The threats were paired with a call to advance the peace process in the Middle East, with the goal of establishing a Palestinian state. In my conversations with many European and American figures, I often remarked that this strategic goal would put an end to a conflict that has lasted for a hundred years. It should not be reduced to a tactical maneuver to distract the Arab and Islamic countries while the west attacked Iran—a tactic that we had been witnessing for over a decade since the bombardment of Iraq in 1991.

Our support of Iran in this respect did not mean that Egyptian–Iranian relations had improved overall during this period. On the contrary, the Iranian effort to improve relations with Egypt had stopped in the previous year, due either to the lack of Egyptian enthusiasm or Iran's escalation of tensions with Bahrain and the UAE. This prompted President Mubarak to travel to Manama and meet with the king of Bahrain to express Egypt's support. As for the UAE, we had always maintained strong relations with them, but the Emiratis began to demand an Egyptian military appearance from time to time so as to reflect Egypt's strong support. In 2009 and 2010, they said they wanted to feel Egypt's commitment to them more concretely. I conveyed these requests to the president and the Egyptian national security services, recommending that we send some land, naval, and air units to participate in maneuvers with them so as to demonstrate our support, espe-cially since they were interested in our economic situation and occasionally responded to our requests for aid. However, I could sense a certain lack of enthusiasm for this idea. Perhaps it was our firm belief that we should not send troops to areas of potential conflict, or to appear to be provoking the Iranians or Iran's supporters within Egypt.

Comments about the need to restore relations with Iran have been made by many observers of Egypt, as if Egypt had no other diplomatic con-cerns. We tried for years to interact with Iran, without any concession on its part. After I left the Foreign Ministry, I was surprised to see my successor rushing to demand an immediate restoration of Egyptian–Iranian relations without any preparation or background knowledge, except for what the situation had been fifteen years earlier while he was Egypt's representa-tive to the UN from 1988 to 1999. The call today for the development of Egyptian–Iranian relations must take into account Egypt's interests within the larger framework of the Gulf States, as well as Iran's relations with the western powers, the latter relations being particularly important for the Egyptian economy and trade. The entire situation must be evaluated in light of how it will actually benefit Egypt. For this reason, and in light of Egypt's interest in maintaining an active presence and good relations in this region, we have also tried, under difficult circumstances, to maintain our presence in Afghanistan. We are eager to use Egyptian soft power to help Afghanistan through technical cooperation programs within the limits of Egyptian capabilities, which are much weaker than those of Turkey or Iran. It must also be acknowledged that Turkey and Iran have a much greater interest in Afghanistan, being much closer to it geographically.

In order to emphasize Egypt's essential, if limited, role in Afghanistan, I attended the ministerial conference in Kabul in July 2010 to support the rule of President Hamid Karzai. I met the Afghan president, who was complaining about the inability of the United States and the European countries to understand the Afghan Islamic thinking and mentality. Since Egypt was about to take over the chairmanship of the Organization of the Islamic Conference in 2011, I suggested a conference of the foreign ministers of Islamic countries, among others, to contribute to a settlement in Afghanistan that would take into account the realities on the ground, knowing that the Afghan forces would continue to resist the presence of western military power.

As my personal relationship with Richard Holbrooke was still strong, I tried to use his influence in the administration, and with Hillary Clinton, to encourage serious steps toward settling the Palestinian cause while maintaining stable Egyptian–U.S. relations. Hence, we cautiously responded to his requests for information on Afghanistan, as explained in chapter four on Egypt's relationship with the United States.

Suffice it to say that Egypt, as a Muslim country in this Muslim region stretching from central Asia to the shores of the Atlantic, is bound to maintain its strongest ties and cooperation with all parts of the Muslim world, as well as with non-Arab countries, including Iran, Turkey, Pakistan, Indonesia, and Malaysia. The most important thing is that these relations should be based on balanced interests, without any attempt by any party to enforce its interests at the expense of another, and that the preservation of Islamic interests in general must be the key factor in managing these relations.

# 11

# CHALLENGES OF EXPANDING THE FRAMEWORK OF THE EGYPTIAN MOVEMENT: EGYPT AND THE WORLD

I held my breath as I watched the presidents of Russia, Ukraine, and Belarus establish the Commonwealth of Independent States in the final days of 1991, calling on their counterparts in the rest of the former Soviet Union, and Kazakhstan in particular, to join them. I knew, of course that the Soviet Union had collapsed under the pressure of the Cold War and the failure of the Russian application of Marxist-Leninist ideologies. It became apparent that the western world, led by the United States, would dominate world politics. The United States, in particular, would enjoy unchallenged hegemony over the international system for a period that was difficult to predict at the time. I imagined that the status of the United States would be equivalent to the Roman Empire in Europe, or the Middle East under the reigns of Emperor Trajan or Hadrian. The first challenge to the United States and the west came quickly, in the form of the Iraqi invasion of Kuwait.

Following his meeting with Saddam Hussein in an attempt to convince the Iraqi president to withdraw peacefully to avoid war with the west, Milos Minic, the last foreign minister of the Socialist Federal Republic of Yugoslavia, was quoted as saying that Saddam Hussein had told him the Soviets were finished, the basic premise of the international balance had disappeared, and that Iraq would work to establish a new balance in the world. But Iraq was destroyed, and U.S. hegemony took root. The range of American and North Atlantic influence expanded in subsequent years, especially with the break-up of the former Yugoslavia into warring republics, and the disintegration of the Warsaw Pact and the accession of many of the newly independent Balkan and East European countries to NATO membership and the European Union.

The superiority of western civilization was declared, and it was said that history was now ending with the victory of liberalism and its values in the world. A flood of publications analyzed the course of international relations at the time, predicting that a clash of civilizations was sure to come. This trend was promoted and defended by Professor Samuel Huntington, then a scholar at Harvard University, in a famous article published in the U.S.-based journal *Foreign Affairs* in 1993, and then in a book later on. Following that, many writers began warning of the danger of an Islamic–western clash. A first attempt to destroy the World Trade Center in New York had failed in 1993, and the west was looking for a new enemy in lieu of the Soviet Union and its theory of governance. An attempt to overthrow communist rule in China was foiled in June–July 1989, depriving the west of what would have been a particularly large victory. The Soviet diplomats with whom I spoke over the next few years complained that the fall of the Soviet Union had left the world in a state of imbalance, and that the west was looking for a fight with us Muslims.

A few years later, the relations of the west with Islamic societies became even more complicated because of the continuing Israeli occupation of Palestine, the popular anger in Islamic countries, and the calls by some who held radical Islamic views to confront the west in a clash that was bound to fail.

I sat down at my desk at the Ministry of Foreign Affairs headquarters in Maspero in the early morning hours of an October day in 2005, to read the reports that had come in since the previous evening. As usual, I started with the top-secret cables, followed by the non-secret ones. I always started around 7:30 a.m. and would finish reading by 9:30 a.m. Then I would start an active workday that lasted until the evening. One of the secret cables from Copenhagen that day grabbed my attention because of its alarming title: "Danish prime minister refuses to receive Arab ambassadors."

I read the telegram carefully, and learned that the ambassadors of the Arab and Islamic countries in Copenhagen had asked to meet with the prime minister of Denmark to discuss something they viewed as a serious threat to Arab–Danish relations, and perhaps the relationship between Islam and Christianity in the west in general. A political cartoonist in Denmark had drawn a number of caricatures portraying the Prophet of Islam as a terrorist, which was extremely offensive to the feelings of Muslims. I looked at these offensive images faxed by our ambassador, all of which had been published in a Danish newspaper, and I was severely provoked. I telephoned our ambassador in Copenhagen, Mona Omar, who narrated the whole story. She said that the Danish prime minister claimed, in response to the ambassadors' request for a meeting, that it was a matter of freedom of expression, and that he could never deny this right to a cartoonist or any other person, adding that Muslims should learn this among other human rights principles.

I immediately asked my assistant for European affairs to summon the Danish ambassador to Cairo on the same day, to inform him of my disgust with this whole situation—both the offensive cartoons, which we viewed as a threat to the stable relationship between our two countries, and their prime minister's response to the situation. The ambassador attempted to justify the situation, and then informed us the next day that the Danish prime minister adhered to his position.

A fierce battle was waged, in the course of which I sent a letter to the UN secretary general to request his intervention with Denmark. I also wrote to the secretary generals of both the Arab League and the OIC, who were already aware of the situation. It seemed to me that I should also communicate with a broader audience about the dangers of ignoring this issue or letting it disturb relations between communities and religions. Therefore, I wrote to the EU foreign ministers, the European Commission, the EU's commissioner for political and security affairs, and the UN High Commissioner for Human Rights. Everyone appeared to be concerned about the possible negative effects of the incident, yet Denmark had expressed no regret. The foreign minister of Denmark tried to justify the country's point of view in more than one telephone conversation and asked to visit Cairo to meet with me, but I had to refuse, because the timing was totally inconvenient.

Gradually the issue began to be publicized. I pointed out to many of the Europeans I met during this period that had Judaism been targeted in any way, or if the prophet Moses been insulted in the same way they insulted the prophet of Islam, I was certain the western and international community would have insisted on a legal trial. Meanwhile, I commissioned our delegation to the UN to submit a draft resolution to the General Assembly, which was in session at the time, on prohibiting the contempt of religion. The proposal met with resistance from European and other western countries. In the end, however, we were victorious, and a resolution was passed concerning this incident.

President Mubarak inquired about the incident after it was publicized in the Egyptian and Arab media. I told him that I had already sent him a memorandum of the situation through the information secretariat. I explained its gravity and what we had done about it. He commented that he had not noticed extensive media coverage of our actions, despite the huge uproar in Islamic and Arab circles. I replied that Egypt was the one that initiated the entire response, and that none of the other Arab or Islamic countries had done a thing.

However, I was concerned about possible negative developments on the Egyptian domestic scene, because prior to the cartoon affair, there had been several disturbing incidents in Alexandria in which Christian churches had been damaged. Therefore, I was in favor of caution in the media coverage. The president listened quietly without commenting, and the battle ran its course.

Part of my statement to the UN General Assembly read: "I wish to comment on the question of the use of freedom of expression to incite hatred based on religion. I emphasize here—with the utmost respect to the importance of freedom of expression—that we reject any characterization of affronts to religions and sacred objects as a legitimate exercise of the freedom of expression." This formulation was repeated in other sessions of the General Assembly, and the world started recognizing how Muslims felt about affronts to Muslim figures and Islamic institutions in the European arena.

The British prime minister proposed a western–Islamic summit in Egypt to discuss the relations between Islam and the west. We were not eager to do this, though, for I believed that more preparation was needed. However, we adopted the concepts of Inter-Civilizational Dialogue and their alliance, as used by many Christian and Islamic circles, which helped to calm the situation, albeit without addressing the roots of mistrust.

Several statements issued by the Pope from the Vatican left us with a very uncomfortable feeling. In the meantime, I received information about the intention of the Grand Imam Sheikh of al-Azhar to visit the Pope at the latter's invitation. I intervened and dissuaded His Excellency the Grand Imam from visiting at this time, because the Pope had recently published a statement criticizing Islam. I could not help but notice, however, that His Excellency wished to go ahead with the visit. I consulted the president, who told him that the timing was inappropriate. This was in 2008, when the Pope had recently spoken about the inappropriateness of Turkey's membership in the European Union, because the EU was a "Christian house." I feared that this flood of hostility could result in a new clash between Christianity and Islam.

In September 2010, I spoke once again before the UN General Assembly, saying:

> The fact that Egypt is part of the Islamic world is common knowledge. We feel the pain of Muslims wherever they are. We share their joys and celebrations; we grieve with them and we feel their pain. There is no doubt that regrettable and appalling incidents against Muslims and Islam are increasingly frequent, and systematic in certain cases. They have ranged from attacks on the symbols and sanctities of the faith to the harassment of Muslims.
>
> In general, we find the west being drawn into a clash with the Muslim world. Such a clash would serve no one except extremists and those who would hold perverse ideas on both sides. It would not be in the interest of security in the world. It would not be in the interests of moderates. In such a clash, the winner is a loser and the victor is defeated.
>
> Need I remind this gathering of the need for coordinated action among the influential advocates of religious, civilizational, and cultural

moderation in order to eliminate the threat before it becomes more ominous and destroys much of everything? We can no longer accept pretexts to condone practices against Islam and its followers—such as the right to freedom of expression—which are surprisingly naive, excessive in essence, and offensive in nature.

Egypt will continue to do its utmost at the political, cultural, and religious levels to address such threats. We call on all countries, in particular their governments, to play their part in highlighting the potential horror of a terrible clash of faiths and civilizations. We call on them to spread a culture of enlightenment based on tolerance, respect for differences, and renunciation of fanaticism, hatred, and zealotry. Laws must be enacted to protect minorities and their beliefs from the aggression of extremists and promoters of strife.

I had been keeping a close eye on the Egyptian domestic scene, fearing an explosion of the internal unity of Egyptian society between Copts and Muslims. I also noticed that many of the western Christian circles, including the Vatican, were paying great attention to the Egyptian developments. We set up a permanent diplomatic working group to study the situation, and then to provide civic leaders with proposals and recommendations for addressing the situation. Their suggestions included increasing the number of Copts in key government positions; acknowledging the radical religious discourse on both the Islamic and Christian sides in general and of some imams in particular; addressing the reluctance of Copts to participate in various government fields; communicating with expat Copts about the situation; and conducting an internal Egyptian community dialogue to discuss, with all frankness and objectivity, the issue of citizenship rights.

I sent these proposals to the president in July 2008. We dispatched a number of missions to the countries of the Egyptian diaspora in the west to conduct open discussions—an effort that continued until the end of my term. The president took an objective view of the situation. He was well aware that any escalation would be dangerous to Egypt, both internally and externally.

I also discussed the topic several times with General Omar Suleiman, because of his role as head of the General Intelligence and his knowledge of many of the secrets of Egypt's internal situation. I found him to be objective in his opinions, and convinced that Egypt needs to encourage greater Coptic participation in the country's affairs. It was his view that extremism on both sides often impedes this objective.

When I became foreign minister in July 2004, I found that the various Egyptian–European negotiations in all fields were moving slowly, despite the conviction of all parties that it was important to develop this relationship. We were looking for economic and commercial gains, but the Europeans were trying to make these advantages contingent on adopting policies that would damage us domestically. The negotiations therefore took a difficult turn.

The Egyptian Cabinet complained that the Foreign Ministry was complicating the situation ahead of the negotiations. Our response was that we totally disagreed with unleashing the Europeans or western powers in Egypt's internal affairs. They applied pressure through the National Democratic Party (NDP), which we resisted.

When we finally signed the agreement in Brussels in 2006, the Europeans said it accurately reflected the balance of interests that I had always sought to achieve in this relationship. We often sought to use our positive relations with the European Mediterranean countries to strengthen our positions before the European Commission, which was negotiating with us on behalf of all the EU countries. The partnership agreement provided for annual economic aid to Egypt, projects to develop the capabilities of the Egyptian industry and economy, training programs, and programs to increase the efficiency of our operations in agriculture, water use, and other areas. Beyond that, the agreement provided an opportunity for Egyptian and European goods to access foreign markets either without fees or with substantial discounts, therefore advantaging both parties over other foreign parties. The volume of Egyptian trade with the EU countries and the other western powers amounts to about four-fifths of Egypt's foreign trade.

As I have said before, Egypt has enjoyed positive relations with the Mediterranean countries of the European Union for many years: France,

Italy, Spain, Portugal, and Greece. Egypt has been a major, and even pivotal, player in the Barcelona process for over a decade. Therefore, when President Sarkozy of France proposed his "Union for the Mediterranean" (UfM), to unite the various circles of the European Union and the Mediterranean countries, Egypt was the first country that France approached.

Egypt agreed, and accepted the UfM's joint presidency with France. The first summit was held in July 2008 in Paris. As we neared the second UfM summit, scheduled to be held in Barcelona under the chairmanship of Spain, the Spanish foreign minister proposed, in connection with this Mediterranean summit, an Egyptian–European summit, or a joint summit with the "European troika" (the European Commission, the European Central Bank, and the International Monetary Fund), on the model of European meetings with China, the United States, or Brazil. Such a proposition, if implemented, could have given Egypt great international momentum, as I believed. The president seemed to agree, until he came to learn that the European leaders, in the course of the Egyptian–European dialogue, might try to address some internal situations and human rights issues. That killed his enthusiasm for the idea, and he asked for the summit to be adjourned. In his defense, some serious obstacles to the Union for the Mediterranean were appearing at the time, in particular Israel's failure to abide by its commitments in the Palestine negotiations, including the cessation of settlement expansion while the negotiations were going on.

President Sarkozy was paying a great deal of attention to his relations with the Egyptian president, and offered him many proposals that reflected France's desire to play a greater role in the international arena, with Egypt as one of its main partners. We did not oppose that as long as it also served our interests. During the summit between Sarkozy and Mubarak at the Élysée Palace in Paris, Sarkozy came up with the idea of a union that would include France, India, Brazil, and Egypt. I enthusiastically approved the proposal and asked the French to go ahead and hold it in 2009 or 2010. But then the grandson of the president passed away, and the president himself required major surgery. And I could sense the French were already moving in another direction.

As the Palestinian–Israeli negotiations became even more complicated, President Sarkozy suggested calling on the Quartet (the Russian Federation, the United States, the UN, and the European Union) to meet with France and Egypt to push forward the stalled peace process, much to the anger of the Russians, who had long been demanding a foreign ministers' meeting or a summit in Moscow. The Americans were concerned about this French effort, born of France's dynamism, afraid it might embarrass them with Israel. For our part, while we did not object to the proposal, we did not express too much enthusiasm so as not to embarrass a friend as important as Russia.

Sarkozy's relationship with Mubarak was marked by unfailing courtesy. The two countries strengthened their relations with one another. Sarkozy would ask Mubarak for his assessments on the general situation in the region, the Palestinian settlement, and how to deal with Bashar al-Assad. He would even sometimes ask Mubarak to mediate with the Saudi king, Abdullah bin Abdel Aziz, as France was concerned about the Saudis' lack of interest in developing bilateral relations. President Mubarak promised to do this, and he kept his word. Mubarak urged Omar Suleiman and me to continue to strengthen our relationship with France. He saw it as our window to the European Union, a source of support for the possibility of expanding the UN Security Council, and a connection to the G8, the G20, and other major groups.

Egypt's strong European relationship was not limited to France; it also extended to Italy, which Mubarak visited repeatedly between 2004 and 2010. Italian presidents and prime ministers also made several visits to Egypt. Trade and tourism were increasing. The Egyptian–Italian axis was finding its place within the strategic framework in the Mediterranean, to the sensitivity of France and other countries. I encouraged the president to proceed cautiously, so as not to lose our connections with any of them. Meanwhile, the Italians were complimenting us enthusiastically. The heads of the Italian government—Silvio Berlusconi, Romano Prodi, and Massimo D'Alema—would go out of their way to demonstrate the strength of the Egyptian–Italian relationship.

I could not believe my eyes when, at a dinner party at the historic Villa Madama in the hills surrounding Rome, I saw Prime Minister Berlusconi playing music and singing to entertain the small Egyptian delegation. The Italians offered to enhance the efficiency and operation of the Egyptian railways, to construct a new high-speed railway line connecting Alexandria and Cairo, and to extend it to Luxor and Aswan.

With the development of Egyptian–European relations, and with Egypt clearly established as a central factor in the European stance toward the Middle East, I proposed to the president that we take the initiative of calling for an Arab–European summit in Cairo to be held every couple of years. The president did not respond, for a reason that I was not aware of back then, although I assumed that he was afraid that the Europeans would raise issues that might embarrass him and the other Arab leaders: human rights, democracy, transparency of governance, and other topics that had begun to enter the lexicon of European contacts with the Arabs. In particular, the European Parliament's criticism of the human rights situation in Egypt in January 2008 had led him to tread cautiously regarding any collective initiatives with EU countries.

The Egyptian president visited Berlin at the end of 2004 and was received by the German chancellor. Once again, as I saw with the French president Jacques Chirac at the same meeting, there was a lot of interest in the Egyptian role in the Middle East and the Mediterranean. This visit reinforced the relationship between the Egyptian president and the new German chancellor, Angela Merkel. Mubarak traveled more than once to Berlin, and Merkel came at least once to Cairo. Although our relationship with the Germans was not as friendly as our relationship with the French or the Italians, I believed that the importance of German influence on European attitudes regarding many regional and international problems required us to continue paying attention to the country, regardless of the occasional difficulties of the stereotypical 'tough' German personality. However, the relationship cooled a bit when Mubarak refused to attend the G8 summit in Heiligendamm, Germany in 2008, rightly assuming that the Germans were prepared to prioritize South Africa over Egypt among the African countries, with possible implications for the expansion of the Security Council. Mubarak did pay a visit of several hours to Germany in early 2009 to reinvigorate relations with Merkel.

As the Palestinian settlement efforts deteriorated in the summer and fall of 2010 after the Washington summit in September of the same year, Mubarak suddenly asked to visit Berlin. I did not see the point of this sudden interest in traveling to Italy and Germany to save the peace process. Mubarak spent several hours in Berlin, asking Merkel to use her influence to pressure Israel to stop building settlements in the Palestinian territories in order to save the peace process and the negotiations that were being planned for after the Washington summit. The German chancellor took a rather tough line with the president that evening. She had just arrived a few hours earlier from New York, where she had attended the UN General Assembly. Unless he had specific proposals, they could have talked on the phone, she told him. The only thing we wanted to ask of Germany was to mobilize the influence of the European Union to pressure Israel.

Aging affected the president's performance during his last three years in office, 2008–10. However, I continued to push for more presidential appearances on the European scene to protect the interests of Egypt. During this period he was still refusing to visit Britain. His meetings with the British prime minister Gordon Brown, first in Sharm al-Sheikh in January 2009 and then in the Italian city of L'Auila that same summer at the G8 meeting with the emerging powers (Brazil, India, Mexico, South Africa, and Egypt), were also rather reserved. This may have been because Mubarak did not know Brown personally, the way he knew other leaders. Mubarak also traveled to Turkey, Greece, Slovenia, and Croatia. I would have liked him to include Romania, Bulgaria, Hungary, and Austria, in order to bring them into the circle of our attention once again. I myself visited the Balkans, the Caucasus, and the northern European Union countries.

The Egyptian president had a great deal of appreciation for the Russian president, Dmitry Medvedev, admiring his ability to be firm and decisive. Medvedev had restored Russia to its role on the international stage—or so Mubarak felt. As soon as I became foreign minister, I came to notice the Egyptian president's admiration of Russia, especially its technological capabilities in the production of advanced weapons. He thought of the Russian Federation as a backup option for Egypt, in case relations got too complicated with the west. He did not want to move too quickly in

Russia's direction—he just wanted to keep the door open in case he needed to resort to it. He was interested in every single technological development in Russian nuclear plants. He followed with interest Russia's work at the Bushehr Nuclear Power Plant in Iran, observing that the Russians did not put impossible conditions on their relationship with the Iranians. As the Russian interest in resuming an influential role in the Middle East became vividly clear, we interacted with them, assuring them of our interest in their return to the region so as not to leave it entirely open to the Americans. We knew from experience that the United States cannot always influence Israeli positions.

Mubarak visited Russia twice during these years. The Russian presidents Medvedev and Vladimir Putin were also received in Cairo. As each of these visits approached, the president and I would talk about Russian affairs. The president would remark that the Russians were showing firmness here and decisiveness there in the face of specific issues with the western powers. I used to agree with him, despite Russia's limited capabilities and resources compared to the United States, the other western powers, and China. Although Russia's economic capacity is not much greater than Italy's, its true strengths, the ones we always rely on, were its veto power in the Security Council, its ability to produce advanced weapons, its influence on many of the Central Asian Islamic republics, and its solid relations with China.

We hoped to develop our relationship with Russia in a strategic direction, especially in the political and diplomatic realms. We did, however, want to proceed with a certain amount of caution with respect to military issues and armaments, so as not to provoke the west unnecessarily. Russian Foreign Minister Sergey Lavrov and I exchanged annual visits within the context of the strategic dialogue between the two countries, and we always met at all the events concerning the Middle East or the UN General Assembly that brought us together. As previously mentioned, the Russians agreed to hold an annual meeting of the Ministries of Foreign Affairs and Defense of the two countries. Unfortunately, these meetings never took place.

I would say that the Russians warmly welcomed the Egyptian president. I recall in particular a wonderful dinner in the main hall of the

Kremlin during the president's visit to Moscow in 2006. Putin, too, visited Egypt and attended a similarly wonderful dinner in a presidential hall no less remarkable than the one in Moscow: the main hall in Abdin Palace, where there was no difference between the tsar and the khedive.

As I recounted earlier, I had previously lived in Moscow for three years. I spent many happy evenings at the Kremlin Theater and visited its various museums, such as the Red Army Museum, and the one that housed the clothing and jewelry that had once belonged to the Russian imperial family. I was very familiar with the areas open to the public inside the Kremlin, and I often wandered around its historic churches and read the histories of the sixteenth-century cannons scattered in its courtyard. But my three visits as a member of the Egyptian delegation accompanying the president—the first of which took place in May 1990—allowed me to become familiar with many of the halls that are closed to the public. I particularly remember one specific incident that revealed the sheer simplicity of the Soviet leadership inside the walls of the Kremlin. The usual practice in Moscow was for the members of the Politburo to drive at high speeds through the streets in their Zil cars, all the other traffic having been halted until they passed. I was in the company of Dr. Esmat Abdel Meguid, deputy prime minister and minister of foreign affairs, on a visit to Moscow in September 1990, for the purpose of discussing the crisis between Iraq and the international community after the invasion of Kuwait. We arrived at the Kremlin with our ambassador and entered one of its halls. I could sense some uneasiness among the young Soviet protocol staff as we passed from one hall to another. We sat in a glass-enclosed verdant garden, enjoying the flowers and greenery, not wanting to leave. We were informed that Mikhail Gorbachev, the party's general secretary and the president of the Soviet Union, was running a little late. Suddenly the elevator stopped in the area where we were sitting. Gorbachev emerged, carrying a huge stack of papers himself. He walked quietly toward us, accompanied only by Eduard Shevardnadze, the Soviet foreign minister, of Georgian origin, also carrying his papers himself. They greeted the Egyptian foreign minister and apologized for being late. A working lunch for some members of the Politburo had run beyond the appointment of the Egyptian minister.

They sat down at a small table in front of us, in the same room where President-elect Medvedev had received the Egyptian president in 2008. The point here is that despite all their power and influence stemming from the strength of the Soviet Union or the Russian Federation, behavior of the leaders of the Kremlin inside the palace is characterized by simplicity and lack of ceremony.

In a bid to provide greater freedom of movement for Egypt, especially in light of the difficulties with the United States throughout 2005 and 2006, Mubarak visited the Chinese capital, Beijing, in fall 2006 for the first time in a long while. His Chinese hosts often said that he was the last foreign official to meet Mao Zedong before he died in 1976, when Mubarak was vice-president. Although the Beijing visit came within the framework of the China–Africa summit and many other African leaders were present, the special feeling for Egypt was apparent. I also recall another visit of the president to Beijing, in May 1990, when he met with Deng Xiaoping, who gave Mubarak a message for President George H.W. Bush that U.S. pressure on China was threatening to create chaos in the country in the aftermath of the 1989 Tiananmen Square protests. Any upheaval in China, he said, would lead to chaos across Southeast Asia because tens of millions of Chinese refugees would flee to neighboring countries. We did convey the message and the Americans stopped pressuring China.

That, however, was in another era, for by 2009, thirty years had passed since Deng's reforms, and China had made unprecedented leaps in the history of humanity and civilization. The Egyptian president wanted to encourage the Egyptian–Chinese relationship. China, which had achieved continuous growth for decades at rates of up to 11 or 12 percent per year and surpassed Japan in economic capacity, has always been and will continue to be a major influence in Asian affairs. However, it had a limited presence in the Middle East, and we hoped to change that.

The meetings of the Egyptian–Chinese strategic dialogue were held annually between the foreign ministers in the respective capitals. China has become a major investor in projects in Egypt. However, I occasionally noticed Chinese reservations about the response of the Egyptian government agencies to Chinese requests in the implementation of these projects.

During this period Egypt also took an interest in India, a growing economic power within the BRIC economic group (Brazil, Russia, India, and China, with South Africa joining them later). Mubarak decided to revisit it, ending a long absence and without any particular reason that I knew about. We paid a very successful visit to Delhi in 2008, identifying great opportunities for Egyptian–Indian cooperation, with no negative impact on the good relations between Egypt and Pakistan.

I also pointed out to the president the importance of visiting Indonesia and Malaysia, and of reinvigorating our relations with Japan and South Korea. He would say, "Exactly. Further communication with them is needed, but you have to keep in mind that these visits are cumbersome, even if they're necessary, and we will look into them in time." It was such a rare confession from the president about how his advancing age was affecting him. During this period I made two visits to India on my own, besides accompanying the president on his visit to Delhi. The prime minister of India stressed the importance of continuing to strengthen relations and restoring this bond launched by Nehru and Nasser. For two years I encouraged the Indian foreign minister to hold the Egyptian–Indian Joint Committee meeting in Cairo, since the previous meeting had been held in Delhi in 2007. But the Indian minister was not enthusiastic about this. I visited Japan twice during these years, as well as Indonesia, Singapore, Pakistan, Kazakhstan, and Uzbekistan.

As Brazil became stronger, we sought to strengthen the bilateral relationship and encourage the country to pay attention to Middle East affairs. I visited the Brazilian capital, Brasília, twice between 2005 and 2010, and I encouraged the president to visit there as well. Two dates were scheduled for the visit, but both were canceled. Once again, I was aware that this was due to the aging of the president, who asked how many hours the flight was and whether a stopover could be arranged in some capital halfway between Cairo and South America. I also visited Argentina and Chile. Visits of the Egyptian foreign minister's assistants became more frequent and intense in both the Asian and Latin arenas, which kept them interested in us and our affairs.

I always felt the power of Egypt's influence on the UN stage. For many years, Egypt was active in submitting ideas and draft resolutions. The

Egyptian delegations always commanded attention. From my position at the UN, I would read and hear critiques of my country's diplomatic performance with great astonishment and surprise. According to them, Egypt's regional and international role was waning. What a baseless accusation! My answer was always that Egypt has not diminished, but that other countries have improved their diplomatic performance. I will discuss this issue in more detail in connection with the Palestinian situation in the next chapter.

It is important to state here that even if I must admit to a certain "lack of achievement" in the contest for influence among Middle Eastern and Arab countries, there are two reasons for this. The first is the traditional caution with which these matters have been handled by the Egyptian president. The second is the weakness of our financial resources compared to the enormous wealth of some of our neighbors, including Turkey, Iran, Qatar, and Saudi Arabia.

In any case, I was surprised, one October morning in 2007, as I reviewed the vote on the Human Rights Council membership, to find that Egypt—which had not even submitted its candidacy for membership—had received two votes. I thought this must have happened accidentally. I was further surprised in the following days and weeks by a fierce media attack on attack Egyptian diplomacy, describing it as a failure, that "the Egyptian role has diminished" and the world no longer respects Egypt's capabilities. The president even called me to find out the truth of the matter. I told him, "Mr. President, Egypt did not nominate itself for membership on this important council. We are waiting for the next elections in 2008, and I can tell you our victory then will be overwhelming." He had no reply. The following year, though, he was quick to offer his congratulations, because we won the highest number of votes in the HRC election. It should be said that it is rare for Egypt not to achieve its goal when it seeks nomination to the UN councils, committees, or expert groups. When Dr. Nabil al-Arabi was nominated for the UN International Court of Justice in 2000, he likewise won the highest number of votes, even though his nomination had been entered late.

In this connection, I would like to address the issue of Egypt's nomination of Minister of Culture Farouk Hosni to the position of director general of UNESCO, a subject that has also been surrounded by a lot of irresponsible talk. When the post of director general of UNESCO became vacant in 2009, at the end of the term of its Japanese director Kōichirō Matsuura, some members of the Egyptian government started telling the First Lady that it was essential for Egypt to pursue the position. The president's secretary of information asked me to provide nominations from the Foreign Ministry for the job. There may also have been additional nominations from outside the Ministry of Foreign Affairs. The list of names sent to the president on June 23, 2007 included Farouk Hosni, Mufeed Shehab, Fayza Abul-Naga, Ismail Serageddin, Ahmed Maher, Ali Maher, and Nabil al-Arabi.

A few days later, I was informed that Farouk Hosni, minister of culture, had been chosen as the Egyptian nominee, a candidacy that generated attacks from the Egyptian elite on many pretexts. The Ministry of Foreign Affairs, however, set up a comprehensive plan to promote the candidacy that included obtaining the support of the Arab League, which was achieved; obtaining the support of the African Union, achieved as well; asking Morocco to withdraw its candidate, which they did. Algeria had already abstained from fielding a candidate. Heavyweight countries such as Italy, Greece, France, and Spain approved the Egyptian nomination.

We set out to collect votes. But suddenly Farouk Hosni made a statement that turned everything upside down. He stated that the Egyptian Ministry of Culture was refusing to translate or publish books by Israeli writers or by Jewish writers in Egypt, adding that he would personally burn any Israeli books found in Egypt. The western world promptly set out to bring down the Egyptian candidate. Despite our best efforts, Hosni ended up just one vote short of victory—twenty-nine votes, versus thirty for the rival candidate, Irina Bokova. He had always garnered the greatest number of votes in the preliminary polls, but was unable to win the position. It was a very fierce battle, in which Israel and the United States used all kinds of intimidation and encouragement. In spite of the closeness of the vote, some Egyptian opponents of Hosni's nomination claimed it was a terrible defeat for Egypt. I was really amazed by how some people could confuse their opposition to Farouk Hosni with the importance of supporting the Egyptian nomination.

It remains in this chapter to deal with the issue of human rights, because of the importance that the international community has attached to it over the past two decades. By the time I became permanent representative of Egypt to the UN, I had seen so much attention given to this issue by the UN, and new concepts developed for sensitive issues, such as removing or diminishing the protections of state sovereignty in matters relating to the relationship between a government and its citizens, and the Responsibility to Protect and the right of intervention, which enjoyed prominence in western rhetoric, and which was slowly and quietly pushed before the UN organizations and their agencies. The developing countries were determined not to allow any action to be taken on issues of this kind except by major resolutions in the UN General Assembly or the Security Council.

I was in fact aware of occasional whisperings, here and there, about western and international reservations about Egypt's approach to human rights issues. Therefore, I was determined that Egypt would move cautiously in addressing the human rights situation in other countries that were under sharp criticism from the western world, in order to protect our own image.

In this context, I must make it clear that there is unquestionably a huge distinction between the theoretical concept of human rights as a set of values and principles to be respected and applied to preserve human dignity and provide basic freedoms, and the practical applications of this concept as they are worked out in international negotiations and international policies. Furthermore, these lofty values are generally subjected to double standards, politicization, and selectivity of application in accordance with the practical requirements of international relations.

Let me present an example. I cannot imagine one more relevant to Egyptian public opinion than the issue of freedom of expression and its use to justify the abuse of religions. This issue reveals the depth of the contradictions in the position of western countries, who have set themselves up as the guardians for human rights, severely judging whoever violates their own concept of these rights.

While western countries were adhering to absolute freedom of expression and total rejection of any attempt to regulate it, they refused to recognize the concept of "insulting religions" and maintained that the abuse of religion or belief was acceptable within the framework of freedom of expression. In contrast, Egypt and the other Islamic countries maintained that the guarantee of freedom of religion and belief should safeguard religions from abuse, and that accusing religions of backwardness and linking them to terrorism under the guise of freedom of expression could incite hostility toward the followers of those religions. This could in turn result in acts of violence, similar to what Europe witnessed before and during the Second World War against the Jews. In recent years, some western countries had witnessed increasing discrimination against their own Muslim citizens, culminating in cases of physical violence against Arabs and Muslims, including Egyptians, such as Marwa al-Sherbini, who was killed in Germany by an extremist criminal, blinded by hatred for Islam and Muslims.

It is also remarkable that the western countries, which refused to impose any restriction on freedom of expression, were the same ones whose laws criminalized mere difference of opinion in the historical circumstances surrounding the Holocaust, or merely questioning the number of its victims, despite the obvious violation of the principles of scientific and historical research. And while these countries allowed unrestricted criticism of religions, especially the Islamic religion in the aftermath of September 11, 2001, as a form of freedom of expression, we find the very same countries condemning any criticism of Israeli policies or the practices of the World Zionist Organization as a form of anti-Semitism. The goal is to sanitize Israel's actions and policies toward the Palestinian people under the guise of protecting the Jewish race from persecution or correcting historical errors that occurred in Europe in the first half of the twentieth century.

This topic also includes restrictions in Europe against Muslims' practices of their religious rituals and the decisions in some countries to prevent the construction of mosques' minarets, amid campaigns of hatred topped by photographs depicting those minarets as rocket launchers. It is regrettable that this happens in the countries that complain day and night about the rights of religious minorities in Arab and Islamic countries, exploiting the tiniest sectarian or ethnic incident to defame those countries in the international arena.

The above incidents, I hope, show the extent of the contradiction that lies within any discussion of human rights. Few countries, western or eastern, consistently apply their own values or standards in the field of human rights, where political considerations tend to be the first, if not the only, criterion everywhere.

Whether serving Egypt in the UN or as foreign minister, I have always tried to follow a consistent line. My aim has been to defend the uniqueness of Egyptian society and its prevailing ethical and moral system, and to protect it from foreign intrusions that would attempt to destroy the cultural and religious heritage of the Egyptian people.

There have been criticisms from Egyptians themselves to this approach that we adopted. Since January 25, 2011, some have even claimed that the Ministry of Foreign Affairs should not have attempted to defend these exclusively Egyptian concepts. I must confirm that the first responsibility of the Egyptian foreign ministry is the defense of Egypt and its principles in all areas. Neither the minister nor the ministry should hesitate to act under the pretext of caution or exposure to criticism. The minister, along with his ministry, must defend his country and society, whatever the counter-pressures may be.

In the course of my work, I have been faced with a great deal of intransigence, torn between foreign countries that seek to impose their own values on us, viewing human rights as nothing but a weapon that is unsheathed in order to impose certain visions or win certain political concessions, and on the other hand, internal Egyptian entities that view human rights as a direct security threat and a tool for interference in the internal affairs of the country. Caught between the two sides, the Ministry of Foreign Affairs sought to convince the western world that Egypt is entitled to its cultural uniqueness, which we will not allow to be derogated, while simultaneously trying to convince our fellow Egyptians that not everything that comes from outside is pure evil, and that many human rights principles work well for the Egyptian people and deserve to be applied.

Following the latter principle, the Ministry of Foreign Affairs exerted considerable effort to amend the state of emergency that has been in force for many decades in Egypt. I have monitored the great attention paid by the international community and external forces, as well as by civil society and human rights organizations, both internally and externally, to the importance of lifting the state of emergency. Fully aware that the Egyptian Ministry of Interior was continuing the state of emergency under the pretext of protecting society from thugs and rioters, we drafted a proposal that was sent to the president and all of the relevant state agencies. The draft called for limiting the scope of the state of emergency to cover only cases of fighting terrorism. We also warned against extending the state of emergency on the same basis that the state had followed for decades, or else the criticism of Egypt that would result would be extremely damaging. The state of emergency was subsequently modified to apply only to terrorism, and then to drug-related crimes as well. We succeeded in convincing the Egyptian security services that the Egyptian government should agree to receive a number of special rapporteurs on specific human rights issues. Previously, the security services, especially the Egyptian Interior Ministry, had refused entirely to accept them.

Despite the weakness I sensed in the internal position on human rights, my instructions to the delegations of Egypt to human rights conferences and negotiations was to adopt a balanced approach, asserting the rights of individuals while also emphasizing the duties and responsibilities of citizens toward society. We also stressed the importance of the historical, cultural, and intellectual specificity of Egyptian society, its vast diversity and richness, and its remarkable contribution to human civilization. We did not intend to limit our role to standing on the receiving end of the teachings and values of other societies.

Our mission was not easy at all, especially with the end of the Cold War and the unilateralism of the western world on the international scene. The UN gave the west the impression that it was the right time to impose its value system on developing societies. Since the early 1990s, the UN has held a large number of conferences that sought to redefine human rights principles in line with the western way of thinking. But throughout my work in New York and Cairo between 1999 and 2011, we resolutely pushed back against those attempts, regardless of the framework in which they were placed or the façade they tried to hide behind. We succeeded in forming an alliance of developing and Islamic countries to reject attempts to change the concept of family so as to accommodate gay coalitions that the west sought to include within the framework of the family. We also contributed to the failure of western attempts to pass draft resolutions trying to include homosexuality within universally recognized human rights as a first step, to be followed surely by pressuring states that do not recognize this behavior as a human right. In this particular case, we faced not only the western countries, but also the UN Secretariat itself, which viewed this campaign as a new opportunity to prove its openness to advanced western values and prove its allegiance to the major donor countries of the UN. We have often objected to the complicity of the UN Secretariat with western countries in their efforts to pass such resolutions.

It is surprising that western countries found any kind of foothold within Egyptian society to promote these concepts on the grounds of personal freedom. We found Egyptian human rights organizations attacking the official positions in this regard, characterizing them as an aggression against these personal freedoms. They even issued statements that try to deceive Egyptian public opinion by focusing on generalities, while their real positions were expressed only outside Egypt, away from the eyes of the Egyptian citizen. It is regrettable that the positions of these organizations, their sources of funding, and their real purposes have not been exposed before Egyptian public opinion, except within the context of the dialogue that took place in Egyptian society in January 2012.

The issue of capital punishment is another striking example of the contradictions in western attitudes toward human rights. The International Covenant on Civil and Political Rights, adopted by the UN in 1966, states that everyone has the right to life and that no one shall be deprived of this right arbitrarily. This text is at the heart of the years-long international debate about the legitimacy of the death penalty. Western countries demand the abolition of the death penalty based on the first part of the text, whereas the second part of the same text shows that the prohibition here is not to deprive a person of the right to life, but the deprivation of this right arbitrarily. Western countries also ignore the fact that the same article of the International Covenant refers to the legal standards that must be met in death-penalty cases, meaning that the International Covenant did not call for the abolition of this penalty, but only the establishment of guarantees governing its fair application.

The contradiction in this case stems from the fact that the western countries that seek to abolish the death penalty on the basis of the sanctity of human life and the impermissibility of taking it for any reason are the very same countries that promote abortion as a human right, even though abortion is a violation of the right of the fetus to life. If the life of a convicted criminal is to be spared, what about the life of a fetus that has committed no sin, and has not even been born yet?

The examples of western contradictions in the field of human rights are numerous and varied, but I would conclude with one related to a cause dear to the heart of every Egyptian and Arab Muslim, the Palestinian cause.

The countries that defend the human rights of minorities and ethnic nationalities within the Arab and Islamic countries turn a blind eye to Israeli violations of the basic rights and freedoms of Palestinians in the Occupied Palestinian Territories in a daily and systematic manner. This happens in full view of the 'civilized' world, which clothes itself in the guise of a teacher, guide, and critic of human rights in developing countries. Every time Egypt and the other Arab countries submit a draft resolution to the UN General Assembly condemning the Israeli violations of human rights, it meets with automatic opposition from the west. The western bloc regards it as a politicization of the Palestinian cause and an attempt to derail the peace process. Even countries such as Australia and Canada deny Palestinian human rights by talking about the "suffering of the Israeli population from Palestinian violations."

I would like to cite one significant instance of this contradiction. In February 2009, the Human Rights Council in Geneva reviewed the human rights situation in Israel, and the Egyptian delegation delivered a harsh statement vigorously condemning Israel's violation of human rights. However, we found no reference whatsoever, in the overwhelming majority of the western statements, to the conditions of the Palestinians under Israeli occupation, but only the situation of women and children in Israel, and other issues that are far removed from the political situation of the Palestinians.

The position of the Egyptian human rights organizations on Israeli practices is something I continue to find confusing. None of the Egyptian organizations has ever, in any UN meeting, criticized the Israeli practices against the Palestinians, despite the fact that these same organizations are eager to talk about the next item, dealing with human rights in one or more Arab countries. After all these years, I am still unable to comprehend this contradiction and selectivity, and to find an explanation for the silence of these Egyptian organizations with respect to a cause that is, as I have said, as close to the hearts of all of us as the Palestinian cause.

I am quite certain that with the major transformations that are taking place in Egyptian society and governance, and for years to come, many of the positions we defended and the issues we supported will continue unchanged because they represent the special value system of the Egyptian people, which cannot and should not be given up under any circumstances.

# 12

# CHALLENGES OF A PEACEFUL SETTLEMENT

O ver the course of 2008, a great deal of information was circulated that Israel—which was humiliated in the Lebanon war and failed to achieve many of its military objectives in the face of Hezbollah militias—was looking for a way to rehabilitate itself, eyeing the Gaza Strip as a possible area for carrying out a major military operation to destroy the military capabilities of Hamas, which was in power in the Gaza Strip. An extendable six-month truce agreement was in effect, which the Egyptian General Intelligence brokered between Israel and the Palestinian organizations. However, Hamas announced that it would not agree to an extension. Whenever we heard any rumor about Israel's intention to carry out military action, we would hasten to talk to its officials in Cairo or Tel Aviv, asking them not to push matters in the direction of escalation. Some officials in Israel and the United States said that Israeli military action would aim at destroying Hamas's infrastructure, and thereby enable the Palestine Liberation Organization (PLO) to regain control of the Gaza Strip. Whenever I read such reports in the telegrams received from our missions in western countries, I could not help but feel surprised by the superficiality of this way of thinking, which, according to its adherents, reflected the belief that the United States—in accordance with the Annapolis Declaration of November 2007—wanted to end Hamas's control of the Gaza Strip, in order to advance the peace settlement. Other western circles favored handing over the administration of the Gaza Strip to the Arab League or Egypt. We strongly rejected all these suggestions that were maliciously circulated behind the scenes.

Despite all this talk about upcoming military operations or attempts to hand over the Gaza Strip to an authority other than Hamas, I noticed that the rocket-launching operations were increasing after the expiration of the truce period, which had not been extended by the resistance organizations in the Gaza Strip. My assessment was that Hamas was trying to influence the selection of the next Israeli government by facilitating the victory of the Likud hard-liner Benjamin Netanyahu against Tzipi Livni and her Kadima party, who had said that she favored a two-state solution—Israel and Palestine—on the historic territory of Palestine. Throughout my readings and assessment of the situation, I concluded that if the firing of rockets into Israel's Negev desert and mortars into the nearby Israeli villages continued, Hamas and the resistance organizations would put Ehud Olmert's government, weak as it was, in an unenviable position, forcing him to take military action to show the strength of Livni and Ehud Barak and get their government reelected in March 2009.

As the bombing increased in the second half of December 2008, Omar Suleiman spoke with Hamas leaders in Palestine and also in Damascus, asking that the situation not be escalated. Meanwhile, we in the Foreign Ministry contacted the Israelis, the United States, and the European powers to warn them that there would be serious consequences if the situation continued to deteriorate. In parallel to the reports of the chief of General Intelligence, I took it upon myself to speak with the president confidentially. The president suggested inviting Livni to Cairo to discuss the situation. In my opinion, inviting Ehud Barak, the defense minister, would have been more effective, but it might also have sent the wrong message to some people. Livni responded that she would not be able to travel to Egypt before Thursday, December 25. The president received her that Thursday morning in the Ittihadiya Palace. The moment she saw us, Omar Suleiman and myself, Livni said, with great consternation, "They [Hamas] launched forty rocket attacks against us yesterday." She added that she had been informed just before taking off to Cairo of the missile launchings on villages in southern Israel. Her tone left me feeling pessimistic. Then Livni asked to meet with the president in private, a tactic that always irritated me. Although Mubarak would always brief us about closed-door meetings he held with foreign officials, which was his typical style in dealing with his subordinates and senior officials, this approach tends to weaken the influence of his assistants in their relations with other parties.

Fifteen minutes later, Omar Suleiman and I were invited into the meeting. The president said that Livni said that they could not remain silent about these provocations and that they would respond, while he stressed the need for restraint and asserted that the grave situation threatened an explosion which would negatively affect the Annapolis process. He added that he would ask the two of us to talk with the Palestinian side to get them to stop the bombing.

A press conference was held in which Livni threatened and sulked, and I said that Egypt was against escalation and rejected all acts of violence on both sides. As she was leaving the press conference, perhaps because she was tense, Livni nearly fell over on the palace stairs and I grabbed her hand so she wouldn't slip on the marble. A picture showing me holding her hand appeared the next day. My wife said, "This photograph will turn people against you." I exclaimed, "Should I let her fall?" and she replied, "Let her fall."

Later I read Condoleezza Rice's memoirs, published in November 2011. I found out that when Livni told her on that Thursday that Israel would respond militarily to Hamas's provocations, Rice did not ask her, despite all our calls, to stop military operations until all other options had been tried. It must be acknowledged here that the Bush administration, and Condoleezza Rice in particular, did not object to the Israeli military action either in July 2006 in Lebanon or in December 2008 in Gaza. As a matter of fact, everything that has been written in the many articles and books about these two battles clearly shows that the U.S. administration was always looking for a suitable opportunity for Israeli military action to accomplish its objectives. Both times, I assured Rice and the Europeans that Israel would never be able to destroy Hezbollah or Hamas, no matter how much time it was given. However, the U.S. administration would not listen unless it came under pressure in Lebanon or Gaza. There is no doubt that the close personal relationship between Rice and Livni had an impact on the U.S. position, especially after they were appointed foreign ministers of their respective countries.

Immediately after Livni's visit, Omar Suleiman sent warnings to Hamas about the impending Israeli operations, and told them that we might succeed in stopping the Israeli military action only if the shelling stopped immediately from the Palestinian side. In fact, it was difficult to know exactly what factors were driving the decision-making in Hamas and the other organizations back then. I believed, at the time, that it was not unlikely that Syria or Iran might have had a hand in the deterioration of the situation. Perhaps Hamas was imagining that it would come out with increased influence and power after the war, as Hezbollah had done.

Suleiman made a direct call to his Syrian counterpart in Damascus, pointing to the importance of avoiding further deterioration. But his efforts failed to achieve their objectives.

I was in my office on the morning of December 27, 2008 when the satellite television channels broadcast heavy air raids on Palestinian police stations in Gaza. I was shaken by the magnitude of the losses. I was surprised that the Palestinians, after all our warnings, had failed to take even ordinary precautionary measures to spread out their personnel and equipment so as to make them more difficult to target.

My thoughts were consumed with how we should deal with the new situation, as the attack was already launched. I believed the safest measure was to call for a ministerial meeting of the Arab League immediately. Afterward, we would ask the Security Council to attempt to contain the situation and broker a cease-fire. Of course, I did not know, at that moment, the time frame in which the Israelis were planning to continue their air operations against the Gaza Strip, or whether it would turn into a ground operation, as some Israeli press reports had indicated.

Egypt began to be attacked and criticized, as if we were the ones attacking Gaza. I responded in a press conference, in the presence of the Palestinian president Mahmoud Abbas, after a meeting with the Egyptian president. I explained that Egypt had warned the Palestinian forces on the ground in Gaza of what was likely to take place, and that the intentions of Israel were written out and clear to all. I received calls from some Arab ministers to discuss the situation. The Jordanian foreign minister said that they had the same idea of an immediate extraordinary meeting of the Council of Ministers of Foreign Affairs. I promptly talked to the Arab League secretary general Amr Moussa, who moved quickly.

I had a conversation with the president that afternoon about the outcome of contacts with the Arab foreign ministers and the Arab League. I added that I was monitoring the attempts in the media to hold Egypt responsible for the coming confrontation, which I hoped would not be as long or as destructive as the battle in Lebanon. The media discourse then dedicated itself to "What will Egypt do?" I fully understood the president's reaction that we should in no way be involved in a situation we had not created. We also began to discuss the status of the Rafah crossing and the other crossings between Israel and Gaza. The president said he had instructed Omar Suleiman and the rest of the relevant government departments to facilitate the passage of all medical aid and other emergency assistance through Rafah.

The president called again in the evening. He had received a telephone call from President Abdullah Gül of Turkey, asking about our reading of the situation and its prospects, and expressing his deep alarm at the barbaric Israeli attack. Mubarak had promised the Turkish president that he would dispatch me to Ankara the next morning to present our views on the situation. I met with the Turkish president, Prime Minister Erdogan, and Foreign Minister Ali Babacan. I found the entire government of Turkey very angry at what was happening. They said, "We have been deceived by the Israelis. They have even been in intensive contact with us, and through us with President Bashar al-Assad, to approve the key agreed-upon elements between Syria and Israel to return to negotiations according to the settlement agreement between them." They added that Istanbul had been hosting negotiators from both sides, with the Turks acting as intermediaries. Among the Turks, Erdogan was the angriest in his demand to take measures. I formulated some ideas that the Turks could use to promote an integrated position acceptable to all parties. My plan consisted of an immediate cease-fire, a call on both parties to calm down, consideration for opening border crossings according to new rules, and resumption of peace efforts. Gül and Babacan said it was essential to push Hamas, and I quote him, to "use rationality and maturity to arrive at practical positions."

I informed the Turks of what we intended to do with the Arab countries in the next meeting, due in two days, and of our plan to approach the Security Council. There was a rumor at the time that Syria and Qatar were promoting an Arab summit, and I told them that I did not agree with this proposal, since it would be rushing the Arabs to a high-level meeting without knowing how things would proceed. The opinions of all sides on the issues of the Security Council and the cease-fire would have to be considered before a summit could be convened. I fully and sincerely believed that the focus would be on Egypt to take the necessary measures to address the Israeli aggression. I was also aware of the president's instructions to be careful not to get involved in the situation.

Ali Babacan said he also did not want to rush into an Arab summit. He felt that the Arab foreign ministers and the Security Council should be allowed to deal with the conflict before resorting to other options.

The statements of Sheikh Hassan Nasrallah, the secretary general of Hezbollah, made it clear that he was plotting against Egypt in order to drag it into the confrontation. I fended him off in the media. I objected to the increased pressure on Egypt to allow the use of the Rafah crossing freely and without restrictions to transfer weapons, equipment, and ammunition to the resistance factions, which completely violated the peace agreement between Egypt and Israel. The Egyptian authorities were organizing the collection of large amounts of humanitarian aid at Arish Airport and setting up a process to transfer this aid to the Gaza Strip, either through the Rafah crossing, which was governed by specific rules that I will explain later, or through the Kerem Abu Salem and al-Ouja crossings on the Egyptian–Israeli border, if the shipments could not easily be transferred through the Rafah crossing. Egypt agreed, and even offered, to treat the wounded Palestinians in the hospitals of Arish and other hospitals in Egypt, while waiting for the ministerial meeting of the Arab League.

I was running on a treadmill in a room attached to my office, watching the satellite television stations, when suddenly breaking news appeared on the screen: Qatar was calling for an immediate summit and Syria supported it. It was to be held in Doha the following Tuesday. It was now Wednesday, December 31, and the fierce Israeli shelling continued unabated.

As usual throughout this crisis, contacts with the president were nonstop. He called at 4:00 p.m. to request a verbal report on the situation. I asked him whether the emir of Qatar had contacted him. "Why?" he asked. I answered, "Because Qatar is now calling for an Arab summit, and I expected that they would talk with you in advance to assess the situation." The president was surprised by Qatar's indifference toward us. Half an hour later, he called again, saying, "This is really strange. Even King Abdullah bin Abdulaziz has not been informed! I called him a few minutes ago and found out the emir of Qatar had not contacted him either." I remarked, "Mr. President, breaking news on Al Jazeera Television reads that the emir of Qatar has contacted a dozen Arab leaders and that there is general acceptance of the idea of the summit." He replied that he would not go because the goal was to embarrass Egypt and Jordan and put them in a dilemma by blaming them for the confrontation while they keep enjoying their trips to London and other European capitals.

For the third time in two hours, Mubarak telephoned and said that the emir of Qatar had just now contacted him, at 6:00 p.m., to confirm the summit, adding that it sounded as if he were summoning the president of Egypt. Mubarak had explained to the emir the proposed Egyptian approach of convening the Arab foreign ministers' meeting first, and then going immediately to the UN Security Council for a cease-fire resolution. After that, we would monitor the developments. If we failed to get this cease-fire resolution, we would then decide what the next step should be. The emir of Qatar replied that there was no harm in holding the ministerial meeting, and that it would be a step along the way to the summit.

The Arab ministerial meeting was held, and the Arab ambassadors in New York were called upon to immediately request an urgent meeting of the UN Security Council. On my part, I contacted the foreign minister of France, which held the presidency of the Security Council at that time

(January 2009). He replied that he would consult with the rest of the Council members, especially the permanent ones, adding that President Sarkozy would like to go to Cairo as soon as possible to assess the situation. I conveyed this request to the president, and he agreed to receive the French president on January 3 in Sharm al-Sheikh. I informed the French side of the approval. Then I contacted the foreign ministers of the United Kingdom, Russia, and China to urge them to support an emergency meeting of the Council. I also talked to Condoleezza Rice; our relationship had improved on the personal level over the past two years. She was about to leave office within two weeks, to be replaced by Hillary Clinton, the new secretary of state in the administration of the incoming Democratic president Barack Obama on January 20, 2009.

I had enjoyed a particularly strong relationship with Russian Foreign Minister Sergey Lavrov, as we had served as permanent representatives of our countries in New York since May 1999. He was a professional, seasoned diplomat with great confidence in himself and his country's ability, as well as extensive knowledge of the issues, accumulated during his long career, including several terms in New York. Lavrov expressed his full support for a Security Council meeting, saying, "Ahmed, you must be careful how you handle this situation. It is a dangerous position and you must beware of everything." I assured him we were counting on Russia's assistance to address the difficult situation facing us all.

The Chinese foreign minister made clear his absolute support for the cease-fire and said that he would tell the Chinese delegation to the UN to coordinate with us. I had agreed with Prince Sa'ud al-Faisal, as well as with the Jordanian foreign minister, on the importance of controlling the Arab diplomatic position. The priority of the Arab action was to focus on the meeting of the Security Council before anything else. In this context, an unprecedented battle took place: Qatar and its diplomats tried to buy their way to obtaining the approval of countries to hold an Arab summit in Doha on the date set by the emir. Most of us were in favor of waiting, and the majority ended up not supporting the summit to be held at that time. Prince Sa'ud and I worked together, with the participation of our leaders. We explained to our Arab brothers our point of view, which insisted that any such summit should be held within the framework of the Arab League. Most Arab governments agreed with our view, which led to a delay in the convening of this summit. This situation was the first stage in a battle in which Qatar decided to formulate an Arab position against Egypt and Saudi Arabia, in contrast to the history of Arab diplomatic work within the framework of the Arab League, which will be discussed later.

President Sarkozy arrived in Sharm al-Sheikh early on January 3, 2009. On the same day, Israel intensified its operations by launching a ground offensive against the Gaza Strip. The French president urged Egypt to advance specific ideas for reaching a cease-fire, which we had already been doing in our contacts with different parties. Mubarak agreed, saying that we had reached a few conclusions that we intended to announce before the Security Council convened.

The French president left immediately for Israel for discussions with the Israelis, and then returned to Sharm al-Sheikh the next day for another meeting with the Egyptian president. He brought up the importance of controlling the tunnels between Egypt and Gaza, apparently expecting Egypt to pledge to do so. The Egyptian president naturally objected.

I did not participate in this second meeting, since I had left for New York on January 4 after the Security Council decided to meet in an open session on January 5. I was there for two days with a group of capable Arab ministers to promote the Arab position before the Council: the president of Palestine, Mahmoud Abbas, the foreign ministers of Palestine, Saudi Arabia, Jordan, Bahrain, Libya, UAE, and Morocco, and the Qatari minister of state, among others.

After the French president left Sharm al-Sheikh on February 5, Mubarak launched an Egyptian initiative that aimed at controlling the situation through an immediate cease-fire, the opening of safe corridors for relief aid, immediate meetings to reach an agreement that would prevent further escalation, and a call on the Palestinian Authority and the resistance factions to reconcile their differences, since we had made a great effort to achieve this particular goal.

The Arab ministers held a series of meetings with the permanent members of the UN Security Council. They also met with the U.S. secretary of state and with the British foreign minister, David Miliband, who played a strong and positive role over two whole days to achieve consensus on a draft resolution demanding a temporary cease-fire pending a final cease-fire agreement that would lead to Israel's withdrawal from the Gaza Strip. Under Arab and international pressure, which was particularly effective due to the close coordination between the Arab ministers, we drafted a resolution that could be palatable to the United States. However, I was informed by one of the Arab foreign ministers that a European minister had, surreptitiously, complained to him of an Arab state that was trying to convince European countries not to pass the draft resolution in the Security Council, and that further consultations were still needed. I was taken aback by this piece of information, conveyed by this well-informed minister who had open contact with everyone.

Vigorously and efficiently, France's foreign minister, Bernard Kouchner, and the president of the UN Security Council pressured the Americans, stressing that the international community should not leave its responsibilities in the hands of Israel, which was already in trouble because its ground and air offensive against the Gaza Strip had failed to meet its intended objectives, although they had inflicted heavy losses. As we approached the vote on a draft resolution that could actually be passed, I was told by the French minister that the French president wished to preside over the session during which the draft resolution was to be adopted. I commented that waiting for the French president to arrive in New York would require more time, which would threaten to undermine the emerging consensus on the draft resolution and might lead the Americans to alter their position to object to the resolution, especially since Israel had become aware of this resolution, which Britain was planning to sponsor. As soon as David Miliband informed me of his country's intention to sponsor the draft resolution, I expected it to pass, for it was hard to imagine that the United States would object to a draft resolution presented by Britain, its main ally. I also told Kouchner that I could not agree to postpone the vote for a day and a half or two, as he suggested. My approach was calm, complimentary, and understanding of the French considerations, but the matter was much greater than France's individual interests. Kouchner said he agreed, and even went so far as to criticize President Sarkozy's personal motives in this regard. I felt that the French minister was under heavy pressure from his president. I also had the impression that he was about to resign, or perhaps was threatening Sarkozy and the Élysée Palace to do so.

Late on the night of February 6, during these intensive contacts in the hours preceding the vote on the resolution, I received a call from the president. At the time, I was sitting in an Arab consultation session with the members of the Security Council—the Arab ministers and the members of the Council were working day and night to get the resolution passed. I spoke very quietly on the mobile phone with President Mubarak's secretary, telling him that I was in a very sensitive meeting, that I had already briefed the president an hour or more ago that things were on the way to a breakthrough, but that these highly critical moments required me to stay in the consultation hall, and I would contact them within a few minutes when things were stabilized. I ended the call, but the secretary called back and said it was urgent. I had to leave the room and enter one of the interpretation rooms attached to the consultation hall. The French minister Kouchner was in another room nearby speaking loudly to someone in Paris, possibly even screaming at them. President Mubarak's voice came through the mobile phone, very clear, although we were all in this hall underground in the General Assembly building. The President asked about the situation. I updated him and told him that the vote on the draft resolution would take place that night, within an hour or less, and that we were waiting for it to be translated into all the official UN languages.

I was surprised when the president said that President Sarkozy had asked him to agree to postpone the vote for two days so that he could convince Olmert, the Israeli prime minister, to accept the resolution. The French were under intense pressure from Israel and America, and Sarkozy wanted to be present to preside over the Council during this important session. The president asked for my opinion. I immediately replied without thinking that if we agreed to Sarkozy's request, we would lose our credibility with everyone and our losses would be severe, especially since the decision was about to be made tonight. I added that I had spoken with Rice just a few minutes earlier, and had learned that the Americans were prepared to allow the resolution to pass that night, although they themselves would abstain due to the Israeli pressures on them. The president therefore asked me to inform the French minister that we could not agree to the French president's proposal and that the vote should go ahead as planned. I commented that I had already informed the French of our position half an hour ago. The president asked Kouchner to inform Paris of Cairo's position. I got the feeling that he did not want to speak directly with the French president. It was late at night in both Cairo and Paris, but it was clear that both presidents were following the matter very closely. Hossam Zaki, my competent assistant and the spokesman for the Ministry of Foreign Affairs, was present while I was speaking with the president; his face and his reactions reflected anger, surprise, and dismay. I told him that Mubarak was merely asking about the current state of affairs and was not ordering us to do anything. I immediately informed my French friend of our official position and he expressed his full agreement, against the wishes of his country's president.

The foreign ministers of Saudi Arabia and Jordan were both highly active, a shining example of commitment to the balanced Arab position during all the consultations. The long, hard hours ended with a vote in favor of Resolution 1860 calling for a cease-fire. Prince Sa'ud and I delivered speeches. We were the only ones among all the Arab ministers participating in this evening session who spoke before the Security Council: the Saudi minister spoke in his capacity as the six-month rotating president of the Arab Foreign Ministers Council, and I participated because of Egypt's role in the region and its efforts in the Israeli–Palestinian conflict. In addition, the resolution that was adopted by the Security Council had been an Egyptian proposal that was based on our initiative to end the fighting in Gaza that was launched by the Egyptian president. I had worked hard to have a reference to it included in the resolution. Here again I give credit to the efforts of my young assistant, Hossam Zaki, who helped draft the resolution and saw to it that the references to the Egyptian initiative were included. It was a triumphant night.

I immediately sent a cable to the president that analyzed the resolution's provisions, along with some recommendations for the course of the Egyptian diplomatic work during the following days. I believed this would be difficult and sensitive work, as it would require exerting a certain amount of international pressure on Israel to respect the resolution. In the end, it took ten more days to enforce the resolution.

Prince Sa'ud said that he would be leaving for Paris aboard his own plane two hours later. I asked him, "Won't you take me with you? I want to get to Cairo as soon as possible to get to work on implementing the resolution." The prince was very welcoming as usual, for I had traveled with him on his private plane more than once, going to or from important meetings. I let the British foreign minister and the secretary general of the Arab League know that I was leaving right away with the Saudi prince, and they quickly asked to accompany him too. Then the Jordanian minister joined us as well. It was such a fruitful trip. We discussed many ideas for coordinating our work on the next phase of the cease-fire.

During these difficult days, Cairo witnessed a lot of visits by high-profile foreign figures who all sought to achieve a cease-fire. The Turkish activity was very clear. The advisor to Ahmet Davutoğlu, who was the Turkish prime minister at the time, wanted to coordinate the Turkish contribution with Omar Suleiman, which we did not mind. The Turks were moving cautiously, so as not to give the impression that they were seeking to downplay or hijack the Egyptian role. By dealing with all of these foreign visitors in person, we were able to tighten our grip on many aspects of the situation in Cairo. Meanwhile, a conference of some of the Arab leaders was held in Doha. To our surprise, the conference favored the withdrawal of the Arab Peace Initiative. None of the decisions of this summit, held outside the Arab League, was recognized in Egypt, Saudi Arabia, the United Arab Emirates, or most other Arab states.

The pressure on Israel to observe the cease-fire continued, as did the passage of Egyptian and foreign humanitarian aid through the Rafah crossing, and the transport of wounded Palestinians for treatment in Arish hospitals. The Egyptian health minister, with much of Egypt's medical capability under his command and that of the Palestinians, was on hand to supervise the situation.

The days passed, heavy and full of tension. Everyone in Egypt and the Arab Islamic world—if not the entire world—demanding an immediate cease-fire. On January 17, 2009, as the Bush administration was inching toward its end, due to leave the White House on January 20, Washington suddenly announced the signing of a memorandum of understanding (MOU) between Israel and the United States on measures to stop the supply of arms and ammunition to Hamas and the Palestinian resistance organizations. This MOU had a regional dimension, designed to prevent weapons from reaching Gaza, and an international dimension, that sought to consolidate international public opinion to control the provision of weapons to Hamas. I declared Egypt's rejection of the MOU and affirmed that Egypt would not be bound by it. I contacted Condoleezza Rice in Washington; she was hosting Livni, who was in Washington to sign the MOU. When I expressed our astonishment at the MOU, she replied that the United States was trying to please Israel in order to get them to accept a cease-fire.

Through the U.S. ambassador to Cairo, Rice sent us a paper outlining a regional and international mechanism to deal with smuggling operations. These U.S. efforts, backed by the EU, were aimed at encouraging Egypt to participate in them. They proposed a mechanism for an international monitoring and supervision group, asking Egypt to engage in that effort by requiring Egyptian border guards to fight smuggling. Threats were made to cut U.S. aid if Egypt did not comply. Some Europeans voiced some irresponsible ideas about placing international or western forces on the Egyptian–Palestinian border. I made public statements asserting firmly that Egypt would not accept the presence of European or any other foreign forces on its territory. If anyone insisted on it, those forces would be confined to a strip of land inside Palestine, against the will of the Palestinian personnel already there. A few days later, it was revealed that the Israeli–U.S. MOU also provided for maritime force against any ships carrying arms and ammunition in the Red Sea or the Mediterranean. We responded that we would refuse to allow any foreign forces in Egyptian waters. During those difficult days, I was in constant contact with the European commissioner for foreign affairs and defense, Javier Solana, explaining the dangers and urging him to warn his fellow European ministers, with whom I was also in direct contact, not to join Israel in its siege of the Gaza Strip. I repeatedly made it clear that our opposition to this European–American mechanism did not mean that we wanted arms and ammunition passing to Gaza through our territories in Sinai. But we believed that allowing this kind of military presence would gradually lead the Europeans to stand with Israel against the Palestinians, which should not be allowed. Nevertheless, the Europeans continued to hold meetings for the international monitoring and supervision group in Europe and in Canada.

We were invited to send Egyptian military personnel and diplomats to the meetings that were held to discuss the operation of this monitoring mechanism, but turned them all down. However, I asked all our missions in these countries to carefully monitor all the findings and conclusions of these meetings. In this regard, I would like to describe a one-day visit I made on January 25—after the cease-fire—to attend a meeting of EU foreign ministers in Brussels to discuss the course of events. I told Solana that I would attend in order to present our point of view. Solana decided to expand the invitation to include the foreign ministers of Palestine, Jordan, and Turkey. I warned the Europeans against sending their troops to the Gaza Strip or to the Egyptian–Palestinian border inside Gaza, in the so-called Philadelphia, or Salah al-Din, Corridor. This is a segment of land stretching from the Mediterranean Sea to the convergence of the Egyptian, Palestinian, and Israeli borders. It is fourteen kilometers long and five hundred meters wide and lies inside Palestinian territory adjacent to the Egyptian border with the Gaza Strip. I told them that if they wanted to deploy forces in that area, they should expect losses to their soldiers, because the Palestinians would fire at them. I added that any shooting might cause casualties on the Egyptian side of the border, which we would never tolerate, and that they needed to be careful in this regard. The European ministers realized the deceptive trap that Israel was orchestrating for them.

In a side conversation, during the working dinner that followed the meeting, I warned the foreign ministers of the Netherlands and Denmark, who were pushing hard for these ideas, "You will only have yourself to blame if you draw Israel into this position and get many of your soldiers killed, for they will be killed. And we will also defend our armed forces on the other side of the border." The two ministers expressed their gratitude for my explanation of the dangers facing their soldiers, and this reckless proposal was stopped.

In the midst of this crisis, I received a telephone call from my friend Dr. Nabil al-Arabi, who proposed that Egypt declare a freeze on the peace treaty with Israel, in protest against the battle of Gaza and the criminal acts committed by Israel in Gaza. I was surprised by the simplicity with which he spoke about the proposal, without making any mention whatsoever of the serious consequences it would have for Egypt. It would affect every aspect of our relationship with Israel, including the QIZ agreement, which provides Egypt with hundreds of millions of dollars' worth of trade with the United States. It would also undoubtedly damage our relationship with the United States. Al-Arabi did not mention whether this proposal meant that the Egyptian army should not comply with the military protocols of the treaty and the limits on ground troops inside Sinai. I listened patiently to al-Arabi, who was angry at what was going on, but told him that I could not, in any way, recommend to the president that we freeze the peace treaty, unless there was a clear danger to Egyptian interests from Israel or a threat to our territory from its army. I added that I was as angry and distressed as he was by what I had seen of Israel's tactics, but although I would convey his message to the president, I could not accept the proposal. Finally, I reminded him that the battle of Gaza in January 2009 was not waged in isolation from the battle of Lebanon in July–August 2006, for it had the same goal: to disturb Egypt's stable position in the 1979 Egyptian–Israeli peace treaty. In my opinion, Iran's hand was not far from the situation, for we had been monitoring its actions throughout 2008. Al-Arabi said that he sent the president a written note on the subject through his information secretary, the competent Ambassador Suleiman Awad. I was in regular, intensive contact with Ambassador Awad, as with the interior minister, the defense minister, and the General Intelligence chief, sending them daily, detailed information. That evening I asked Awad whether the president had received the memo al-Arabi had sent him. He said that the president was surprised by the proposal and rejected it immediately, remarking that anger and loss of perspective would not benefit anyone, but would instead inflict serious harm on us.

I was later surprised by the statements made by al-Arabi, immediately after he became foreign minister in March 2011, in which he condemned Egypt's disgraceful attitude during the Gaza war. I was sorry to hear this statement from my successor, who even went as far as saying that Egypt had committed a war crime. I was taken aback, and Omar Suleiman was extremely distressed. I learned that high-ranking and influential military sources were equally angered by this irresponsible statement, which was an accusation against all the national security services.

The Rafah crossing was open to individuals at all times, but through specific procedures. The crisis that unfolded following Turkey's dispatch of the so-called Freedom Flotilla in June 2010 changed the situation for Egypt. We decided to expand the operating hours of the Egyptian crossing and to allow all Palestinians to cross during daylight hours. After the January 25 revolution, some people demanded a change in the status of the crossing, and claimed that they had succeeded. The fact of the matter, so as to clarify the situation, and to ensure that Egyptian policy is not determined on the bases of populist passions, is that the operating time of the Rafah crossing was extended for only one hour, and the traffic increased by only fifty individuals per day.

On the morning of January 16, I read an encrypted cable from our ambassador in Paris to the effect that President Sarkozy and his aides were looking into the possibility of coming to Egypt, perhaps accompanied by other high-profile European officials, to try to put further international pressure on Israel to accept Resolution 1860. I had an interview in my own office with the editor in chief of *Rose al-Yusuf* newspaper, Abdullah Kamal, at this time. He kept talking and asking questions, which I answered absentmindedly. I was a million miles away, mulling over Sarkozy's idea and how we could put it into effect if we accepted it. I told Abdullah Kamal I had a lot on my mind, and asked him to stop the interview and consider that his questions and my answers never took place. I asked him to move to another nearby room for a while, or to resume the interview the next day. I called the president's secretary. As Kamal was leaving my office, the president's voice came on the line much faster than I expected, and I had to begin my conversation him while Kamal was still in the room. A little later

I saw him coming back as if he were trying to get a press scoop, because he had heard me mention Sarkozy's idea to him. I informed the president of the proposal and suggested inviting the French president to a summit in Sharm al-Sheikh. I also offered to issue to the foreign ministers of the major European powers our invitation to their heads of state or government to participate in a summit to marshal international opinion to exercise pressure on Israel, which was contemplated by Sarkozy. Strangely enough, the president agreed instantly without any discussion. With Sarkozy's approval, we agreed to expand our contacts with the Italians, especially since Italian Prime Minister Berlusconi and the Egyptian president were very close friends. Mubarak said that he himself would get in touch with Berlusconi, after he talked to Sarkozy, while I, on behalf of the Ministry of Foreign Affairs, was to invite the Spanish prime minister, the British prime minister, and the German chancellor.

The president called back within fifteen minutes to say that both Berlusconi and Sarkozy had accepted his invitation to Sharm al-Sheikh for the day after tomorrow. I proceeded to call the foreign ministers of Spain, Britain, and Germany. My contacts with the Germans and the British indicated that they were reluctant to participate, especially after German Chancellor Merkel consulted with British Prime Minister Gordon Brown. I therefore got back in touch with the foreign ministers of France and Spain, asking them to notify Germany and Britain that Italy, Spain, and France would definitely be attending the summit. Sarkozy did this, and an agreement was reached to meet in Sharm al-Sheikh. To my surprise, the entire process took only a few hours. Thus Egypt became the focal point of international attempts to implement resolution 1860 and effectuate a cease-fire in Gaza.

That evening the summit was announced. I then received a call from the Turkish foreign minister saying that Prime Minister Erdogan would like to participate. I called the president and recommended that he invite Turkey, which had been in constant contact with us throughout the days of the Israeli attack, especially between the prime minister's advisor, Ahmet Davutoğlu, and Egypt's intelligence chief, Omar Suleiman. Surprisingly enough, the president asked us to invite the Turkish president, Abdullah Gül, instead of Erdogan, because the latter had made some sharp statements during the Gaza siege about Egypt's responsibility to break it. After much talk with my Turkish counterpart, the Turks finally accepted our invitation to Abdullah Gül and not Erdogan.

The Turkish prime minister was a bit reluctant to come because of a bad experience at the Davos–Middle East meeting in Sharm al-Sheikh in May 2008, when he was to be received by President Mubarak at his residence. Erdogan was accompanied by a large number of Turkish security personnel who were determined to accompany the prime minister with their weapons into the room in which he would meet the president. But Egyptian security rejected this, and the Egyptian Republican Guard prevented it with its typical strictness. The Turkish foreign minister and the prime minister's advisor complained. I placated them by pointing out that the army and the Republican Guard were not familiar with the protocol niceties. The Turkish army, I added, would probably have acted in the same manner were the situation reversed. The situation was thus resolved.

The summit received considerable coverage in the media, and I felt that the whole thing was a huge success for Egypt, which had been unfairly criticized for weeks. The Egyptian actions resulted in both parties agreeing to abide by the cease-fire as long as the other side did. The fighting stopped after three weeks, during which Mubarak made four major statements about the Egyptian position. Among the victims of the conflict was the Egyptian–Qatari relationship, because Al Jazeera launched a sharp media attack on Egypt and stirred up Egyptian public opinion, or at least some segments of it, against Egypt's management of the crisis, assigning a great deal of the responsibility to me. As a result, I was compelled to appear on television with the prominent Egyptian broadcaster Amr Adib on February 27, 2009, in one of my most frank and candid conversations about this situation that occupied Egypt for two months.

I went to Kuwait in the last days of February 2009 to attend the Arab foreign ministers' meetings held in preparation for the Arab Economic Summit. The resulting statement of the Arab foreign ministers included an assurance that Arab countries would adhere to the Arab Peace Initiative. We also affirmed the support of the Arab countries for the UN Security Council mandate for Egypt to resume its efforts to secure a final cease-fire between Hamas and Israel, to bring the various Palestinian factions together, and to reconcile Hamas and Israel; the adoption of this mandate was a huge Egyptian success.

At this same meeting, the Omani minister of foreign affairs, my friend Yusuf bin Alawi, a powerful and sophisticated figure, told me that he followed with considerable sadness the tension between Egypt and Saudi Arabia on the one hand and Qatar on the other over Qatar's attempts to hold an Arab summit in Doha, despite the lack of enthusiasm on the part of Egypt and Saudi Arabia. To restore Arab unity, he suggested that the statement of the economic summit should include a reference to the outcomes of the Doha summit, which had not involved a large number of Arab countries. I was surprised. How could Egypt or Saudi Arabia agree to the outcomes of a summit that we had resisted because it required a major shift to the fundamental premise of Arab foreign policy; namely, pursuing peace with Israel as a strategic objective of the Arab world. Accepting the outcomes of that summit would also have required Egypt and Jordan to adopt new positions that rejected peace and called for war and confrontation—and Egypt would definitely be expected to fight. Naturally, I rejected Yusuf bin Alawi's proposal. This was followed by a similar attempt by Sheikh Hamad bin Jassem, the Qatari prime minister, to convince me of adopting the outcomes of the Doha Summit at the Arab Economic Summit. I refused, and the situation became complicated. There were ongoing attempts to find a satisfactory resolution for both the Qatari and the Egyptian–Saudi sides. The ministers met with me and Prince Sa'ud. The closing session of the economic summit was adjourned. The Kuwaiti foreign minister tried to find a way to conclude the summit with a clear decision in support of the Palestinian position. Egypt and Saudi Arabia said that we supported the Palestinians with everything we had, but we would not agree to include in the summit's statement a reference to the Doha outcomes, which contradicted our positions.

The emir of Kuwait met with the president of Syria, the prime minister of Qatar, Prince Sa'ud, and the secretary general of the Arab League to examine the issue. The Kuwaiti minister, Sheikh Dr. Mohamed al-Sabah, who is a dear friend, asked me to attend the meeting, and I went with him.

The secretary general presented the situation and suggested that we find a more neutral formula on the Doha outcomes to be adopted by the summit. I refused, and a civilized confrontation took place between me and Sheikh Hamad bin Jassem, which ended in an agreement to omit any decision from the summit on the Palestinian issue, but also with the adoption of a general statement expressing the summit's support of the Palestinians.

That evening we returned to Cairo, and I presented a full report to the president, who had attended the opening session of the summit for a few hours and left the same evening. All along, I had been keeping him abreast of the developments in Kuwait. He emphasized that the ideas we had opposed in the Doha outcomes should not be accepted in any way in Kuwait.

Egypt announced a conference on the support and reconstruction of Gaza, scheduled for March 2, 2009 in Sharm al-Sheikh. I met with the U.S. secretary of state in advance and invited her to attend the meeting, and she agreed. We were in favor of meeting with the Palestinians, who had prepared a long list of possible economic projects. This list had been presented to the World Bank and all other parties who might potentially contribute to them. It was a high-level meeting, with both the French president and the Italian prime minister in attendance. The United States offered $600 million for the reconstruction of Gaza. However, progress came to a halt when the discussion turned to the mechanism for spending these funds. The western powers refused to allow the projects to be under the supervision of Hamas in Gaza, and demanded the return of the PLO to the Gaza Strip. We did not reach a conclusion and the effort ended.

The crisis in Gaza had significant effects on the Arab world. Qatar had attempted to hijack inter-Arab cooperation and to re-orient Arab policy in a direction that conflicted with the basic principles of Egyptian foreign policy and the Egyptian role during the thirty years since President Sadat's visit to Jerusalem and the peace treaty with Israel.

By the time I was appointed minister of foreign affairs in July 2004, the Second Intifada had ended as Israel escalated its attacks on the Palestinians and besieged the Palestinian president in his headquarters in Ramallah. (It is interesting to note that this building was a prison during the British occupation of Palestine.) At this point, international efforts to reach a final settlement had ceased, except for the truce achieved by the Quartet (the Russian Federation, the United States, the UN, and the European Union) with an active Egyptian contribution. Our priority at this stage was to ameliorate the suffering of the Palestinians and push Israel to lift its siege; return to implementing the Oslo agreement; and restore the Palestinian Authority's control over all cities, as had been the case until September 2000.

In November 2004, the president asked Omar Suleiman and me to meet with Ariel Sharon and other members of the Israeli government in order to pursue these goals. Israel and the Israeli government were no strangers to me. I had accompanied Foreign Minister Amr Moussa twice on quick visits to Israel between 1997 and 1999, before I was posted to New York. I had also visited Jerusalem for a few days as a member of the Egyptian delegation led by Foreign Minister Mohamed Ibrahim Kamel to negotiate with Israel in January 1978.

We landed at Lod Airport early in the morning in a small Mystère plane. The Israeli foreign minister, its chief of protocol, and the head of the Egyptian section of their ministry drove us to Jerusalem in their fully armored four-wheel-drive vehicles. The corresponding journey during my visit in 1978 is described in *Witness to War and Peace*. The road was lined with many ruins, barren rocky hills, some hilltop settlements, and a group of old and poor Arab villages. We arrived at the headquarters of the government and were received by Foreign Minister Silvan Shalom, who escorted us to meet with Prime Minister Sharon. I had previously met Sharon in his office when he was foreign minister. Amr Moussa had met him in 1999, although he refused to shake hands with him because Sharon's hands were stained with the blood of Palestinians and Egyptians. Still, the Israeli Minister complimented him at the time, and they shook hands at the end of the interview. On the handshake issue specifically, Hossam Zaki, who at the time of this visit to Israel in 2004 was serving as an assistant to Amr Moussa at the Arab League, drew my attention to the importance of not extending my hand to shake hands with Sharon. He advised me to let the Israeli prime minister get close with his hand stretched out to me; I should salute him, but with my arm close to my body. (I noticed afterward that the photographs showed clearly that the Egyptian foreign minister was extremely reserved with the Israelis.)

From the moment we landed at the airport until we entered the prime minister's headquarters, I noticed that Omar Suleiman was very familiar with all the Israeli officials, who welcomed him warmly, especially the members of the security services who were involved in the consultations. The Egyptian–Israeli relationship at the time was under the sole control of the General Intelligence Service, because the Egyptian ambassador, Mohamed Bassiouni, had been withdrawn in protest of Israel's actions against the Palestinians in 2001. I was not in any way satisfied with this situation and did not intend to accept it indefinitely. As a matter of fact, the responsibilities of this diplomatic relationship had been placed in the hands of the General Intelligence even earlier, following the clash between Amr Moussa and President Mubarak in October 2000 at the Sharm al-Sheikh summit, where Amr Moussa disagreed intensely with the president over meeting with U.S. Secretary of State Madeleine Albright in private and accepting her proposals on how to stop the fighting between Palestinians and Israelis without consulting the foreign minister. I believe that was when the president decided to remove Amr Moussa from the Foreign Ministry and, months later, nominate him for the Arab League. I met Amr Moussa in December 2000 during my vacation from New York and told him, "You have to prepare yourself to leave the Foreign Ministry. I am following the situation and I think the president holds a grudge against you due to your stance at the Sharm al-Sheikh summit." He replied, "But I have often told you that I would not stay for more than ten years in office before leaving it for another position, haven't I?"

I would say that the control of General Intelligence over the Egyptian–Israeli relationship also stemmed from the fact that the peace process and efforts to achieve a final settlement to the Israeli–Palestinian conflict had ceased since the Bush administration came to power in January 2001. The U.S. president and senior aides were convinced that as long as Yasser Arafat remained at the head of the PLO, there would be no political settlement. Bush himself even said that peace would depend on changing the Palestinian Authority, an idea with which we did not agree and which we resisted. In order to prevent further conflict between the Israelis and Palestinians, the U.S. agencies, especially the Central Intelligence Agency, took responsibility for pursuing the objectives of maintaining truce between the two parties and rebuilding the Palestinian security services. It was only natural, then, that the role of the Egyptian General Intelligence was amplified, because of its long experience in working with the Palestinian, the American, and even the Israeli governments.

I myself needed to concentrate on the responsibilities of the Egyptian foreign ministry regarding bilateral relations and the resumption of negotiations. Therefore, I was happy to leave the security-related aspects of relations with Israel to the General Intelligence, so that I could focus on the economic and political aspects of the Egyptian–Israeli relations. I was aware that this would take a lot of time—although at that time I did not know how much. Now I can say that it took at least a whole year, during which I was criticized and attacked by the Egyptian media and some anti-government elements, who said the Egyptian foreign ministry had no business dealing with such vital issues.

The peace process and the efforts to reach a settlement, however, remained within my purview and that of the Egyptian foreign ministry. From the moment the peace process was relaunched, in 2007, it was under our full control, with the consent of the president and the head of the General Intelligence Service.

In this regard, I would like to say that General Omar Suleiman understood these situations carefully, and the two of us cooperated fully and honesty to preserve Egyptian interests, as well as the rights and welfare of the Palestinians. I recall making several statements at the end of 2004 that might have seemed overly critical of Israel. General Omar Suleiman said that the Israeli security services were asking us to soften these statements, because the Egyptian–American consultations on Qualified Industrial Zones were at their height. The proposed agreement would allow the QIZ industrial products into the U.S. market either without tariffs or with significant price reductions, provided that at least 10 percent of the components of the manufactured output originated in Israel. I told General Omar Suleiman that I fully understood this, but I could not remain silent in the face of the many Israeli provocations. From then on, while my positions themselves remained unchanged, I tried to restrain our statements in a way that would serve our international and regional interests and also oblige Israel to take our reactions into account. The president spoke to me about this, several days after Omar Suleiman raised the issue with me, pointing out that our statements should not sound like an ongoing attack on Israel. So I reduced their intensity for some time, even though I had committed myself to respond appropriately to any Israeli actions against the Palestinians.

We entered the consultation room attached to the office of the Israeli prime minister accompanied by the Israeli foreign minister and Sharon's senior assistants. A minute or two later, Sharon himself made his appearance. He had a huge body, a faint voice, and sharp eyes, one of which was obviously crossed, especially at close range. He welcomed us, and explained Israel's unwillingness, under any circumstances, to accept acts of violence committed by the Palestinians, whether in the West Bank or Gaza against the settlers, or attacks by suicide bombers in Israel itself. He added that he would always respond with equal violence. He complained about Egypt's lack of control over the border with Gaza and the smuggling of weapons through the tunnels, demanding that we put an end to it.

I spoke about the necessity of achieving a de-escalation between the two parties to allow for the relaunching of the peace process in order to return to the situation that had prevailed before the beginning of the Second Intifada in September 2000. I said, "It is important to have an international mechanism, supported by the Quartet, Egypt, and Jordan, to act immediately against any deterioration in the situation and to prevent the deepening of differences." Sharon listened and did not comment on the proposal. He said only that he agreed to a de-escalation only if the Palestinians ceased attacks against Israel. He noted, however, that he would attack what he described as "ticking bombs," by which he meant any Palestinians Israel considered posed a threat, and whom they would kill or detain.

I said that this approach would be a provocation to the Palestinians and would prompt them to respond against Israel, which would complicate the situation and impede the truce. Sharon responded sharply, "I will not allow any threat to the security of Israel or its citizens, and we will move to counter any action by the Palestinians." Omar Suleiman described Egypt's efforts to achieve the truce and to control the tunnels. "But Egypt needs to increase the presence of border guards by a full battalion in this area of the Egyptian–Palestinian border," he elaborated. At this time the U.S. Congress had begun to threaten reductions in U.S. economic and military support for Egypt if it did not fully control its borders. In fact, some features of the new American position had already begun to appear, in terms of the transfer of military aid for the purchase of hardware and equipment—at high prices—to improve border control.

Sharon also mentioned the idea of complete separation between the Palestinians and the Israelis. His detailed thinking, however, did not emerge at the time. I asked him to elaborate, and he answered, "They should not be allowed to enter Israel, and we should enter into their areas. And we would separate from each other." I wondered whether this meant they would have their own state, but he did not comment further. The following months showed that Sharon was thinking of a full withdrawal from the Gaza Strip, and the full withdrawal of the settlements and their residents into Israel. These settlements occupied about 40 percent of the territory of the Gaza Strip at the time. Israel also said it was considering building a canal extending from the Mediterranean along the Egyptian–Palestinian border—fourteen kilometers—to prevent smuggling, and it also began building a wall inside the West Bank to separate the two sides.

In the weeks that followed the visit, as Sharon's intentions to make a full withdrawal from Gaza were confirmed, we proposed holding an international conference in Egypt to discuss the followup to the withdrawal, to set up guidelines to regulate contacts between Palestinians and Israelis during the withdrawal process, and to restore the Road Map, which was first introduced by the Quartet in 2002.

We were concerned that Israel would try to claim, by withdrawing settlers and its forces from the Gaza Strip, that it had implemented Security Council Resolution 242 adopted in November 1967. We therefore made it very clear that this withdrawal did not represent an end to the occupation of the Gaza Strip because Israel had retained its control over its airspace and territorial waters. We also rejected the idea of establishing a maritime canal in the Philadelphia Corridor along the border, because of its serious impacts on the ecology of the area, including the groundwater that supplies the farms, the Palestinians, and us in Egypt.

The period leading up to the start of the Israeli withdrawal from Gaza produced a number of analyses. Some of these warned that the withdrawal would negatively affect the future of the Palestinian settlement. Others argued that the withdrawal would lead to a situation where the Palestinian Authority was required to establish full control over the Israeli–Palestinian border. Some expressed concern that the withdrawal would lead to the implementation of Sharon's basic ideas of separation, which would include a fifteen-year settlement during which the regional situation might change in a way unfavorable to the Palestinians. Still others feared that the ultimate Israeli goal would be to get rid of the chronic headache that was Gaza by transferring the entire responsibility for it to Egypt. Some analyses predicted that the withdrawal would lead to an international public-opinion victory for Israel, which could widen the rifts among the various Palestinian factions.

In a bid to improve Israel's international standing, the United States proposed an international conference that would be attended by Israel and all the Arab countries and that would be held immediately after the Israeli withdrawal. I informed the Americans of our rejection of this plan. Sources in the UN were talking about the importance of full withdrawal, which would include the right of the Palestinians to operate the airport and the seaport and to ensure safe passage between Gaza and the West Bank—that is, a return to the situation as it was in September 2000. Israel rejected this vision because it was concerned that the airport would be used to threaten Israeli cities if a hijacking similar to the destruction of the World Trade Center in New York in September 2001 were to take place. I expressed my cynicism about this Israeli thinking.

Israel said it intended to remain in the Philadelphia Corridor to make sure it was not being used to smuggle weapons or allow Palestinian militants into the Gaza Strip, meaning Hamas and its men, who could carry out operations against Israeli towns and villages near the Palestinian–Israeli border. We told them that an Israeli presence on the Egyptian–Palestinian border inside the Gaza Strip meant that Israel would be at the Rafah crossing between Egypt and Palestine, which would mean continued Israeli occupation and control, and that they would have to withdraw completely from the Palestinian territories. We talked to the Americans, who understood the situation. The U.S. secretary of state, Condoleezza Rice, was working actively to secure a Palestinian–Israeli–European agreement that would secure Israel's exit, yet ensure that the crossing would not be misused by placing European observers, who would be asked to monitor the whole area. Thus Israel withdrew from the Rafah area and the border, which in turn encouraged Egypt to consider the possibility of turning Rafah into a transit point for Palestinian trade, not just for persons.

We were not aware then of what was going to happen between Hamas and Fatah, on the one hand, and the Israeli invasion of the Gaza Strip in the following years, on the other. We spoke with the Palestinians about the importance of deepening their security control over all the borders of the Gaza Strip and preventing its use in any attacks against Israel, as if we had read the future and foreseen the invasion and destruction that occurred in December 2008 and January 2009 because of rockets fired from the Gaza Strip.

In many of his conversations with me, Omar Suleiman talked about this Israeli exit, saying that this withdrawal represented an opportunity for the Palestinians that should not be wasted under any circumstances. A real effort had to be exerted not only to assure the outside world of the ability of the Palestinian Authority to control the Strip and to reassure Israel that no hostile actions would be committed against it from the Strip, but also to rebuild it economically and equip its infrastructure, following the lead of Singapore, Hong Kong, and other places where similar withdrawals of occupying powers had taken place. It should be noted that, the idea was appealing, especially since the international community was ready to provide sufficient financial support to the Palestinians to achieve this goal. Unfortunately, things did not turn out for the best. The covered farms built by Israel in the Gaza Strip, which had achieved such high productivity of exportable vegetables and fruits, had been allowed to fall into ruin. It was a disappointing blow to my full conviction of the ability and determination of the Palestinian community in Gaza to rebuild the Gaza Strip and its cities.

I found in this Israeli withdrawal a good opportunity to demand that Israel continue to ease its grip on the West Bank; otherwise the residents of the West Bank would resist the Israeli presence and the continued stalemate in the peace process.

As we returned to Cairo that night, I agreed with Omar Suleiman that it was important for us to visit Yasser Arafat in Ramallah, to demonstrate Egypt's support for him and to connect with him during his siege. The president approved, and Suleiman arranged the visit with the Israelis. We arrived at Lod Airport, once again, to take the armored cars provided by the Israelis. As we approached Ramallah, we exchanged the Israeli cars for Palestinian ones. At Arafat's residence in the Muqata'a, we found him standing in front of the main door of his residence, accompanied by a large number of Palestinian and international media figures. I observed the difficult conditions in which the Palestinian leader was living, though no symptoms of illness that ended his life within weeks of our visit were yet visible.

It was a successful visit that confirmed Egypt's support for the Palestinian leader. I could see that Arafat was capable of controlling all the people of Palestine. I witnessed his firm and calm talk with all the elites we met. The luncheon was an opportunity to hear them express their deep gratitude to Egypt and its people for supporting them. During this meal, which was a bountiful feast, I sat to the right of the Palestinian president, who served me a variety of the best Palestinian dishes.

We left in the same way we came. As we moved through the city of Ramallah, I noticed that—in spite of all that it had gone through—the city looked as clean as European cities bordering the Mediterranean. I should say here that Omar Suleiman and I visited the city again in 2010, but this time in a Jordanian helicopter that flew us from Amman to Ramallah. As we flew over the city, I noticed that there were many more buildings and its streets had become crowded with modern cars. During the 2010 visit, it occurred to me that we should have traveled to Arafat directly to Ramallah like this, and not through Israel, but the circumstances did not allow that at the time.

This was not my first meeting with Arafat. I met him with Dr. Esmat Abdel Meguid in New York in 1974 when he addressed the UN General Assembly. I met him again at the Egyptian foreign ministry headquarters in 1998 when he visited Amr Moussa, and finally several times in 1999 and 2000 in New York when I was the head of Egypt's delegation to the UN. He was a very intelligent and stubborn person who believed strongly in the demands of his people; he was also capable of maneuvering against his enemies, as well as with his friends. When I took over the Foreign Ministry, I noticed that President Mubarak had reservations about him because of some of the positions he had taken during the signing of the economic and financial agreements between the Palestinians and the Israelis in 1994. Mubarak displayed this attitude again when Dr. Nasser al-Qudwa, Arafat's nephew and the Palestinian foreign minister in 2005–2006, requested that Cairo be the headquarters of the Yasser Arafat Institute for Arab Studies. Al-Qudwa wanted Mubarak to participate in the opening ceremony of the institute, but the president refused, despite many attempts on my part and that of the head of the General Intelligence.

Arafat then fell ill and quickly departed our world. Omar Suleiman and I were sent by the president to accompany the body to his final resting place in Ramallah. We took off in helicopters from Arish Airport after our arrival in the C130 plane that was to carry the martyr Arafat to Arish. As the two helicopters approached Israeli territorial waters, several Israeli helicopters appeared and asked our planes to follow them into Israel and then to the Palestinian territories. Once again, I could see the modernity of the cities and rural areas of Israel. As we were landing near the Muqata'a, I was surprised by the presence of thousands of Palestinians on top of buildings and light poles, and in the streets and the landing area itself. The situation as we landed felt dangerous to me; on our way back, the Egyptian pilots admitted having the same fears.

Thousands gathered around the two planes, rushing toward the dead president in a scene that seemed like an abduction of the body from the plane. Heavy gunfire started in all directions. The door of our plane had been opened and I went out, but the intensity of the fire forced me to get back in, lest I should be hit by a stray bullet until the situation was under control. The pilot was speaking through the aircraft's microphone, asking people to stop firing near and under the plane, so as not to be hit by ricocheting bullets. However, one of the plane's fan blades was hit, although the damage was not serious enough to endanger the plane. As the shooting and commotion around the plane continued, I saw that we could not wait much longer, because the evening was approaching and it would be very difficult to take off in this difficult atmosphere. I finally left the plane, accompanied by Major General Omar Suleiman. I was afraid that he might become involved in some sort of incident because of the press of the crowd.

We entered the nearby building and met the Palestinian leadership, at the forefront of whom was Abu Mazen and all the dignitaries of Palestine. We spent less than thirty minutes with them before returning to the plane. Our takeoff was extremely difficult because people were still firing randomly into the air. The same Israeli aircraft that had escorted us before flew near us throughout the return journey. As soon as I arrived at my home, which was near Almaza Airport, the president called, and I gave him a full report. Suddenly he asked, "Weren't you afraid of the shooting? How did you get out of the plane with gunfire everywhere?" He had watched the entire event on the satellite channels. I felt some fear, I said, but I had to complete the mission. "Amid bullets!" he exclaimed, and I said once again that the mission had to be accomplished. He replied, "It's bullets, Ahmed. Bullets." I was astonished that the president spoke so frankly, since he was the one who had seen so much shooting over the years.

The Palestinians elected a new leader of the Palestine Liberation Organization and then a president of Palestine and the Palestinian Authority. As this new situation unfolded in Palestine, we in Egypt found it an opportunity to advance the peace cause, which had been completely stalled. In January 2005, I suggested to Omar Suleiman that we begin to promote the idea of a Palestinian–Israeli meeting in our presence, to reach a comprehensive framework for the next phase of action. I also submitted the proposal to the president. Now that a new Palestinian president had been elected, it was time to insist that Israel take a series of steps, including stopping its violations against the Palestinian territories under area A (which was under the full control of Palestinian security), returning to the borders of September 28, 2000, relieving the daily suffering of the people, and releasing prisoners held in Israeli prisoners.

My proposal also included involving the Quartet in order to ensure that our initiative enjoyed international support and had an international dimension. It was equally important to persuade the Palestinian factions to declare a truce or accept a de-escalation with Israel. Omar Suleiman set to work and communications with the Israelis and Palestinians intensified. We began to prepare for a meeting between Abu Mazen and Sharon in Sharm al-Sheikh in February 2005, for the purposes of agreeing on a truce, enabling the new Palestinian president to rebuild the Palestinian security institutions that had been destroyed during the intifada years, to return to the September 2000 borders, and to prepare for negotiations on a comprehensive settlement.

When Sharon arrived at the president's residence in Sharm al-Sheikh, I think that all of us on the Egyptian side of the room noticed that he seemed perhaps fearful of what was coming. Gradually he began to relax. He started by saying that as his plane was approaching Sharm al-Sheikh, he informed the pilot that the destination was Sharm al-Sheikh, not the big city they were approaching. The pilot confirmed that it was. Sharon asked us, "How did you do that? How did you create a big city with all these hotels and facilities in such a short time?" He had not been in Sharm al-Sheikh since 1981. The president told him he would arrange a tour of the city for him after the consultations.

The Palestinians sat down with the Israelis and an agreement was reached as to how to move ahead. This Sharm al-Sheikh conference was an important step in the return of the two parties to discussions. I briefed the Americans and the Europeans on the proposed Egyptian approach. Shortly thereafter, in March 2005, there was a conference in London, to gather support for the Palestinians to build their institutions.

Mubarak believed that Sharon had the ability and power to convince Israel—if he wanted—to reach an understanding with the Palestinians. Sharon always said that he had fired Netanyahu from his post as finance minister when he objected to the Gaza pullout. Therefore, Mubarak advised the Palestinians not to try to fight him because he was the person most capable of responding to their demands. Despite the momentum that was beginning to build in the peace process, the U.S. administration was still cautious about making a serious effort. U.S. action was limited to rebuilding Palestinian security capabilities, urging the Israeli administration to reduce the number of roadblocks to make life easier for the Palestinians (although without much in the way of results), and persuading them to allow the Palestinians to receive fifty armored vehicles and two helicopters as a grant from the Russian Federation. Under pressure, the Israelis agreed. That was in 2005, but when I left my position in March 2011, no vehicles or aircraft had been allowed into the Palestinian territories from Jordan.

This evasion revealed the reality of Israeli intentions, at least to me. In 2005, the Palestinians were meticulously implementing the basic elements of the first phase of the Roadmap, as presented by the Quartet. As the Palestinian parliamentary elections approached, I asked for an assessment of the situation. The reports of the Foreign Ministry's experts expressed doubts about the ability of Fatah to defeat Hamas, which had decided to participate in the 2006 legislative elections. Hamas then won a majority, thus putting everyone, except Hamas, in a difficult predicament. Hamas was demanding that it hold executive authority while adhering to its policies of refusing to recognize Israel and resisting the occupation by all means. At the time, I believed that the Palestinian president, Mahmoud Abbas, should have insisted that Hamas recognize the Arab Peace Initiative and the two-state solution before it was even allowed to participate in the vote.

Prior to the January 2006 election, the Palestinians were determined to give the residents of East Jerusalem the opportunity to vote. It was said at the time that the Palestinian leadership hoped Israel would not permit it, so that the election would be canceled and the situation would be stalemated. But the U.S. administration intervened with Israel—according to many sources—to allow the Palestinian demand to be met, and stressed the importance of holding the elections.

Once again, things were moving in the direction of a Hamas government for the Palestinian Authority. The west refused to deal with Hamas, unless it declared in advance its recognition of Israel, its commitment to the two-state solution, and acceptance of the agreements signed by the PLO with Israel since the Oslo agreement. I told the Europeans and the Americans that their position was contradictory and had complicated the peace process; how could they promote democratic elections and then oppose the results? The peace process was therefore halted for nearly a year and a half, during which strife erupted between the Palestinian factions, despite all the Egyptian efforts to bridge the gap between Hamas and Fatah. The new Palestinian foreign minister, Mahmoud al-Zahar, arrived in Cairo on a tour that also included some other Arab countries, and the president asked me not to meet with him. The man had become a reality, I told him. We must deal with Hamas as part of the Palestinian national fabric, and seek to influence it if we could, particularly as it had been voted into a position of power and decision-making, just as I had told the Europeans. Omar Suleiman explained that our attitude toward him stemmed from his failure to visit Cairo first, only stopping in on his way to other countries. I therefore had to stay in my country house in Qaha in Qalyubiya Governorate, so that I could claim I was not in Cairo to meet him, much to the outrage of the Egyptian media. And indeed, I believed they had every right to their displeasure. However, I made up for this occasion by receiving him during several other visits to Cairo. I also received the Palestinian prime minister Ismail Haniyeh and the Hamas leader Khaled Meshaal.

In one of our meetings with Zahar, in May 2006, in Tahrir Palace in Cairo, the former palace of the Egyptian foreign ministers, he said that the Palestinians were the owners of all the land of historic Palestine. I informed him of the importance of modifying his position and declaring the commitment of Hamas and its government to the Arab Peace Initiative, which would gradually open the way for them to be recognized internationally, instead of becoming isolated. The success of the Palestinian national action, under any banner, is in the interest of Egypt, I said, while Zahar listened in silence. Our relationship with him began to strengthen from that point. He recognized my sincere emotions toward the Palestinian cause and my relentless efforts to rid the Palestinian land of occupation.

Khaled Meshaal gave an important media interview in January 2006, in which he stated the need to liberate Jaffa and Haifa, and promised that aggression against any Arab or Islamic country would lead to an escalation of the resistance in the occupied territories. I took advantage of our meeting in December 2007, also at the old Foreign Ministry headquarters and away from media attention, to tell him that I was speaking to him with all sincerity and honesty, based on my family's history in the fight against Israel. His talk about Jaffa and Haifa would in no way open a path for Hamas or result in any progress, and the Israelis would stick to their plans for further settlement in the Palestinian territories. I added that before the Palestinians awakened to the real situation, history would have passed them by, and stressed the absolute importance of declaring their readiness to negotiate with Israel by recognizing the country and demanding in advance that they recognize the Palestinians. I was impressed by Meshaal's personality and by his ability to talk and debate. I even told him, "You will, someday, be the president of Palestine if you take a positive attitude toward the negotiations and achieve the Palestinian dream. But surely you should not waste Palestinian national action for non-Palestinian interests." I had no doubt that the man understood my meaning. I referred to his media interview in January 2006, saying, "This position connects you to Iran, which is said to be controlling you, as well as Hezbollah. You have to preserve the Palestinian decision as your own, not coming from some other foreign power, even if it is Arab or Islamic." He listened carefully but denied that they were linking their fate with any other country. I asked him to cooperate with the Palestinian president Mahmoud Abbas, who had extensive experience in the pursuit of Palestinian interests. I had followed Abbas's performance for many years since he had visited Dr. Esmat Abdel Meguid in his office at the Egyptian foreign ministry in 1989, when the subject was the so-called proximity talks between the Palestinians and the Israelis. I emphasized that Abu Mazen was a great patriot and Meshaal agreed, but he commented that Fatah was resisting the recognition of the election results and thus putting obstacles in front of the Hamas government.

I used to receive phone calls from Meshaal from Damascus when the situation in Gaza deteriorated after Hamas won the elections and Israel carried out military operations against the Gaza Strip, including the December 2008 attack. He kept asking Egypt to intervene with Israel to stop its operations or to allow the passage of more raw materials and aid to the residents of the Gaza Strip. My response was always that he must trust that we were doing whatever was within our power to stop the aggression.

As a result of Egypt's lack of enthusiasm about Hamas, its leaders sought, at the beginning of their journey to power, to open up to all other countries that would agree to a relationship with them, such as Iran, Turkey, and Russia. In this way, we lost a good opportunity to influence them. Yet we succeeded in attracting them to us at a later stage, when Egypt exerted great efforts to help Hamas and Fatah form a real national unity government.

I also tried to make the western world and the Quartet understand that their demands on Hamas were influenced by the Israeli position. While recognizing the importance of these demands—recognizing Israel, stopping acts of violence, acknowledging the signed agreements and the Arab Peace Initiative—the western powers also needed to encourage Hamas to develop its positions by opening a dialogue with it, especially since we had noticed some signs of softening in the positions of Meshaal, Haniyeh, and others. Unfortunately, there was little progress on the international level, and the Palestinians were pushed into the tragic scene of mid-July 2007 when armed confrontations broke out between Fatah and Hamas.

Israel began in 2006 to stir up obstacles to the new Palestinian government. I learned in November that the Palestinians were concerned that Israel would cancel the Paris Protocol on Gaza and stop the trade between the Gaza Strip and the West Bank. I contacted the General Intelligence, and ordered our ambassador in Israel to raise the issue with the Israelis and warn them against this behavior. Unfortunately, I noticed that certain Arab parties, especially Qatar and Syria, tried during the Arab League ministerial meeting in September 2006 to persuade the League to recognize the Rafah crossing as an Egyptian–Palestinian border and to abandon the crossings agreement. They also did not want to comply with the Palestinian–European agreement on the presence of observers. I rejected this proposal, pointing out that by doing so, we would appear to be helping the Israelis to cancel the Paris Protocol, from which the Palestinians were obtaining huge sums of money that was being spent on the development of the Gaza Strip. The proposal would also lead Israel to sever the organic link between Gaza and the West Bank cities. Finally, it would allow Israel to claim that it had implemented Resolution 242, ending the occupation of Palestinian Arab territories, and Israel would move to settle the West Bank while leaving some land for the so-called Jordanian option, in the sense that Jordan is Palestine.

My meeting with Haniyeh in November revealed that Hamas was behind the joint Syrian–Qatari move, backed by Sudan, to modify the nature of the Rafah crossing. He asked to turn the crossing into a commercial corridor and to establish a Palestinian industrial zone inside Egypt in Sinai, where factories would be constructed by Palestinian workers who would enter in the morning and return to the Strip in the evening. He also mentioned their desire to export Palestinian gas from Egypt in the future, and also to facilitate the transport of Palestinian exports from the Rafah crossing to Arish or Port Said. For my part, I explained the concept of the Palestinian–Israeli trade agreement, the Paris Protocol, and the consequences of changing the status of the crossing. In any case, I promised to study their proposals, although I made it clear that it might be difficult in the near future to establish this industrial zone within our territories.

During my meeting with Haniyeh, I did not discuss the proposals that were appearing in the Israeli and U.S. press to conclude an Egyptian–Israeli–Palestinian agreement pursuant to which Israel would obtain land in the West Bank, while Egypt would give land in Sinai to the Palestinians in return for Israel handing over land to Egypt in the barren areas of the Negev desert. Indeed, these ideas, as well as the conversion of Rafah into a commercial crossing, were among the Egyptian concerns when the Palestinians, encouraged by Hamas, invaded Egyptian territory after the destruction of the Egyptian border wall on Wednesday, February 23, 2008. The Palestinians had been firing at five or six of the Palestinian–Israeli crossings, yet at the same time asking Egypt to upgrade the Rafah crossing. We viewed the picture more comprehensively. Hamas was seeking full legitimacy through us. We were receiving information about the intention of Hamas to clear the Egyptian–Palestinian border by removing the walls that Egypt and Israel had constructed since 1982. The Egyptian security and defense services regarded this move as dangerous, because it would make Egypt responsible for the Gaza Strip and its residents, while relieving Israel of the pressures of the occupation.

Suddenly, the Egyptian walls were blown up and Palestinian bulldozers entered our territories to remove the rubble. The Egyptian state felt the weight of the situation. I received from the United Nations Relief and Works Agency for Palestine Refugees (UNRWA) a report that thousands of Palestinian citizens had crossed into Egypt and reached a number of Sinai cities. Another report the same evening estimated the number of Palestinians who had crossed the border at 300,000. During a conversation with the president on Wednesday evening about the deterioration of the situation on the border, I mentioned this number to him, and he reacted in disbelief: "What are you saying? What is this talk?" This is from the UNRWA reports, I said. He replied that reports he had received from the security services had given the number of 30,000. The president inquired again on Thursday afternoon about the situation. I meticulously checked the information I had received, for fear of giving him incorrect or exaggerated numbers. I said the numbers had increased to about 750,000 people, according to the most recent UNRWA reports as of Thursday noon. I sensed his tremendous concern about the numbers. We were worried that some of them would arrive at the Suez Canal, and we were afraid at the time of attempts to impede navigation in the canal. The president immediately ordered the National Security Committee to convene on Friday morning. We met in the Ministry of Defense. The recommendation was to proceed quietly, to absorb the Palestinians calmly, to work toward their gradual return to the Gaza Strip, and to intensify the Egyptian military presence on the roads and within the cities. The situation was controlled within a week.

The president met with the ministers and senior officials in charge of national security on Saturday morning and emphasized the importance of not allowing this situation to be repeated, which meant that the concrete wall on the Egyptian side would have to be reconstructed and the military and security presence increased. He also decided to take firmer action against any future attempt to violate the border or destroy the wall, which was rebuilt within a short period of time. The president confirmed that the use of weapons is the responsibility of the minister of defense, and that no one should open fire without his authorization. The president himself would decide how many more troops to assign to the area. Some members of the groups were asking to use heavy weapons, such as tanks, despite the fact that the peace treaty with Israel does not permit it. A decision to breach the treaty can be made only at the presidential level, and only after all other measures were exhausted. These were difficult moments, especially because of the ongoing Israeli demands for Egypt to take responsibility for the Strip and its economy, and Israel's desire to exchange land among Egypt, Palestine, and itself.

In media reports a few weeks later, there were indications that the Palestinians were planning to destroy the border and cross into Sinai again. I said that whoever violates our border and walls will have his legs broken. This caused a wave of anger from some supporters of Palestine in Egypt. I had to wonder why the Egyptian mind would prefer the interests of the Palestinians over the security of the land of Egypt. Still, the message reached the Palestinians and Hamas, and no one tried to breach the border again. I will not even mention the absurdities to which the Egyptian soldiers were exposed during these weeks.

Omar Suleiman continued his efforts to improve relations between Fatah and Hamas in the Gaza Strip and the West Bank. Syria joined in as well. Syrian Foreign Minister Walid al-Muallem proposed holding meetings with Egypt and Syria in Damascus, perhaps to provoke Egypt. We were not enthusiastic about the idea, and it died away. Tension was rising inside the Gaza Strip between the two rivals in the early weeks and months of 2007. We discovered a lot of money being funneled into the Gaza Strip for the benefit of Hamas from Iran, Qatar, and others. Finally, in June 2007 the two sides clashed violently and Palestinians killed each another for the first time in the history of the conflict. In Egypt, we naturally viewed this as a real threat to the dream of a Palestinian state, as its two factions were moving apart from each other. Egypt moved its diplomatic office from Gaza to Ramallah. I took advantage of this change to secure the presence of an extremely powerful Egyptian mission staffed with competent diplomats.

Back in June 18, 2007, two days after the expulsion of Fatah from Gaza, I had submitted an assessment of the situation to the president and the General Intelligence, and a list of the policies that Egypt should adopt: maintaining a minimal relationship, to be reactivated with Hamas at a later stage; continued Egyptian commitment to help the Strip economically; emphasizing the importance of not taking positions that would tend to divide the Palestinian people; taking steps to avoid the displacement of people into our territory—as if I were predicting the onslaught of Palestinians into Egypt that took place at the beginning of 2008; keeping the Rafah crossing open to the Palestinians, despite the fact that the European observers had decided to withdraw immediately after Hamas took control of the crossings; and finally, to use all available means to control the Egyptian–Palestinian border.

There was talk about sending an international or Arab force to the Philadelphia Corridor. The idea of digging a canal along the border was also raised. We rejected both of these ideas, because the major goal was to protect Israeli security without risking damage to any of the other parties, especially Egypt. Some Europeans said that their personnel could return to the Gaza Strip to monitor the crossings if Hamas allowed the Palestinian Authority's Republican Guard to remain only at these crossings, while Hamas continued to control the rest of the Strip. This proposal was rejected by Meshaal and Haniyeh. Within days of my first memorandum on the situation of the Strip, and with a new appreciation of the dimensions of the situation, I sent another proposal to the president and all the relevant state agencies: it is important to encourage Hamas to act responsibly within the Strip; we should agree to let Hamas control the Palestinian–Egyptian border in exchange for allowing the passage of individuals through Rafah; the Kerem Shalom Crossing in the Egyptian–Palestinian–Israeli triangle would continue to be the transit point for all commercial shipments into the Gaza Strip. In this memorandum, I emphasized the need to support the Egyptian security presence and to prepare for possible major relief operations if the situation deteriorated in the Strip or if Israel attacked. I further advised that we begin to seek reconciliation between Fatah and Hamas, although it would not be achieved in the near future because of the positions of Syria and Iran and their control over Hamas's decisions. Hence the importance of an Israeli–Hamas truce, which had actually been achieved for a period of time until Israel attacked the Gaza Strip in December 2008.

Egypt thus put forward its ideas to achieve reconciliation and both parties accepted them, but the results on the ground showed only that Hamas wanted to maintain control over Gaza without any concessions to the other side, and also change the status of the Rafah crossing.

Meanwhile, we were actively seeking to form a Palestinian government of national unity. The United States and Israel, however, claimed that such a government would lead to a halt in the peace negotiations between the Palestinian Authority and Israel, which were being conducted with the help of America and the Quartet, as long as Hamas refused to respond to the demands of the Quartet. Fatah, too, was wary of losing U.S. and western support.

At this point, Israel returned to talk about ideas and proposals it had already discussed with Presidents Sadat and Mubarak about handing over the Strip to Egypt. I was very surprised to see these proposals return, given the completely new circumstances of Hamas's control over the Strip. I therefore rejected all of them, and stressed instead the importance of returning to the inter-Palestinian Hamas–Fatah accord in order to ensure the return of the Palestinian Authority to the Strip. The president was one of the strongest opponents of holding Egypt responsible for the Strip. He regarded it frankly as a trap.

The Egyptian efforts toward reconciliation resumed with the full encouragement of the international community, even though the United States was not very enthusiastic about either this reconciliation or the formation of a national government that would include representatives from Hamas. For this reason, the United States withdrew its support for the Palestinians and its efforts in the peace process.

The presidency of Abu Mazen was due to end in January 2009, and Egypt supported its extension by a decision from the Arab League until the parties agree to hold new elections. The Egyptian delegation drafted the Arab League Council resolution in this regard.

I had an excellent group of young people in the Foreign Ministry who were helping in this effort: Ali Erfan, who spent several months with me; Ezzedine Choukri Fishere, who effectively handled the dossier of the Palestinian crisis for two years; and Hossam Zaki, who went on to serve Egypt's interests for many years.

It is appropriate at this point in the chapter to address in some detail the peace process—or, perhaps more precisely, the absence of a serious effort to achieve a Palestinian settlement. The president paid close attention to the Palestinian issue, yet I noticed early in the process that his focus was mainly either on the internal Palestinian situation, or the desire to avoid Israeli–Palestinian clashes, particularly because their negative effects on Egypt, both internally and externally. Even though President Mubarak listened attentively to our ideas for advancing the peace efforts, he did not study the details. I believe there are two reasons for this lack of attention to details. First, he had seen and heard many ideas and proposals over the course of thirty-five years that failed to achieve the dream of a Palestinian state. Second, he may have reached the conclusion that Israel would agree to peace with the Palestinians only on its own terms: a fragmented Palestinian state that is completely under Israeli hegemony, both economically and in terms of security. Therefore, all talk of an 'evolution' in Israel's thinking about a Palestinian state is merely a maneuver for wasting time in order to enable Israel to continue to settle the Palestinian territories in the West Bank.

Despite this Egyptian concern, and the lack of confidence that Israel was serious about peace—an attitude that I vehemently criticized before the General Assembly in all its public sessions over the years—we had to keep the pressure on Israel and the United States, and remain determined to pursue our goal of establishing a Palestinian state with contiguous and integrated territory alongside Israel. Unfortunately, my belief at the beginning of 2006 was that the year would not witness a lot of action, either because there was no real U.S. intention to move the situation or because of my lack of confidence in the abilities and influence of Israeli Prime Minister Ehud Olmert, whose views and positions cast doubt upon the credibility of his commitment to achieving a peaceful settlement. But I was also convinced that we were like a cyclist, who has to keep pedaling or else he falls off. In March 2006 I sent the president an assessment of the situation, which included my observation that there would be no serious movement this year. It was therefore important to resume our dialogue with Hamas to avoid the repercussions of the continued stagnation of the peace process and to prevent the further expansion of Iranian influence in Gaza, while concurrently, encouraging Fatah to reorganize itself and adhere to the truce with Israel, along with a continued call for a resumption of the peace process. Finally, I suggested that the president consider an initiative, similar to that of President Sadat during a visit to Israel, that Israel would withdraw from the Palestinian territories and accept the idea of a Palestinian state in return for Palestine's recognizing Israel and accepting peace with it. My proposal to the president also mentioned the importance of allying with King Abdullah II of Jordan, the king of Morocco, Abu Mazen, and the emir of Qatar. The resident was not convinced. "They will fear the consequences of failure," he said. Perhaps he did not want to take such a sensitive risk, but I saw it as a serious possibility for making progress.

As the UN General Assembly approached in September 2006, Arab ministers were again deliberating the danger of the stalemate in peace negotiations. The secretary general of the Arab League spoke energetically about the need to keep the issue moving, going so far as to threaten to withdraw the peace initiative. I objected to this threat, but I did not oppose presenting a unified Arab position before the Security Council, despite my conviction that the general situation and the inter-Palestinian rifts would make it easier for Israel and America to escape pressure and not respond to the Arab proposal.

During a visit to Cairo in September, Brent Scowcroft, the national security advisor to former U.S. presidents Ford and George H.W. Bush, spoke about the need to move things forward by asking the United States, the Quartet, or the Security Council to determine the major elements of a final Palestinian settlement—the so-called End Game. These elements would include land, borders, refugees, security, and water, among other things. Scowcroft suggested that President Mubarak talk to Bush, either through a message or in direct contact, about joint Egyptian and American action on this proposal. I presented the proposal to the president, but he was not enthusiastic. I admit that the difficult relations between him and the U.S. president at the time kept him from believing that the idea could be implemented.

The Arab ministers headed to New York, and we spoke before the Security Council. Our presentation caused some tumult, and we came back empty-handed. Nothing was accomplished, since the United States did not react positively to the statements made to the Security Council by members of the Arab delegation.

I communicated with Condoleezza Rice, calling on the United States and the Quartet to provide a comprehensive vision of the situation and the settlement, adding to the Roadmap that had been agreed upon internationally in 2002. I stressed the need for agreement on the ultimate goal of the settlement, with a clear reference to the End Game in a Security Council resolution or in a declaration adopted by the international community and both parties of the conflict. However, things did not move forward. As we entered 2007, still dealing with the continued Palestinian rift and our attempts at reunification, a Saudi initiative known as the Mecca agreement was signed by Hamas and Fatah, much to the consternation of the Egyptian president because the Saudis had not coordinated with us on this plan that was actually an extension of Egyptian efforts. I discussed the issue more than once with the president and with Major General Omar Suleiman. I learned the president was convinced that the Saudi effort would last for only a short time and then stop in favor of other concerns, and indeed, the idea was never actually implemented.

Whenever we suggested that the Americans move things forward, they would try to bring us back to the idea of a meeting of the Quartet, the Israelis, the Palestinians, and an Arab presence in the form of an Arab Quartet. The underlying purpose of the idea was easy to grasp: normalization of Arab-Israeli relations before Israel would seriously commit to any position on the Palestinian settlement. During these contacts with the Americans and others, I maintained that the Arabs should take no step toward Israel in the absence of real progress on the Palestinian track, and that any step agreed upon by the Arabs with respect to Israel must be based on the agreed-upon peace process. In a bid to keep the United States from winning concessions from the Arabs without similar concessions from Israel, I presented to the president an integrated plan for action during 2007, with Egyptian–Arab coordination, focusing on improving the situation on the ground and supporting the Palestinian president. The plan consisted of three stages of action: agreement on the general framework and objectives of the negotiations; establishing a de-escalation on the ground, restoring the status to what it was before September 28, 2000, and ending the construction of settlements and the Israeli separation wall in the West Bank; and finally, as an Arab response to Israel's commitment, a meeting of the Arabs, Israel, the Quartet, and others to discuss the Arab initiative and launch Palestinian–Israeli negotiations based on the existing peace agreements.

Egypt sought to reach an agreement with the other Arab countries on a specific approach to the steps we would take to reinvigorate the peace process. The Arab Foreign Ministers Council agreed that the foreign ministers of Egypt and Jordan would visit Israel to relaunch the peace initiative and explain it to the Israelis. We went and returned without achieving anything tangible. Israel reiterated its general desire to achieve peace and its overall acceptance of the concept of a Palestinian state, without, however, outlining its detailed view on how to achieve these objectives. We continued to talk with the Americans about the need for an international meeting. So we were surprised when the Israeli prime minister proposed a regional summit to discuss the Arab initiative; the United States supported it. I studied the proposal and decided that it represented progress on the part of Israel. However, there was no guarantee that Israel was not aiming only to open contacts with the Arabs without making serious concessions to the Palestinians. With American support, the Palestinian president was invited to meet with the Israeli prime minister in Sharm al-Sheikh in June 2007; Egypt and Jordan would also take part. The goal was to get Israel and the Palestinians back to negotiating. The Americans were finally willing to deal with the Palestinian issue. The U.S. secretary of state had made frequent visits to the region to discuss key elements of the settlement.

We received information that the Israeli–Palestinian discussions were becoming serious about the elements of the Palestinian state, its borders, the portions of the West Bank that Israel wanted to keep, and other questions of land exchange. Despite our lack of confidence in Israel's intentions, I was beginning to see progress in addressing the issues of borders, lands, maps, security, and the implementation of the Roadmap through to the establishment of a Palestinian state. Rice came to Cairo to urge the Arab states to take steps toward Israel. We replied that any Arab step must adhere to the terms of the settlement and Israel's fulfillment of its side of the bargain: stop the settlements, ease the life of the Palestinians, stop the construction of the separation wall. We also required a U.S. guarantee of Israel's adherence to the eventual agreement. I met Israeli Foreign Minister Tzipi Livni in Sharm al-Sheikh and in New York. The Israeli strategy was that they would not disclose their exact position on the borders of the Palestinian state until they were assured that the Palestinians would agree to Israel's refusal to allow Palestinian refugees to return to Israel except in extremely limited numbers.

I received a call from Rice in the last week of July 2007, informing me that President Bush was going to call for an international meeting in the United States because they had made some progress in persuading the parties to pursue formal negotiations. Rice added that their goal was to achieve a real breakthrough in 2008 so that by the time the Bush administration ended in January 2009, a settlement would have been reached. I was surprised by this optimism, which reflected a complete lack of understanding of the complexities of the issue. However, I encouraged them to make every effort, because any progress in achieving peace could only bolster the role and influence of Egypt within the region. We therefore agreed to support the conference, and presented a comprehensive framework paper setting out Egypt's vision of a settlement. We also asked the United States to provide a full and clearly worded American plan for the time frame and the final objectives of the negotiations, which should not exceed one year. Rice's response was that the Arabs needed to encourage Olmert, who felt vulnerable to criticism and attack from Israeli right-wing political parties. I believed that Rice's suggestion was no more than another attempt in American's ongoing effort to make gains for Israel on the normalization of relations with the Arabs. I replied that the Egyptian and Arab position was that we cannot agree to Israel's demand to return to the conditions that existed in 1995, unless Israel was willing to return to the status of the situation on September 28, 2000, before the eruption of the Second Intifada.

I resumed my attempts to discover the real Israeli vision. Rice's information indicated that they had made some progress, although the Palestinian reports to us did not reflect this growing American optimism. I met again with Israel's foreign minister Livni whose positions frankly contradicted what Rice had told me. Livni said that we should not expect the international meeting to produce an understanding on the final solution, and that the only settlement of the refugee issue could be the one that Israel proposed. The sole purpose of the meeting was to restart the negotiations. I pointed out that there were only two months left before the meeting, and therefore we needed to reach an agreement on the outlines of the final settlement. The detailed negotiations would be conducted for several months in 2008, with the expectation of tangible and serious progress, which would allow the Arabs to approach Israel with specific measures. I asked Livni to return to the lines of September 28, 2000; oddly enough, she referred me to Defense Minister Barak. I told her that I was speaking in the political framework with my Israeli counterpart and I had nothing to do with the defense minister. To my surprise, Livni then said that the Palestinian refugees, in exercising their right of return, would return to the Palestinian state we would agree to, rather than Israel. She added that there should not be excessive optimism about this international meeting, whose date and location had yet to be determined.

After this conversation with Livni, I contacted Rice again and informed her that the Israeli minister had not been reassuring in terms of their intentions. I emphasized once again how important it was for the United States to present a specific, detailed vision of the final form of settlement, along with an overall framework for it, based on which the negotiations would be conducted over a limited time span, perhaps a year. Time proved that the United States was unable to meet this demand, due to Israel's own opposition and the influence of the Jewish lobby in America, which supports Israel's vision.

The conference was finally scheduled for November 28, 2007 in the American city of Annapolis. As the date approached, I received evidence of a major American effort to persuade the Kingdom of Saudi Arabia to send its foreign minister, Prince Sa'ud al-Faisal. This suggested that the Arab countries were trying to decide whether to attend the meeting or not. An Arab ministerial meeting was held in Cairo, days before the conference, to discuss the situation. After extensive discussion, we reached the conclusion that the meeting should not be foiled by the absence of the Arabs, despite the mounting evidence that it might merely be an attempt by the U.S. administration to improve its image a year before the end of its term. Our decision was to go, and to try to obtain as much benefit as possible for the Palestinians.

As usual, Rice was fully aware of what was going on in the Arab meetings, which no longer amazed me after decades of working with the Americans, who always had their sources reporting every single Arab move to them. She called late at night, only a few minutes after the Arab meeting ended, to say that she hoped we could help them with Syria, which was opposed to attending the meeting in Annapolis. I called the Syrian foreign minister, who said that Syria was willing to participate, that the meeting would also address other paths to peace, not just the Palestinian one. Walid al-Muallem and I both spoke on the phone with Rice. The secretary general of the Arab League was following the situation calmly as we stood together in the courtyard of the headquarters of the Arab League. He hoped that Syria would not be absent from the Arab gathering, which had decided to participate and present a clear Arab position regarding peace in the Middle East before the international community, which reflected the demands of the Palestinians. The Americans suggested that the invitation to the Annapolis meeting would include a reference to other possible settlements, namely the Syrian and the Lebanese. Syria accepted this approach.

I had felt all along that Syria could not detach itself for so long from the Arab consensus; it would suffer considerable diplomatic losses. Its participation would give it an additional opportunity to engage with the United States on the difficulties of bilateral relations, Syria's position on Iraq, its relationship with Iran, and incentives that the United States could offer for the Syrians to change their positions.

I represented Egypt at the Annapolis meeting, which was attended by a large number of foreign ministers of important countries, as well as the Palestinian president and the Israeli prime minister. The closing statement revealed that the Israelis continued to resist committing to a clear formulation of the details of the Palestinian state, which were to form the basis for negotiation toward a Palestinian state within one year. Once again, I spoke to the members of the Quartet, and Rice in particular, to encourage all the parties to keep working so as to reach an agreement within twelve months. However, I quickly spotted two events that vividly illuminated the underlying reality. First, in December 2007 Rice again demanded that the Arab parties confirm their willingness to coexist with Israel before the Jewish state agreed to any final settlement on a Palestinian state. Second, the United States maintained an unnecessarily slow pace in the negotiations during the remaining weeks of 2007 and the first months of 2008. I concluded that the Annapolis meeting and the effort that followed would not achieve the desired goal. The Arabs also sought to pressure the Americans into formulating their vision of the final settlement and presenting it in the form of a resolution to be adopted by the Security Council. Israel, however, intervened in Washington, which shut down that effort.

I continued to follow the situation during Rice's four or five visits to the region in the first six months of 2008. The Palestinians informed us that Israel was asking them to give up 8 to 10 percent of the West Bank in return for simply defining their vision of a Palestinian state. Abu Mazen refused, stating that he could accept an exchange of territory between the two countries of no more than 1.9 to 2 percent. Parallel to this, we knew from many sources about Syrian–Israeli negotiations being conducted through Turkey to settle the issue of Golan. Rice informed me in May 2008, in connection with a meeting in London to support the Palestinian economy, that great progress was being made in the negotiations, and that therefore the United States did not intend to present its "vision" of the outcome, as it had previously promised. At about the same time, I noticed that the Israeli prime minister had asked Russia not to proceed with a ministerial meeting in Moscow, following the Annapolis meeting, which had been agreed upon between Rice and Lavrov with the consent of a number of parties directly involved in the negotiating process, and which had been tentatively scheduled for November 2008. I seemed to see a link between the request for postponement and a rumored military action by Israel against Gaza in light of Hamas's positions on Israel. I felt anxious, and asked Omar Suleiman to warn Hamas against any escalation. Unfortunately, its leadership did not listen to our advice.

In August 2008, Rice visited the region again. She talked about Palestinian–Israeli border demarcation issues, and said that the security measures that were being considered would require a third party, possibly the Americans or some other major country. The American view on the refugees was that they would be compensated, meaning that the right of return would not be guaranteed.

I met Rice again on September 22, 2008 in New York at the UN General Assembly. She said that the two sides had reached an understanding on security measures as part of the peace process. Israel had agreed that the basis of the settlement would be the 1967 lines in the West Bank and Gaza. Still under discussion was the territory called "No Man's Land," an area of about fifty-two square kilometers. According to Rice, Israel had also agreed that the Palestinian state would include the Jordan Valley and the Old City of East Jerusalem. I did not like this wording, because the Old City does not mean all of East Jerusalem, and we had to insist on giving all of East Jerusalem to Palestine. Rice said the exchange would involve 7 percent to 8 percent of the West Bank, adding that the border between the countries would be "ugly," meaning it would have a lot of twists and turns. Finally, she said that Israel would agree to the Palestinian flag being raised over the Old City, and to the existence of a joint administrative system for the city. I combined this report of Rice's with other U.S. statements I had seen that there might be a time lag, perhaps of several years, between the conclusion of an agreement and its date of implementation, so as to proceed in a gradual way.

We were now under considerable time pressure, especially that the Bush administration was coming close to leaving office in January 2009. The month of October passed without a final agreement. As a consequence, the Palestinians understandably resisted many of the Israeli proposals despite pressure from the United States. Meanwhile, we tried to relieve this pressure by supporting them in their demands and publicizing the Egyptian positions, which we hoped would strengthen the Palestinians' resistance. Throughout this period, I observed what I was convinced was close cooperation, if not full coordination, between the Americans and the Israelis. Yet it never crossed my mind that the extent of this collusion was as great as was revealed by Rice's memoirs, published in 2011, about her experience as secretary of state in dealing with Sharon, Olmert, Livni, Barak, and other Israeli leaders.

In any case, fearing that all of our previous efforts had gone to waste, I asked Rice to list all the elements of progress in a statement before the Security Council. She did not respond. I therefore asked her to leave a briefing or a written summary of what was done during the post-Annapolis negotiations for the incoming Obama administration, as a reference for their efforts to pursue a final settlement. I have been informed that Rice did in fact leave for Secretary Clinton a full thirteen-page report on what had been done in the Annapolis process. I spoke about the report with members of both administrations, old and new, and they acknowledged it. However, all of a sudden everyone began to deny its existence, and in 2009 we started a new effort on a different course.

Within a couple of days of taking office, the new U.S. administration appointed the former senator George Mitchell as its representative to deal with the Palestinian issue. Mitchell worked actively to achieve a real breakthrough in the settlement effort. He visited the region, and held meetings with the president, Omar Suleiman, and myself. He listened to our ideas and did not talk much, apart from repeating how he had managed to broker peace between the parties in Northern Ireland, despite the fierce and historic hostility between them. As aware as I was of the different circumstances, cultures, and experiences of the Palestinian and Israeli sides, as well as the historical background of the conflict, I listened to him politely and attentively and told him that he had to deal with Palestine in isolation from his experience in Northern Ireland. I said encouragingly that his 2001 report on the need to stop Israeli settlements in the Palestinian territories was a suitable starting point. However, what was needed—and was particularly vital now, as he began his work—was for him to present his specific vision of the final settlement he envisaged for ending the conflict, which I called the "End Game," based on the previous administration's report. He listened attentively. Then he went on to meetings in Israel, Jordan, and Palestine. When he came back to Egypt, he said, "Everyone is saying that stopping the settlements is the basic requirement to start with." Omar Suleiman and I responded that that approach was wrong and would lead nowhere. From that early moment, it was clear that we disagreed with Mitchell and that we were asking him to do something he could not do, namely putting forward a comprehensive U.S. vision that Rice had promised but had been unable to accomplish.

On the other hand, some Palestinians suggested turning to the UN to declare a Palestinian state. I replied that the Palestinian state had been declared in Algeria in December 1988. Still, there was no reason not to go ahead with it, for if we got a vote of support from the UN Security Council, Palestine could join the UN as a full member, not as an observer, as it was now. The situation had still not been resolved in 2009.

Then Benjamin Netanyahu, the eternal hard-liner, succeeded in forming a new government in Israel, further complicating an already complex situation. And we all began from the beginning—not an unusual experience in the area of Palestinian–Israeli negotiations. Experience suggests that whenever there is some sign of progress, Israel will change its government, which then says it is not bound by the positions of the previous government. And then we would start all over again, and so on.

One of the victims of the new Israeli government was the concept of the Union for the Mediterranean (UfM), which fell through because of Israel's decision to appoint Avigdor Lieberman as foreign minister, who held a hardline, far-right, anti-Palestinian view. I told the president that I would never meet him, talk to him, or even greet him anywhere. The president understood, and once again turned the Egyptian–Israeli issue over to Omar

Suleiman, who even held talks with this hardline minister. Omar Suleiman subsequently visited Israel to urge the new government to work with the Americans and with us to achieve a breakthrough in the peace process. The Israelis told him that they were in favor of peace but would not abide by what the previous Israeli administration agreed to, and then turned the discussion to Iran and its nuclear threat. We made it clear that we disagreed with them. Then they broached the subject of the so-called recognition of Israel as a Jewish state by the Palestinians. The U.S. administration supported the Israeli policy on this point. Israel, as usual, managed to raise controversial but secondary issues, so as to distract the parties from the real effort to reach a settlement. Israel's president, Shimon Peres, took an active interest in the subject despite the fact that his powers do not provide him with any authority in the matter. He told us that he was siding with Egypt and the Palestinians with a full mandate from Netanyahu. Still, progress was impeded because of Israel's determination to officially name Israel as the "Jewish State" and to get the Palestinians to recognize it as such.

While the Israeli prime minister clung to hardline positions, the new U.S. administration returned in June 2009 to suggest to the Arab countries various measures they could take to encourage Israel to resume negotiations. The old rhythm was back again. We met with the Palestinian president in Riyadh in the presence of the foreign ministers of Saudi Arabia, the United Arab Emirates, and Jordan, and we affirmed our position that any steps toward Israel could only be achieved through the Arab Peace Initiative, with Israel fulfilling its side of the deal in accordance with the Roadmap.

I spoke again with Hillary Clinton, the U.S. secretary of state, whose relationship with me and my staff had gradually been consolidating. I told her that the solution was for America to present an integrated vision of a settlement and a framework for the solution. Her response was: you may like some of what we will present, and you may not like some. And I replied that that was okay. Yet she was still talking about the traditional U.S. position of negotiation between the parties, with the U.S. role limited to encouraging agreement. They did not view the concept of the End Game as feasible. In accordance with this policy, the U.S. administration called for a summit in Washington between the two parties, with the participation of the United States, Jordan, and Egypt, and it was agreed to return to negotiations. However, everything stopped once again when Israel resumed building settlements. We asked again for the Americans to pressure Israel. Some senior administration officials told us that they were convinced that Prime Minister Netanyahu would make no concessions to the Palestinians. President Obama felt the same way.

We wanted to emphasize the importance of an agreement on the border between the two countries, which would determine the status of the lands under their respective territories. This would also resolve the issue of settlements, as Israel would not be able to build on any land beyond its recognized borders. Israel continued to maneuver—its permanent strategy. If they were feeling too much pressure, they need only ask the United States not to go beyond specific lines that Israel considered vitally damaging to its interests, and the United States would stop.

It has always been my conviction, as a result of my participation in many negotiations, that the unity of the Palestinians is the key to success. It is the only way that the Palestinians and their negotiators will succeed in persuading the Israelis that the only solution is for Israel to accept the basic elements of the Palestinian vision. Otherwise, the conflict will drag on indefinitely, with serious consequences for the stability of the Middle East. On the other hand, I also believe in the necessity of moving and not allowing the situation to freeze, because stagnation will enable Israel to seize the West Bank and unilaterally impose a decades-long settlement.

What remains here is to briefly address the Egyptian–Israeli relations. I say it loud and clear: Any serious and sophisticated relationship with Israel will be governed mainly by what happens with the Palestinian problem. If things go well and the Palestinian state emerges, the Egyptian–Israeli relationship will improve. If things remain the same or the relations between the Palestinians and the Israelis deteriorate, Egypt's relations with Israel, regardless of the peace treaty, will also suffer. It is also essential for Egypt to try to separate the Egyptian–American relationship from Egypt's ties with Israel. This we have tried to do, by all available means, over the years, but both the Americans and the Israelis endlessly worked against it. This has become clear whenever the Egyptian–Israeli relationship was unusually complicated, or whenever Israel wanted something from Egypt: Israel would pressure Washington to intervene on its behalf. The Americans have repeatedly asked us to adopt positions that we had categorically rejected, thus complicating our relationship with them. As a result, Egypt has always sought to separate the Egyptian–American relationship and protect it from the ongoing tricks of Israel.

# 13

# CHALLENGES OF THE
# FINAL FORTY-FIVE DAYS

The second Arab economic summit ended routinely in Sharm al-Sheikh on January 19, 2011 without achieving substantial results. President Mubarak went to the airport to bid farewell to some of the leaders who decided to leave the same night. I was standing with General Omar Suleiman, head of the General Intelligence Service, discussing the conference and the calls for large, peaceful demonstrations on January 25 in Tahrir Square that had been propagated on social media sites. I asked him if he had informed the president about these events. He said that he did not want to bother him during the two days of the summit but that it was time to present the situation to him. We approached the president, who was standing alone on the tarmac, and Omar Suleiman told him that he had an important subject that needed to be discussed, referring to the news about the coming demonstrations on January 25. The president did not show much interest and his comments revealed that he did not really care, but he did not reveal whether Omar Suleiman was the first to talk to him about this matter or whether he had been informed earlier by the Egyptian Interior Ministry. Omar Suleiman suggested holding a meeting with the leaders of the main government agencies to discuss the subject and establish procedures in case something needed to be done. The president showed no sign that he was worried about how the situation might develop, though the events in Tunisia had happened just a few days earlier.

I thought the president's reaction was quite strange. On the flight back to Cairo that same night, I told Omar Suleiman that the president did not seem bothered at all by the coming events, and that maybe it was his extended experience in ruling the country that made him confident about handling these challenges. I added that his unaffected attitude actually made me more worried. Suleiman replied that he would give him more information that evening after we arrived in Cairo, to try to get him to take more interest.

The days passed heavily between January 19 and 25. I remained in contact with the president as usual, passing along to him all the incoming foreign policy information that required his attention. I attended more than one meeting where the president hosted foreign guests. The president never talked about the planned demonstrations.

The demonstrations did in fact take place on Tuesday, January 25. I called the president on Wednesday, January 26 to ask for his permission to travel to the African Summit in Addis Ababa the following day. The president said that he was not going to allow the prime minister to travel to the summit to head the Egyptian delegation, as previously decided. Therefore, I was to head the Egyptian delegation and to come back on January 31, or at the end of the summit if it ended earlier. I did not talk to him about the January 25 demonstrations and he sounded very calm during the call. I thought that his decision to cancel the prime minister's trip to Addis Ababa three or four days before the African Summit revealed his concern about the situation.

I traveled to the summit and followed the events in Egypt through phone calls with Omar Suleiman. He informed me on the evening of January 28 that the situation had become very grave in Cairo. Things had got out of the control of the Interior Ministry, and the army had been deployed to restore order, in accordance with the plans that had been prepared. Suleiman had been chair of the Military Plans Branch in the Operations Division of the Armed Forces for years, and had often talked about his role in preparing the army's emergency plans for internal situations such as the January 28 demonstrations. When Prime Minister Ahmed Nazif and his cabinet were dismissed and General Ahmed Shafiq was asked to form a new cabinet, I informed Cairo that I would return on January 30, a day before the summit ended, so as to allow the new prime minister to choose the new foreign affairs minister. I did not know at the time that the president had directed the newly appointed prime minister him to keep me as foreign minister, as was later announced.

During my stay in Addis Ababa, I received two phone calls from Hillary Clinton, the U.S. secretary of state, inquiring about the situation in Egypt. Except for what Omar Suleiman had said during my several calls to him, I did not have much to tell her. Clinton referred to the importance of dealing wisely with the situation and letting the peaceful demonstrations run their course. She also added that the president needed to announce measures, which she did not specify, in order to avert a possible crisis. I promised her I would deliver her message to Cairo. I told Omar Suleiman everything she said, and he replied that the Americans were contacting all authorities in Egypt to express their views.

I informed the office of the president and his secretary of information of my arrival in the evening and did not attempt to present any reports about the African Summit. I did send him a brief report about it on the morning of January 31. The same night, I stood near my house in Heliopolis with some of the people who joined the popular committees, which were forming at the time to provide security in various neighborhoods in the city. In the morning I was informed that I must be at the Ittihadiya Palace before 11:00 am to participate in the swearing-in of the new cabinet. Up to that point, I had not talked to the incoming prime minister, Ahmed Shafiq. I met him in the palace that morning. He was extremely busy convincing some of the people he had chosen to join the government and to accept the ministerial positions they were offered, and the chief of staff of the president's office was helping him.

I met Vice-President Omar Suleiman in front of the outer stairs of the side gate of the palace; he had arrived a few moments before. I was astonished that he did not use the main gate of the palace as the president does, but I did not comment on this. I learned from the security guard accompanying him that there had been an attempt to shoot him during the previous night in the Roxy area of Heliopolis, which he confirmed to me personally later on. I was deeply disturbed by this news.

As I entered the office of the president's chief of staff on the ground floor of the palace, I noticed that Gamal Mubarak, the president's son, was moving back and forth between the office of the president and that of his chief of staff. That was a strange sight, since the president's son had rarely appeared in the corridors of the palace before. I was sure he was there because of the crisis.

I told Omar Suleiman that the president needed to consider speaking to the nation directly to present a careful and mature analysis of the situation and to announce some concessions that might save the deteriorating situation. The vice-president said he talked to the president all the time, but he was deeply embarrassed about suggesting any course of action, lest the president mistake his intentions and think that he, Omar Suleiman, was seeking personal gains or advantages. I volunteered to talk to the president myself, and maybe to his son, who had obviously imposed his authority on the situation. Suddenly, as I was on my way from Omar Suleiman's office on the first floor to ask to meet with the president, I found myself face to face with Gamal Mubarak. I told him that the situation was dangerous and that the president must speak to the nation to explain it. Gamal replied that he was supervising the preparation of a statement that would be delivered in the evening. I insisted that there should be no delay since the situation had become so grave. The president made the statement late at night, thus losing many of the advantages that could have been achieved had it been made earlier. I must admit here that the interference of more than one hand and more than one way of thinking in the phrasing of all of the president's statements during this crisis definitely had a harmful impact, not only on the way ideas were expressed and their consequent effectiveness, but also, and mainly, in terms of timing, which was characterized by continuous delay and sluggishness.

During the early years of my work as foreign minister, my relationship with Gamal Mubarak did not go beyond that of an important minister and the son of the president, who was said to have wide ambitions to work in politics and maybe to rule the country. This relationship had gradually developed after I saw him on board a British Airways flight from Cairo to London that I had taken en route to Cuba in 2006. Gamal Mubarak sat in front of me and pulled out a book about strategy by Basil Liddell Hart, which I had read in its Arabic translation back in 1964. He said that the book was great and very useful, and we talked for a while about the most important books in this field. I could see he had a real interest in reading, so I suggested some other good books. At the end of the flight, he invited me to join him for lunch in Cairo when I got back, and I accepted. When he accompanied the president on visits to places like Rome, Paris, and Washington, he often talked during the flights about his latest readings, all of which were major books which had had an impact when first published years ago.

At the swearing-in, the president's head chamberlain asked the new and old ministers to line up to enter the hall. This was the third time I had done this since 2004. I noticed that, like the first two times, the president was really uninterested. Then we went to the main meeting hall where the president chaired the first meeting of the new government, which was rather short. Though the president gave some general instructions, which he read from cards prepared by the information secretary, he looked remote and consumed in his own thoughts. He greeted me and asked whether I had anything to tell him about the summit. I briefly replied that I did not have much to say and that it was not different from other summits. The president ended the meeting and left immediately for his office. Though he looked calm, I sensed he was carrying a mountain of worry and pain.

The minister of defense approached me on his way out of the hall. Our relationship was based on mutual respect and affection, and he knew that I was infatuated with the military and that I had always wanted to serve as an officer in the Armed Forces. In our discussions, I often talked about the Egyptian wars with Israel in Sinai or other matters related to regional military security. To me, he was a professional leader who carefully pondered all matters and considered all their angles before making a decision. He asked me, "What do you think about what is happening nowadays in the country?" I replied, "The situation is really dangerous, and all of us need to understand it and deal with it very carefully and delicately." He said sarcastically, "I have heard people talk about the need to use the military to control the situation with force." I replied, "The army does not fire on the people under any circumstances, or it would lose its credibility." "Definitely!" the defense minister, replied as he left the hall.

I spoke more with Omar Suleiman about the attitudes of foreign countries. I told him that I could hear that the United States was speaking in two different voices: that of the White House, which had adopted a strict attitude toward the government in Egypt, and that of Secretary of State Clinton, who was showing some flexibility. He commented that this was the traditional American way of role-distributing.

That same evening, we waited for the statement of the president, which was delayed twice. I fell asleep, and was suddenly awakened by a call from the president's closed-circuit telephone around 2:00 a.m. It was Gamal Mubarak calling. He asked whether I had listened to the president's statement, and I said that I had not been able to keep from falling asleep. He said that the statement was great and that the feedback he had received indicated the presence of a new spirit. I listened to the president's emotional statement.

In the morning, there were rumors that some people intended to demonstrate in support of the president. Egyptian and foreign radio stations talked about a huge demonstration. During the day, I could see from the window of my office in the headquarters of the Ministry of Foreign Affairs a small demonstration led by camels and horses that passed in front of the building toward the Television Building nearby and then approached Tahrir Square. I became anxious; what if the demonstrators started a fight? My son Kamal called, screaming wildly, "How could such a thing be allowed? They are setting the country on fire and the unity of the country will be lost."

I called the vice-president to inform him of what I had seen from my office window, and to tell him that he needed to intervene in any way he could. The phone was answered by his secretary. He said that the vice-president was in extended meetings with some representatives of the opposition. It was then that I realized that it was all over for the president, and that it was only a matter of time before he would have to give up his power. I gave my evaluation of the situation clearly to the vice-president on February 2 or 3. He listened quietly and said that he too could see this, but his position dictated that he could not appear as if he was pushing the president out of power, so as not to give him the impression that he was seeking any personal advantage. The truth was that all he wanted was to achieve peace and quiet for the country and bring it out of that dark crisis.

Once again the days passed heavily. I was summoned to the president's office several times to take part in meetings with foreign ministers and envoys of various countries. The president looked calm but deeply affected by the crowds of people in the streets. Omar Suleiman, on the other hand, was consulting groups from the opposition to find a way out of the crisis. Meanwhile, the revolution went on. I was asked to give an interview for Al Arabiya television by presenter Randa Abul Azm, and I agreed; it was aired on February 7. She asked what I thought were the reasons for the revolution going on in the Egyptian cities. I gave several reasons: the president's advanced age, which weakened his decisiveness; the growth of Gamal Mubarak's power; and the constant speculation about his desire to rule after his father, or even during his father's lifetime. I would add here that the president had come to depend on, or even to submit to, the opinions of his son, who was always with him, both in the palace and at home. This had become obvious to me when in a previous conversation with the president I suggested to him the need to take certain measures to address popular demands and to demonstrate that the government was attentive to public opinion. The president's response to my proposals had been: "Talk to Gamal."

Of course, I did not talk to Gamal about these proposals. As Gamal's power and authority expanded, talk of his possible ascension to the presidency became incessant. I was adamantly opposed to this idea, which was a sentiment that I shared with Omar Suleiman during our long flights alone. After much observation and reflection, I had come to the conclusion that there had been an attempt to impose the president's son as ruler of the country. This attempt would have surely failed if it had been made after the death of the president, because the Armed Forces and the majority of the national security agencies would never have agreed, and they would have been backed by the people. Had the president attempted to impose his son on the country during his rule, the situation would have been dangerous too. I told Omar Suleiman that I would not continue work if that happened, and he said that he would not either. He added that the situation would then depend on the minister of defense. He said, "They want to get rid of me and the minister of defense, and they have already tried, and it will not be the last attempt." I sensed that, by "they,"

Omar Suleiman was alluding to the president's wife and some of the other people surrounding him.

Every time the name of the president's son was mentioned as a successor, the president would absolutely deny any such intentions. I used to send him any communications we received from our missions about this subject, especially when they mentioned the resistance of the public and the Armed Forces. One day, I was surprised to hear him say unreservedly, "Do they think I am crazy enough to put my son, my own son, in such a position, such a prison? Impossible!" Despite this, I believe that all indications led to the conclusion that the president's son was seeking to build up a political base that would make it possible for him to assume authority at any moment. I saw members of the Cabinet talking to him as if he were either the next president or the one who had the authority and power to get their decisions approved. They sought his support because the president often listened to his point of view, except in matters of personnel appointments, which he reserved for himself.

Throughout my years as foreign minister, I worked just as any Egyptian foreign minister should, through a direct channel to the president of the country and no one else, and through constant coordination with national security agencies, never indulging in partisan alliances with other ministers and major officials. In 2005, Dr. Ahmed Nazif had been reappointed as prime minister, one year after his initial appointment. In this second cabinet, I started to notice the presence of some politically competing currents or camps, or even personal competitions. I did not pay much attention to such matters, though I did keep an eye on them so as not to allow them to influence our foreign policy in any way. In 2010, when the president was forcefully denying that he wanted to see his son ruling the country, I once suggested that he might encourage his son to seek public elected office, which would take him away from the policy committee within the ruling National Democratic Party. For example, Gamal could perhaps run for a seat in the People's Assembly or Shura Council for the Heliopolis constituency. I was surprised by the president's reply: "That's a terrible idea! They would cut him into pieces; don't you know what happens in the Assembly?" I kept silent about it after that.

In my analysis of the situation for the Al Arabiya television interview, I mentioned that the elections for the People's Assembly in October 2010 had contributed greatly to the anger of all the political forces that were denied representation and political presence, since the ruling party had received almost all the votes. I did not mention in this interview that I was talking to the president's chief of staff during the second round of these elections, and he also expressed great concern about the ruling party's predominance in Parliament. I suggested that he should tell the president about this justified concern. He replied that he did not want to be subjected to the hostility of the president's son, since the president told him everything.

I happened to be in the palace the day on which the second round of the results of the parliamentary elections were announced. I was attending the ceremony during which the president receives the credentials of some foreign ambassadors. I casually brought up the danger of the domination of a single party in the People's Assembly, and hinted that the president might find it advisable to take steps to address that critical situation. I tried to express indirectly my deep concern and the reasons for caution. This was my usual style whenever I talked to the president about matters that did not directly relate to my responsibilities, knowing that he could always sense what I wanted to convey to him. What I had in mind in this case was to annul the second-round results in order to find a way to make room for the other political parties. He calmly answered that the opposition parties were "cartoon" parties with no power or influence and that he could not give them seats in Parliament just to keep up a good appearance; they must be capable of earning the seats themselves.

In the interview for Al Arabiya television I also mentioned that the performance of the Egyptian police had become provocative to all Egyptians. I did not mention, though, that even my sons and I, like the rest of the citizens of the country, were sometimes subjected to the harassment of police officers, who behaved like little gods in the Egyptian streets. Some of them were corrupt and indulged in favoritism.

The Egyptian government had also been unable to deal with many of the problems of its people, despite its strong economic performance. Furthermore, the growing political alliance between capital and those in

power resulted in a general impression that the system had become corrupt, which, given my status as foreign minister, I was not in a position to
verify. The media often discussed this impression of wrongdoing, but neither the government nor the president did anything to counter it.

The interviewer finally came to the moment of truth and I was asked
the hard question: "How can the country get out of this impasse?" I
answered that the president had prepared a roadmap, according to which
the vice-president was to take over authority and presidential elections
were to be held within six months, thus keeping the state stable and the
society in balance. However, if things continued on the current revolutionary road, the Armed Forces would have to take control of the situation in
order to secure the safety of the country, in accordance with its national
responsibility. Some people misinterpreted what I said as threatening to
unleash the army on the revolution, which was not at all what I meant. All I
ever wanted was the stability and well-being of my country.

As the decisive moment approached, I learned that the president was
planning to give an address on Thursday, February 10 to announce that
he was stepping down and handing over his authority to Vice-President
Omar Suleiman for a transitional period. During the preceding days,
there had been continuous pressures on the president that led him to
that decision. We waited for the statement, which was delayed. When
it finally came, it was confused and did not offer a clear-cut end to the
problem, which intensified everyone's anger. I believed that the phrasing
of the statement was an attempt on the part of the president's son to beat
around the bush.

Early on the morning of Friday, February 11, I called the vice-president and the prime minister and asked them to consider holding a meeting
of the national security group in order to discuss the situation and to send
a message to the people about the presence of a governmental authority,
despite the president's inconclusive statement of the previous evening and
his imminent departure to Sharm al-Sheikh. I had been informed by Omar
Suleiman that the president was to leave before the noon prayer. The prime
minister asked me to go to Ittihadiya Palace at 1:00 p.m. to take part in the
meeting, which I had advised them to hold earlier.

The presidential guards had closed all the roads leading to the palace, and I found it very difficult to reach it. For the first time, I noticed a number of citizens standing by the barbed-wire and iron barriers, shouting against Mubarak's rule. I managed to enter through the main gate, normally used only by the president. I came to the conclusion that things had really changed and that Mubarak's rule was completely overthrown.

Before entering the interior hall, I encountered the prime minister, who said that the palace was in danger of being stormed and that the guard forces were advising everyone to leave immediately. He invited me to go to the Presidential Guard headquarters near the palace. There I found the vice-president, who had left the palace earlier, and the minister of interior, who said that the president had already left for Sharm al-Sheikh at 11:00 a.m. and that his family were to catch up with him in two hours. Omar Suleiman then called the president as we stood there. The president told him to inform the minister of defense, Field Marshal Mohamed Hussein Tantawi, that he was now in charge of the affairs of the state. Thus the vice-president realized that his role had ended too. He called the field marshal, and I understood from Suleiman's side of their conversation that Tantawi was cautious about implicating the army in this matter. The vice-president then called the president and asked him to call the field marshal and give him instructions himself. The vice-president continued to serve as an intermediary, calling each of the men in turn. It was finally settled that the vice-president and the prime minister would go to the headquarters of the Ministry of Defense to settle the matter. They would declare that the president had relinquished his powers and assigned the military council to run the state.

The declaration was postponed because of the delay of the departure of the president's family. I went out of the gate of the Presidential Guard headquarters with the vice-president and the prime minister at 6:30 p.m. to find thousands of Egyptian youth and families celebrating the moment. I thought apprehensively about the unknown future and went back to work.

On the morning of Monday, February 14, I received a phone call from Field Marshal Tantawi, asking me very gently to meet him whenever it was convenient for me. I replied that I would be glad to see him at whatever time and place he set. We met on the first floor of the headquarters of the Ministry of Defense in the room next to his office at 12:00 p.m. He said that he hoped I would continue to serve as foreign minister, but also wanted me to be the Military Council's advisor for foreign affairs. I said that I had always performed whatever task I was assigned with the spirit of a soldier fighting for his country, and assured him that I would always do my very best despite the hard conditions and the unknown future that the whole country was facing.

I left the office for my apartment in Heliopolis; my wife had returned from her family's house in Qaha in Qalyubiya Governorate, where she had spent the days of the revolution. She said that she and many of her relatives and friends believed that it was time for me to resign my position, to allow the Military Council to choose their own foreign minister. I told her that the field marshal and the Military Council wanted me to continue doing my job. What was more important to me, I told her, was my feeling that I did not run away from my responsibilities or abandon ship in the time of danger, which I expected would continue for long months, or even years. I told her a story that I had always found amazing. It was based on a shot from actual recorded footage of the sinking of a heavy German cruiser under the leadership of Admiral Graf Spee in the waters near the Falkland Islands in the South Atlantic Ocean in 1915, after a fierce battle with British battleships. Four or five of the German sailors stood on the surface of the sinking cruiser, which had capsized and was sinking to the bottom of the ocean, carrying the flag of imperial Germany. They never left the flag; they went with it to the bottom and drowned. It was a story of sacrifice for the sake of one's country and it touched a chord for me; I felt that I must not run away from my duty until it was the right time to be released from it.

My work continued under very difficult circumstances. A ministerial reshuffle took place and a new cabinet was formed. Prime Minister Ahmed Shafiq said that some of the new ministers had asked that I be dismissed from my position. I replied that I received my assignments from the Military Council, which was the only authority that could remove me from service. I decided to present a lecture about Egyptian foreign policy and the challenges that it would face in the coming years. I spoke for an hour in that first meeting of the council. After the lecture, those who had wanted to end my term expressed their deep appreciation for the information, news, and analysis I shared with them, about which they could have had no idea when they were not yet members of the Cabinet. Even after that, there were more requests that I end my term, along with other leading ministers. The situation of the German sailors always comes into my mind again, and I come to the conclusion that the whole cabinet, not just a few other ministers and me, would probably not last for long anyway; that was one of the features of revolutions everywhere.

On February 13, I received a letter from the prosecutor general asking me to address the judicial authorities in the many countries that wanted to freeze the accounts of a number of senior Egyptian government officials. The letter was dated February 12, the day after the president stepped down. I assigned the necessary work to my office and to other departments of the ministry. I replied to the letter of the prosecutor general on February 14, 2011 telling him that the Ministry of Foreign Affairs had contacted all the foreign embassies in Cairo and informed them about his request. On the same day, we also informed all Egyptian embassies and missions in the relevant countries to contact the authorities there to freeze these accounts.

The prosecutor general sent a separate request to freeze any property and accounts of the president and all his family members that might be in foreign countries. I took the necessary action immediately, and informed his office the next day that the job was done. We soon began to receive replies from all these countries through their embassies in Cairo or our missions abroad. I feel that it is important to register these facts here as a reply to the many people who have accused the Foreign Affairs Ministry of failing to do what was required in this respect. Such an accusation, of course, has nothing to do with the truth; I appreciated the seriousness of this matter and the fact that it was likely to become a major issue in the future. I kept copies of all the correspondence about the procedures followed in collaboration with the prosecutor general in order to immobilize the possessions of anyone who was accused of illegal acts.

The main crisis I faced during the few weeks between the start of the Libyan civil war on February 17 until I left the Ministry of Foreign Affairs on March 5 was securing the safety of hundreds of thousands of Egyptians who wanted to leave Libya safely. The Ministry of Foreign Affairs formed a very efficient working group to supervise their transport by air, sea, and land. That required a great effort that revealed the true character of the Egyptian diplomats and administrative officials in Benghazi, Tripoli, Tunis, and Cairo.

Egyptians were accused by Qadhafi's men, especially his son Saif al-Islam, of being involved in the armed rebellion. I issued a press release ridiculing these accusations and warning the government and the ruling authorities in Libya against harming Egyptians, and they got the message. I was extremely cautious in handling this crisis. When a meeting of the Council of Arab Ministers proposed to the UN Security Council to intervene against the government in Libya, I strictly refused. My main concern was not to expose the Egyptian community in Libya to any reprisals from Qadhafi.

During this period, I received a call from the minister of finance, Samir Radwan, who was having difficulty providing $250 million for Egypt's purchases of gas. Five ships were already in the Egyptian ports, he said, and the Saudi company that owned the shipment was requesting full payment before unloading. I called Prince Sa'ud al-Faisal, but he was not available, so I called Prince Muqrin bin Abdulaziz, the head of Saudi intelligence, and Prince Bandar bin Sultan, both of whom were in Morocco with the Saudi king. I described the problem to them and hoped that the king would give the five shipments to Egypt as a gift. In less than two hours, all three princes called back to say that there was only one gas shipment in the port in the Red Sea and that King Abdullah had decided to give it as a gift to Egypt. That was a generous gesture from Saudi Arabia during the hard time Egypt was passing through.

By the end of February 2011, I had completed the work of the Arab Ministerial Meeting. Around 10:00 p.m., I received a call at home from the former secretary of the president, saying that the president wanted to talk to me. That was the only call I received from him after he stepped down. He asked about what was going on in Libya. We talked for a few moments. He said that Qadhafi would resist and give everyone a hard time because he was obstinate, hard-hearted, and malicious. The call ended and I was carried away by thoughts and distant memories.

# CONCLUSION: CHALLENGES OF THE PAST AND THE FUTURE

I served as minister of foreign affairs for almost seven years. I shouldered the same responsibilities that were borne by the previous foreign ministers who had worked with President Mubarak since October 1981: Kamal Hassan Ali, Esmat Abdel Meguid, Amr Moussa, and Ahmed Maher. I think that all of them sensed how cautious the president was in dealing with Egyptian foreign policy issues. He was careful not to take risks and sought to examine every aspect of a subject carefully, even if this led to delays in making a decision or addressing an issue. I had witnessed this approach to administering Egypt's foreign policy since the earliest days of Mubarak's presidency, which had coincided with the Israeli invasion of Lebanon in June 1982. Israel had just completed its withdrawal from the Sinai several weeks earlier, which was perhaps the reason for Egypt's extremely cautious approach in addressing this enormous crisis. However, the general caution in engaging with foreign relations continued after that. When a crisis erupted in Sudan, including the outbreak of the second civil war between northern and southern, we moved cautiously in addressing that situation too. Then two further incidents happened: the hijacking of the cruise ship *Achille Lauro* in the Mediterranean and an EgyptAir flight to Malta. These crises were managed under the direct supervision of President Mubarak, and it became apparent to me that Egypt's approach had not improved much since the crisis of the assassination of Yusuf al-Siba'i and the killing of Egyptian soldiers in Cyprus in 1978.

Then the Iraqi invasion of Kuwait happened in 1990. During this crisis, Egypt gave up its traditional caution and emerged as the major influential power in the region. With the end of that crisis in 1991, Cairo began to take an active role in influencing the policies of the region. This was not achieved through confrontations or threats of war, nor was it achieved by seeking to impose on Israel a settlement to the Palestinian crisis that was based on the Arab perspective. Rather, we sought to reach a political settlement through negotiations, an approach that the Arab world had adopted as its strategic choice in addressing the Arab–Israeli conflict.

By 2002, I could see from New York, where I was serving as Egypt's permanent representative to the UN, that Egypt had given up some of its leading role. The Saudi crown prince Abdullah, not Egypt, introduced the Arab Peace Initiative that was adopted by the Arabs at the Beirut Summit in 2002. Meanwhile, Egypt was unsuccessful in its attempt to pass a proposal to reform the Arab League and improve inter-Arab cooperation at the Arab Summit in Tunis in 2004. Today, I honestly believe that at that time, Egypt began to be preoccupied with the question of the presidential succession, since the president was over seventy-five and his interests were moving in other directions. From 2004 to 2011, I noticed that, as the president got older, he became less inclined to travel abroad. Even his readiness to engage in political, economic, cultural, or philosophical discussions grew weaker. He managed situations and made decisions based on his extensive experience and his intimate knowledge of Egyptian domestic matters and the Arab situation. I realized he was not like the Chinese leader Deng Xiaoping, who transformed China through great advances and launched a new revolution that equaled what Mao Zedong had done. President Mubarak was not like Lee Kuan Yew, the leader of Singapore who imposed changes on his people with an iron fist in order to implement his reform programs, nor was he like Mahathir Mohamad, the leader of Malaysia, who carried out a deep reform program like a dictator, but with the consent and participation of the whole community.

Egypt failed where Korea and Malaysia succeeded. It was said that the Egyptian people were different from the peoples of East Asia, who were bound by a system of values and religion that made them sanctify work, discipline, self-denial, readiness to emulate, openness to others, and the ability to benefit from the experience of others. To these claims I would reply that this is a haughty and racist point of view. These Asian nations, which are now described as "the emerging tigers" and whose growing economic strength shifted the balance of economic and military power to the east at the beginning of the twenty-first century, had been described by the west in the first half of the twentieth century as "the sleeping people" for more than two centuries.

Hence the conclusion: progress is achieved by studying the experiences of others, and taking the road toward progress and modernity while taking into consideration the particularities of the people. The president did not realize that ruling for long decades would necessarily end by either death, failure, or the fall of the regime by revolution. He did not take into account that his son's succession to the presidency could never happen in an open world in the wake of the information revolution that transformed our age.

The president did not read the fate of Tito, Franco, Salazar, Marcos, Suharto, and many others, and he was not supported by a party that possessed a clear vision for the future and a philosophy of development. Therefore, even the minimum needs of the society—the eradication of illiteracy, which affects 40 percent of the population, and the rule of justice and law for all—could not be met.

I often talked about the situation in Egypt with people whose ethics I trusted, like my friend Ambassador Suleiman Awad. In 1998, we had many discussions about the failure of comprehensive development in Egypt while other nations had succeeded in achieving progress and development. We believed that the absence of a philosophic vision of governance was the reason behind that failure. Instead of introducing to our people a new value system as other leaders did, we focused solely on infrastructure. For decades the president concentrated on statistics of electricity and cement production, construction of industrial areas and highways throughout the country, and so on, while insufficient attention was paid to building Egypt's human capital through education, fighting corruption, the rule of law, and community participation in governance. As mentioned before, we failed to eradicate illiteracy and to carry out strict projects of population control. Perhaps because I have repeatedly read Arnold Toynbee's encyclopedia *A Study of History*, I have always wondered why Japan succeeded while Egypt failed, especially since we started before the Japanese. Was this failure due to being closer to the west and in a continuous clash with it since the advent of Islam? Japan, on the other hand, was always ready to emulate and transfer all that was western as long as it did not undermine the Japanese personality. I had many questions and explanations for what happened, though discussing them might be out of context in this short conclusion to this book. To be honest, a serious analysis of this crucial question would, in my opinion, reveal how to connect Egypt better to the advanced world, and prevent it from stagnating or diminishing.

I must go back to the concept of Egyptian foreign policy during the age of President Mubarak, especially its final years. Egyptian diplomacy was constrained by many of the transformative developments that occurred in the early twenty-first century and the emergence of new concepts in international affairs. Themes such as good governance, transparency, democracy, and human rights had come to dominate global discussions. Egypt was also struggling to achieve economic development that would ensure that it would become part of an international economic system led by the western world with its vast network of information that was freely available. We were also locked in an unceasing race in which every Asian and African country sought to achieve development and growth. The Saudi GDP was twice that of Egypt, with only half the population; the Turkish GDP was four times that of Egypt with almost the same population. All similar comparisons led to the same conclusions: frail policies, lack of firmness, lack of resources, and the absence of a philosophical vision led to a general feeling that Egypt's foreign policy was not achieving the desired goal of representing Egypt as an effective and influential country.

The truth is that Egyptian foreign policy was an honest and authentic reflection of the internal Egyptian conditions. In spite of this, it managed to maintain an effective presence with very limited resources. Despite all the restrictions, Egyptian foreign policy secured a major role for Egypt on the regional and international levels that only an ungrateful person could deny, and it did this without taking risks that could have wasted its resources, except when the good of its people was at stake.

During these years, Egypt was often compared to other countries. Much has been said about Iran and its influence on the policies of the region, but those who admired Iran were listening only to its confrontational statements that challenged and defined the west. They were blind to the international isolation and the economic hardships that caused such suffering in the Islamic Republic.

Some Egyptian elites looked up to Turkey with a great deal of admiration. The Turks were having diplomatic battles with Israel and were moving to build coalitions with Syria, Jordan, Libya, and other countries. Many of the elites thought Egypt should emulate the vigor and vitality of Turkish foreign policy, but they failed to notice Turkey's rising economic strength and the consequent search for markets for its products. That was the real source of the Turkish awakening. Nor did these critics pay attention to the existing influences on Turkey: NATO and its strategic policies, and the west in general.

Some Egyptians wanted to build Egyptian pride by returning to the policies of confronting Israel. I was of the opinion that we must defend vital Egyptian interests in the face of any country. The decisive criterion here, though, was taking care of our own vital interests and not those of other regional countries. We needed to hold on to the general framework of peace with Israel as long as it did not pose any direct or indirect threat of any kind to Egyptian national security.

Throughout my seven years as foreign affairs minister, Egypt's internal tensions led to attempts from within Egypt to undervalue its attitudes and policies. Hence came the accusations that Egypt was responsible for the division of Sudan, the fragmentation of Somalia, and even the occupation of Iraq. The voices that made these claims did not take into consideration that Egypt, with its limited resources that could not even meet the needs of its people, was not a superpower that could shoulder all the responsibilities of the Arab, Islamic, and African states in the region.

Since the revolution of January 25, 2011, many people have talked about a new foreign policy for Egypt. In this context, I must reply that Egypt's history, geography, culture, and regional role have imposed stable attitudes and policies on the country for dozens, if not hundreds, of years.

Arab, Islamic, Christian, African, Asian, and Mediterranean Egypt has been a melting pot, assimilating other civilizations, interacting with the western world, and always open to others. Egypt has always competed for status and a commanding role in the vast region that extends from Iran in the east to Morocco in the west, and from the Mediterranean coasts in the north to the shores of Lake Victoria and the Great Lakes in the middle of the African continent in the south.

To conclude, I have to say that for a great country like Egypt, its international and regional status and the effectiveness of its foreign policy cannot be maximized unless it first achieves comprehensive successes domestically. Once this is done, Egypt will easily find its effectiveness and ability to influence its neighbors and the whole region. However, if Egypt does not adjust its outlook or decides to go back to timeworn policies as a means of salvation, it will only find itself bogged down in populism, demagoguery, lies, deceit, and maybe even clashes with regional or international enemies in a bid for status and authority. Neither status nor authority can be achieved except through change, hard work, perseverance, and commitment to a system of fair and objective laws that apply equally to all Egyptians without distinction.

The belief, held by some commentators, that Egypt must make significant changes to its traditional attitudes, policies, and orientations will only lead to more wasted potential and resources and will not achieve the desired goals. The elements that govern the current international equation will not change overnight, but over decades, if ever.

I must add here that taking unconsidered chances or relying on improvisation will always cause us to pay dearly. We have many examples to learn from in our policies from the 1960s and mistakes that we should never repeat. We should understand the timeless adage: no permanent enemies, no eternal friendships, but definitely everlasting and constant concern for the long-term welfare of the people of Egypt. Their interests will be best served by a mature foreign policy that is certain of its objectives and aware of the limits of its resources.

Finally, it is my great hope that this book will achieve its desired goal of informing those interested in Egyptian affairs about the implementation of

Egyptian foreign policy during the harsh period of the last years of President Mubarak's rule. I hope readers can benefit from the lessons and attitudes that formed the Egyptian vision all those years, so as to preserve the vital interests and the national security of the country that all of us Egyptians love.

# INDEX

25 January Revolution 144, 402, 441–54, 459–60; 11 February 2011 450; Ittihadiya Palace 450–51; Mubarak's statements 446, 450–51; Tunisia 441; *see also* Ministry of Interior; People's Assembly elections 2010; Supreme Council of the Armed Forces

Abbas, Mahmoud 129–30, 337, 389, 416, 417, 418, 420, 426, 428
Abdel Meguid, Esmat 12, 13, 63–64, 65, 81–83, 84, 86–87, 243
Abd al-Nasser, Gamal 9, 19, 20, 23, 25
Abdul Aziz, King Abdullah bin 454, 318–19, 322, 323, 324, 331, 332, 337–38, 392
Abdulaziz, Prince Muqrin bin 454
Abul-Naga, Fayza 31, 32, 178, 202, 225–26, 229, 230–31
Aboul Gheit, Ahmed; Cyprus diplomatic mission 52, 54–56; Military Technical College 48–49; Russian diplomatic mission 50, 52, 63–63, 67–71, 374; *Witness to War and Peace* 2, 56, 59, 66, 84, 85, 407; *see*

*also* Cyprus; *al-Musawwar*; Salah, Laila Kamal al-Din
Abou Zeid, Mahmoud 196, 206, 207–208
Abu Mazen *see* Abbas, Mahmoud
Afghanistan 360–61
Africa: relations with Egypt 26–27, 90, 101, 178–79, 180–81, 200, 243–259
African Union (AU) 175–76, 77, 82, 183–84, 185, 189–90, 249, 258–59, 267–68, 272; Abuja summit (2005) 178–79, 181, Ezulwini Consensus 179–88; Sirte conference (July 2005) 182–83, 258–59, 298; summits 253, 255 257–58; *see also* Burundi; Common Market for Eastern and Southern Africa (COMESA); Egyptian Fund for Technical Cooperation with Africa (EFTCA); Kohare, Omar; New Partnership for Africa's Development (NEPAD); Nigeria; Nile Valley; Rwanda; South Africa; Sudan; Tanzania; Uganda; UN Security Council
Akol, Lam 266, 268

Algeria 179, 181–82; 2010 FIFA World
　Cup match 334–225; relations
　with Egypt 335–36; *see also* New
　Partnership for Africa's Develop-
　ment (NEPAD)
Ali, Hassan Kamal 39, 67, 72, 73–74,
　76, 77, 78–79, 80–81, 82–83,
　325–26
Allam, Mohamed Nasr Eldin 208,
　209–210, 214, 221
Al Thani, Hamad bin Jassim bin Jaber
　270, 294, 405, 406
Annan, Kofi 175–76, 221, 268
al-Arabi, Nabil 100, 215, 266, 377,
　401–402
Arab Peace Initiative 323, 398, 404,
　418, 419, 421, 430, 438, 456
Arafat, Yasser 24, 76, 85, 106, 414–15;
　death 129, 415–16;
al-Assad, Bashar 121, 295, 296, 305–
　306, 307–309, 314, 308, 320–22,
　329, 331–32, 333–34,
　337, 338, 390
Atatürk, Mustafa Kemal 47, 72
Awad, Suleiman 109, 110, 155, 186,
　187, 189, 401, 457

Bahrain 292, 320; see also Forum for
　the Future; Gulf Cooperation
　Council (GCC)
Baker, James 86, 221
Barak, Ehud 387, 432
Barcelona Declaration *see* Union for
　Mediterranean (UfM)
Barcelona Process *see* Union for Medi-
　terranean (UfM)
al-Bashir, Omar 37, 98, 99–100, 189,
　198, 199, 264–68, 271, 272–74, 275,
　276, 279, 284, 285, 288, 289; *see also*
　International Criminal Court
El-Baz, Osama 29–31, 65, 66, 84
Berlusconi, Silvio 92, 370–71
Biden, Joe 357, 358

Boutros-Ghali, Boutros 26–27, 33, 66,
　67, 74, 78, 87, 170, 178, 244–45;
　"An Agenda for Peace" 170–71 173
Brazil 103, 171, 183–84, 190–91, 376;
　*see also* BRIC; IBSA Forum; UN
　Security Council
BRIC 104, 190, 376; South Africa 104;
　*see also* Brazil; China; India, Russia
Britain 100, 172, 192, 312, 353, 395,
　403; British Empire 19–20;
　occupation of Egypt 203, 304;
　relations with Egypt 104, 372; *see
　also* Group of Eight Industrialized
　Nations (G8); Nile Valley: 1929
　Agreement; UN Security Council
Broader Middle East initiative 128,
　143–44, 150
Burundi 208, 214–15, 217, 218,
　224–25; *see also* Nile Valley
Bush, George H.W.: administration 84,
　119, 150, 146
Bush, George W. 118, 159, 124, 134,
　143, 150, 153, 319, 431; adminis-
　tration 124, 125, 134, 145–47, 148,
　153, 154, 167, 388, 399, 408–409,
　418, 428–29, 431, 436; Bright
　Stars maneuvers 120, 428–29, 431;
　State of the Union 2005 148; State
　of the Union 2006 148; *see also*
　Broader Middle East initiative

Camp David Accords 64, 66, 67, 74,
　118, 125, 153, 341, 391
Canada 400; *see also* Group of Eight
　Industrialized Nations (G8)
Central Intelligence Agency (CIA) 36,
　168, 408–409
Chad 260, 266, 270, 271, 274, 280
Cheney, Dick 133–34, 137, 150
Cheney, Liz 143–44, 150
China 28, 126, 154, 171–72, 188, 363,
　373, 375, 456; relations with
　Egypt 42, 78, 188, 280, 375; *see*

*also* BRIC; Forum on China-Africa Cooperation; UN Security Council

Clinton, Hillary 154, 156–50, 164, 165, 156, 157, 158, 287, 358, 361, 406, 436, 438, 443, 446

Cold War 20, 55, 170, 362, 382

Colin Powell 105–106, 118–21, 127, 128, 261, 297

Common Market for Eastern and Southern Africa (COMESA) 197, 199, 245, 247, 249

Congo 207, 208, 209, 217; *see also* Kabila, Joseph

Cyprus: coup d'état 63; Israeli influence 56

Denmark 363–64; anti-Prophet Muhammad cartoons 343, 364–65; Egyptian ambassador to Copenhagen 364; *see also* Rasmussen, Lars

Dlamini-Zuma, Nkosazana Clarice 252

Egypt: Christian population 365, 367–68; GNP 28; human rights 481–83; state of emergency 381–82; *see also* Egyptian Air Force; Egyptian Armed Forces; Egyptian Fund for Technical Cooperation with Africa (EFTCA), Egyptian General Intelligence; Egyptian Ministry of Interior; Egyptian Ministry of Irrigation; The General Company For Research & Ground Water (REGWA); Mubarak, Hosni; People's Assembly

Egyptian Air Force 44–45; Royal Air Force 44–4

Egyptian Armed Forces 36, 45–46; presence in Sudan 265, 268–69; *see also* Egyptian Air Force; Supreme Council of the Armed Forces

Egyptian Fund for Technical Cooperation with Africa (EFTCA) 27, 181, 244, 247–48, 250–51, 256, 259

Egyptian General Intelligence 34–38, 62, 108, 168, 219, 223–24, 228, 229, 255–56, 263, 269, 275–76, 299, 301, 321, 322, 326, 332, 368; Israel 386, 408–409, 437–38; *see also* Ali, Kamal Hassan; National Security Council; Suleiman, Omar

Egyptian Ministry of Interior 442, 449

Egyptian Ministry of Irrigation 195, 196, 205; *see also* Abou Zeid, Mahmoud; Allam, Mohamed Nasr Eldin

ElBaradei, Mohamed 158

Erdogan, Recep Tayyip 103, 344–45, 390, 403–404; Zapatero-Erdogan initiative 345

Eritrea 228, 257, 266; relations with Egypt 247; *see also* Ethiopia

Ethiopia 196, 200–203, 204, 206, 207, 210, 212–16, 217, 220, 223–28, 229, 233, 257, 280–81, 287; and Eritrea 201, 202, 228, 250; tripartite cooperation with Egypt and Sudan 202, 212, 228; *see also* Mesfin, Seyoum; Zanawi, Meles

European Union (EU) 27, 139, 140–41, 362, 368–69, 399–400; relations with Egypt 368–72; Turkey 366; *see also* Nile Valley: Nile Basin Initiative; North Atlantic Treaty Organization (NATO); Quartet; Union for the Mediterranean (UfM)

Fahmy, Ismail 29–30, 64, 65–66, 83

al-Faisal, Prince Sa'ud 106, 293, 308–309, 313, 314, 316, 322, 323, 324, 330, 393–94, 397, 405, 433, 454

Fatah 413, 418, 419, 420, 421, 424–26, 428, 429; *see also* Hamas; Israel; Saudi Arabia: Mecca Agreement;

Palestinian Liberation Organization (PLO)
al-Fiqi, Mustafa 13, 347
Forum for the Future 143–44; *see also* Broader Middle East initiative
Forum on China-Africa Cooperation 210, 212–13, 248, 250–51, 280
France 169, 172, 191, 192, 274, 288–89, 296, 311, 321–22; relations with Egypt 20, 76, 369–70, 372; relations with Syria 296, 321–22 *see also* Group of Eight Industrialized Nations (G8); Kouchner, Bernard; Quartet; Sarkozy, Nicolas; Union for the Mediterranean (UfM); UN Security Council

Garang, John 260, 261–62, 263–64
Gates, Robert 151
Gawally, Mohamed Hassan 73, 80, 82–83
General Company for Research & Ground Water (REGWA), The 197
Germany 24, 171, 172, 186, 183–84, 111–12, 371–72; *see also* Group of Eight Industrialized Nations (G8); UN Security Council
Ghalib, Morad 50, 52–53, 56–57
Ghana 254; *see also* Annan, Kofi
Ghorbal, Ashraf 81–83
Gration, Scott 165–66, 275, 276, 288, 289
Group of Eight Industrialized Nations (G8) 90, 128, 131, 191, 193; G8 Foreign Ministers Conferences 134, 136, 137, 139, 159–60
Group of Twenty (G20) 162, 193
Gül, Abdullah 103, 342, 344, 345, 390–91, 403–404
Gulf Cooperation Council (GCC) 24, 85, 283, 293, 294, 304, 309,

320; relations with Egypt 23, 95, 181, 360
Hadley, Stephen 133–35, 151, 302
Hamas 149, 304, 316, 332, 386–89, 399, 406, 412–413, 418–26, 429, 435; relations with Egypt 419, 420–21 *see also* Fatah; Haniyeh, Ismail; Iran; Israel: Gaza war 2008; Meshaal, Khaled; Palestine Liberation Organization; Saudi Arabia: Mecca Agreement
Haniyeh, Ismail 419, 422, 424
Hariri, Rafik 293–94; assassination 131, 295, 321, 322; and Mubarak 294; *see also* Hariri, Saad; Syria
Hariri, Saad 330–31, 333
Hezbollah 304–318, 321, 329–30, 333, 348, 353, 386; and Egypt 391; *see also* Iran; Israel; Israel: Second Lebanon War; Nasrallah, Hassan; Palestine; Palestinian National Authority; Syria; UN Security Council: Resolution 1559
Higher Committee of Nile Water 205, 210, 211–13, 215, 225, 269
Holbrooke, Richard 159–60, 166, 361
Hosni, Farouk 158, 377–78
Hussein, Saddam 84, 298, 362

IBSA Dialogue Forum 90, 103, 190–91
India 171, 172, 186, 183–84, 186, 188–89, 376; *see also* BRIC Countries; UN Security Council
Intergovernmental Authority on Development (IGAD) 249, 260, 261
International Atomic Energy Agency (IAEA) 147, 347, 348, 349, 355, 356–59; *see also* Nuclear Non-Proliferation Treaty (NPT); Iran; Israel
International Conference in Support of the Palestinian Economy for the Reconstruction of Gaza (2009) 156, 406

International Conference on the Great Lakes Region (ICGLR) 249
International Criminal Court (ICC) 90–100, 189, 266, 268, 272–73, 274, 279, 284; *see also* al-Bashir Omar; Sudan; al-Arabi, Nabil; Ocampo, Luis Moreno
Iran 22, 24, 105, 108–109, 157, 161, 165, 166, 292, 298, 304, 306–307, 310, 312, 320, 323, 324, 340–42, 346–48, 350–55, 359–360, 426, 428, 459; and Bahrain 292, 348, 359; Bushehr Nuclear Power Plant 6, 127, 147, 149, 157, 161, 292, 312, 320, 342, 348, 349, 350, 352, 353–55, 359; al-Islambouli, Khaled mural 347; relations with Gaza 348, 352–53; relations with Hezbollah 306–309; relations with Israel 353–55; relations with United Arab Emirates 292, 348, 359; revolution 341; *see also* Ahmadinejad, Mahmoud; International Atomic Energy Agency (IAEA); Mottaki, Manouchehr
Iraq 24, 292, 293, 297–302, 303–304, 327–28, 336–337, 362–63; invasion of Kuwait 84–86, 456; Neighboring Countries of Iraq 105, 197, 297–98, 342, 348; *see also* Hussein, Saddam; al-Sherif, Ihab
Islamic Republic of Iran *see* Iran
Ismail, Mohamed Hafez 57, 58–62; *see also* National Security Council
Ismail, Mustafa Osman 200, 232, 266, 268, 271, 273, 275, 277
Israel 8, 20, 24, 72, 76, 158, 168, 354–55, 380; 1967 war 51–52, 54, 58; 1973 war 59, 60; activity in southern Sudan 282–83, 286; Gaza war 2008 344, 386–405, 413, 420–21; Negev Nuclear Research Center 339, 342, 348–50, 355, 356–57; occupation of

Southern Lebanon 72, 76–77, 78, 455; relations with Egypt 5, 8, 77, 125; relations with African nations 222–23; relations with Syria 72, 303, 305–306, 311, 313; Second Lebanon War 149, 304–318, 386, 401; *see also* Barak, Ehud; Fatah; Hamas; Hezbollah; Livni, Tzipi; Netanyahu, Benjamin; Olmert, Ehud; Palestine; Palestine Liberation Organization; Palestinian Authority; Peretz, Amir; Shalom, Silvan; Shamir, Yitzhak;
Italy 171, 172; 403 relations with Egypt 191, 370–71; *see also* Group of Eight Industrialized Nations (G8); UN Security Council

Japan 24, 171, 172, 183–84, 186, 188–89, 458; relations with Egypt 188–89, 376; *see also* Group of Eight Industrialized Nations (G8); UN Security Council
Jordan 84, 95, 321, 405, 410, 422, 428; *see also* Muasher, Marwan

Kabila, Joseph 218
Kamel, Mohamed Ibrahim 65–66, 74–75
Kandil, Hassan 68, 71
Karti, Ali 270, 271, 284–86, 288
Kenya 196–7, 200, 208, 217, 219, 283; relations with Egypt 201–202, 219; relations with Uganda 198; *see also* Israel, Lake Victoria
Khalifa, Sheikh Hamad bin 294, 319, 405–406
Khalil, Mustafa 66–67
Kiir, Salva 264, 268, 275, 281–82, 288, 289, 290
Konare, Omar 253, 268
Kouchner, Bernard 218, 274, 395–97
Koussa, Moussa 96, 325

Kuwait, 181, 320, 323, 331, 404–405; *see also* Arab Economic Summit; Gulf Cooperation Council (GCC); Iraq

Lake Victoria 197, 198, 460; *see also* Kenya; Uganda
Lavrov, Sergey 354, 373, 393, 435
League of Arab States 270, 273, 283, 301–302, 316, 330, 336–37, 387, 394, 421, 426, 433, 456; Arab Economic Summit 331, 403, 404–406; *see also* Abdel Meguid, Esmat; Moussa, Amr
Lebanon 142, 307, 321, 329–31; Sabra and Shatila massacre 73, 76–78; Taif Agreement 296; *see also* Hariri, Rafiq; Hariri, Saad; Hezbollah; Israel: occupation of Southern Lebanon; Israel: Second Lebanon War; Nasrallah, Hassan; Syria: occupation of Lebanon; Syria: Taif Agreement; UN Security Council: Resolution 1559
Libya 35, 36–37, 95–98, 180, 189, 230, 232, 252, 253, 258–59, 266, 271, 274, 290, 324–27, 336–37, 350; civil war 453–54; *see also* Koussa, Moussa; Qadhafi, Muammar; Yemen
Livni, Tzipi 307, 387–89, 399, 431, 432

Maher, Ahmed 11, 13–14, 32–33, 65, 66–67, 89
Makhlouf, Abdel Hadi 57–59, 60, 62
Mbeki, Thabo 221, 252, 290
McConnell, Mitchell 164, 436–37
media; Adib, Amr 404; Al-Arabiya 447, 449–50; Al Jazeera 16, 315, 332, 392, 404; Egypt 98, 136, 142, 222, 234, 267, 409, 450, 250–51, 324, 335, 365, 419; *Foreign Affairs* 111, 363; *al-Musawwar* 3–8; Palestine

414, 419–420; *Rose al-Yusuf* 402; United States 139–41, 389–90
Medvedev, Dmitry 164–65, 372, 373, 375
Merkel, Angela 192, 371–72, 403
Mesfin, Seyoum 200–201, 202, 223, 226, 228; *see also* Ethiopia
Meshaal, Khaled 419–21
Mexico 171, 192; *see also* UN Security Council
Mitchell, George 436–37
Morocco; King Hassan II 79–80
Mottaki, Manouchehr 297–98, 346–47, 348
Moussa, Amr 11–12, 13, 30, 33, 34, 39, 65, 78–79, 83, 86, 87, 89, 128, 178, 245, 256, 260, 337, 390, 433
al-Muallem, Walid 305, 306, 308, 309, 313, 321, 322, 424, 433
Muasher, Marwan 147, 390, 397, 430
Mubarak, Gamal 38, 94, 134, 135, 137, 140, 444–45, 446, 447–48, 449, 457
Mubarak, Hosni 9–10, 13, 26, 29–30, 32, 39–43, 74–75, 86–87, 90–96, 100, 101, 103–104, 105, 107–10, 118, 120–23, 127, 133–41, 154–56, 161, 164, 186, 187, 189, 210, 217, 221, 230–31, 253–55, 265, 288–89, 294, 296, 300–301, 304–308, 312, 318–19, 321–24, 329, 330–34, 336, 337, 338, 344–45, 353–54, 357–58, 365, 367, 369, 370–72, 376, 387–88, 389–90, 392, 394, 396–97, 401, 402–404, 406, 408, 415, 416, 417, 419, 423–24, 426, 427–29, 437, 441–51, 453, 454, 455–58, 461; African summits 27, 90, 101–102, 105, 121–22, 178–79, 246, 253, 255; and Aboul Gheit 12–13, 33–34, 92–93, 99–100, 107–108, 136–37, 273; assassination attempt 2004 27, 34, 90, 246; and Barack, Obama 157, 159, 162–65; and

Bush, George W. 153–54; and
Qadhafi 97–98; and United
Nations summits 26, 90, 108; *see
also* 25 January Revolution; Awad,
Suleiman; El-Baz, Osama; Hariri,
Rafik; Mubarak, Gamal; Mubarak,
Suzanne; Museveni, Yoweri;
Obama, Barack; Reagan, Ronald;
Shoukry, Sameh; Suleiman, Omar
Mubarak, Suzanne 13, 94, 378, 448
Museveni, Yoweri 197–99, 211, 225–26,
230–31, 261; and Mubarak, Hosni
197–98,; *see also* Uganda; Kenya

Naivasha Agreement *see* Sudan: Com-
prehensive Peace Agreement
Nasr Company 219, 245
Nasrallah, Hassan 306, 307, 317, 391;
*see also* Hezbollah
National Council for Human Rights 159
National Security Council 61–62,
109–11; Aboul Gheit 57–62, 83;
*see also* Egyptian General Intelligence; Ismail, Mohamed Hafez;
Suleiman, Omar
Nazif, Ahmed 17, 40–41, 89, 139–40,
209–210, 211, 213, 248, 255, 258,
442, 448; *see also* Higher Committee of Nile Water
Negroponte, John 146, 151
Netanyahu, Benjamin 387, 417, 437–39
New Partnership for Africa's Devel-
opment (NEPAD); 191, 192, 202,
249, 253; *see also* Algeria; Nigeria;
Senegal; South Africa
Nigeria 25, 173, 174–75, 179, 182–83,
184–85, 187–88, 189–90, 250,
258, 298; 2005 emergency Arab
summits 185–88; relations with
China 182–83; *see also* African
Union; New Partnership for Africa's Development (NEPAD); UN
Security Council

Nile Valley 5, 26, 98, 101, 166,
195–234, 247, 255, 280–81, 289,
290; 1929 Agreement 203–204;
1959 Nile Waters Agreement 166,
203, 205, 226–27, 232, 281; Comprehensive Framework Agreement
196, 204–232, 255, 280, 287,
290; Great Lakes 204, 211, 220;
Nile Basin Initiative (NBI) 196,
204–234; *see also* Burundi, Ethiopia; Higher Committee of Nile
Water; Rwanda; Sudan; Tanzania;
Uganda
Non-Aligned Movement 57, 91,
172–73, 174, 243–44, 249, 251,
273, 346, 353; 1983 summit in
Delhi 78–79
North Atlantic Treaty Organization
(NATO) 22, 84, 111, 120, 126–28,
257, 311–12, 340, 343, 352–53,
363; meetings attended by Aboul
Gheit 127; *see also* Turkey
North Korea 163, 172, 331, 350
al-Nour, Abdul Wahid 267–68, 274;
*see also* Sudan People's Liberation
Movement
Nour, Ayman 122–24, 125, 131–32,
133, 134–36, 139, 141, 145, 150,
155–57
Nuclear Non-Poliferation Treaty
(NPT) 29, 125–26, 136, 342,
348–50, 355, 356–59; Israel 29,
125–26, 342, 348, 356–57, 358;
North Korea 357; Review Conference of the Parties to the Treaty
on the Non-Proliferation of
Nuclear Weapons 136, 356–58; *see
also* International Atomic Energy
Agency; Iran, Israel, Russia

Obama administration 155–57, 159,
274, 436, 438–39; *see also* Clinton,
Hillary

Obama, Barack 154–157, 162–63, 285, 287, 439; address to Islamic and Arab World 156–157, 159, 161–63; Mubarak 123, 154, 161–63, 164

Ocampo, Luis Moreno 272–73

Olmert, Ehud 305–306, 387, 396, 427, 431

Organization of the Islamic Conference (OIC) 80, 249, 277, 360–61; Egypt membership 244

Palestine 73, 76–77, 129–30, 337, 348, 384–440; Annapolis Conference 333, 433–34; Annapolis Declaration 386–87, 388, 436; End Game 428, 437, 439–40; membership at United Nations 437; Palestine War 1948 44–45; Paris Protocol on Gaza 421, 422; settlement 5, 6, 8, 13–14, 36, 76–77, 84, 87, 105–106, 122, 129–30, 165, 292, 348, 369, 370, 372, 380, 384–85, 386–440, 456, 459; see also Arafat, Yasser; Lebanon: Sabra and Shatila massacre; Palestine Liberation Organization (PLO); Palestinian Authority; al-Qaddumi, Farouk

Palestine Liberation Organization (PLO) 76, 386, 407, 408, 412, 413, 416–19; see also Fatah; Hamas; Haniyeh, Ismail; Palestinian Authority

Palestinian National Authority 36, 76, 85, 395, 412, 413, 425–426; see also Abbas, Mahmoud; Arafat, Yasser; Central Intelligence Agency (CIA); Fatah; Hamas; Palestine Liberation Organization

Panetta, Leon 154, 168

People's Assembly 448; 2010 elections 449

Peretz, Amir 305–306

Philadelphia Corridor 412–13, 425, 440; see also Hamas; Hezbollah; Palestinian National Authority; Rafah crossing

Putin, Vladimir 164, 273–74

al-Qaddumi, Farouk 76

Qadhafi, Muammar 36–37, 95–98, 189, 230–32, 252–53, 258, 290, 324–27, 337, 454; see also Yemen

Qatar 157–58, 270–72, 294–95, 309, 316, 336, 337–38, 392, 393–94, 404–406; Arab summit in Doha 391–94, 398, 405–406; relations with Egypt 332, 404; relations with Hamas 421–22, 424; relations with Syria 320, 330, 391, 392; see also media: Al Jazeera; Al Thani, Hamad bin Jassim bin Jaber; Khalifa, Sheikh Hamad bin

Qualifying Industrial Zone (QIZ) 126, 145, 313, 401, 409

Quartet 370, 407, 410–411, 417–18, 421, 426, 429; Road Map 411, 418, 429, 430, 431, 438; see also European Union; Russia; United Nations; United States

Rafah 390, 391, 398, 402, 413, 421, 422–23, 425, 426; see also Hamas; Hezbollah; Nasrallah, Hassan; Philadelphia Corridor

Rasmussen, Lars 343, 363–64

Rice, Condoleezza 121, 129–33, 136, 139, 141–42, 144, 147, 148, 149–50, 151, 153, 268, 295–96, 298, 306, 307, 310, 388–89, 393, 396–97, 399, 413, 429, 431–32, 435, 436; speech at the American University in Cairo 141

Riyad, Mohamed 65–66

Ross, Dennis 161; see also Iran

Russia 28, 103, 139, 154, 172, 349–50, 354, 372–75; invasion of Afghanistan 69; relations with Egypt 19–21, 28 71, 154, 372–75; Soviet Union 68–70, 71, 79, 84, 149–50; power plants 373; *see also* BRIC; Group of Eight Industrialized Nations (G8); Medvedev, Dmitry; Lavrov, Sergey; Putin, Vladimir; Quartet; UN Security Council
Rwanda 208, 210, 216, 222–23, 255; *see also* Nile Valley

al-Sadat, Anwar 9, 21, 59, 61, 64, 65–66, 67, 71, 74–75, 347
Salah, Kamal al-Din 53, 301
Salah, Laila Kamal al-Din 15–16, 17–18, 52, 53, 55, 56, 63–64, 88, 108–109, 301, 388, 452; *see also* Salah, Kamal al-Din
Sarkozy, Nicolas 191, 192, 321–22, 326–27, 369–70, 393, 394, 395–97, 402–403
Saudi Arabia 23–24, 85, 96, 97, 323, 324, 454; Mecca Agreement 429; relations with Egypt 304, 314, 318–20, 324, 329; relations with Syria 330–32; *see also* Arab Peace Initiative; Abdulaziz, King Abdullah bin; al-Faisal, Prince Sa'ud; Abdulaziz, Prince Muqrin bin; Sultan,
Senegal 189, 258; *see also* New Partnership for Africa's Development (NEPAD)
Shafiq, Ahmed 144, 442, 443, 451, 452
al-Sharaa, Farouk 85, 106, 130–31, 293, 295–96, 318, 322
Sharon, Ariel 129–30, 407, 410–11, 412, 417–18
al-Sherif, Ihab 129, 298–301
Shoukry, Sameh 31, 42, 166
Solana, Javier 399, 400

Somalia 108, 292; civil war 255; Ethiopian intervention 202, 228; piracy 257, 323; relations with Egypt 255–57; *see also* New Partnership for Africa's Development (NEPAD)
South Africa 25, 173, 174–75, 179, 183, 184–85, 187, 192, 247–48, 251–52, 258, 298; P5 159; *see also* African Union, Dlamini-Zuma, Nkosazana Clarice; Mbeki, Thabo; UN Security Council
South Korea 172, 376
Sudan 26, 35, 81, 95, 98, 99–101, 165–66, 179, 189, 196, 208–209, 212–13, 214, 215, 216, 221, 224–25, 226–27, 229, 232, 255, 257, 260–291, 325–25, 334–35; Abyei referendum 165–66, 261, 275–76, 277, 278, 281, 284–87, 288, 289, 290; Abuja Agreement 267, 270, 283, 286–87, 288; aid from Egypt 265–66, 269–70; civil war 84, 99–101; Comprehensive Peace Agreement (CPA) 260–62, 266, 267, 272, 274–75, 278–79, 280; Darfur 263, 264–66, 267–68, 272 276–77, 279–80, 286, 292; government 262–63, 266, 267, 268, 271, 274–75; National Congress Party 287; southern Sudan 100–101, 165, 217–18, 226, 231–34, 250, 260–62, 268, 277, 278, 282–83; relations with Egypt 35, 334–35; western interference 264–66, 276; *see also* African Union; Akol, Lam; al-Bashir, Omar; Garang, John; Ismail, Mustafa Osman; Karti, Ali; Kiir, Salva; Nile Valley; Nimeiry, Jaafar; Omar, Magdy Abd al-Moneim; Sudan People's Liberation Movement (SPLM); Taha, Ali Osman; UN Security Council

Sudan People's Liberation Movement
(SPLM) 260, 263, 264, 267–68,
287; see also al-Nour, Abdul Wahid
Suleiman, Omar 34, 36, 37–38, 62,
95–98, 99, 101, 107, 108, 110, 122,
138, 140, 149, 151, 155, 159, 160,
161, 162, 164, 165, 166–67, 167–68,
202, 208, 224, 228, 256, 263, 271,
272, 274, 275–76, 282, 284, 289,
299–300, 313, 319, 325, 332, 368,
370, 387–88, 389, 390, 398, 402,
407–11, 413, 414, 415–16, 419, 424,
429, 435, 436–38, 441–42, 443,
444, 446, 447–48, 450, 451; see also
Egyptian General Intelligence
Supreme Council of the Armed Forces
252–53; see also Tantawi, Mohamed
Hussein
Syria 24, 85, 95, 293, 295–97, 302–303,
304, 305–306, 311–12, 313–14,
317–318, 320–21, 329–32, 342,
350, 390, 392; assassination of
Hariri, Rafik 296, 302–303, 306,
309, 311, 320, 321, 329; Damascus
Declaration 24, 30, 85, 106, 306;
nuclear reactor 358; relations with
Egypt 320–22, 331, 333; relations
with Saudi 309, 317–18, 321–22;
Taif Agreement 296, 303; withdrawal from Lebanon 293–94,
295–97, 302–303; see also al-Assad, Bashar; al-Muallem, Walid;
al-Sharaa, Farouk; UN Security
Council: Resolution 1559

Taha, Ali Osman 260, 275, 285, 288–89
Tantawi, Mohamed Hussein 451–52
Tanzania 200–203, 206, 210, 216, 219
224–25, 232–33
Touré, Ahmed Sékou 80, 244
Turkey 22–23, 72, 175, 337, 339–41,
324, 331, 342–46, 390–91, 398,
403–404, 459; Freedom Flotilla
402; and Israel 342–43, 344, 345,
390; relations with Egypt 60, 103,
390, 403–404; relations with the
Middle East 103, 343, 344–45,
434; relations with the west 22,
23; see also Erdogan, Recep Tayyip;
European Union; Gül, Abdullah;
North Atlantic Treaty Organization (NATO)

Uganda 196, 197–200, 206, 209, 211,
216, 219, 222, 224–26, 230–31;
media 196; Owen Dam 198; see
also Nile Valley; Museveni, Yoweri
UN (United Nations) 24–26, 62–64,
76, 78, 80–81, 83, 87, 139, 169–94,
216, 217, 268–69, 285–87, 288,
458; 59th General Assembly 108,
265; 65th General Assembly 285;
African representation to 25–26;
Egyptian presence 91, 376–78;
Human Rights Council (HRC)
377, 384; see also Boutros-Ghali,
Boutros; North Atlantic Treaty
Organization (NATO); Pérez de
Cuéllar, Javier; Quartet; Treaty on
the Non-Proliferation of Nuclear
Weapons; UN Security Council
UN (United Nations) Security Council
24–5, 63, 79, 169–71, 264–65, 266,
273, 284, 289; expansion 103–104,
169–94, 298; Resolution 242 411,
422; Resolution 1559 293, 296–97,
310, 311, 315, 318, 323; Resolution 1701 317; Resolution 1860
392–93, 394–99, 402, 403–404;
P5+1 248, 251–52; see also African
Union; Brazil; China; Germany;
India; Italy; Japan; Mexico; Nigeria; Russia; South Africa
Union for the Mediterranean (UfM)
27, 98, 191, 192, 321, 327, 368–69,
437;

United Arab Emirates 23, 320, 398; aid
to Egypt 319; relations with Egypt
359; *see also* Gulf Cooperation
Council (GCC)
United States 21, 27–27 76, 77, 86,
105–106, 117–168, 276, 284,
286, 288, 297–98, 310–11, 314,
320, 353, 355, 356–58, 362–63,
412, 429, 432–35, 446; aid to
Egypt 124–25, 142–43, 145–49,
150, 151–52, 153, 154, 157, 167,
168, 319, 439–40; invasion of
Afghanistan 118–20, 125, 159–60;
invasion of Iraq 24, 106, 119–20,
125, 131, 139, 214, 328; Israel 125,
399; and the Muslim Brotherhood 148; relations with Egypt
6, 86, 117–168, 274–75, 297, 303;
relations with Saudi Arabia 148;
relations with Syria 106, 119–21,
130–31, 292, 295–96, 302–303,
313; War on Terror 118, 148, 153;
*see also* Baker, James; Biden, Joe;
Broader Middle East Initiative;

Bush, George W.; Camp David;
Central Intelligence Agency
(CIA); Cheney, Dick; Cheney, Liz;
Clinton, Hillary; Gates, Robert;
Gration, Scott; Group of Eight
Industrialized Nations (G8); Nile
Valley; Hadley, Stephen; Jones,
James; McConnell, Mitchell;
Mitchell, George; Nour, Ayman;
Obama, Barack; Reagan, Ronald;
Ross, Dennis

WikiLeaks 358
World Bank 204, 206, 211, 212, 214,
216, 221, 224, 233, 406; *see also*
Nile Valley: Nile Basin Initiative;
Zoellick, Robert

Yemen 292, 324–25

Zanawi, Meles 200–201, 202, 212–213,
217, 223–24, 226–29, 233
Zebari, Hoshyar 107, 303–304
Zoellick, Robert 193, 221, 224